The Life & Pontificate of
POPE PIUS XII

The Life & Pontificate of
POPE PIUS XII
BETWEEN HISTORY &
CONTROVERSY

Frank J. Coppa

The Catholic University of America Press
Washington, D.C.

Copyright © 2013
The Catholic University of America Press
All rights reserved

Library of Congress Cataloging-in-Publication Data
Coppa, Frank J.
The life and pontificate of Pope Pius XII : between history and
controversy / Frank J. Coppa.
   pages ; cm
Includes bibliographical references and index.
ISBN 978-0-8132-2015-4 (cloth) —
ISBN 978-0-8132-2016-1 (pbk.)
1. Pius XII, Pope, 1876–1958.
2. Popes—Biography.   I. Title.
BX1378.C64 2013
282.092—dc23
[B]   2012033239

To the memory of Professors Hans Rosenberg
and Hans Trefousse, who influenced my undergraduate
historical studies at Brooklyn College,

John K. Zeender and Manoel Cardozo of
the Catholic University of America, who provided guidance
and friendship during my graduate study

CONTENTS

Abbreviations	ix
Introduction	xi
1. The Pacelli Family: A Counter-Risorgimento Clan in a National Age	1
2. The Child Is Father of the Man	23
3. The Making of a Diplomat	47
4. In Germany, 1917–1929	74
5. Secretary of State to Pius XI, 1930–1939	101
6. Confronting the Second World War	124
7. The "Silence" during the Holocaust	152
8. On Palestine and Israel	174
9. The Cold War: Pius XII Finds His Voice	199
10. Traditionalism and Modernity	221
Conclusion	245
List of Encyclicals of Pope Pius XII	265
Bibliography	267
Index	301

ABBREVIATIONS

AAES   Archivio della Sacra Cogregazione per gli Affari Ecclesiastici Straordinari

AAS   *Acta Apostolicae Sedis*

ADSS   *Actes et documents du Saint Siege relatifs à la seconde guerre mondiale*

ANM   Archivio della Nunziatura Apostolica in Monaco

ASS   *Acta Sanctae Sedis*

ASV   Archivio Segreto del Vaticano

AS   Archivio Storico

b   busta, or envelope

PE   *The Papal Encyclicals*

pos   posizione, or position

PP   *Papal Pronouncements. A Guide: 1740–1978*

RDHSWW   *Records and Documents of the Holy See relating to the Second World War*

SS   Secreteria di Stato

INTRODUCTION

> Even before Pius XII died in 1958, the charge that his papacy had been friendly to the Nazis was circulating in Europe.... It sank for a few years under the flood of tributes from Jews and gentiles alike, that followed the pope's death, only to bubble up again with the 1963 debut of *The Deputy* ... [which] was fictional and highly polemical, claiming that Pius XII's concern for Vatican finances left him indifferent to the destruction of European Jewry.

EUGENIO MARIA GIUSEPPE GIOVANNI PACELLI, born March 2, 1876; ordained a priest April 2, 1899; elected the 260th pope on his sixty-third birthday, March 2, 1939; and died October 9, 1958, has emerged as the most controversial pope of the twentieth century. Although long studied, his turbulent pontificate remains one of the least understood in recent times. In part this has flowed from the grave problems it had to confront, including the Second World War, the Nazi genocide of the Jews, the political collapse of Europe, the march of communism, the cold war, and the threat of nuclear annihilation. Not surprisingly, evaluations of his responses to a host of problems have varied both in time and place.

However, contentious assessments did not always prevail. During his papacy, and its immediate aftermath, he was hailed for his asceticism, saintly persona, and his efforts on behalf of

---

Epigraph is from David G. Dalin, "Pius XII and the Jews," in *The Pius War: Responses to the Critics of Pius XII*, ed. Joseph Bottum and David G. Dalin (Lanham, Md.: Lexington Books, 2004), 13.

the stricken during the Second World War. His broad knowledge, interest in science, and support for technological innovation, modernization, and liturgical reform was applauded inside and outside the Church on both sides of the Atlantic and led some to proclaim him the "first modern pope."

Despite the anti-Catholicism in the United States, many Americans appreciated the role this pope played in the Second World War and the cold war that followed, applauding his early and persistent condemnation of communism. *Time* magazine praised Pius XII for combating totalitarianism while editorials in the *New York Times* applauded his "courageous" campaign against anti-Semitism.[1] His vision and call for a new international order to supersede the chaotic one that had led to more than half a decade of destruction, and the political collapse of Europe, was likewise appreciated. This positive image was reflected in the obituaries following his death in 1958, in which he was acclaimed in the West as the "pope of peace" and "crusader against communism and materialism." In fact he invoked peace in a number of messages before the outbreak of the Second World War, during that conflict, and after the war when a series of other wars raged in Europe and abroad.[2] He was also praised for having rallied the "Church's spiritual vigor" against the evils of the age, respected for his campaign against nuclear weapons, and applauded for his support of European integration and the United Nations. Described as a paternal pastor, he was said to have made all the ills of the world his concern.[3]

Jews as well as Christians were among his most ardent admirers. Golda Meir, the Israeli foreign minister at the time, paid

---

1. See "Religion: Peace and the Papacy," cover story in *Time*, August 16, 1943, and "The Pope's Message," *New York Times*, December 25, 1941, p. 24, as well as "The Pope's Verdict," *New York Times*, December 25, 1942, p. 16.

2. See *Dum gravissium* of March 3, 1939, his first message to the Catholic world and one that called for peace; *Norunt profecto* of October 1940 that called for relief from war; and *Auspicia Quaedam* of 1948 that also invoked world peace.

3. "Pope Pius Arrayed Catholicism's Spiritual Strength against Materialistic Forces," *New York Times*, October 9, 1958, p. 22.

tribute to the dead pope for his efforts on behalf of the Jewish people during the decade of their misery and martyrdom. She, and other Jews, regretted the loss of this "humanitarian" peacemaker, whom they honored, appreciated, and respected. The Jewish-German scientist Albert Einstein, at the close of 1940, thanked the Catholic Church and its leaders for their solitary efforts on behalf of the persecuted Jews.[4] The chief rabbi of Rome, Israel Zolli, was apparently so inspired by, and grateful for, the papal efforts on behalf of the Jews that at the end of the war he converted to Catholicism and took the Christian name Eugenio in the pope's honor. He described the intense impact and influence of this pope on his life in his volume *Why I Became a Catholic*.[5] Pinchas Lapide, for his part, judged Pius XII "the greatest benefactor of the Jewish people."[6] These Jewish figures were not alone in their genuine and profound esteem for Pope Pius XII.

At his death Jewish leaders joined Catholic figures in eulogizing this pope for his wartime programs on behalf of the persecuted and humanitarian assistance to the victims of the conflict deemed nothing less than a "crusade of charity." Gratitude was expressed by deed as well as word and led to a series of donations including one by the World Jewish Congress in recognition of the passionate and persistent work of the Holy See in rescuing Jews from Fascist and Nazi persecution. During the Second World War and the early years of the cold war, Jewish-American publications such as the *American Israelite* and the *Jewish Advocate* honored Pius XII for his humanitarian campaign. The Jewish press reflected the sentiments of a host of Jewish organizations including the American Jewish Joint Distribution Committee.[7]

4. "Pius XII," *Time*, December 23, 1940, p. 38.
5. Previously published by Israel Zolli as *Before the Dawn* (New York: Sheed & Ward, 1954).
6. Hubert Wolf, *Pope and Devil: The Vatican Archives and the Third Reich*, translated by K. Kronenberg (Cambridge, Mass.: Harvard University Press, 2010), 15.
7. This was an umbrella organization for a number of Jewish philanthropies, many of which likewise applauded this wartime pope for his "mission of mercy" and efforts at saving thousands of Jewish lives.

Subsequently, a combination of historiographical factors, literary developments, ideological considerations, and the need to assign responsibility for the Holocaust contributed to a radical transformation of his reputation. His role during the Second World War and the genocide of the Jews was first seriously challenged during the revelations of the Eichmann Nazi war crimes tribunal in 1961, which brought home to many the terrible consequences of the brutal and widespread genocide which was until then not widely known. The revelations shocked political and religious leaders as well as the masses in Europe, America, and the Middle East. As the frightening details of the *Shoah*, or Holocaust, became public, and the search for responsibility commenced, Pius's role was questioned and his positive image gradually eroded. His legacy was challenged as critics denounced his cautious diplomatic responses, appeasement, conciliation, indirect criticism, and limited actions against the satanic Nazi regime. Discounting, sometimes virtually ignoring, the difficulties the pope then confronted, critics weighed his cautious actions against the gravity of the horrendous crimes and genocide committed by Hitler's Reich.

This evolving critique was broadly popularized by Rolf Hochhuth's play *Der Stellvertreter, The Deputy: A Christian Tragedy* (1963) —which had its American premiere in New York in February 1964. This drama, by the thirty-one-year-old playwright, presented a dramatic if less than accurate or objective account of Pius XII's behavior during the Holocaust, increasingly deemed a central feature of the war years. Translated into more than twenty languages, the play, which appeared first in Berlin, blended fact and fiction to denounce papal "inaction," "silence," and "impartiality" in the face of the brutal Nazi genocide. Even worse, this drama depicted Pius XII as a cold and calculating figure preoccupied by narrow clerical concerns, institutional constraints, and the Vatican's financial interests, who reportedly ignored the plight of the Nazi victims, and was basically indifferent to their suffering.

The performance and publication of Hochhuth's play, which combined fact and fiction, ignited a war of conflicting interpretations of Pius's limited actions and alleged silence. The drama found adherents who readily accepted its central contention that a "callous" Pius XII, insensitive to the plight of the Jews, failed to raise an authoritative public voice on their behalf during their brutalization at the hands of the Nazis. His alleged "indifference" and "silence" were attributed to a gamut of nefarious reasons—including anti-Judaism and anti-Semitism—which for many were deemed identical. Some Christians as well as Jews concurred with Hochhuth's assessment, including the former priest James Carroll.[8] This critique, in turn, was denounced as nothing less than defamation by defenders of the pope, who argued that Papa Pacelli was not indifferent, anti-Semitic, or silent and did more than most other political figures to assist the victims of Hitler's racism, paranoia, and rage. Pius, although surrounded by the dangerous dictatorial regimes of Mussolini and Hitler, earned praise for his recourse to clandestine means and quiet diplomacy to save tens of thousands of Jews from the gas chambers.[9] No basis was provided, or could be provided, for the number of Jews saved by his actions cited in light of the extreme secrecy that was considered essential for the papal operation.

A number of admirers of Pope Pius XII observed that both the American and British governments were aware of the Nazi genocide of the Jews, and unlike the pope, they had the military means and aircraft to hinder if not halt it. They complained that Washington and London chose to ignore, downplay, and even suppress reports of the Holocaust before the Second World War

---

8. James Carroll, "The Silence," *New Yorker*, April 7, 1997, pp. 52–68.

9. Raffaele Alessandrini, "Washington e Londra di fronte alla tragedia degli ebrei europei. Silenzi e omissioni al tempo della Shoah," *L'Osservatore Romano*, August 14, 2009.

in order to avoid arousing part of their population to favor intervention and thereby create internal dissension.[10] Indeed, some supporters of Pius XII claimed that he did more on behalf of the persecuted Jews than Roosevelt and Churchill combined.

Papal critics did not find these arguments persuasive, arguing that it was not a difficult task to transcend two zeros. Hannah Arendt, the German political philosopher, responded that more was expected of the "Vicar of Christ" than ordinary political figures,[11] and Daniel Jonah Goldhagen found it damning that Pius XII proved no more courageous than the Allied leaders and utterly failed to fulfill his moral and religious obligations.[12] John Cornwell initially proved no less critical of Pius XII than Hochhuth, Arendt, and Goldhagen, depicting the wartime pope as an authoritarian and anti-Semitic figure, obsessed by a determination to preserve papal primacy, who pursued a conservative course to protect the institutional Church's interests. Echoing the Jewish Daniel Jonah Goldhagen, the Catholic John Cornwell also blamed the Church and its leadership for the "unfortunate" course pursued during the war and the Holocaust—branding Papa Pacelli "Hitler's Pope."[13] The priest-historian Kevin Spicer, in turn, has been critical of the German Catholic Church for its relative silence during the Holocaust.[14]

Objectivity is likewise often missing in the pro-Pius camp, with some of its writers having their own predetermined agenda: to exonerate and absolve this pope from the "black legend" fabri-

---

10. One can find a virtual catalogue of the various reasons that the states, churches, and organizations gave for their inaction in combating Nazi atrocities in the papers of James Grover McDonald found in the Lehman Archive of International Affairs housed at Columbia University, in New York.

11. Gerhard Besier with the collaboration of Francesca Piombo, *The Holy See and Germany*, trans. W. R. Ward (New York: Palgrave/Macmillan, 2007), viii.

12. See Daniel Jonah Goldhagen, *A Moral Reckoning: The Role of the Catholic Church and Its Unfulfilled Duty of Repair* (New York: Knopf, 2002).

13. John Cornwell, *Hitler's Pope: The Secret History of Pope Pius XII* (New York: Viking Press, 1999), 4.

14. See his volume *Hitler' Priests: Catholic Clergy and National Socialism* (DeKalb: Northern Illinois University Press, 2008).

cated by his enemies and restore the reputation they have unjustly tarnished. One of Pius XII's most ardent defenders has been Margherita Marchione, of the Filippini Sisters, who has long pressed for his beatification.[15] In a steady stream of works, she provides a spirited defense of Pius and his response to the Holocaust,[16] asserting that the accusations launched against him are without foundation and the charge of anti-Semitism both unfair and unfounded. She insists that Pius XII was neither indifferent nor inactive in the face of the genocide, but preferred quiet diplomacy to public confrontation, arguing that a more forthright and forceful condemnation of Nazi and Fascist anti-Semitism would have made things worse for the Jews.[17] In an article titled "Setting the Record Straight on Pope Pius XII and the Jews," she posited that he had been made the "scapegoat for the crimes and inaction of others"[18] During the course of several decades, she has tirelessly continued the defense of Pius XII and pressed for his beatification.

A combative attitude prevails outside the faith as well as within it, with Jews as well as Christians sharply divided in their assessment of Pius XII's role during the Holocaust. The Jewish author Dan Kurzman concurs with much of Marchione's assessment, indicating that rather than being "Hitler's Pope," Pius XII was perceived as a bitter enemy whom the Führer seriously considered seizing.[19] Pinchas Lapide, the former Israeli

15. John Thavis, "N.J. Nun Presses for Beatification of Pius XII," *The Tablet* (Brooklyn), December 6, 2003, p. 24.
16. These include, among others, *Yours Is a Precious Witness: Memoirs of Jews and Catholics in Wartime Italy* (1997); *Pope Pius XII: Architect for Peace* (2000); *Consensus and Controversy: Defending Pope Pius XII* (2002); *Man of Peace: Pope Pius XII* (2003); *Pio XII e gli Ebrei* (1999); *Pio XII è veramente un Santo* (2004); *Crusade of Charity: Pius XII and POWs* (2006); *Did Pope Pius XII Help the Jews?* (2007); and most recently "A Hand of Peace: Pope Pius XII and the Holocaust" (2009).
17. "GreetingLine," "Pius XII and the Holocaust," *Vital Theology* 1, no. 13 (October 30, 2004): 7–8.
18. *The Tablet* (Brooklyn), November 6, 2004, p. 28.
19. In this regard, see Dan Kurzman, *Hitler's Secret Plot to Seize the Vatican and Kidnap Pope Pius XII* (New York: Da Capo, 2008).

consul, writes that Pius XII was neither silent nor inactive during the Holocaust and was responsible for saving no less than 860,000 Jews from the Nazi death camps.[20] Like so many other figures cited by both sides, this one too has not and cannot be confirmed. The Jewish historian Jenoe Levai likewise supports and defends Pius XII, as is readily apparent from the title of his book *Hungarian Jewry and the Papacy: Pius XII Did Not Remain Silent* (1968). Rabbi David Dalin has proven even more energetic in championing the cause of Pius and his relationship with the Jews,[21] as has Sir Martin Gilbert—who is also Jewish. Gilbert has defended Pius in *Never Again: A History of the Holocaust* (2000), *The Righteous: Unsung Heroes of the Holocaust* (2003), and *Hitler's Pope?* (2006). Likewise supportive of Pius XII is the Jewish American Gary Krupp and his Jewish wife, who together preside over the pro-Pius Pave the Way Foundation. The two have collected and posted a series of informative documents on the Internet and not surprisingly a majority of them present a positive image of Papa Pacelli.

Regretting the developing controversy which proved bitter and divisive, Giovanni Montini, who had worked closely with Pius XII during the war and became Pope Paul VI in 1963, believed that the documents of the Vatican Archives would exonerate the pope whom he had long and loyally served and very much admired. Consequently, this devotee of Pope Pius partially lifted the usual seventy-five year period of closure in the Vatican Archive and allowed four Jesuits to examine the papers therein—which led to the publication of the eleven-volume *Actes et documents du Saint Siège relatifs a la seconde guerre mondiale.* Their publication, as well as the passage of time, saw the storm over Pius XII's "silence" temporarily subside—but not end. It re-

20. Pinchas E. Lapide, *Three Popes and the Jews* (New York: Hawthorn Books, 1967), 214.
21. David G. Dalin, "Pius XII and the Jews," *Weekly Standard*, February 26, 2001, pp. 31–39.

sumed at the turn of the century during the discussion provoked by the projected beatification (the second step toward the proclamation of sainthood) of Pius XII—whose case for sainthood was opened in November 1965 by Pope Paul. The criticism was compounded by the suspension of the six-member International Catholic-Jewish Historical Commission appointed to study the documents of the *Actes et documents du Saint Siège*.[22] Their call for access to all the files in the Secret Vatican Archive (ASV) apparently angered some in the Vatican and precipitated the suspension.

Meanwhile, opponents of Pius XII's beatification resurrected the dual charges of "silence during the Holocaust" and "impartiality between good and evil" during the Second World War, claiming that his recourse to expediency violated the ethical principles of the faith and proved detrimental to the victims of Nazi abuse.[23] On the one hand he was denounced as "Hitler's Pope," while on the other hand he was hailed as the "hound of Hitler."[24]

It was hoped that the availability of new sources would end this ideological and polemical debate, and contribute to the publication of an objective biography of Pius XII and his policies, transcending the subjective and nonhistorical picture hitherto presented in much of the literature. Others, following the lead of the Catholic-Jewish Commission, complained that a balanced historical account could not be written because much of the essential documentation remained inaccessible. To quiet the outcry, in the early 1990s Pope John Paul II (1978–2005) opened the papers of

22. Included in the group were the Reverend Gerald Fogarty, S.J., of the University of Virginia, Reverend John Morley of Seton Hall University, and Eva Fleischner of Montclair State University representing the Catholic presence and Bernard Suchecky of the Free University of Brussels, Robert S. Wistrich of the Hebrew University of Jerusalem, and Michael Marrus of the University of Toronto accounting for the Jewish presence.

23. Tony Barber, "Calls Grow to Canonise Controversial Nazi-Era Pope," *Financial Times*, July 29, 2006.

24. See, respectively, Cornwell, *Hitler's Pope*, and Gerard Noel, *The Hound of Hitler* (New York: Continuum, 2008).

the pontificate of Benedict XV (1914–1922) for scholarly scrutiny. Subsequently, in 1998, he opened the archives of the Inquisition and that of the Congregation of the Index. This did little to satisfy skeptics who loudly complained of the unavailability of the papers in the ASV for Pacelli's pontificate, which remained essentially shut after the admission of the four Jesuits. To make matters worse, at the end of the twentieth century, the ASV likewise remained closed for the pivotal pontificate of Pius XI (1922–1939) in which Pacelli served as nuncio to Germany from 1922 to 1930 followed by his stint as secretary of state from 1930 to 1939, before assuming the tiara.

Insinuations that the papacy had something to hide prompted the Vatican to undertake the selective opening of the papers of Pius XI, making available hundreds of thousands of pre-Second World War documents while Pacelli was nuncio in Germany and then secretary of state. Those of the Munich Nunciature or the Archivio della Nunziatura Apostolica in Monaco (ANM) and the Archivio della Nunziatura Apostolica in Berlino (ANB) released in 2003 proved most useful in clarifying Pacelli's diplomatic development from 1922 to 1930 and the emergence of his pro-German sentiments. In 2004 the papers of the Affari Ecclesiastici Straordinari (AAES) (Baveria) from 1922 to the beginning of 1940 were made available. Also released were the documents of the Vatican's relations with the German Catholic Center Party. The files of the Congregation for the Doctrine of the Faith, the Archivio della Congregazione della Fede (ACDF), were organized and opened for the pontificate of Pius XI as were the documents in the Archivio della Sacra Congregazione per gli Affari Ecclesiasitici Straordinari (AAES), and both proved useful for understanding the policies and politics of Pope Pius XII.[25] Microfilm copies of part of this material (some ninety-five reels to

---

25. See Frank J.Coppa, *The Policies and Politics of Pope Pius XII* (New York: Peter Lang, 2011).

date) are now housed in the United States Holocaust Memorial Museum in Washington, D.C.

In 2006 Benedict XVI (2005–) decreed that *all* the documents relative to the pontificate of Pius XI—some 30,000 files with millions of pages—be opened to researchers; these included Pacelli's papers while nuncio in Munich and Berlin, and his correspondence with the German bishops while he served as secretary of state.[26] In 2007 Benedict made other documents available—some covering the war period. Included in the released papers were Pacelli's personal notes or "diary" on meetings he had with Pius XI each morning and the notes he made on the pope's meetings with diplomats most afternoons from 1930 to the start of 1939. The first volume of these *Fogli di udienza*, or *Records of Audiences*, appeared in August 2010 in printed form. The volumes are important not only for what Pacelli noted and emphasized, but also for what he chose to ignore.[27] Among the issues that were unquestionably discussed by Pius XI with Pacelli and ignored in the latter's notes are all references to the encyclical *Mit brennender Sorge*, made public in mid-March 1937 and no mention of the anti-Semitic vandalism of *Kristallnacht* in November of the following year.[28] Likewise available are the unpublished minutes of papal meetings, drafted by Monsignor Domenico Tardini when Pacelli was on vacation in Switzerland in September and October 1938.[29]

All these documents permit one to examine and assess the

26. See ASV, Archivio della Nunziatura Apostolica in Monaco, Monsignor Eugenio Pacelli (1917–1925), and Pacelli's letters to the German bishops (1934–1939) during his tenure as secretary of state in ASV, Archivio Storico, Affari Ecclesiastiche Straordinari, Germania (1922–1939).
27. Fogli di udienza, ASV, Affari Ecclesiastiche Straordinari, Stati Ecclesiasici, posizione 430 ff.
28. Sergio Pagano, "Presentazione," in *I 'Fogli di Udienza' di Eugenie Pacell, Secretario di Stato (1930)*, edited by Sergio Pagano, Marcel Chappin, and Giovanni Coco (Vatican City: ASV, 2010), i, xix–xx.
29. Unlike the notes taken by Pacelli, those of Tardini are much more straightforward narrative accounts and more comprehensive rather than selective in their coverage.

policies of Pius XI and Eugenio Pacelli toward Nazism and its anti-Semitic policies from primary sources and diplomatic eyewitnesses of the march of events. Among other things they note the increasing dissension between Pius XI and the secretariat of state on the policy to pursue toward Hitler's regime.[30] A wide range of useful primary and secondary sources—albeit almost all positive—can be downloaded from *pavethewayfoundation.org*.

While archival sources tell us something about what the Catholic Church did or did not do to combat Nazi racism and their genocide of the Jews, they reveal far less about individual motivation, and must be interpreted within the broader historical context. Papa Pacelli did not facilitate the task of the historian attempting to reconstruct his life and pontificate and write his biography. Unlike most other popes of the twentieth century, he did not leave much of a paper trail regarding his personal opinions and sentiments, and he left no personal correspondence, notes, or journals. His *Fogli di udienza* is not a journal but notes on what was discussed in meetings with Pope Pius XI from 1930 to 1938.

The bulk of the papers of Pius XII's pontificate remain inaccessible and the prefect of the Archive indicated in 2004 that it would take at least another twenty years to arrange the millions of pages of this pontificate—a necessary first step before opening them for scholarly scrutiny.[31] Subsequently he has given a more optimistic timetable of eight to ten years, but in the Vatican there is often a broad divide between intent and outcome. However, other sources compensate for the partial availability of the Vatican Archives after 1939, including the papers of Giovanni Montini, who worked closely with Pius XII.[32]

30. Appunti di Tardini, ASV, Affari Ecclesiastiche Straordinari, Stati Ecclesiasici, posizione 560.
31. Conference with the prefect of the Secret Vatican Archives, Monsignor Sergio Pagano, on January 13, 2003.
32. These are catalogued in the Istituto Paolo VI in Brescia.

INTRODUCTION   xxiii

In addition the printed acts of the Holy See since 1909 appear in the *Acta Apostolicae Sedis (AAS)* Rome's equivalent of an official gazette or organ for Vatican documents. It publishes (most often in Latin) the official texts of encyclical letters, apostolic constitutions and exhortations, the decrees and instructions of the sacred congregations, as well as some of the more solemn allocutions of the popes. These printed acts, like the encyclicals letters of the papacy, are available down to the present.[33] *The Pope Speaks: American Quarterly of Papal Documents* publishes a selection of papal addresses and documents in English translation. The official web site of the Holy See offers a virtual treasure trove of Vatican documents not readily available elsewhere including papal addresses, allocutions, speeches, encyclicals, letters, telegrams, and the reports of various commissions.

One can also glean much about the pontificates of both Pius XI and Pacelli's own pontificate from the pages of the *Osservatore Romano. Giornale quotidiano politico-religioso* (OR), the daily authoritative voice of the Vatican. Founded by Pius's grandfather, its first issue appeared in Rome on July 1, 1861. This newspaper reproduces most papal talks as well as official documents in the original Latin text as well as in Italian. From 1890 on, the Vatican has published a daily edition of the journal in Italian, with weekly editions in English, French, Spanish, Portuguese, German, and Polish. Some consider it the closest thing to the official voice of the Vatican because it is owned by the Holy See, and submits all editorial material to a department of the Vatican's Secretariat of State for review. Vatican opinion on issues can often be ascertained by reading the columns of the

---

33. In September 1908, during the pontificate of Pius X (1903–1914), *Promulgandi* (the apostolic constitution on the promulgation and publication of laws and official acts of the Holy See) provided that these would be published in the *Acta Apostolicae Sedis* by the Vatican Press; see *Promulgandi*, September 29, 1908, in *Papal Pronouncements: A Guide, 1740–1978 (PP)*, edited by Claudia M. Carlen (Ann Arbor, Mich.: Pierian Press, 1990), 1.74.

Jesuit-run *Civiltà Cattolica* (CC), which was founded in Naples in 1850, and has been published in Rome since 1888. Although the *Civiltà Cattolica* remains under the direction of the Jesuits, it has long displayed an intense loyalty to the papacy and at times it has served as a virtual "mouthpiece for the popes." There are also the transcripts of Vatican Radio established by Guglielmo Marconi and inaugurated by Pius XI in February 1931. Likewise controlled by the Jesuits since its inception, its broadcasts often reflect the papal stance on a wide series of issues.

Likewise useful for the historian are the printed speeches and discourses of Popes Pius XI and Pius XII. Claudia Carlen has published the *Papal Encyclicals* (PE) from 1740 to 1981 in five volumes. Volumes 3 (1903–1939), 4 (1939–1958), and 5 (1958–1981) are particularly important for the pontificates following Benedict XV. She has also published in two volumes *Papal Pronouncements. A Guide: 1740–1978* (PP). Volume 1 covers the pontificate of Pius XII and includes excerpts from his encyclicals, allocutions, papal addresses, radio messages, sermons, homilies, and decrees. The material collected in the *Annuario Pontificio* (AP) or *Annual Papal Directory* provides valuable historical, ecclesiastical, and biographical information on the modern and contemporary papacy. The encyclical Pius XI commissioned against racism and anti-Semitism *Humani Generis Unitas* (HGU) has finally been uncovered, and the juxtaposition therein of the traditional clerical anti-Judaism with its condemnation of Nazi and Fascist anti-Semitism, is revealing.[34] The "secret encyclical" sheds considerable light on the thought of Pius XI who commissioned it, and the policy of Pius XII, who decided to shelve it.[35] Contemporary newspapers, magazines, and journals provide in-

---

34. Georges Passelecq and Bernard Suchecky, *The Hidden Encyclical of Pius XI*, trans. from French by Steven Rendall (New York: Harcourt Brace, 1998).

35. Frank J. Coppa, "The Hidden Encyclical of Pius XI against Racism and Anti-Semitism Uncovered—Once Again!" *Catholic Historical Review* 84, no. 1 (January 1998): 63–72.

INTRODUCTION xxv

formation on current developments and represent another valuable source of information on papal and Vatican positions.

New memoirs such as that of Harold Tittmann Jr., who was in the Vatican from 1941 to 1944 as assistant to Myron C. Taylor, President Roosevelt's personal representative to Pius XII, offer valuable insights into Pius XII's thought and actions.[36] The memoirs of this eyewitness to Vatican events and the earlier published ones by others close to the pope such as François Charles-Roux, Sister Pascalini Lehnert, Domenico Tardini, Galeazzo Ciano, and Dino Alfieri, among others, also shed light on this pope and his pontificate. The disclosure of a secret agreement made in 1938 by Vatican officials without Pius XI's knowledge, promising not to interfere with Fascism's anti-Semitism, reveals the deep divisions within Vatican circles on how best to respond to the fascist regimes.[37] The division between Pius XI and his two secretaries of state, Gasparri and Pacelli, is described in detail in the reports of Mussolini's spies in the Vatican presently housed in the Central State Archive of Italy, the Archivio Centrale dello Stato di Roma (ACS).

Likewise available are the archives of Italy, Great Britain, Germany, France, and the United States, and the printed correspondence of their representatives to the Holy See with their governments. Useful information on the pontificates of Pius XI and Pius XII is stored in the Archivio Storico–Diplomatico del Ministero degli Affari Esteri italiano (ASMAE) and revealed in the Italian *Diplomatic Documents (DDI)*. Likewise available and useful are the *Documents on British Foreign Policy (DBFP)* and the Public Record Office in London, which contains a wealth of information about developments since 1922. Additional infor-

---

36. Harold G. Tittmann III, ed., *Inside the Vatican of Pius XII: The Memoir of an American Diplomat during World War II* (New York: Image Books, 2004).
37. In this matter, see Angelo Martini, "L'Ultima battaglia di Pio XI," in *Studi sulla questione romana e la conciliazione* (Rome: Cinque Lune, 1963), 175–230.

mation can be gleaned from the Documents on German Foreign Policy (DGFP), from the archives of the German Foreign Ministry, as well as the French Diplomatic Documents (DDF) from the *Archives du Ministere des affaires Etrangeres* (Paris). The Wartime Correspondence between President Roosevelt and Pope Pius XII has been printed and reveals the cooperation as well as the differences between Washington and the Vatican.

These and other sources provide an important background for the origins and development of papal "silence" during the genocide and other policies pursued by Papa Pacelli. In addition, the contentious debate and charge of papal indifference toward the victims of the war has played a part in making available the files of the Vatican Information Service in the Vatican Archives[38] and access to them has been facilitated by the publication of a two-volume work.[39] The papal assistance provided the victims of the conflict has been dubbed a "crusade of charity" by defenders of Pius XII, who posit that he was far from an inactive spectator during the conflagration.[40] Finally, there is a vast and growing secondary literature on Pope Pius XII's position and policies. Since much of this is decidedly partisan and ideologically driven, it must be used with caution.

The debate provoked on the person and policies of Pius XII is documented in José Sánchez's *Pius XII and the Holocaust: Understanding the Controversy*; in Alessandro A. Persico, *Il caso Pio XII. Mezzo secolo di dibatito su Eugenio Pacelli*; and in Joseph Bottum and David G. Dalin, editors, *The Pius War*. While the first two strive for some objectivity, the commentary in the latter's annotated bibliography by William Doino Jr. (pp. 97–280)

---

38. Archivio Segreto Vaticano (ASV), Ufficio Informazioni Vaticano (Prigionieri di Guerra) (1939–1947).

39. *Inter Arma Caritas: Uffizio Informazioni Vaticano per I prigionieri di guerra istituito da Pio XII* (Vatican City: Archivio Segreto Vaticano, 2004).

40. Sister Margherita Marchione, *Crusade of Charity: Pius XII and POWs (1939–1945)* (New York: Paulist Press, 2006).

is decidedly pro Pius, evaluating the literature on the basis of its support of this pope and his pontificate. This is acknowledged by the subtitle of the volume: *Responses to the Critics of Pius XII*. A wide variety of sources have catalogued what Pius XII did and did not do during the Second World War and the cold war that followed, and forms part of the historical record. To be sure there is some disagreement on the impact of what he said and did—although this is not the main source of contention. There is greater disagreement on whether this pope could and should have said and done more. Likewise disputed is the issue of Pius XII's motivation—why he responded as he did. Furthermore, many of the problems in the "historiography" flow not from a lack of sources but from the dismissive attitude and unwillingness of some partisan writers to consider any evidence that contradicts their preconceived notions. The divisive debate has rendered difficult reaching an objective assessment so there is more partisanship than detachment in the "studies" of Pius XII's response to the Holocaust and the other policies of his pontificate.

Finally, few historians have looked at the entire life of Pius XII, or taken into account his formative years before his appointment as nuncio to Munich in 1917. One can no more understand the life and career of Pius XII by examining only a small portion of his life than one can put together a jigsaw puzzle with only a few pieces. In fact, one cannot understand the position and policies assumed by Papa Pacelli during his pontificate without delving into his family, childhood, education, and training. Furthermore, to acquire some perspective one should examine his entire pontificate within the broader context of his life. For many of the authors embroiled in the "Pius War" the focus has been almost entirely on the Second World War and the Holocaust to the neglect of Pius's modernization of the Church and its liturgy, the more than forty encyclicals he wrote, and over one thousand speeches and messages he delivered on a wide variety of subjects both secular and spiritual. The vision and framework of many of his "would-be" biographers remains narrow and restrictive, sensationalist rather than sensitive to his life and development.

We do not need another indictment or hagiographic account of the pontificate of Pius XII but an objective biography and historical examination of his entire life, including his childhood and early career which have long been largely ignored.[41] In the words of one observer, "what we really need now is a new biography of Pius XII during those years, a *nonreactive* account of a life and times, a book driven not by the reviewer's instinct to answer charges but the biographer's impulse to tell an accurate story."[42] His biography should not be restricted to his pontificate; his pontificate not only focused on his "silence." Gary Krupp has written "It's time for our 'historians' to correct this academic negligence and honestly research the open archives."[43] Owen Chadwick has cited the need to separate fact from fiction regarding the biography and pontificate of Pius XII.[44] Another historian has written "What is sorely needed is a detached scholarly work ... free from much of the hysterics that has surrounded Pius XII."[45] This has been largely missing in the massive and growing historiography on this pope. A first step in compiling a broader biography has been taken by Philippe Chenaux for French-speaking readers with the publication of his volume *Pie XII. Diplomate et Pasteur* (2003), translated into Italian but not into English.

The present biographical study, unlike the greater part of the vast and rapidly growing historiography on Pope Pius XII,

41. Emma Fattorini, *Germania e Santa Sede. Le nunziature di Pacelli tra la Grade Guerra e la Repubblica di Weimar* (Bologna: Il Mulino, 1992), 15.
42. Joseph Bottum, "Introduction," *The Pius War: Responses to the Critics of Pius XII* (Lanham, Md.: Lexington Books, 2004), 11.
43. Gary Krupp, "WWII Pontiff—Branded 'Hitler's Pope'—Did Much to Save the Jews, Says a Leading Interfaith Activist," *New York Daily News*, May 3, 2009, p. 27.
44. Owen Chadwick, "Pius XII: The Legend and the Truth," *The Tablet* (London), March 28, 1998.
45. Paul O'Shea, *A Cross Too Heavy: Eugenio Pacelli, Politics and the Jews of Europe, 1917–1943* (Kenthurst, New South Wales, Australia: Rosenberg, 2008), 22.

does not focus on his "silence" during the Holocaust—although it must necessarily address this contentious issue. It seeks to do so within a historical and objective framework rather than a preconceived, ideological one. It is a biography of the man as well as the pope, and probes into the roots of his traditionalism and legalism, his approach to modernity and reformism in Church and society, while examining the factors that influenced his action. It seeks to provide an objective and balanced account of the life of this pope as well as his pontificate for an English-speaking audience. This was no easy task in light of the existing clutter, partisan positions, and combative stance of many of the combatants in the Pius War.

The volume is divided into twelve chapters. Following this introduction, which traces the roots of the controversy surrounding this pope, the second examines his extended family, its service to the Vatican, and the influence it exercised upon Eugenio. The third chapter looks at his early development and education—the boy that produced the man. The fourth, in turn, explores his recourse to diplomacy rather than a pastoral career, while the fifth examines his crucial tenure in Germany as nuncio first to Bavaria and then to Germany, and its impact on his anticommunism and love of the Reich. The sixth delves into his crucial years as the secretary of state (1930–1939) and his policy of conciliation rather than confrontation vis à vis the dictators, while the seventh focuses on his "impartiality" during the Second World War. The eighth and ninth respectively discuss the controversy surrounding papal "silence" during Hitler's genocide and his stance toward the Middle East, Palestine, and Israel. The tenth concentrates on Pius's policies during the cold war, while the eleventh assesses both his reformism and traditionalism. The twelfth, and conclusion, examines the legacy of a pope caught between history and controversy, reform and traditionalism, and modernization in society and modernism in the Church.

ONE

The Pacelli Family

A COUNTER-RISORGIMENTO CLAN
IN A NATIONAL AGE

> In the order of nature, among social institutions there is none higher than the family. Christ elevated marriage, which is, as it were, its root, to the dignity of a sacrament. The family has found and will always find in the Church defense, protection, and support, in all that concerns its inviolable rights, its freedom, the exercise of its lofty function.

OVER THE CENTURIES church and society have often disagreed on various issues and the importance of particular institutions, but have almost always concurred on the crucial role of family in the physical, psychological, social, and religious formation of individuals. "We are not born as the partridge in the wood ... to be scattered everywhere," wrote the American clergyman Henry Ward Beecher, adding that human beings should be grouped together and "reared day by day in that first of churches, the family."[1] He like others recognized that character and personality are largely shaped by the interaction of genetic and environmental considerations, and the family plays a

---

Epigraph is from Address of Pius XII to the "Family Front" Congress, November 27, 1951, in Michael Chinigo, ed., *The Pope Speaks: The Teachings of Pius XII* (New York: Pantheon Books, 1957), 41.

1. H. W. Beecher, "Family," in *The New Dictionary of Thoughts*, edited by T. Edwards (New York: Standard Book Co., 1944), 191.

1

key role in the emergence of both. Despite its profound influence in character development, this crucial aspect has been largely ignored by those examining the life and pontificate of Eugenio Pacelli, who in early March 1939, on his sixty-third birthday, became Pope Pius XII.

In fact, most of the writers embroiled in the "Pius War," from the appearance of Hochhuth's play in 1963 to the present, have neglected the impact of both Eugenio's family and his formative childhood years on his life and career. Paul O' Shea, author of *A Cross Too Heavy*, and John Cornwell, who wrote *Hitler's Pope*, both of whom have devoted a chapter to the Pacelli family in their volumes, are more of an exception than the rule.[2] For the most part "combatants" in the Pius controversy not only overlook his family but tend to ignore his educational background, initial diplomatic activity, his decade of service as nuncio in Germany, and his years as the secretary of state of Pope Pius XI—all vital for an understanding of the man who became pope and the policies he would pursue once he donned the tiara. Both man and pope were long in the making.

Nonetheless, much of the literature and historiography on Pacelli dwells primarily on his papacy. Indeed, a number of writers have narrowed their scope even further. Saul Friedländer, for example, begins his study with the election of Pacelli as pope in March 1939 and ends his work in September 1944.[3] Others bypass even more aspects of Pius XII's papal tenure (1939–1958) to focus on his "silence" during the Holocaust, not realizing that this and other aspects of his pontificate cannot be fully understood in isolation, outside the broader context of his life and times. Small wonder that these narrow and restricted accounts have been compared to a jigsaw puzzle with missing pieces, ren-

2. O'Shea, *A Cross Too Heavy*, chapter 4, 125–50; Cornwell, *Hitler's Pope*, chapter 1, 9–28.

3. Saul Friedländer, *Pius XII and the Third Reich: A Documentation* (London: Chatto & Windus, 1966), xxiii.

dering difficult, if not impossible, an objective and coherent biography of Pius XII.[4]

Some blame the introspective, private, and taciturn Eugenio for the shortcomings in much of the historiography of his life and career, citing his failure to say or write much about himself and for revealing precious little about his personal feelings, inner convictions, and intellectual and religious development. It is true that over the years the inner-directed Eugenio, who from an early age was a loner, did not provide much information on his childhood, which he regarded as a personal matter. Indeed, even when on the verge of death Pius XII ordered his staff to burn those papers he had not reexamined.[5] He was equally protective of his public and private lives, clearly reflected in the notes he took during his meetings with Pius XI.[6] Whether one judges his family's influence as positive or negative, or most influential religiously, politically, culturally, economically, or socially, his numerous relatives clearly played a crucial role in Eugenio's formation, career, and future actions. His traditional and strict Catholic family therefore warrants greater study than it has hitherto received.

Although the Pacelli family's political, religious, and legal roles in the nineteenth and twentieth centuries have been explored, some things are not known about the early origins of the family. Its presence is first recorded in Onano, a little town—some would say a village—of some three thousand in the northern province of Lazio, near Viterbo, on the border with Tuscany. Today its population is even smaller, numbering just over one thousand. While the family lived there, some fifty miles north of Rome, the paternal family surname already had been changed

4. O' Shea, *A Cross Too Heavy*, 27.
5. Maura Velati, ed., *Diari di Angelo Giuseppe Roncalli/Giovanni XXIII. Pater amabilis. Agende del pontifice, 1958–1963* (Bologna: Istituto per le scienze religioso, 2007), ix.
6. See Pagano, Chappin, and Coco, *I fogli di udienza del Cardinale Eugenio Pacelli segretario di stato*.

from Pacella to Pacelli in the seventeenth century—but it is not precisely known when and why this had occurred. We do know that the earliest accounts of the family relate their political traditionalism, deep religious devotion, staunch loyalty and service to the papacy, and their support for both its political and religious rights.

We also know that the standing of the family was enhanced in January 1774 when Maria Domenica Pacelli married Francesco Caterini, son of another prominent Catholic family from the Onano area. Six children resulted from this marriage, the youngest of whom was Prospero Caterini (1795–1881), who would have an important impact on the life and career of Marcantonio Parcelli, who in turn influenced his son Filippo and his grandson Eugenio. The intermarriage and "alliance" between these two families, devoted to the papacy and the papal state, continued. At the turn of the eighteenth century Maria Domenica's brother Gaetano Pacelli married Maria Antonia Caterini, sister of Francesco. Six children also resulted from their marriage.[7]

Their second son Marcantonio (1800–1902), a name in the papal state generally borne by the nobility,[8] and some believe reflective of the family's high aims and great ambitions, was the future pope's grandfather. Born during the Napoleonic Age, his career was advanced by a number of ecclesiastics, establishing a precedent that would be followed by most of his descendants, down to Eugenio and his nephews. Marcantonio's first cousin Monsignor Prospero Caterini, who became Cardinal Caterini in 1853, acted as the entire family's protector and patron. Almost all the biographers of Pius XII mistakenly refer to Prospero as Marcantonio's uncle. He was not. Since Prospero was the son of

7. Pacelli family tree drafted by Vincenzo Pacelli and posted by Randy Pacelli on April 27, 2001, on *http//genforum.genealogy.com/pacelli/messages/97.html*; O'Shea, *A Cross Too Heavy*, 126; Philippe Chenaux, *Pie XII. Diplomate et Pasteur* (Paris: Du Cerf, 2003), 26–27.

8. Nazareno Padellaro, *Portrait of Pius XII*, translated by Michael Derrick (New York: Dutton, 1957), 6.

a Caterini male who married a Pacelli female, while Marcantonio was the son of a Pacelli, who was brother to the female who married the Caterini male that produced Prospero, the two were first cousins.

Prospero found personal fulfillment and a religious vocation in Rome. However, he missed his extended family which remained in Onano and sought to persuade its more adventurous and ambitious members to join him in the capital. To persuade them to venture to Rome, he pointed out the many educational and employment opportunities available there. He noted that to govern and minister to the millions of his subjects and faithful, the pope required a host of collaborators and assistants—both lay and clerical. This need, together with the vast array of schools and institutes that provided training for potential candidates to serve Church and state, offered prospects simply not available in the small and largely rural Onano.

Prospero's invitation was all the more attractive because it was accompanied by an offer of assistance and guidance both in education and employment to those family members who joined him in Rome.[9] In 1819, Marcantonio and his older brother Giuseppe Pacelli, excited and enticed by the promises and prospects dangled before them, accepted Prospero's suggestion that they transfer to the capital. Together the ambitious duo ventured to Rome for educational, economic, and occupational reasons as well as religious ones, above all nourishing the hope of securing positions in the schools and services of the Eternal City. Advised and assisted by their cousin Prospero, they settled in the Rione di Parione district, across the Tiber from St. Peter's, the source of religious inspiration and economic opportunity. While the older Giuseppe, following the example of his sponsor Prospero Caterini, decided to pursue an ecclesiastical career, the

---

9. Thomas McDermott, *Keeper of the Keys: A Life of Pope Pius XII* (Milwaukee: Bruce Publishing, 1946), 30.

younger Marcantonio determined to study canon and civil law. After receiving his doctorate in 1824 he began practicing in the papal court. With the support and assistance of his cousin, in 1834 Marcantonio was made an advocate of the tribunal of the Sacred Roman Rota—charged with dispensing marriage annulments among other things.[10]

Extremely ambitious, Marcantonio quickly displayed an interest and aptitude in financial and legal matters and later served as undersecretary in the Ministry of Finance during the pontificate of Gregory XVI (1831–1846). During his residence in Rome he married and had ten children—some say twelve! Filippo, Eugenio's father, was his second son. In Rome Marcantonio, following the family tradition, showed himself devoted to the papacy and proved a staunch supporter of its temporal power, both of which had been shaken by the French Revolution, the turmoil of the Napoleonic period, and the revolutionary decades that followed. While Marcantonio remained in Rome, the city experienced unparalleled turbulence. He proved sympathetic to, and supportive of, Pius IX (1846–1878), who began his career as a liberal but in the wake of the revolutionary events of 1848–1849 shifted to the conservative camp. Without hesitation Marcantonio followed him there. Sympathetic to the plight of Pio Nono, he unquestionably adhered to his antinationalist, intransigent, and ultramontist views which prevailed in the papal court, rejecting both the republican notions of Giuseppe Mazzini's "Giovane Italia" (Young Italy) and the obvious territorial ambitions of the Savoyard monarchy. By this time he and his family considered themselves as "Romani di Roma" (Romans of Rome), totally loyal to the papal regime for fiscal as well as religious reasons. Consequently they initially rejected all offers to defect to the national cause championed by the Risorgimento, which called for the unification of the peninsula and a united Italy's absorption of the Papal State.

---

10. Chenaux, *Pie XII*, 26.

Marcantonio's dedication to the papacy was reciprocated and rewarded by the papal administration, which appointed him an advocate of the tribunal of the Sacred Rota. He, in turn, revealed the depth of his loyalty following the renewed revolutionary upheaval in Rome at the end of 1848 and the flight of Pope Pius IX and his chief minister Cardinal Giacomo Antonelli to Gaeta in the Kingdom of Naples. Refusing to recognize the Republic over which Giuseppe Mazzini presided, and his disciple Giuseppe Garibaldi defended, Marcantonio joined the pope and his acting secretary of state in exile, serving as Pio Nono's legal and political advisor during this time of trouble and turmoil. Shrewdly and wisely, Marcantonio chose not to compete but to complement the efforts of Antonelli, who arranged for foreign assistance to implement the pope's restoration and the reestablishment of the Papal State. The grandfather of the future Pope Pius XII focused on internal issues, leaving international affairs in the capable hands of Antonelli.

It was the diplomatic maneuvering of the cardinal that led to the military intervention of the Catholic powers (France, Austria, Spain, and Naples), who orchestrated the collapse of the Roman Republic and brought about the papal restoration of 1849.[11] The Piedmontese, distrusted both by Pio Nono and his chief minister, were not invited to participate in either the military intervention or the political restoration. The Turin government they correctly concluded sought territorial expansion in the peninsula and had national ambitions that threatened the temporal power of the papacy.

On the other hand, Marcantonio Pacelli, who enthusiastically supported the demise of the Roman Republic and championed the pope's restoration, was trusted and once again rewarded, this

---

11. For the papal perspective on the Risorgimento and Counter-Risorgimento, see Frank J. Coppa, *Pius IX: Crusader in a Secular Age* (Boston: Twayne, 1979), and *Cardinal Giacomo Antonelli and Papal Politics in European Affairs* (Albany: State University of New York Press, 1990).

time by being named to the Council of Ten charged with the crucial task of punishing and purging the revolutionary enemies of the papal administration, and paving the way for the pope's return to Rome a year later. His ardor in resisting the demands of the nationalist-inspired liberals pleased Pius IX who in 1851 appointed him undersecretary of state in the Ministry of the Interior, a post he held for some two decades. For his loyal service and productive efforts, in 1858 Marcantonio was enrolled in the Nobile di Sant'Angelo in Vado which listed him and his family as notables, an honor that contributed to Pacelli's sense of importance and prestige, which in turn provided access to other opportunities and contributed to his increased loyalty to the papacy.

In the Eternal City the Pacellis eventually settled in an apartment, number 34, on the south side of the third floor of the five-story Palazzo Pediconi on the Via di Monte Giordano (today Via degli Orsini) in the heart of papal Rome. The owners of their rented residence, still called a palace, confronted by financial difficulties, had been constrained to convert it into an apartment building, housing not one but a number of families. It provided the Pacellis with a number of advantages: its rental was less expensive than the newer constructions, it was close to the Chiesa Nuova, built on the site of the sixth-century Chiesa di Santa Maria di Vallicella, where they regularly worshipped, and was less than a mile away from the Vatican—where they were employed. Their apartment was large—it had twelve rooms—and a certain decadent charm, but remained unheated, even during the coldest days of winter. To make matters worse, none of the stone floors of the drafty rooms was carpeted. In it religious signs and symbols prevailed over elegant décor and included a shrine to Mary which housed a picture of the Madonna painted by Eugenio's paternal uncle, Vincenzo Pacelli, reflecting the religious beliefs and traditional values of the apartment's inhabitants.

The future Pope Pius XII was born on March 2, 1876. His

birth came during the last period of the long, troubled, and turbulent pontificate of Pope Pius IX, whose Counter-Risorgimento sought unsuccessfully to preserve the papacy's temporal power by resisting his state's absorption into a united Italy. Politically perceptive, Eugenio quickly understood that despite Pius IX's intransigent opposition to the Risorgimento, and his restoration following the revolutionary upheaval of 1848–1849, this pope proved unable to prevent the loss of most of his state during the unification of the peninsula (1860–1861). Nor was he able to retain even a remnant of the papal state or preserve his temporal power after Rome was seized by the Italians in 1870. As a result Pio Nono's long pontificate would have a profound influence on his grandfather Marcantonio, his father Filippo, and Eugenio and his brother Francesco. It appears that the failure of the papal policy of intransigence was one of the factors that played a part in moving the young, impressionable, and sensitive boy to shun intransigence for accommodation, which he found useful in childhood and beyond. It was a trait he acquired in his family long before he entered the religious life or the diplomatic service of the Vatican.

Eugenio was the third child and second son, of the lawyer Filippo Pacelli and grandson of Marcantonio, of the "black" or papal faction that opposed the Italian seizure and annexation of the Papal State. The family's distinction stemmed not from wealth or noble status, but from their long and loyal service to the Vatican. Both for religious and economic reasons the elders in the Pacelli family steadfastly refused to recognize the Italian Kingdom's incorporation of the papal state. The total loss of the Vatican's temporal power from 1860 to 1870 had fiscal as well as political and religious implications, so that those who served it could not be, and were not, highly paid.[12] Consequently the

12. For a scholarly examination of Vatican finances, see John F. Pollard, *Money and the Rise of the Modern Papacy: Financing the Vatican, 1850–1950* (Cambridge: Cambridge University Press, 2005).

Pacellis, like so many others in this group employed by the Vatican, while not poor, were far from prosperous.

They were deemed "blacks" because they sided with the papacy and the Church in opposition to the "whites," who supported the national state which had absorbed the pope's territory during the unification of the peninsula, and the opportunistic "grays," who straddled the fence. Marcantonio Pacelli abstained from any contact with the Italian authorities who seized Rome from papal control. Not so his son Filippo (1837–1916), Eugenio's father. Eventually he, and other members of the family, pragmatically abandoned Marcantonio's strict intransigence and came to terms with the new Italian state. Indeed, Francesco Pacelli, Eugenio's older brother, negotiated the Lateran Accords of 1929 which included a treaty, Concordat, and financial settlement with Mussolini's Italy. It led to the sovereignty of Vatican City and played a key role in the reconciliation between the Vatican and the Italian state. The Pacellis thus played a part in the reestablishment of the temporal power—albeit on a very reduced scale. Their devotion to the pope remained constant, although with the passing of time they were reconciled to the loss of much of the papal state. They did so without challenging Marcantonio who continued to hope for a second restoration.

Born into this pious Catholic family which recited the rosary before supper each evening, the Pacellis remained religiously orthodox while some of its members became politically pragmatic. Eugenio was quickly baptized two days after his birth by his paternal great uncle Don Giuseppe Pacelli in the parish Church of Santi Celso e Giuliano in the Via del Banco San Spirito. Early baptism was customary among the very religious families of Rome, and particularly important in Eugenio's case for as an infant he was judged less than healthy. It was widely believed and deemed a dogma that those who were not baptized could not enter heaven and at best might enter a state of limbo. This conviction contributed to Eugenio's early baptism. His godfather for this crucial sacrament was Filippo Graziosi, the brother of his mother; and his godmother was Donna Teresa Pacelli, the sister of his father. From the first, and continuing throughout much of his life, his extended family had a profound influence on the young Eugenio who would later serve as an altar boy for his cousin Don Vincenzo Cirrili at the Chiesa Nuova, the parish Church of the Pacellis which housed the body of the Italian saint Filippo Neri (1515–1595), who Eugenio greatly admired.[13]

Eugenio, like his older brother and two sisters, was profoundly influenced by his parents' religious beliefs and practices along with those of his extended family. Their belief in the unity of the faithful was reflected during his pontificate in his encyclical letter of June 29, 1943, *Corporis Christi*, in which he expounded on the nature of the Church and the unity of the faithful in terms of the Mystical Body of Christ.[14] The family's devotion to the Sacred Heart was outlined by Pius XII in his *Haurietis aquas* of May 15, 1956.[15] Their appreciation of sacred music was reflected in his encyclical *Musicae Sacrae* of December 25, 1955— the first encyclical in the history of the Church that dealt exclusively with the subject of sacred music.[16]

Eugenio also totally absorbed his family's Marian convictions and was especially influenced by his mother's devotion to Mary. This explains some of his actions when he assumed the tiara, and his placing his pontificate under the special patronage of the Virgin. In the years that followed he would become the most Marian pope in Church history. His encyclical of May 1, 1946, discussed the prospect of defining the Assumption of the Blessed Virgin Mary as a dogma of faith.[17] Two weeks later in his radio address "Bendito seja" of May 13, 1946, he praised the Portuguese for

---

13. Alden Hatch and Seamus Walshe, *Crown of Glory: The Life of Pope Pius XII* (New York: Hawthorn Books, 1957), 34.
14. *AAS*, vol. 35 (1943), 193–248.
16. Ibid., 5–25.
15. Ibid., vol. 48 (1956), 309–53.
17. Ibid., vol. 42 (1950), 782–83.

their coronation of the Madonna of Fatima, which helped provide support for the Immaculate Heart of Mary.[18] Subsequently he praised the people of Chile for their devotion to the Virgin.[19] Supported in his endeavor to proclaim the Assumption of the Virgin Mary, at the beginning of November 1950 he released the dogmatic bull *Munificentissimus Deus* which officially defined the dogma.[20] His mother who daily led the family in reciting the rosary made her children supportive of its recitation and led to Pacelli's call in *Ingruentium malorum* of September 1951 for other families to do likewise.[21] Devoted to the memory of his mother, in 1953 Pius XII ordered a Marian Year for 1954—the first pope to do so. That same year he proclaimed the "Queenship of Mary" in his encyclical *Ad Caeli Reginam* which explored and explained her contribution to Redemption.

The pervasive family's influence, which played an influential role in Eugenio's Marian devotion and religious formation, was seen to play a less positive one in other areas. It has been claimed that at times the family's influence and most notably its role in the Counter-Risorgimento and intransigent defense of the temporal power apparently had a negative impact on the impressionable and sensitive Eugenio. In fact, some suspect that the combative stance the Pacelli elders assumed during the course of the Church-state conflict may have led the young Eugenio to withdraw into his interior world and later played a part in leading him to shun confrontation and conflict which he deemed counterproductive. In the words of Domenico Tardini, who years later served as a close associate and his undersecretary of state, Pacelli preferred conciliation to confrontation and sought to persuade rather than impose. It was a trait he displayed at home and school in his childhood, long before he entered the Vatican's diplomatic service, donned the tiara, or had to respond

18. Ibid., vol. 38 (1946), 264–67
20. *PP*, 1.138.
19. Ibid., vol. 43 (1951), 122–24
21. *AAS*, vol. 43 (1951), 635–44.

to Nazi atrocities during the Holocaust.[22] In 1893, at the age of seventeen, he confessed that as a child he saw evil spirits that he perceived had diabolical intentions surround his bed. His response was to hide under the blankets.[23]

His paternal grandfather, Marcantonio, was convinced that the struggle between the papacy and its liberal and nationalist opponents was not only political and military but psychological and educational as well. For this reason he felt that the papacy had to present its case to the public to combat the "propaganda" and "lies" of the nationalist and liberal press which sought to undermine the temporal power. Motivated by the need to educate the public and nourishing the hope of preserving the sliver of territory the papacy retained, in 1861 he played a crucial role in the formation and publication of the newspaper *L'Osservatore Romano*. Subtitled *Giornale politico-morale*, it was a frankly apologetic newspaper committed to the political and moral defense of the papacy, its temporal power, as well as the Church as a whole. Marcantonio served as the initial director of the journal originally created to preserve what remained of the papal state as well as advance the interests of the transnational Church in an age of liberalism and nationalism. The first issue of the *Osservatore Romano* appeared on July 1, 1861, following the proclamation of the Italian Kingdom which sought to make Rome—which was then still under papal control—the capital. Later his grandson Eugenio concluded that radio, television, and motion pictures could play a similar educational and positive role for the Church and the papacy. However, in the nineteenth century neither the columns of the *Osservatore Romano* nor the condemnations of liberalism and nationalism in Pio Nono's encyclical *Quanta Cura* of 1864 and the attached "Syllabus of Errors" proved able to preserve papal control over Rome.

22. Ibid., vol. 46 (1954), 625–40.
23. See "I Pacelli" in O'Shea, *A Cross Too Heavy*, 125–50.

Following the Italian seizure of the Eternal City in September 1870, during the course of the Franco-Prussian War, Marcantonio once again remained loyal to Pope Pius IX, who locked himself in the Vatican. In the bitter Church-state conflict that erupted during this troubled pontificate, Marcantonio refused to accept the new Italian regime. Instead he supported the Vatican's opposition to unification, dubbed the Counter-Risorgimento, serving the cause of the self-imposed "prisoner in the Vatican." Marcantonio shared Pio Nono's antinationalist and ultramontist call for a restoration of the pope's temporal power as a solution to the "Roman Question," and sought to transmit these sentiments to his entire family. Once the Counter-Risorgimento proved unsuccessful, if not counterproductive, this led some members of the Pacelli family to quietly modify their stance. The "restoration" that the pope and the Pacellis fervently prayed for never materialized.

Some family members tenaciously clung to what Italian patriots derided as a "lost cause," remaining firmly entrenched in the papal camp. Like others in the black aristocracy they did not adjust easily to the new "liberal" Italian order. They were scandalized by the anticlerical outbursts in Rome and the rest of the peninsula, the confiscation of Church and papal properties, the disbanding of religious orders, and the drafting of priests and other religious into the army following unification. To protest these "sacrilegious" and "scandalous" developments, like other members of the black aristocracy composed of bourgeois and aristocratic papal adherents, they shunned the national colors of red, white, and green, and proudly donned the papal colors of white and gold. To protest developments in Rome they kept their shutters permanently closed to avoid viewing the "sad state" and "tribulations" of the Eternal City. A determined traditionalist, Marcantonio donned a yellow ribbon roseate while in public to display his loyalty to the papacy. Other families of the black aristocracy wore only one glove, symbolic of the missing pope, while others placed an empty chair in a prominent corner of their apartment to draw attention to the pope who could not be with them, but remained a virtual prisoner in the Vatican.

Filippo Pacelli (1837–1916), the third child and second son of Marcantonio, and the future pope's father, born September 1, 1837, shared his father's religious fervor and pro-papal stance. He was a member of a Franciscan Tertiary—an association of lay Catholics connected to the mendicant and other religious orders that administered to the poor and like his father perceived the need not only to assist the masses but to educate them. Privately, however, he questioned the wisdom of Pio Nono's recourse to total intransigence. Both he and his brother Francesco favored a more pragmatic and flexible approach to the Italian state they regretfully but realistically regarded as a permanent fixture. However, Filippo who shared his father's interest in the law as well as his living quarters, kept his sentiments to himself, but later indirectly transmitted them to his children. In October 1871, the thirty-four-year-old Filippo Pacelli married the twenty-seven-year-old Donna Virginia Graziosi (1844–1920). She also was a member of a traditionally black Italian family from Acquapendente near Viterbo, and not far from Onano. She came from a noble and ultramontist family known for their piety and service to the Church and papacy. Two of Virginia's sisters became nuns and two of her brothers priests.[24] Like the Pacellis the Graziosi had moved to Rome, but more for religious reasons than economic ones.

They too remained devoted to the papacy and likewise supported the Counter-Risorgimento. Virginia was widely perceived and described as a "saintly," "sensitive," and an extraor-

---

24. Considerable information on Eugenio Pacelli's childhood was provided to me by Eugenio Pacelli, a third cousin of the pope, during the course of an interview on April 27, 2006. A useful published source for Eugenio's early years is the *Articoli per Il Processo* (Rome: Vatican Press,1967), information gathered by the Jesuits for Pacelli's beatification and canonization.

dinarily "pious" woman. Her siblings who entered the religious life, maternal aunts and uncles to Eugenio, reinforced the positive image, benefits, and importance of the religious life for him. One of his uncles was a missionary in Brazil—something to which the sensitive Eugenio did not aspire after having heard of the violence to which missionaries were at times subjected. Distressed to hear that some who served the Church were brutally tortured and some even crucified, the precocious five-year-old confided to his older sister Giuseppina that he wanted to be a martyr—but without the nails.[25] Some have suggested that this childhood dread of pain remained with him and later led him to fear the retribution of the fascist dictators and inspired his conciliatory course. This is an interesting supposition but one that has not been, and perhaps cannot be, confirmed. What is known, however, is that Eugenio eventually found less extreme and painful measures than martyrdom to express his devotion to the faith and the Church.

Religious, legal, financial, and political issues were nightly discussed at home and piqued the interest of both Francesco and Eugenio, influencing their outlook and subsequent development. His grandfather and father, as well as other uncles and cousins, also stressed the importance of the law—civil, canon, and international—to which both he and his older brother were attracted.

Filippo and Virginia had four children, two boys and two girls: Giuseppina (1872–1955), Francesco (1874–1935), Eugenio (1876–1958), and Elisabetta (1880–1970). At an early age Donna Virginia led these children in prayer, especially the rosary, and introduced them to the picture of the Virgin in the small chapel of the Madonna della Strada in the Church of the Gesù, which Eugenio later regularly visited on his solitary walk home from school. He would spend hours there and sometimes engrossed

---

25. Hatch and Walshe, *Crown of Glory*, 32.

in prayer did not return home for lunch. His mother understood and forgave him for not doing so. She noted that his Marian devotion provided a spiritual nourishment that more than compensated for a missed meal.

"The family that prays together stays together" was the slogan later adopted by the Roman Catholic Rosary Crusade. It proved true for the Pacellis, who devoted considerable time to prayer and charitable acts, and were attracted to the clerical life. His mother had the greatest influence on Eugenio, her only child to enter the religious life. However, her influence was subtle and psychological rather than overt and obvious, and was partially countered by her husband who favored the study and practice of law for both his sons. However, none of the children were constrained to enter one vocation or the other. In fact, Francesco married and embarked on a legal career which pleased his father; both his sisters also married. Eugenio was torn between the law and the religious life—and some believe he eventually and ingeniously managed to blend the two.

Marcantonio shunned national politics in accordance with Pius IX's *non expedit* of 1868 which deemed Catholic participation in Italian political life inexpedient. In 1886, his successor Pope Leo XIII (1878–1903) issued the *non licet* which virtually prohibited Catholic involvement in the affairs of the "illicit Kingdom."[26] Filippo, dean of the Confraternity of Lawyers of the Consistory, found it expedient for parental reasons to support the ban on Catholic participation in the national political life of the peninsula. When he had the time, he distributed religious literature in the various parishes to stem the tide of dechristianization he believed was being promoted by anticlerical elements allied to the national regime. Privately, he did not share his father's intransigence regarding the Italian Kingdom and believed that eventually and inevitably there would be a resolution of the bitter

26. Frank J. Coppa, *The Modern Papacy since 1789* (London: Longman, 1998), 135.

Church-state conflict. This sentiment he transmitted to his two sons, both of whom later enthusiastically supported the Lateran Accords of 1929, which effected the reconciliation between the Catholic Church and the Italian state. In fact, Francesco Pacelli, with his younger brother's encouragement, alongside Cardinal Gasparri, negotiated the settlement.

Since the papal prohibition did not extend to local and regional politics, Filippo served as a member of Rome's city council for some two decades from 1886 to 1905. He also joined the Roman Union, a clerical electoral alliance to defend and further Catholic interests in municipal affairs and elections. In fact, it was his political activity and diplomatic intercession that restrained the Italian authorities from closing the Roman retreat house of Ponterotto.[27] At the same time Filippo presided over the Catholic Action group that promoted Christian doctrine in the parishes of Rome and distributed religious literature to the poor, both to assure their eternal salvation and to affirm and secure the Catholic nature of the Eternal City. From his grandfather the young Eugenio learned the impact and importance of the press while his father revealed the need for political pragmatism and activism in the defense of the papacy and the Church in Rome. From both, and perhaps most of all from his mother, he acquired a sense of compassion and learned the need to provide instruction for the less fortunate members of society.

Filippo Pacelli followed his father in pursuing a legal career in the service of the Vatican, emerging as dean of the lawyers practicing before the Sacred Rota, one of the Church's highest courts, and aided Pope Leo XIII (1878–1903) in providing a resolution to the Spanish-German dispute over the Caroline Islands in 1886. He also shared his father's fiscal ability by presiding over the Istituto per le Opere di Religione (IOR), or "The Insti-

---

27. Jan Olav Smit, *Angelic Shepherd: The Life of Pope Pius XII* (New York: Dodd, Mead, 1950), 9.

tute for Religious Work," commonly called the Bank of Rome. Founded in 1887, it helped manage papal finances following the total collapse of the Papal State in the decade from 1860 to 1870, and the papacy's refusal to accept the stipend offered as compensation under the terms of the Italian Law of Papal Guarantees of 1871. Pius IX was advised that his acceptance of such funds would signify his acquiescence in, as well as his acceptance and legitimization of, the seizure. Filippo Pacelli clearly understood and supported the papal rejection of money which compromised the Holy See. However, unlike the intransigents, he was receptive to accepting funds and assistance from the Kingdom of Italy that had no strings attached.

A pragmatist, as well as a devout Catholic, Filippo proved selective in his adherence to papal opposition to the national state. Consequently, he practiced law in the civil courts of the new Italian government, with which he had been reconciled, as well as in the papal court. Subsequently, he became legal counselor for a number of important Italian industrial firms as well as financial institutes, thereby enhancing the family's standing and economic position. His second son Eugenio "inherited" his father's pragmatism. Filipppo also had a strong interest in the arts and science and apparently transmitted this, as well as his pragmatism, to his two sons.[28] His second son was particularly fascinated by the technological developments of his age and this likely contributed to his later love of Germany.

Along with the study of law the Pacelli family focused on banking and finance, which increased their income and influence. Although it consumed considerable time and effort it returned substantial dividends. In addition to his father's example, Filippo also followed the path of his brother Ernesto, who served as a key financial advisor to Leo XIII. During Filippo's genera-

28. In this regard, see Filippo Pacelli, *Sulla tutela del patrimonio artistico e scientifico* (Rome: 1891).

tion they not only provided advice and assistance to the Vatican but helped to fund state activities and enterprises.[29] Despite these heavy responsibilities and a hectic schedule, Filippo found time for active membership in the Third Order of Saint Francis, deeply committed to the pastoral task of teaching the catechism to local children and distributing spiritual reading material and pious tracts to the poor in a number of parishes. He, along with his wife, served as a religious model for all their children.

Eugenio's uncle Ernesto Pacelli served as a key financial advisor to Popes Leo XIII, Pius X, and Benedict XV as well as serving as the founder and president of the Banco di Roma (1880–1914) which provided funds for the Vatican and support for various Catholic causes and newspapers throughout the peninsula. He also functioned as a vital though unofficial link between the Italian state and the Holy See. Among other things, he secured funds from the Italian government for Leo XIII following the collapse of the Banco Romano, which had served the Papal State. Ernesto ingratiated himself with prominent members of the curia including the influential Pietro Gasparri by offering advice, loans, and credit. These Vatican officials, in turn, were indebted to him and members of his family and reciprocated the favors. This would later prove beneficial to the careers of Filippo's two sons Francesco and Eugenio.

Filippo, like many other fathers, hoped both his sons would follow in his footsteps and serve as lawyers for the Vatican as well as practice before the state courts. This was one of the main reasons he sent them to the state-run and leading liberal secondary school in Rome, the Ennio Quirino Visconti Lyceum. Here Filippo's two sons received a broad classical education, which put them in touch with the world their grandfather shunned. Eugenio's generation followed the family tradition in preserving their

---

29. Gabriele De Rosa, *Storia del movimento Cattolico in Italia. Dalla Restaurazione all' Età giolittiana* (Bari: Laterza, 1966), 544.

commitment and connection to the Vatican, while adopting their father's pragmatic attitude toward the Italian state. They sought a reconciliation with the Rome government without alienating the Vatican. His older sister Giuseppina married the director of the Bambino Gesù, the Vatican Hospital for Children, while his younger sister Elisabetta married the papal chamberlain and administrator of the goods of the Holy See. His older brother Francesco was called upon to negotiate a number of agreements for the Vatican, including the crucial Lateran Accords with Mussolini's Italy in 1929. Unlike their paternal grandfather, they rejected his negative intransigence and proved willing to operate within the state structure—which they regarded as a reality they could not and did not ignore.

In return for their dedication and service to the Vatican they were compensated by being granted important posts, generous honors, as well as modest salaries. Eugenio apparently absorbed the Pacellis' dedication to the papacy, the need for family solidarity, along with his father's pragmatism and his grandfather's ambition. Witnessing the assistance the Pacelli, Graziosi, and Caterini clans provided their relatives, Eugenio did the same when he was in a position to do so. Thus Francesco, Eugenio's brother was made a marquis, and his three sons, who were Pius XII's nephews, were made princes. Although the titles were granted by King Victor Emmanuel III of Italy, Eugenio's input proved crucial. Furthermore, Prince Marcantonio and Prince Giulio were inducted into the Pontifical Noble Guard, while Prince Carlo was made general councilor of Vatican City. The Pacellis proved able to provide legal and financial guidance to all the popes from Pius IX onward because most male members of the family were well versed in civil, ecclesiastical, and international law, as well as financial matters.

Their friends and relatives in high Vatican circles also helped the Pacelli family succeed. With the passage of time their talent and training, as well as the patronage bestowed upon them, combined to make the next generation of the Pacelli both wealthy and influential. Pius XII, who contributed to their ascendancy, was criticized by some who resented his "revival of Nepotism."[30] It was but one of the many charges launched against Pius XII and his pontificate. Others soon followed.

30. George L. Williams, *Papal Genealogy: The Families and Descendants of the Popes* (Jefferson, N.C.: McFarland, 2004), 134.

TWO

The Child Is Father of the Man

> My heart leaps up when I behold
> A rainbow in the sky:
> So was it when my life began;
> So is it now I am a man;
> So be it when I shall grow old,
> Or let me die!
> The Child is father of the Man;
> I could wish my days to be
> Bound each to each by natural piety

IN 1958, WHEN PIUS XII DIED, Father Robert Lieber, his private secretary who had been as close as anyone else to the solitary, shy, and often aloof pope, commented on the figure he had faithfully served for some four decades. This German Jesuit, one of the few figures whom Pacelli befriended and persuaded to accompany him on his return to Rome, noted the close tie between the boy and the man, pointing to the importance of probing his formative years in order to understand his later policies, positions, and personality.[1] This assessment has been challenged by a few but ignored by most of the combatants in the "Pius War," who have neglected these crucial years in the formation

---

Epigraph is from William Wordsworth, "My Heart Leaps Up."
1. O'Shea, *A Cross Too Heavy*, 135–36

of the future pope. Even worse, some have probed his early years only to discover the roots of his sanctity while others have examined his youth in order to uncover the origins of his pontifical "failures." The selective use of sources by some, and their outright abuse by others, has contributed to the confusion concerning Pacelli and his pontificate.

It is obvious that over several decades ideological considerations and biases have conspired to frustrate an objective historical inquiry into Pacelli's life and pontificate. Since the taciturn and very private Pacelli said little, and wrote even less, about his youth or the development of his personal opinions and sentiments, a number of writers have projected their own image on the young Pacelli that harmonized with their later positive or negative assessments of the man and his ecclesiastical career. Such a priori judgments have not been seriously challenged by the few school-assigned boyhood essays he wrote on his self-image. They have been preserved because they were not in his possession and therefore survived his ordered destruction of personal papers. Having survived, they provide some insight into his inner thoughts and attitude, albeit of a very limited nature.

To further complicate the quest for an objective assessment of Pacelli, as an adult he did not keep a personal diary, and produced no memoir historians might draw upon. The recently found "diary" in the Secret Vatican Archive (ASV) is really a record of topics discussed during his various early morning meetings with Pius XI, who Pacelli served as secretary of state from 1930 to 1939, and appropriately titled *Fogli di udienza*. While it is important in telling us considerable about Pacelli as Pius XI's secretary of state, it reveals virtually nothing about the boy who became the man. Some have claimed that this paucity of personal revelations and sources is largely responsible for the lack of an objective assessment of Pacelli's crucial prepapal life and career or serious examination of the factors that shaped the man who became pope. This may have played a part is discouraging some from writing about this formative period, but it does not explain why a number of serious authors have not probed the available material that sheds light on his first years, family life, and early career.

A series of sources reveal that Eugenio was influenced by his great uncle, grandfather, father, cousins, and brother, all of whom served the papacy as clergy, lawyers, political and financial advisors, and administrative officials. Born and bred within this environment, it is hardly surprising that Eugenio early on likewise thought of serving the Vatican and the Church in one capacity or another. He was well qualified to do so. During his childhood he was seen to be not only bright and possessing a prodigious memory, but mature and determined, extraordinarily well behaved, and disciplined. He was perceived as aristocratic in his bearing and demeanor as well as self-confident—some said proud and stubborn.

From an early age Eugenio did not interact much nor trust most outside his family circle. When the circumstances or his career constrained him to remain apart from his relatives, he created a surrogate family. From his first years he was less than healthy, which paradoxically proved advantageous for the boy because it led his extremely religious mother to lavish special attention on him, according him privileges denied his siblings. As a consequence she exercised the greatest influence on Eugenio. Eugenio was also influenced by his broad and liberal secondary education that piqued his interest in science and technology as well as astronomy, and contributed to his conclusion that faith and reason were not in conflict but reinforced one another. His secondary education also introduced him to a fund of secular literature that complemented the religious reading his parents and other relatives recommended along with those suggested by the clergy of his local parish.

He perceived his solitude not as a burden but a blessing and found refuge in literature and music. He read constantly and widely including popular literature along with religious tracts. He read and reread the classic works of Saint Augustine, Cicero, Dante, and Manzoni along with a series of volumes on astronomy, biology, the physical sciences, and technology. In 1889, at the age of thirteen, in an assigned essay, he wrote that a good book was his best friend.[2] His favorite spiritual reading was *The Imitation of Christ* by Thomas à Kempis, the fifteenth-century monk. Through the intercession of his mother, he was even granted permission to read at mealtime, another privilege not extended to his older brother and two sisters. Both his mind and memory were superb, providing some compensation for his frail body, enabling him to memorize multiple pages of material following a single reading—which impressed those who came into contact with the boy. The clear though very small handwriting he had as a child persisted throughout his life, which makes reading his notes difficult though not impossible. At times he had difficulty deciphering his own script and therefore had frequent recourse to the typewriter, which he found eminently useful both in terms of clarity and the preservation of his privacy, which was a lifelong priority—some said obsession.

A number of observers have mistakenly assumed that Eugenio's assumption of high ecclesiastical office, culminating in the papacy, led to his social isolation, aloofness and sense of superiority. In fact, the inner-directed Eugenio revealed all these characteristics as a young boy. Although some individuals exhibit a profound transformation in personality as they age and mature, such was not the case with Eugenio who essentially retained the same basic personality from childhood. An introvert from a young age, he remained a solitary figure, who said little about himself. "He was different from other children of his age, he was

2. See "I Pacelli," in O'Shea, *A Cross Too Heavy*, 125–50.

nearly always alone," one observer noted "He preferred to keep to himself—to remain detached ... the boy seemed to find his own company sufficient."[3] By temperament he was introspective and reclusive, and like his parents passionate about the Catholic Church, to which he gave his total loyalty and first obedience, and expected other Catholics to do the same. As a child he was profoundly impressed with both the trappings and message of Catholicism. His faith was reinforced by his family life which revolved around the activities of his parish church of Santa Maria di Vallicella where the Pacelli's regularly worshipped and where Eugenio served as an altar boy. Popularly known as the Chiesa Nuova since its reconstruction, it was run by the Oratorian fathers. It was here, in October 1886, at age ten, that Eugenio made his First Holy Communion at a mass celebrated by the cardinal-vicar of Rome, and family friend, Lucido Maria Parocchi, who was also devoted to the Virgin Mary. The young Eugenio liked to walk, almost always alone, to visit the many churches of the eternal city, to which he had initially been introduced by his mother. These visits represented a spiritual as well as physical exercise for the religious, sedentary, and studious youngster. The precocious boy reportedly was impressed by the inscription over the door of Rome's church of Santa Maria della Pace "Opus justitiae pax" (Peace is the work of justice), which he later adopted as his motto, and contributed to his sense of social justice, which has often been overlooked, by a number of his critics.[4] From an early age Eugenio had revealed a certain spirituality, so while other boys were playing soccer and other contact sports, Eugenio preferred to play at "saying mass," at an altar his mother helped him set up complete with candles. When a sick aunt was distressed as well as depressed because she could not attend religious services, the young boy immediately and happily provided a substi-

3. O'Shea, *A Cross Too Heavy*, 124.
4. "Pope Pius Arrayed Catholicism's Spiritual Strength against Materialistic Forces," *New York Times*, October 9, 1958, p. 22.

tute celebration which included a homily at "his altar."⁵ He committed himself to serving others as did both his parents—but on his own terms and in accordance with his talent and interests.

He sympathized with those souls who were kept out of heaven and confined to purgatory, and sought to provide his assistance. Among the sacrifices made by the boy on behalf of these "unfortunate souls in purgatory" was to resist eating his favorite foods and to stop drinking the fruit juices he craved. His self-diagnosed health and digestive problems, determination to exercise self-control, as well as religious considerations, led him to carefully restrict and limit his meals. His rigid diet and frequent abstinence as a child continued into adulthood and prevailed even on festive occasions as he carefully considered what he ate and when he did so. Later, he routinely diluted his wine with water. This restricted diet helps to explain his later lank physique: though just under six feet tall in adulthood, he only weighed 125 pounds. The abstaining child became the ascetic adult who carefully watched and weighed what he ate and imbibed.

Eugenio's spiritual life was directed first and foremost by his mother, the former Virginia Graziosi (1844–1920), who was devoted to the Virgin Mary, supervised the children in prayer several times a day before the shrine to the Virgin in their home, and led the family in reciting the rosary before supper each evening. She thus provided the inspiration for Eugenio's lifelong devotion to Mary and proved instrumental in making him a "Marian pope." He apparently also derived many of his other religious convictions and sense of entitlement from his mother; his pragmatism and legal interests from his father Filippo Pacelli (1837–1916); and his ambition and loyalty to the papacy from his grandfather Marcantonio Pacelli (1800–1902). Later the Oratorian priest Father Giuseppe Lais of the Chiesa Nuova also contributed to Eugenio's spiritual development by helping him

5. Cornwell, *Hitler's Pope*, 18.

comprehend the inspirational literature his father distributed. The young boy responded positively to this instruction, virtually memorizing a number of these spiritual tracts from cover to cover. Critics later charged that while he memorized the words he often failed to internalize the message.

Eugenio's dedication to the Virgin Mary, prayer, sacrifice, and the Eucharist or mass, which characterized his early religious life, remained with him in later years.[6] His mother, who was deeply committed to the education of her children, early-on home-schooled Eugenio and his siblings. When Eugenio reached the age of four in 1880, she supplemented his education at home by enrolling him in a nursery school. She did so largely because she was concerned about her younger son's solitary nature and isolation, believing he needed to socialize more and interact with other children his own age. With this objective in mind, he was enrolled in the kindergarten and elementary school run by Sister Prudence and Sister Gertrude of the French Sisters of Providence in the Piazza Fiametta in what is now the Via Zanardelli. The sensitive, often ailing, boy missed his parents' company and despite his mother's sustained efforts and encouragement, and the prodding of the sisters, the youngster did not socialize much with the other children. This self-imposed social isolation persisted during the course of his subsequent education and beyond, largely because he found solitude comforting, allowing him to arrange his thoughts and convictions.

A creature of habit, Eugenio was initially perturbed by the family's departure from the "Palazzo" Pediconi in 1880 to new quarters in the nearby Via della Vetrina, which became the family residence for the next three decades. Although the new apartment like the old one was spacious and some of the rooms had

---

6. Eva Fleischner, "The Spirituality of Pius XII," in *Pope Pius XII and the Holocaust*, edited by Carol Rittner and John K. Roth (Leicester: Leicester University Press, 2002), 124.

a view of the Tiber River and the Castel Sant' Angelo—which they seldom saw for they kept their windows shuttered to protest the Italian seizure of Rome—Eugenio initially found the change disruptive, especially since a number of the other houses on the new street seemed rather different.[7] After his three year stay with the sisters, in 1883 his parents transferred him to the Marchi Institute. This private Catholic elementary school in the Piazza Santa Lucia dei Ginnasi was near the entrance to the Jewish quarter, again not far from his home. It was a small, two-room school, with four teachers: Signor Giuseppe Marchi, his wife, and brother, who was a priest. The fourth member of the staff was not related to the family. What Eugenio thought of the school, the nearby ghetto, or the Jews of Rome he did not indicate, and is not known.

What is known is that the founder and director of this school was given to anti-Judaic outbursts, denouncing the "hard-hearted Jews" for what they did and what they failed to do. Some believe that this influenced the boy who would become pope, helping to explain his "inaction" during the Holocaust. Aside from those who believe in guilt by association, the impact of these anti-Judaic and anti-Semitic outbursts on the young Pacelli is pure conjecture. There is absolutely no evidence that Marchi's anti-Jewish diatribes infected the young Eugenio any more than did the antipapal and anti-Catholic rhetoric spewed in his subsequent school. In fact, during his high school years one of Eugenio's closest friends was the Jewish Guido Mendes with whom he maintained contact after graduation. Later, when Italian Jews were threatened by Mussolini's anti-Semitic legislation, Pacelli, as Pius XI's secretary of state, enabled the Mendes family to find its way to Jerusalem.[8]

Upon graduation in 1885, at the young age of nine, he entered the secular school system, which he attended from 1885 to 1894,

7. Chenaux, *Pie XII*, 28. Padellaro, *Portrait of Pius XII*, 10.
8. Owen F. Cummings, *A History of the Popes in the Twentieth Century* (Lewiston, N.Y.: Edwin Mellen Press, 2008), 65.

completing his classical studies program in the Ennio Qurino-Visconti Institute, housed in the building of the former Collegio Romano, located in the Piazza Santa Lucia dei Ginnasi, close to the Piazza Venezia. Attendance at a state school was quite extraordinary for children of the "black nobility" who objected to the anticlerical and anti-Catholic indoctrination they heard prevailed therein, and feared might prove detrimental to the faith of their children. Apparently Eugenio's father did not share this concern, confident in the Catholic formation of his boys, and pragmatically enrolled them in this state-run institution because he considered it the best school in Rome, capable of providing an excellent preparation for the study of law and the legal career he envisioned for both his sons. His attendance in this large, secular school, whose students were boys from the age of nine to eighteen, was made easier by the fact that his older brother Francesco was already in attendance and knew the ropes. During his attendance Eugenio further developed his lifelong interest in science and technology and evolved his own coping mechanisms, learning to ignore challenges to his religious beliefs and firm convictions to avoid what he considered pointless and counterproductive debates. Then, as well as later, his lack of response to opinions contrary to his own did not mean he accepted, or much less embraced, them. Rather, he simply found it prudent to avoid confrontations that might prove detrimental to his interests, or in which he might not prevail. He preferred to preserve rather than squander his energy, devoting his time and efforts to subjects that mattered to him.

There was no hint of anti-Semitism in the self-portrait he was asked to compose in school by Ignazio Bassi in 1889 at the age of thirteen, which admittedly and deliberately focused on his physical attributes more than his intellectual framework and inner beliefs.[9] First as a child and later as an adult, the self-assured

---

9. Gianni Padoan, Pio XII: "Con lui—dissse Hitler—farò I conti doppo!" *Historia*, November 1989, p. 19, n. 144.

Eugenio was little prone to ponder over his beliefs much less to reveal them to those outside the family circle. Sometimes he did not divulge his thoughts even to them. He wrote with a certain degree of detachment and objectivity:

> I am of average height. My figure is slender, my face rather pale, my hair chestnut and soft, my eyes black, my nose rather aquiline. I will not say much of my chest, which to be honest, is not robust. Finally, I have a pair of legs that are long and thin, with feet that are hardly small.[10]

He concluded his assigned self-assessment by acknowledging that physically he was a fairly mediocre youth who did not like to have others contradict him—although he forgave those who did so. He also acknowledged his love of music, literature, and the Latin language. On a more personal level he admitted to being possessed by a certain impatience which he sought to control.[11] These were traits and characteristics that would prevail throughout his life and pontificate, as would his tendency to have recourse to circuitous language both in private matters and public affairs.

Eugenio remained more or less silent in the face of the nationalist, anticlerical, and antipapal sentiments often manifested in classes and corridors of his new school, which like most state-run institutions banned religion. This silence did not imply adherence to this blatant anticlericalism and anti-Catholicism. Rather, the self-controlled and extremely confident young student thought it best not to challenge nor question the assertions of his teachers and fellow students, preserving a pragmatic quiet or early "silence." His essay in defense of St. Augustine was the exception that proved the rule and contributed to his subsequent cautious response to challenges to his system of beliefs. As a youngster, and later as an adult, and even as pope, he often

---

10. Cornwell, *Hitler's Pope*, 19.
11. Padoan, *Historia*, November 1989, p. 22, n. 144.

avoided confrontation by ignoring sentiments he did not share, preferring to concentrate on matters within his control. Early on he pragmatically adhered to the Italian proverb "La meglia parola e quella che non e detta," the best word is the one that is not uttered or it is best to leave certain things unsaid. He developed a reticent stance as regards his interior life and opinions lest their exposure undermine his aims and frustrate his ambitions. This strategy proved successful in high school where he was supported by teachers who were clearly liberal as well as those who were rather more conservative. Silence, he found, proved more productive in school and society than counterproductive discourse.

Pacelli was able to impress his teachers in this liberal state school both by his intelligence and his strict focus on the subjects studied. Furthermore, though ideologically committed he was not ideologically identified. He was a good student whose prodigious memory, diligence, and persistence enabled him to absorb material quickly and to learn a series of languages including French, English, German, Spanish, and Portuguese in addition to his native Italian.[12] His linguistic skills and training would later prove eminently useful in both his diplomatic career and his pontificate.

In 1894, the year he graduated from the Ennio Qurino-Visconti Institute with honors, he went on a retreat at Saint Agnese on the Via Nomentana and formalized the decision, which he had been seriously pondering for some time, to enter the priesthood. *Mi farò prete* (I will become a priest) he succinctly informed his parents upon his return from the retreat. His decision and choice of vocation did not surprise his mother and father or his siblings, for the usually uncommunicative Eugenio had within the family circle openly expressed his desire to become a priest since the age of twelve, and his younger sister Elis-

---

12. Padellaro, *Portrait of Pius XII*, 15.

abetta noted that the entire family believed that "he had been born a priest."[13] His mother, who played a central role in his religious formation, was particularly overjoyed.[14] Filippo, who had long favored the study of law for his two sons, did not contest Eugenio's decision or attempt to dissuade him, but respected and supported Eugenio's choice. In fact, Filippo pragmatically weighed the advantages that would accrue to Eugenio and the entire family from his second son's decision to enter the clergy.

A number of considerations rendered his son's decision palatable. First, Filippo had long been aware of Eugenio's desire to become a priest. Furthermore, he was convinced that the priestly life suited his second son, and was satisfied that his older son did follow his suggestion and entered the legal profession. For Filippo's wife, Eugenio's decision was the realization of a dream. Consequently, both parents approved and supported his vocation, but concerned about his frail health and persistent digestive difficulties, they insisted that he continue his education in Rome, where they could closely observe him. This more than suited the young Eugenio, who was devoted to his family and particularly attached to his mother.

His father's decision to accept and support his son's plans to pursue religious study proved crucial. Filippo, dean of the Sacred Roman Rota, wielded considerable influence in the Vatican and the papal court. His backing, along with that of the family parish priest Don Pietro Monti, as well as the candidate's outstanding grades and personal prudence and discretion, assured his admission to the seminary. At the end of 1894 he enrolled in the State University of Rome and subsequently donned the black cassock and entered the oldest college in Rome, the Almo Collegio Capranica of the Lateran University, in preparation for the priesthood, and the Gregorian University for the study of

---

13. Chenaux, *Pie XII*, 33.
14. Charles Hugo Doyle, *The Life of Pope Pius XII* (New York: Didier, 1945), 19.

theology and law—in which he, like his father, grandfather, and older brother had a great interest and considerable aptitude.

The Roman diocesan seminary, founded in 1456 by Cardinal Domenico Capranica, initially appealed to Eugenio for a number of reasons. It was less than half an hour's walk from his home, was Rome's oldest, and in the eyes of many the most prestigious seminary in the Eternal City and offered the most varied education. It had a limited enrollment of no more than fifty students and admission was highly competitive. A wide variety of classes and lectures were held at other colleges in Rome, but none was held in the residence hall. All of this, as well as its renowned reputation in Italy and abroad, appealed to Pacelli. In the first classes he enrolled in Pacelli once again proved to be an exceptionally gifted student with a quick mind and extraordinary memory. However he suffered from claustrophobia and resented the restrictions that hampered his activity. His physical frailty was aggravated by his cramped living quarters which consisted of a tiny room with a small window and a narrow bed. He resented the big bronze bell outside his room which blasted the seminarians out of their slumber at six in the morning. It initiated the rigid routine of the day which Eugenio found disruptive and distressing.

He also disliked and was disturbed by the prohibition of visiting family without prior permission and authorization.[15] Finally, he found the food served in the hall "intolerable." His unwillingness to accept the diet of the seminary and rejection of the greater part of each and every meal served, soon took a toll on his already fragile health as he lost weight and caught lingering colds and severe coughs. Some believe he used the food and his fasting as a visible manifestation and convenient pretext for his real opposition, having to reside at the seminary in the midst of strangers rather than at home with his family. Whatever the basis of

---

15. Alden Hatch and Seamus Walshe, *Crown of Glory: The Life of Pope Pius XII* (New York: Hawthorn Books, 1957), 42–43.

his opposition, within a matter of weeks Eugenio was clearly unhappy at the Capranica, and freely, loudly, and continuously expressed his dissatisfaction to his parents. No silence here.

While Eugenio resented the closed quarters, the regimentation, and the rigid routine he complained most about the food provided. Almost from the first days of his entry, Pacelli constantly criticized the meals served at the Capranica which he judged "unacceptable." His catalogue of complaints prompted his parents to deliver weekly "care packages" to satisfy their son's fastidious appetite and help sustain Eugenio who rapidly lost weight, became visibly thinner, and appeared more sickly, weak, and dispirited with each visit. His loud, persistent, and troubling cough frightened his parents, especially his mother, who feared it would result in a life-threatening tubercular condition. However, his parents' attempt to solve the problem and reconcile their son to the seminary by providing home-cooked meals proved unsuccessful. The family's food deliveries did not reconcile Eugenio to seminary life, for he also disliked the noisy resident hall in which he was housed with his fellow seminarians and did not take to communal living. He especially resented the imposed agenda and regimentation and sought an alternative. Eugenio was determined to continue his preparation for the priesthood—but on his own terms.

Psychological and physical problems contributed to his digestive difficulties and rendered more pressing his incessant and increasingly desperate pleas to prepare for the clerical life outside the Capranica.[16] His vocal and visible unhappiness contributed to a cycle of depression which profoundly distressed his mother. This led her to second and support her "sick" son's increasingly urgent and constant appeals for a transfer. His father, pressed by his wife to help their ailing and despondent son, used his in-

---

16. "Pope Pius Arrayed Catholicism's Spiritual Strength against Materialistic Forces," *New York Times*, October 9, 1958, p. 22.

fluence to intervene on his behalf to secure an unprecedented alternative path to the priesthood for him. Pacelli happily left the Capranica "for health reasons" in the summer of 1895 to continue his studies elsewhere after a welcomed restful interlude with his family at Onano. He was able to do so because Pope Leo XIII granted Eugenio an extraordinary dispensation, allowing him to continue his seminary education as a day student at the Jesuit-run Ateneo Pontificio di S. Apollinare, established by Pius IV (1559–1565) in 1565.

The Apollinare suited a delighted Pacelli not only because it was close to his home but primarily because he could return to his household each evening, allowing him to enjoy the company of his parents and siblings in familiar surroundings. Equally important, at home he would be served food he deemed acceptable and he considered conducive to preserving his good health. Perhaps most important of all, at home he was not subject to the regimentation of seminary life and could withdraw to his room whenever he wanted for the solitude he often craved and needed to read his books, play his violin, and plan his schedule for the following day, without having to provide any explanation or answer to anyone for his increasingly reclusive behavior. His conduct as student and seminarian reflected his youthful aversion to being told what to do, how to do it, and especially when to do it. His mother's intervention had liberated him from these constraints and he appreciated this freedom that he was not prepared to surrender—and which he managed to retain.

For recreation the young seminarian continued to read widely including works on science and technology as well as religious tracts, collect coins and stamps, play his violin, and occasionally in the company of his parents and siblings visit the family home at Onano. This satisfied his need to learn at his own pace in a congenial environment. He certainly did not miss the communal life and collegiality enjoyed by resident students at the seminary, which he deemed more of a burden than a blessing. As a result he did not know—and some said did not care to know—his fellow seminarians. "Pacelli was a loner who did not seek out the company of others," wrote one of his biographers, adding, "he was content to be with his family, read his books and say his prayers."[17] Not surprisingly, the seminarian who was content to remain within the bosom of his family while a student, as pope would later adopt his housekeeper, private secretary, and confessor—all of whom he brought from Germany—to serve as a sort of surrogate family to whose company he could withdraw. It was habit rather than vanity or a superiority complex that led Pacelli, when he became pope, to take his meals alone. For Pacelli solitude was a need that with the passage of time became a virtual necessity.

The personal freedom the Apollinare offered him trumped the fact that its philosophical orientation was eclectic, exposing Eugenio to a number of conflicting ideological frameworks, which did not disturb the young seminarian who was secure in his beliefs and convictions. At the school he was influenced by Riccardo Tabarelli (1851–1909), professor of dogmatic theology, who was a convinced Thomist, as well as by Francesco Faberj (1869–1931), professor of sacramental theology, who was an avid opponent of Scholasticism. Once again, Eugenio displayed a certain natural diplomacy in his ability to preserve good relations with both, pragmatically and diplomatically alienating neither. Surprisingly supported by instructors of decidedly different ideological outlooks, in 1895 he received tonsure, the rite of initiation to the clerical state.

The following year, at the age of twenty, he accompanied Father Giuseppe Lais to Paris to attend a conference on astronomy, in which he had a lifelong interest. His visit to France led to a further appreciation of the work of the scientific mind and

---

17. O' Shea, *A Cross Too Heavy*, 138.

method, and the importance of their contributions to mankind if used properly. He proved remarkably able to compartmentalize and adhere to both his faith and reason. In the months after his return from Paris he received the minor holy orders: porter, lector, exorcist, and acoloyte followed by the three major orders: subdiaconate, diaconate, and finally the priesthood.[18] His academic ability and exceptional exemption from the residency requirement enabled him to easily and quickly complete his studies and receive his degree in sacred theology in 1899 and on April 2, Easter Sunday of that year, at the age of twenty-three, he was ordained a priest. The ordination was performed by Monsignor Francesco di Paola Cassetta (1841–1919) the vice regent of Rome and another influential friend of the Pacelli family, which as in the past did not hesitate to ask for favors for their sons.

Having been granted the extraordinary privilege of studying for the priesthood while living at home, Eugenio was now privileged to be ordained alone, rather than bunched with the other seminarians. According to his wishes, the twenty-three year old priest, devoted to Mary since childhood, said his first mass alongside Father Lais at the side chapel of the Virgin in the Basilica of Santa Maria Maggiore on Easter Monday, April 3, 1899. Convinced of the righteousness of the Catholic faith as taught by the Church, he committed himself to defending both the institution and its teaching.

Following his ordination, Eugenio was favored once again when he was made an assistant to the pastor of the church of Santa Maria in Vallicella, also known as the Chiesa Nuova or "New Church," where he offered his second mass. This was an assignment he sought. He did so because this church was near the family residence, was the church where his parents regularly worshipped, and where he had served as an altar boy after 1886.

18. Ralph McInerny, *The Defamation of Pope XII* (South Bend, Ind.: St. Augustine Press, 2001), 7.

It was also the residence of Father Giuseppe Lais, the renowned astronomer who headed the astronomical club known as Il Circolo della Chiesa Nuova which continued to interest Pacelli. Located in what is now known as the Corso Vittorio Emmanuele, its parishioners ranged from the wealthy to the poor. While some of his biographers maintain that the young priest longed to remain involved in the saving of souls at the parish level, and only reluctantly answered the call to do otherwise, others suggest that this is essentially a pious legend. The latter group claim that from the first Pacelli welcomed, indeed sought, entry into the church's diplomatic service. What we know for certain is that soon after his ordination the intellectually inclined priest decided to limit his pastoral role to continue his studies. With his family's support and approval, he returned to the university, and within two years attained a doctorate in civil and canon law summa cum laude.[19] Apparently a number of figures in the curia concurred that Pacelli's learning and personal diplomatic manner could be put to better use for the Church and papacy than having him locked in a parish assignment.

This view was shared by a number of influential clerics in the curia and above all by Cardinal Vincenzo Vannutelli (1836–1930), a longtime family friend, and Monsignor Pietro Gasparri (1852–1934), who Mussolini later deemed the greatest diplomat he had ever met. While serving as secretary of the Congregation of Extraordinary Ecclesiastical Affairs, considered the first department of the Secretariat of State, Gasparri sought the collaboration of Pacelli and played a crucial role in directing and facilitating his ecclesiastical and diplomatic career. It was Gasparri who put an end to the rumors and speculation that circulated in the Vatican about the path Pacelli's career would or should take. Reportedly, one night in February 1901, while Eugenio was enjoying another quiet evening at home playing the violin, while

---

19. Besier with collaboration of Piombo, *The Holy See and Germany*, 1–2.

his sister Elisabetta accompanied him on the mandolin, there was a loud knocking at their door. When it was opened, the family was reportedly surprised by the unexpected visit of Monsignor Gasparri. Having heard the rumor that Pacelli wanted to continue his parish ministry, Gasparri allegedly said in a booming voice, "So you want to become a shepard," and not permitting time for a response, added, "I want you to become a sheepdog to shy away the wolves."[20] This supposed encounter has not been challenged nor has the part played by Gasparri in directing Pacelli's future ecclesiastical career been seriously disputed.

Nonetheless, the story that Gasparri was constrained to employ all of his legendary power of persuasion to convince the reluctant twenty-five-year-old priest to abandon his parish pastoral plans and enter the diplomatic service of the Church, is questionable, indeed doubtful. Supposedly Gasparri did so by persuading the "impressionable" young prelate that by fulfilling the Church's diplomatic mission, he would also be helping to save souls, and that all work and efforts on the Church's behalf was ultimately pastoral work. Reportedly he also assured Pacelli that he would have plenty of time to continue and fulfill his pastoral mission.[21] In fact, Pacelli was constrained to reduce his pastoral work in order to meet his legal and diplomatic assignments, and all indications suggest he did so willingly. As a child, student, seminarian, and priest, Pacelli did not readily submit to situations he disliked and from a young age was accustomed to charting his own course. It is highly unlikely that Pacelli would have entered the diplomatic service had he not found it congenial and eminently suited for his personality, education, and training. The law and diplomacy had long been major interests whose study and experience he continued to pursue.

Consequently while some believe that Gasparri was con-

20. Kees Van Hoek, *Pope Pius XII, Priest and Statesman: A Biography* (New York: Philosophical Library, 1945), 31.
21. Smit, *Angelic Shepherd*, 29.

strained to resort to a series of reassurances and promises to "lure" Pacelli into the diplomatic fold, others suggest that Gasparri was preaching to the converted for Pacelli had long considered the diplomacy of the Catholic Church eminently important and most interesting. It is believed by many that he had actually sought and welcomed his appointment to the Vatican Secretariat of State in 1901—less than two years after his consecration as a priest. Clearly, once there, he felt at home and advanced rapidly. In 1902, he received his doctorate in canon and civil law, writing a thesis on the nature and importance of concordats. This would provide Eugenio with the theoretical foundation for his later negotiation of concordats.

In 1903 he was promoted in the Congregation of Extraordinary Ecclesiastical Affairs presided over by Pietro Gasparri and given the rank of *minutante* or senior clerk, responsible for drafting letters for the papacy's international diplomatic missions. Subsequently, in 1904 he was made a papal chamberlain and granted the title of monsignor. In 1905 he was named a domestic prelate which made him a member of the pope's official household. He was also asked to teach canon law at the Apollinare, where he was appointed acting professor of canonical institutions. Following the suggestion of his mentor Gasparri once again, he resigned his position at the Apollinare to accept one at the Accademia dei Nobili Ecclesiastici to provide training for future Vatican diplomats, another assignment he found congenial. In 1904, he was once more drafted by Gasparri, this time to assist him in the revision of the code of canon law—a task that Pacelli willingly accepted and that would last for more than a decade.

Along with Gasparri a number of popes including Leo XIII (1878–1903), Pius X (1903–1914), Benedict XV (1914–1922), and Pius XI (1922–1939) all recognized Pacelli's extraordinary intelligence, linguistic skills, perseverance, and loyalty, and sought his advice and service in international affairs. It is true that

Pacelli, following in his father's footsteps, was made a prefect of the Congregation of St. Ivo whose lawyers were committed to assisting deserving but poor clients without charge. However, unlike his father, who devoted considerable time and energy to the program, Eugenio's ever-increasing administrative and diplomatic responsibilities severely restricted his participation in the charitable program. Despite an occasional and largely formal protestation in favor of a more pastoral ministry, over the years he never refused a diplomatic mission for a pastoral one. He did not protest when Pius X called upon him to assist in the resolution of a number of internal issues in the Church including the elimination of the right of exclusion claimed and exercised by the Holy Roman Empire, France, Austria, and Spain and used by Austria in 1903 to veto the election of Cardinal Rompolla as pope. Utilizing his legal expertise, Pacelli willingly and ably provided the juridical and historical justification for the elimination of this "right" in future conclaves.

Pius X also sought his assistance in his conflict with the liberal leadership of the Third French Republic and his battle against modernism. Regarding the first issue, Pacelli concurred with the pope that the French, who had separated Church and state, had acted illegally in unilaterally abandoning the concordat, providing Pius with the material for his encyclical *Vehementer nos* of February 1906 denouncing the French action. It expressed convictions that both the pope and Pacelli shared, claiming that "the same rule applied to the concordat as to all international treaties, viz., the law of nations, which prescribes that it cannot be in any way annulled by only one of the contending parties."[22] It was a belief that Pacelli firmly adhered to during the age of dictators, even after Hitler unilaterally and continuously

22. Harry C. Koenig, ed., *Principles for Peace: Selections from Papal Documents from Leo XIII to Pius XII* (Washington, D.C.: National Catholic Welfare Conference, 1940), 118.

violated the Reich Concordat of 1933 which Pacelli negotiated. Pacelli's services were again invoked when Pius X assigned Gasparri the task of composing a "white book" cataloging the Vatican's complaints against the French violations of the concordat and especially their separation of Church and state. Convinced that the academically inclined and legally trained Pacelli could ably tackle the task, Gasparri, occupied by a number of other assignments and responsibilities, promptly delegated it to him. Consequently the volume on the Vatican's troubled relationship with the French Republic was largely the work of Pacelli.

During the pontificate of Pius X, Pacelli seconded and quietly supported the papal position on the question of modernism. He not only approved the penalties and actions imposed upon its adherents but sought to reinforce and expand the arsenal of repressive measures that might be employed against this "heresy." Unlike the more liberal prelates, Pacelli had no quarrel with the papal condemnation of the movement in the encyclical *Pascendi*, issued in September 1907. In fact, Pacelli proved to be a zealous prelate determined above all to defend the purity of the faith and the integrity of doctrine. From 1906 to 1911, Pacelli collaborated with Umberto Benigni (1862–1911) in combating modernism. A series of letters in the archive of Monsignor Benigni reveal the very close collaboration between Pacelli and the anti-Semetic founder of the secret and repressive League of Saint Pius V.[23] However, despite the assertions of some, there is no evidence that Pacelli shared the anti-Judaism or anti-Semitism of his biased collaborator. Prudence, it is believed, apparently influenced Pacelli's decision not to criticize his superior.

On the other hand, Pacelli did share Benigni's determination to preserve the orthodoxy of the Church and its ministers and in doing so was clearly in the antimodernist camp—though he did not broadcast the fact. His opposition to modernism was

---

23. Chenaux, *Pie XII*, 73.

reflected not only in his strict orthodoxy but also in the fact that while others were persecuted for their association with it, Pacelli continued to receive promotions and honors. Indeed, his work alongside Benigni in the Congregation of Extraordinary Affairs in the Secretariat of State revealed at once his diplomacy and resiliency. Pacelli's various Vatican assignments constrained him in 1908 to reject the offer to teach canon law at the Catholic University of America in Washington, D.C.[24]

In March 1911 Pacelli became sottosegretario, or undersecretary, of the Congregation of Extraordinary Ecclesiastical Affairs and the following year he was selected to serve as an advisor to the Holy Office of the Inquisition, assigned the responsibility of safeguarding the teaching of the Catholic Church in matters of faith and morals. Once again his antimodernism was not publicly displayed, for the pragmatic and prudent prelate did not wish to anger or alienate those who remained sympathetic to the movement. In part this conduct foreshadowed the course he would later pursue toward the atrocities of the Second World War and the Holocaust. More public was his collaboration with his major patron and future cardinal Pietro Gasparri in the revision of the code of canon law (*Codex Iuris Canici*), again at the behest of Pope Pius X. It would absorb a good deal of Pacelli's time and efforts for more than a decade. Critics complained that Pacelli's contribution led to a top-down relationship and an unhealthy centralization in the Church. Furthermore, granting the pope the sole right to nominate bishops was seen to increase the already great power the papacy wielded. The inclusion of the antimodernist oath therein disturbed others who believed it stifled debate.

Undoubtedly, Pacelli sought to strengthen the power and position of the vicar of Christ who had lost the protection offered

---

24. "Young Cleric Declined Professorship in U.S." *New York Times*, October 9, 1958, p. 22.

by his state. Having heard his grandfather's complaints about the callous mistreatment of Pius IX during the Risorgimento and its aftermath, Pacelli saw the need to shore up the position of the pope in the Church so he could more effectively deal with the increasingly secular society of the outside world. Pacelli, in part, also achieved this objective through his work on the revised code of canon law in which he strengthened the pope's standing vis-à-vis the other bishops and Church bodies. Nineteenth-century developments also influenced his diplomatic training from 1899 to 1901, which emphasized secrecy in negotiations and the inviolability of finalized treaties, strengthened by the conviction that the rules of formality reigned supreme.[25] These characteristics and criteria derided by certain twentieth-century critics attracted rather than discouraged Pacelli, who found they suited his penchant for secrecy perfectly and were reflected in his subsequent diplomatic career. He was convinced that realism rather than idealism was central to diplomacy, and appreciated the need to balance ethics and expediency.[26] In fact, Pacelli would soon become the quintessential nineteenth-century diplomat scrupulously cautious in word and deed, and elegant in style and manner. A born negotiator and diplomat, he apparently believed that all problems could best be resolved by compromise and conciliation.[27] It was a stance he would pursue during the course of his developing diplomatic career in Rome and the Reich.

25. Charles R. Gallagher, "Personal, Private Views," *America*, September 1, 2003, p. 9.
26. Chenaux, *Pie XII*, 69.
27. Anthony Rhodes, *The Vatican in the Age of Dictators (1922–1945)* (New York: Holt, Rinehart and Winston, 1973), 182.

THREE

The Making of a Diplomat

Athough Eugenio entered Vatican diplomacy as an *apprendista* or junior clerk at the age of twenty-five, a remarkably rapid and brilliant career awaited him alongside Cardinal Gasparri.

E UGENIO'S ABILITY, discretion, fluency in more than half a dozen languages, negotiating skills, determination, self-confidence, and above all his loyalty to the Church hierarchy was widely recognized and highly valued in the curia. The recognition of these traits contributed to his increasing diplomatic role and responsibilities. It was clear that Pacelli's temperament, training, interests, and institutional loyalty combined to secure his position in the Secretariat of State. Undoubtedly his career was also promoted by his family connections so he advanced not only because of *what* he knew—which was considerable—but also because of *who* he knew. His success commenced with the help of Cardinal Vincenzo Vannutelli, who was friendly with his family; the intervention of Pietro Gasparri, who presided over the Congregation of Extraordinary Ecclesiastical Affairs and had long been indebted to the Pacelli's for legal and financial considerations; and the support of Leo XIII's secretary of state, Cardinal Mariano Rampolla. With their backing, and that of others in the curia, in 1901 he was admitted as an apprentice into

Epigraph is from Emma Fattorini, *Germania e Santa Sede. La nunziature di Pacelli tra la Grande Guerra e la Repubblica di Weimar* (Bologa: Il Mulino, 1992), 17.

the Congregation of Extraordinary Ecclesiastical Affairs, a suboffice of the Vatican Secretariat of State, to which it reported. Considered the training ground for Vatican diplomats, here Eugenio acquired invaluable diplomatic experience to complement his innate ability and his scholarly knowledge of both civil and canon law.

Eugenio's early administrative efforts were bolstered by the enthusiastic recommendations of his superiors, who admired his broad knowledge, self-assurance, and regal bearing. These positive reports led Leo XIII to dispatch him to London following the death of Queen Victoria in 1901 to convey the papal condolences to her son and successor, Edward VII. Pius X, who succeeded to the papal throne in 1903, and his secretary of state, Raphael Merry del Val, likewise appreciated the potential of Pacelli in the promotion of Vatican interests and called upon him to perform various tasks and frequently sought his opinion. Over the years Pacelli collaborated with a string of secretaries of state and clerics of differing persuasion including Cardinal Mariano Rampolla, Cardinal Raphael Merry del Val, and above all Cardinal Pietro Gasparri.

Unquestionably, one of Eugenio's major assets was his ability to collaborate with individuals of the most diverse personalities, principles, policies, and political programs. In the Secretariat of State Pacelli worked with the ultraconservative, secretive, and anti-Judaic Monsignor Umberto Benigni (1862–1934), who railed against the "Jewish-Masonic" sects and conspiracies, edited the anti-Judaic newspaper *La Voce della Verità* or "Voice of Truth," conducted a clandestine campaign against modernism and its adherents—and ended his life as a Fascist.[1] Some believe he transmitted both his anti-Judaism and his anti-Semitism to Pacelli.[2] This conjecture is more or less based on the fact that

---

1. Frank J. Coppa, *The Papacy, the Jews, and the Holocaust* (Washington, D.C.: The Catholic University of America Press, 2006), 112, 130.

2. Sergio Minerbi, "Pius XII: A Reappraisal," in *Pope Pius XII and the Holocaust,*

Pacelli preserved an effective collaboration with him. However, there is no evidence to suggest that Pacelli's beliefs and convictions were influenced by his association with the extremely biased monsignor.

Others have noted that when Pacelli entered the Secretariat of State at the turn of the century, it was not only anti-Judaic but anti-Semitic[3] and this colored his outlook. This accusation emerged because Pacelli did not challenge those who espoused such prejudiced views. However, this silence, like his earlier ones, reflected his desire to avoid the adverse consequences that he feared might flow from confrontation—especially with one in a position of power. His failure to challenge their biases did not imply consent, but rather revealed that Pacelli pragmatically sought to avoid fights that might prove detrimental to his career and interests—a trait he had displayed and employed since childhood.

From an early age Pacelli possessed an extraordinary ability to coexist and collaborate with those who harbored very divergent beliefs, learning not to contradict opinions he did not share by keeping his own views private to avoid "counterproductive" confrontations. Adherence to such silence did not prove difficult for Pacelli, whose temperament and personality favored privacy and secrecy. The fact that he preserved a cordial relationship with an anti-Semite or an anti-cleric should not lead to the conclusion that he espoused the biases of either. Pacelli simply transposed the conciliatory and cautious approach he had developed over the years in his private life and interpersonal relations to his official duties and his diplomatic assignments. In the diplomatic realm this technique often proved useful and was highly valued by some, but deemed morally problematic by others.

Although some questioned the appropriateness of this "di-

---

edited by Carol Rittner and John K. Roth (Leicester: Leicester University Press, 2002), 85–86.

3. Joseph Adler, "The Dreyfus Affair," *Midstream* 48, no. 1 (January 2002): 31.

plomacy of silence" for the Holy See, Pacelli's efforts found a legion of supporters in Vatican circles. This too helped place his career on the fast track. He was appointed to the prestigious Congregation of Extraordinary Ecclesiastical Affairs upon the recommendation of its secretary Pietro Gasparri, who thought highly of this ecclesiastic, who soon became his protégé.[4] Among other things, Pacelli collaborated with Gasparri in the crucial drafting of the new code of canon law from 1904 to 1917, assuming the bulk of the burden, which was much appreciated by the cardinal. Not all were pleased by what he produced. Critics complained that this code worked to establish a "top-down" power relationship in the Church, and blamed Pacelli for laying the foundation of this authoritarian structure. Pacelli did play a part in this development, but he reflected rather than originated this structure which was advanced by the papacy, the curia, and the hierarchy. His ardent acceptance of the prevailing clerical power structure, and determination to assure and perpetuate it, earned him the trust of the upper echelons in the Church and furthered his career.

It would be wrong, however, to assume that pragmatism rather than principle always determined and dominated Pacelli's policy. In fact, at times he had recourse to pragmatic means to implement his principles. This approach likewise proved eminently successful and personally advantageous. As earlier noted, in return for his loyal and competent service in 1905 Pope Pius X (1903–1914) made Pacelli a papal chamberlain and bestowed the title of monsignor. Convinced of Pacelli's ability and reliability, in 1908 Pius X sent him to London once again, this time to attend the nineteenth Eucharistic Congress. Three years later he was once more dispatched to the British capital for the coronation of George V. These trips not only increased Pacelli's visibility abroad but better enabled him to understand the English political structure, and the policies

---

4. Chenaux, *Pie XII*, 52.

that island nation might pursue. At the same time these ventures increased his prestige at home and abroad.

As a consequence Pacelli's intellectual ability and broad knowledge of Church law was recognized not only in the Vatican, Italy, and Europe but across the Atlantic in the United States as well. His enhanced reputation led the rector of the Catholic University of America to invite Pacelli to become professor of Roman law at the pontifical university in Washington, D.C. The intellectually inclined prelate was flattered and tempted by the invitation, but was constrained to reject the offer due to the "fatherly prohibition of the saintly Pontiff, Pius X."[5] Apparently, at this juncture he was already deemed a valuable asset the Vatican was reluctant to lose. He was called upon to teach international law and ecclesiastical diplomacy at the school for papal diplomats in Rome and did so willingly from 1909 to 1914. In 1912 his cooperation with Benigni brought dividends and he was appointed to replace him as assistant secretary of the Congregation of Extraordinary Ecclesiastical Affairs or acting secretary of the Vatican foreign office. Two years later, in 1914, he assumed the direction of this important congregation as its secretary.

Long an advocate of concretizing and legalizing the liberty and rights of the Church by formal accord,[6] he was selected by Pius X to negotiate a concordat with the Kingdom of Serbia. The agreement he concluded provided a number of guarantees for the faith but antagonized the Austrians and were therefore deemed by some dangerously counterproductive. It was signed on June 24, 1914—four days before the assassination of Archduke Franz Ferdinand at Sarajevo by a Serb nationalist, which prompted Austria-Hungary to attack Serbia, sparking the First World War. It was believed that Pacelli's accord with Serbia

5. The 1958 article that reported this offer and its rejection was titled "Young Cleric Declined Professorship in U.S.," *New York Times*, October 9, 1958, p. 22.
6. See Eugenio Pacelli, *La personalità e la territorialità delle leggi, specialmente del Diritto Canonico* (Vatican City: Poliglotta Vaticana, 1912).

antagonized Austria-Hungary and this has led John Cornwell, among others, to conclude that his agreement played a part in provoking Austria-Hungary to attack Serbia—leading to the outbreak of the First World War. In Cornwell's words "the Serbian Concordat undoubtedly contributed to the uncompromising terms that the Austro-Hungarian Empire pressed on Serbia, rendering war inevitable."[7] In his mania to condemn Pacelli, Cornwell's virtually ignores the long-held contingency plan of the Austrian military to wage a preventive war against Serbia. The ultimatum was not a spur-of-the-moment decision, but another reason and pretext for implementing the military's contingency plan and final solution for Austria's nationality problem.

Dreading the prospect of a European-wide conflict, the grief-stricken and depressed Pius X died on August 20, 1914. In early September Giacomo della Chiesa, who had recently been made a cardinal, became Pope Benedict XV (1914–1922).[8] Elected for his diplomatic expertise—as Pacelli would be elected on the eve of the Second World War—he emerged as an "apostle of peace" in a divided continent. Cardinal Pietro Gasparri became his secretary of state and the thirty-eight-year-old Monsignor Eugenio Pacelli served as secretary of the Congregation for Extraordinary Ecclesiastical Affairs, a post analogous to that of undersecretary of state.

The new pope, no less than his two immediate predecessors, appreciated and had recourse to Pacelli's widely recognized competence, perhaps more so than Leo XIII or Pius X because there was a certain affinity between the new pope and Pacelli, both of whom were less than healthy as children and constrained to attend schools close to home. Della Chiesa and Pacelli also possessed remarkable memories and intellectual abilities and were prone to follow set and vigorous daily routines. Both attended

---

7. Cornwell, *Hitler's Pope*, 51.
8. ASV, SS, Morte di Pontificie conclavi, Bendetto XV.

the Capranica and studied at the Gregoriana and earned doctorates in canon and civil law and theology. Like Pacelli, Benedict taught at the Accademia dei Nobili Ecclesistici and manifested a great interest in diplomacy and its potential use on behalf of the Church. Finally, the careers of both were advanced by patrons who brought them into the Secretariat of State. Small wonder that Pope Benedict and Eugenio Pacelli, kindred spirits, found themselves in accord on most internal and international issues and pursued similar paths and policies, a fact that is often shunted aside by those seeking to heap greater responsibility upon the shoulders of Pacelli.

Benedict XV was elected on September 3, 1914, too late to take any step to prevent the outbreak of war. The new pope called upon both Gasparri and Pacelli—whose very name connoted peace—to help preserve papal "neutrality" and assist him in the onerous task of restoring tranquility to the Continent—no small responsibility. Often forgotten and sometimes deliberately neglected is the fact that Gasparri, who became secretary of state in October 1914 after the premature death of Cardinal Domenico Ferrata, was the chief architect of the policy of "impartiality" the papacy adhered to during the course of the two world wars. It was a policy that allowed the pope as Vicar of Christ to denounce principles and even policies in general, without naming particular parties or embroiling the Church in partisan politics or favoring one side over another in conflicts. This policy of impartiality was supported by Pope Benedict and Monsignor Pacelli.

The vast majority of the Vatican's "diplomatic experts" concurred with Gasparri, Benedict, and Pacelli that impartiality was the only policy the Vicar of Christ could and should pursue, for the faithful were found in both camps and only an impartial pope would he be trusted and able to broker a settlement between the combatants. Furthermore, supporting one side against the other would jeopardize the unity of the Church and require Benedict to firmly establish the political, legal, and moral guilt of one camp and the innocence of the other—clearly not his principal aim. Pacelli steadfastly supported this stance during the course of the First World War, and later as Pope Pius XII, adopted, and adhered to it during the Second World War. Adherence to impartiality provided the rationale for Pius XII's public silence during the latter war and the Holocaust.

The insistence on impartiality instead of neutrality was not simply a stylistic play on words but reflected the tension between diplomacy and morality, and religion and politics. Benedict explained that the Holy See was not, and did not want to be, neutral, in the European war, but had the duty to remain impartial.[9] Apparently this distinction was constructed to quiet the pope's conscience and assure the Christian world that the pope could, would, and should make moral judgments. However, he would not necessarily act upon them by making political decisions or public pronouncements or supporting one state in a conflict against another. Benedict, Gasparri, and Pacelli hoped thus to illustrate that impartiality did not mean indifference to ethical considerations. This allowed Benedict to quietly and indirectly render a moral judgment of the German violation of Belgian neutrality, permitting him to remain politically silent while diplomatically seeking redress and restoration. While broadly supported in the curia, Benedict's and Gasparri's insistence on impartiality provoked criticism in the Church as well as outside it. Early on, some denounced the notion that the Vicar of Christ could make moral judgments but not issue any public condemnation to seek redress of an obvious wrong. This complaint would later surface in the face of Pius XII's public silence toward Nazi aggression and the Holocaust.

---

9. "Pope Eager to Convince the World at Large of His 'Absolute Impartiality' in the War," *New York Times*, July 24, 1916.

The nature and use of impartiality in the First World War, and later in the Second World War, although extremely important, has been little studied. During the Second World War it was employed to justify the public "silence" of Pius XII. In the earlier conflict none of the belligerents understood or appreciated the distinction between neutrality and impartiality, which was perhaps only comprehended by three individuals: Pope Benedict, who utilized it; Secretary of State Gasparri, who devised it to prevent the pope's moral indignation from leading to some precipitous political outburst with unfortunate consequences; and the secretary of the Congregation of Extraordinary Ecclesiastical Affairs, Pacelli. During the course of the Second World War, Pacelli inwardly condemned the Nazi invasion of Poland but did not publicly denounce it. In fact, Pacelli would later also repeat Benedict's claim that he had condemned all the atrocities perpetrated during the conflict, even if he did not name those responsible for these crimes.

This construct developed by Benedict and Gasparri, in collaboration with Pacelli, was justified by the Vatican because it allowed the pope to denounce principles while remaining silent on particular practices and policies, thus assuring papal neutrality. It was hoped it would allow Benedict XV to play the part of an honest broker in the search for peace and aid a stricken humanity during the First World War. Subsequently this encouraged Pacelli, who became Pope Pius XII in 1939, to do the same during the Second World War—but at a greater cost and with far graver consequences. Both popes hoped that by preserving the papacy's "absolute impartiality," it would be trusted by both camps and could more readily influence the course of events. This did not occur. It was rendered difficult the summer and fall of 1914 due to the restricted outreach of the Holy See,[10]

10. David Alvarez, *Spies in the Vatican: Espionage and Intrigue from Napoleon to the Holocaust* (Lawrence: University of Kansas Press, 2002), 127.

and the fact that neither of the belligerent camps was pleased by Benedict's election. Indeed, both sides questioned his and the Vatican's motivation.

Despite his proclamation of impartiality and humanitarian desire to end the suffering and turmoil, there was widespread suspicion of papal intentions in both camps. Rome was most suspicious of all, fearing that the papacy really sought to undermine the work of the Risorgimento and restore the temporal power by destroying the liberal Italian state created by Camillo di Cavour, Giuseppe Garibaldi, and Victor Emmanuel of Piedmont-Sardinia—as well as the forgotten figure of the Risorgimento, the Contessa di Castiglione.[11] It had acquired the pledge of its allies to keep the papacy out of the peace conference and supported a series of spies within the Vatican. Some Protestants in Britain worried about the Vatican's religious designs, while in Berlin Benedict was suspected of being the pro-French *franzosiche Papst*. His failure to condemn German aggression in general, and the invasion of Belgium in particular, was resented in Paris where he was denounced as *le pape boche* sympathetic to the Central Powers.

The suspicion of both camps did not discourage Benedict from attempting to reestablish peace nor prevent him from issuing a series of exhortations to the powers to reach a settlement, including those of September 8 and December 6, 1914; May 25, July 28, and December 6, 1915; March 4 and July 30, 1916; and January 10 and May 5, 1917. During the first year and a half of his pontificate, Benedict XV issued more than forty appeals for reconciliation, all of which fell on deaf ears. Nonetheless, Pacelli fully supported these efforts, appreciating the need to preserve papal impartiality in order to act as an effective mediator. He understood Benedict's motivation and neither publicly nor privately did Pacelli question Benedict's failure in 1914 to condemn

---

11. Frank J. Coppa, "The Contessa di Castiglione: The Forgotten Figure of the Risorgimento," *Italian Quarterly* (Winter–Spring 2004): 47–53.

the German violation of Belgian neutrality or his decision in 1915 not to publicly condemn the Turkish genocide of the Armenians. Like Benedict and Gasparri, Pacelli appreciated the need for papal impartiality for the mediation of peace and the preservation of Catholic unity.[12] This course had the overwhelming backing of the curia and College of Cardinals with only a small but vocal minority denouncing it as the triumph of diplomacy over morality, of prudence over principle.

Benedict and Pacelli also concurred on the need to keep Italy out of the conflict: the first during the First World War and the second during the Second World War. Benedict's main objective was to restore peace and in the interim mitigate the suffering of combatants and civilians—again a program strikingly similar to the one Pacelli would adopt during the course of the Second World War. During the first conflict Pacelli gained experience in providing relief for war victims when Cardinal Gasparri commissioned him to contact the belligerents for the exchange and reparation of prisoners of war as part of the papal "apostolate of charity." Benedict's relief program also called for the hospitalization of wounded prisoners and civilians, provision for visitation rights, and decent burial in individual, marked graves for the fallen.

Benedict also sought material aid in the form of money, clothing, food, and medicine for those rendered destitute by the war. His own charitable effort and generous assistance to the victims of the conflict virtually bankrupted the Vatican treasury. In addition to providing material aid, a papal bureau was established for locating prisoners, informing their families of their location and condition, and providing the mechanisms and means for the exchange of letters.[13] The Vatican's entire wartime "mis-

12. For Benedict's peace efforts, see in the Archivio Segreto Vatican (ASV), the Archivio Particolare Benedetto XV, and in the Segreteria di Stato (SS), the Spoglio Benedetto XV.
13. Walter H. Peters, *The Life of Benedict XV* (St. Paul, Minn.: Bruce Publishing, 1959), 179–86.

sion of mercy" was coordinated by the Congregation of Extraordinary Ecclesiastical Affairs, over which Pacelli presided.[14] This massive relief effort would provided invaluable experience for his pontificate's "crusade of charity" during the Second World War.

Initially charged with supervising the papacy's ambitious relief program, Pacelli was subsequently entrusted with a broader political role and responsibility—especially as regards the pope's peace initiatives. Pacelli shared the pope's belief that Italy's entry into the war would prove detrimental to its people and dangerous for the Church and the papacy, and concurred with Benedict's decision to discourage such an intervention. Since Italian nationalists were calling for "unredeemed Italy," namely, the Austrian-held provinces of Trent and Trieste, the pope and Pacelli sought to persuade the Habsburg state to make territorial concessions in return for monetary compensation, hoping this would discourage the Italians from entering the conflict.[15] This plan followed the suggestion made by Mathias Erzberger, leader of the Catholic Center Party in Germany, during his February 1915 visit to the Vatican. Erzberger proposed that to discourage Italian intervention the Austrians might be persuaded to turn the Trentino over to the pope, who would then transfer it to the Italians, eliminating the pretext for Italy's intervention in the war.

To garner Austrian support for this territorial transfer to Italy, in 1915 the pope and Gasparri dispatched Pacelli, who spoke German, as the Vatican's special envoy to the multinational Habsburg Empire. Pacelli was sent to the Austrian capital to assist Monsignor Raffaele Scapinellli, the apostolic nuncio to Vienna, to negotiate with Emperor Franz Josef regarding concessions to make to Italy to keep her out of the war. The papal envoy was known to be sympathetic to German culture—an im-

14. Smit, *Angelic Shepherd*, 35.
15. *New York Times*, February 7, 1922, p. 4.

portant asset for this assignment. In the Vatican note to Franz Josef introducing their emissary, Gasparri indicated they were sending a representative who had their complete confidence. This did not matter much to the old emperor, who was more concerned with the message rather than the messenger. During the meeting, Pacelli accurately concluded that the Austrian emperor was not prepared to make a priori territorial concessions and that diplomatic and military decisions were not made in Vienna but in Berlin, suggesting that any proposal for the Central Powers' consideration required German consent, and therefore any future envoy should be dispatched to Berlin rather than Vienna.

The failure of Pacelli's mission to Vienna, followed by Italy's entry into the conflict in May 1915, exposed the precarious position of the Vatican inside one of the belligerent countries. In the eyes of critics this compromised not only its impartiality but also the security of the Holy See. This led some to propose the transfer of the Holy See from the Vatican in Rome to a more neutral and safe environment such as Switzerland, Liechtenstein, or Monaco. The Roman Pacelli strongly, one might say vehemently, opposed such a move but moderately, calmly, and diplomatically proposed less drastic measures in his response to his fellow Italians Benedict and Gasparri.

This prospect of an Italian infringement continued to haunt the curia, which inspired another diplomatic initiative on the Vatican's part. Despite the earlier promises made by Vatican officials that they would not raise the Roman Question, and repeated reassurances provided to the Italians that they would not do so, the documents in the Vatican Archive reveal that Vatican diplomats took steps in that direction. In the summer of 1915 these diplomats issued a highly secret circular to all the Vatican's representatives abroad, in Catholic as well as non-Catholic countries, urging their governments to make every effort to help resolve the

Roman Question. Pacelli was embroiled in the campaign, as is revealed in his correspondence with the Bavarian minister to the Holy See, Otto von Ritter.[16] The Bavarians, hoping to enlist the support of the Holy See for their own diplomatic efforts to combat centralization in Germany, championed the internationalization of the Roman Question.

Although Pacelli accepted the need for a reordering of the position of the papacy, he responded cautiously and pragmatically to the proposal for international intervention regarding the pope's precarious position in Rome at that time. On the one hand, he agreed that all the powers with Catholic populations should be concerned about the difficult situation of the Holy See, but, on the other hand, he insisted that the difficult and delicate European situation and the war's division required extreme caution and prudence.[17] For this and related reasons he had serious reservations about convoking an international Catholic Congress during the war, even if it were presided over by a neutral state such as Switzerland. Pacelli did not consider such a step opportune at the moment. He knew how sensitive both belligerent camps were to any departure of the Holy See from its absolute impartiality, having been assigned the task of explaining why an article in the *Osservatore Romano* had indirectly criticized the invasion and occupation of Belgium. Pacelli hinted that the Roman Question might better be addressed at the end of the war during the peacemaking process, in which he assumed the Vatican would participate.[18] At this juncture he and the curia were unaware of the Allied determination and decision to exclude the Vatican from any role or even any participation in the peacemaking process.

Nonetheless, Pacelli's call for caution had considerable merit and reflected the reality that both the French and Italians were

16. Otto von Ritter to Pacelli, August 23, 1915, AAES, Bavaria, 21, n. 99.
17. Pacelli to Otto von Ritter, September 1, 1915, AAES, Bavaria, 21.
18. Pacelli to Otto von Ritter, November 3, 1915, AAES, Bavaria, 21.

suspicious of the Holy See's activities and closely monitored its diplomatic moves. Indeed, in order to keep abreast of Vatican developments, the Italian government retained a number of clerical and lay agents on its payroll to spy on its every maneuver. Through these means in November 1915 the Allies learned that Benedict XV was soliciting the advice of various cardinals on whether, when, and how to seek a seat at the peace conference. Clearly, he was unaware that earlier Italian concerns had resulted in Article 15 of the Treaty of London of April 26, 1915, which the Italian foreign minister, Sidney Sonnino, had insisted upon, and specified that the Holy See would not be permitted to play any part in the peacemaking process. Only at the beginning of 1916 did the Vatican learn of the Allied commitment to Italy. Pacelli was assigned the task of responding to the exclusion. He complained to the Allied Powers as well as the United States that the prohibition of its participation was not only offensive but unjust. It also required a reassessment and readjustment of Vatican diplomacy. The Italians in turn denounced Benedict—in Italian "Benedetto"—as "Maledetto," or the damned one.

At the end of 1916, when the Central Powers dispatched a note to the Allied Powers and the pope suggesting the opening of peace negotiations, the Holy See reacted cautiously, largely because of the skepticism of the secretary of state, Gasparri. Pacelli, on the other hand, privately proved more receptive to the German initiative and proposed pursuing it to see what resulted—but he was neither willing nor able to challenge his superior. Ultimately, the Vatican did not respond to the German initiative because it feared that its support might be seen as favoring the Central Powers. This accusation was deemed plausible in light of the fact that the pro-German Joseph Caillaux, a former French premier, ventured to Rome to obtain Vatican support for the German plan. Benedict refused to meet with him, not wishing to jeopardize his absolute impartiality and because he was on the verge of launching his own peace initiative. The papal proposal called for the replacement of military force by moral right and national self-interest by international cooperation. It reflected the internationalism of the prewar pacifist peace movement, which sought a peace of compromise without conquerors or conquered, invoking the restitution of occupied territory and the *status quo ante bellum*.

Both the curia and Benedict perceived Pacelli as the ideal candidate to present the outline of the papal peace proposal to the Germans. For one thing he had earlier indicated that any peace negotiation required the consent of the Germans, while Gasparri, another potential envoy, was needed at home to direct Vatican diplomacy. In fact, the pragmatic secretary of state, Pacelli's major patron, harbored a certain pessimism about the prospect of the papal peace initiative, and sought to spare his sensitive protégé the humiliation of another failure by keeping him at home, working on the completion of the code of canon law. However, the unexpected death of Giuseppe Aversa, the Vatican's first emissary to Germany, followed by Benedict's insistence on sending Pacelli to fill the vacant post, constrained Gasparri to dispatch him to Germany.[19] In April 1917, the pope and Gasparri agreed to have Pacelli present the outline of the papal peace proposal to the Germans. To ensure a proper hearing, Benedict appointed him apostolic nuncio to Bavaria, whose residence was in Munich, but at the same time he was also accredited to the Imperial Court at Berlin.

Pacelli's nomination was welcomed by the Bavarians and most other Germans. What was surprising was the speed with which the Vatican moved to implement his delicate diplomatic assignment. On May 13, 1917, Benedict personally consecrated Pacelli with the honorary title archbishop of Sardes, in the Sistine Chapel, to make the still young prelate a more respectable

19. Besier with the collaboration of Piombo, *The Holy See and Hitler's Germany*, 9.

negotiating partner. It was one of the hundreds of sees that existed only on paper and imposed no pastoral responsibilities that might hinder Pacelli's diplomatic duties. The ecclesiastical title and office were conferred for political rather than pastoral considerations. Nonetheless, Pacelli thought it prophetic that on the very day of his consecration the Virgin Mary, to whom he had been devoted since childhood, appeared to three illiterate children in the small town of Fatima, in Portugal.[20]

The consecration ceremony was attended by a number of key cardinals from the curia, including Gasparri, Merry del Val, Raffaele Scapinelli, and Cardinal Andrea Früwirth—a virtual chorus of Pacelli admirers. After the ceremony he was warmly embraced by the pope and cardinals, who wished him well and prayed for the success of his crucial mission. The newly minted archbishop left Rome for Munich on May 20, 1917, occupying two train compartments: one for his person and another holding some sixty cases of groceries to sooth his sensitive stomach while away from home. It was only on the eve of his departure that the Italians, who made all the train arrangements, alerted the Vatican to the exorbitant cost of carrying the prelate and his food in private and separate compartments, as Pacelli stipulated.[21] He considered it a small price to pay for his time away from his home and family.

Although optimistic regarding the papal peace proposal, Pacelli did not share the pope's haste in venturing to Bavaria, making two stops in Switzerland en route to Germany. The first was at Lugano, the small Swiss city across the Italian border, where the representatives of Austria, Bavaria, and Prussia to the Holy See had withdrawn in May 1915, when Italy had entered the war. Their departure pinpointed the fact that the Holy See no longer had a state that could provide refuge for the represen-

20. The children were Lucia dos Santos and her two cousins Francisco and Jacinta. While all three saw her, only the girls heard her.
21. Chenaux, *Pie XII*, 107–8.

tatives of the combatants. Here he met his friend the minister from Bavaria, Baron Otto von Ritter, and the minister from Prussia, Otto von Mühlberg. This stop was justified for the two alerted him to a number of difficulties they foresaw he would confront in Germany that might undermine his efforts to win support for the pope's projected peace initiative. Their warnings did not appear to discourage Pacelli, who remained supremely confident in his negotiating skills and power of persuasion.

His second stop was the abbey of Einsiedeln, where he met Monsignor Rudolf Gerlach, who had earlier ingratiated himself with Benedict and Pacelli and had been made a papal chamberlain. When the Italians produced convincing evidence that the Bavarian priest was central to the German intelligence operation in Italy, Benedict reluctantly let Gerlach go, consenting to have the Italians transport him to Switzerland. Despite the scandal, the prelate retained the confidence of the Holy See which continued to consult him as Pacelli did during his stop at the abbey. Word of these meetings confirmed the Allies' suspicion of the pro-German proclivity of the Vatican and reinforced their view that Benedict was the *"Boche* Pope." Their mistrust was supported by the reports of the Italian agents who at times exaggerated their findings in order to justify their salaries from the cash-strapped Italian government.

Pacelli, for his part, remained convinced that he could sell the papal peace proposal to the Germans—whom he considered a rational people. He reached Munich on May 25, where he received a quasi-royal reception, presenting his credentials to King Ludwig III of Bavaria a few days later. Toward the end of June, Pacelli commenced his peacemaking mission when, accompanied by Cardinal Felix von Hartmann, he arrived in Berlin and settled in the nunciature in Briennerstrasse, opposite the building that Hitler later converted into his Brown House.[22] Soon

---

22. "Search for Peace Marked His Reign," *New York Times*, October 9, 1958, p. 23.

thereafter he met with the German chancellor, Theobald von Bethmann-Hollweg, and discussed the necessary preconditions for a negotiated settlement as outlined by Pope Benedict. These included (1) the limitation of armaments, (2) the establishment of international tribunals, (3) Belgian independence, and (4) leaving contentious issues such as Alsace-Lorraine to be settled by the contending parties. The chancellor, acknowledging that the pope could play a major role in the peacemaking process, personally approved Benedict's preconditions, posing no objections to his peace proposal.

Overconfident of his diplomatic ability and nourishing illusions as to what he could accomplish,[23] Pacelli believed his mission would end successfully. In fact, he jumped to the conclusion that the chancellor's positive reaction to his presentation signified the German government's approval of the papal preconditions for peace. Consequently, he was convinced that a major hurdle had been overcome and the first steps necessary for the opening of peace talks had been accepted by the German government. Furthermore, Pacelli predicted that the peace plan would be supported by most Austrian and German Catholics. In fact, much of this was wishful thinking on his part. In his euphoria he virtually ignored the chancellor's admission that though Germany wanted peace he was uncertain if the time was ripe for its negotiation. Accentuating the chancellor's positive responses while discounting his doubts, the nuncio convinced himself that the war-weary Germans would back the pope's peace proposal. Pacelli was unaware that Bethmann-Hollweg's approval was an expression of his own opinion and failed to inquire whether the chancellor had consulted the kaiser or the military. Nor did he know that soon the chancellor would be constrained to resign by the emperor, the military that still believed they could win the

23. J. S. Conway, "The Vatican, Britain and Relations with Germany, 1938–1949," *Historical Journal* 16 (1973): 148.

war, and the conservative classes that feared the internal consequences and ramifications of acknowledging defeat.

Some believe that the veteran and "wily" chancellor deceived the young and relatively inexperienced prelate, who had a lot to learn.[24] Others claim it revealed that while Pacelli's intellectual and theoretical understanding of diplomacy and international affairs was unrivaled, the interpersonal relations of the aloof archbishop were less than ideal. Both these assumptions are less than fair as regards Pacelli. Bethmann-Hollweg did not know that generals Hindenberg and Ludendoff were plotting to force his resignation, that Erzberger had lost confidence in his leadership, and his opinions would soon be discounted. Consequently how could Pacelli, an outsider, know that a change of government was forthcoming? Finally, Pacelli was not aware of the military situation on the Eastern Front which favored the Germans and understandably rendered them far less likely to make a priori concessions to obtain peace.

In the specific instructions Gasparri dispatched to him on June 13, Pacelli was instructed to meet with the German emperor and assess if he were willing to recognize the independence of Belgium and return Alsace-Lorraine to France. On June 29 Pacelli ventured to the kaiser's military headquarters at Kreuzach with Lorenzo Schioppa, the chief political advisor at the Munich nunciature, to present the pope's letter to Wilhelm II outlining the papal peace plan. The kaiser frowned as he read the pope's message invoking German concessions and his remarks, in turn, did little to reassure the nuncio. Wilhelm further disturbed Pacelli, who favored papal impartiality, by complaining that Benedict had failed to use his infallibility to condemn the "atrocities of the Allies." On key issues the kaiser proved evasive and questioned crucial aspects of Benedict's proposal including the future of Belgium as well as French claims on Alsace-Lorraine, jumping from

---

24. Peters, *The Life of Benedict XV*, 142.

one point to another in rapid succession. Finally, he shocked the sensitive nuncio by suggesting that Pope Benedict die a martyr's death in the quest for peace. This apparently struck a nerve for Pacelli, who as a child wanted to be a martyr—but did not want to suffer.

As usual, Pacelli did not reveal his anger and inner sentiments nor contradict or correct the egocentric emperor, keeping his feelings and disappointment hidden. This pleased Wilhelm, who might not have liked the pope's message but was impressed with the messenger, whom he later described in his memoirs as "aristocratic," "distinguished," possessing "great intelligence" and "impeccable manners,"[25] and who understood German even though he could not speak it fluently. This may have been the case in 1917, but later, during the course of more than a decade in Germany, he did acquire a fluency in speaking the language he loved. Indeed, it was the only language he later used in speaking to Sister Pascalina, his housekeeper, even though she had become fluent in Italian.

Pacelli, for his part, was less than impressed with the Kaiser, who shattered his illusion that his mission would end successfully. Very likely this contributed to his negative impression of Wilhelm II, whom he found fanatical, distracted, incoherent, and far from normal.[26] Whether this last assessment was an indirect reference to the rumors of the emperor's latent homosexuality or simply a reference to his bizarre behavior is not known. What is known is that the enormous self-confidence Pacelli displayed since childhood survived and prevailed in this matter, for he convinced himself that others were responsible for the unfortunate turn of events including the German emperor and Matthias Erzberger, the leader of the Catholic Center Party. Pacelli complained that Erzberger did not provide real help in getting

25. Chenaux, *Pie XII*, 110, 143.
26. Pacelli to Gasparri, June 30, 1917, in Archivio della Sacra Congregazione per gli Affari Ecclesiastici Straordinari (AAES), Germania, 415.

the pope's plan approved and later judged him more of a liability than an asset.[27] Like most others in the curia and most notably Gasparri, Pacelli, descendant of a long line of lawyers, preferred legal to political solutions and tended to increasingly blame the parties for the Vatican's failure to achieve its goals. Indeed, he grew increasingly suspicious of political parties, even Catholic ones, and preferred to assure the rights and independence of the Church by means of concordats.

Pacelli's distrust of political agreements was confirmed by the replacement of Bethmann-Hollweg in mid-July followed by the Reichstag's adoption of its own peace resolution days later, which also invoked a "peace without annexations and indemnities."[28] Since it did not seem to conflict with Benedict's suggestions, Pacelli continued to press Benedict's peace initiative. During the course of a secret meeting with the new chancellor, Georg Michaelis, on July 24, Pacelli revealed the memorandum to be delivered to the belligerents which included all the points of Benedict's peace note of August 1, 1917. This proposal reiterated both Benedict's aims and plans for ending the war including his determination to preserve absolute impartiality; to do the utmost good without distinction of persons, nationality, or religion; and finally to neglect nothing that might hasten the end of the calamity. Later the kaiser boasted that he had provided the inspiration for the papal peace note—an assertion Pacelli felt constrained to contradict. Nonetheless, a good part of the political class in the Allied camp found it convenient to believe the kaiser's contention—later providing another pretext for their rejection of the papal peace proposal.

During the nuncio's ongoing discussion with the German

---

27. Pacelli to Gasparri, July 15, 1920, Archivio della Nunziatura in Monaco (ANM), posizione 328, fascicolo 1, folio 41.

28. Avro Manhattan, *The Vatican in World Politics* (New York: GAER Associates, 1949), 149.

government, little was conceded by the new chancellor Michaelis —whom Pacelli rather mistakenly described as sincere and anxious to find a solution to the present international problems. In fact, he reflected the stance of the military and was not prepared to make any commitment on restoring Belgian independence as a basis for negotiation. Inevitably Pacelli's remaining optimism that the Germans would accept the papal preconditions for the opening of peace talks began to fade before the harsh reality. Following the collapse of Russia and the German military's determination to impose the punitive treaty of Brest-Litovsk (March 1918) upon the fallen empire, the prospect of their acceptance of the papal peace proposal or even that of the Reichstag appeared slim. Generals Erich Ludendorff and Paul von Hindenburg, who increasingly made political as well as military decisions, categorically rejected the notion of sacrificing either Belgium or Alsace-Lorraine prior to any peace negotiations. A disappointed Pacelli returned to Rome empty-handed and had to report that the Germans had failed to make any commitment to the pope's plan. Sensing that Benedict was determined to press on, he encouraged the pope to proceed with his peace proposal.

The specific terms the pope proposed for the conclusion of peace included (1) a simultaneous and reciprocal decrease in armaments, (2) international arbitration to replace the recourse to war, (3) free intercourse of peoples and liberty of the seas, (4) the reciprocal renunciation of war indemnities, (5) evacuation and restoration of all occupied territories, and (6) the resolution of political and territorial claims between Italy and Austria and France and Germany to be determined in a spirit of equity and justice. Finally, (7) the pope called for the use of equity and justice to determine other territorial and political disputes, particularly those concerning Armenia, the Balkan states, and Poland. The program called for first the suspension of the fighting, second the reduction of armaments, and finally the institution of arbitration to resolve differences.[29] Although just, it was an unrealistic plan for terminating the conflict which had aroused anger and animosity in both camps.

Not surprisingly, from the first neither of the belligerent camps proved receptive to Benedict's idealistic but vague terms. The new German chancellor, Georg Michaellis, drafted a vague statement that promised that his government would support every effort of His Holiness which could be reconciled with the interests of the German people. The American secretary of state, Robert Lansing, was more forthright in his rejection, indicating that the Allies could not "take the word of the present rulers of Germany."[30] The reaction of the English, French, and Italians to Benedict's peace proposal proved equally dismissive. At this juncture neither belligerent camp envisioned a peace without victory. Although not responsible for the failure of the mission, it left Pacelli physically and psychologically exhausted.

Subsequently the Americans, who had become cobelligerents alongside the Allies, would succeed where the "impartial" Holy See had failed. As war weariness increased and the prospect of an Allied victory increasingly depended upon the Americans, for the European Allies were militarily and economically dependent upon the United States, the Allies pragmatically proved more inclined to follow the idealistic proposal introduced by the American president, Woodrow Wilson, than that of the pope. Wilson's "fourteen points" of January 1918, which elaborated upon the pope's seven suggestions, appeared borrowed from Benedict's proposal and deemed by some equally unrealistic. The American plan called for (1) renunciation of secret diplomacy, (2) freedom of the seas, (3) removal of economic barriers between nations, (4) reduction of armaments, (5) impartial adjustment of

29. *Dès le Début* (To the Belligerent Peoples and to Their Leaders), August 1, 1917, in Koenig, *Principles for Peace*, 29–32.
30. Peters, *The Life of Benedict XV*, 11, 156.

colonial claims, (6) evacuation and restoration of Russian territory, (7) restoration of Belgian sovereignty, (8) evacuation of France and the return of Alsace-Lorraine, (9) redrawing the Italian frontier along national lines, (10) autonomy for the peoples of Austria-Hungary, (11) evacuation of Montenegro, Rumania, and Serbia, (12) self-determination for the peoples of the Ottoman Empire and freedom of navigation through the Dardanelles, (13) establishment of an independent Poland with access to the sea, and finally (14) creation of an association of nations to govern international relations.[31]

Pope Benedict, Cardinal Gasparri, and Nuncio Pacelli, having failed in their efforts to end the conflagration, supported all the points of the American proposal, including the reorganization of international life and the creation of a League of Nations to prevent future conflicts. Subsequently, the Covenant of the League formed the first part (Articles 1–24) of the treaties of Versailles (with Germany), Saint-Germain (with Austria), Trianon (with Hungary), and Neuilly (with Bulgaria). Meanwhile, Benedict expressed the hope that Catholic Poland would be restored as Wilson prescribed and allowed to resume its place in the family of nations.[32] Anticipating this development, in April 1919, the Holy See recognized an independent Poland. While the Vatican applauded the restoration of this Catholic country and the creation of the League of Nations, its Secretariat of State decried the fact that most of the other points upon which Germany had surrendered were violated during the peacemaking process, and found the treaty both unfair and counterproductive, observing that the Germans had real cause to complain. These sentiments were shared by Pacelli who spent the last year

---

31. "The Fourteen Points," January 8, 1918, in G. A. Kertesz, ed., *Documents in the Political History of the European Continent, 1815–1939* (Oxford: Clarendon Press, 1968), 347–49.

32. Benedict XV to Archbishop Kakowski of Poland, October 15, 1918, in Koenig, *Principles for Peace*, 255–26.

of the war traveling throughout Germany dispensing Vatican funds to provide food and clothing to its suffering population, with whom he openly sympathized.

Until Pacelli moved to Munich he had lived with his family, and he particularly missed his mother's presence and cuisine in Bavaria. Therefore he welcomed the addition of Sister Pascalina Lehnert, who was moved from her teaching position in Swabia and added to the staff of the nuncio. While there is no indication of impropriety on Pacelli's part, it was extraordinary that the papal envoy be permitted to have a nun who was eighteen years his junior to head his household. Indeed, critics charged it was contrary to the code of canon law Pacelli himself had earlier drafted—but this apparently did not disturb or deter him. Critics claimed this attitude reflected his sense of entitlement nourished by the privileged position he had enjoyed since childhood.

Disregarding criticism and gossip, Pacelli retained the service of Sister Pascalina, originally assigned to him for only two months. Once she achieved a good rapport with the aloof nuncio, he found steps to ensure she would remain at Eugenio's side until his death. Although his junior by almost two decades, the twenty-three-year-old sister served as a sort of mother substitute and confidant as well as his cook, housekeeper, and secretary, first in Munich, then in Berlin, and finally in Rome. Her presence made it easier for Pacelli, who missed his mother, to remain in the Reich and better able to tackle the diplomatic duties that Benedict thrust upon his shoulders. In the spring of 1918 he implored the pope to give him permission to return home to visit his ailing mother. His request was granted, and Pacelli remained in Rome from March 16 to April 3, 1918, where he briefed Benedict on the German situation on March 24, 1918, and met with Gasparri on a number of occasions.

Although frustrated by the rejection of his peace initiative, the pope continued his diplomatic efforts to secure justice for the vanquished as well as the victors. Early in January 1919,

Benedict XV met with Woodrow Wilson, the first president of the United States received by a pontiff, and the two discussed prospects for peace and the need to construct a new basis for international relations. Like Wilson, Benedict favored a reorganization of such relations, noting the inability of the prevailing international anarchy to peacefully resolve conflicts. He had adhered to this stance since the beginning of his pontificate and in 1914 appealed to the nations of the world to find some other means of resolving differences and disputes. Deploring the violation of international law, Benedict believed this contributed to the carnage of the First World War and sought a new code of conduct to assure a more tranquil future. Cardinal Gasparri expressed similar sentiments when he had elaborated upon the papal peace proposal of August 1917, focusing on Benedict's call for a new world order which included "the suppression, by common accord, of compulsory military service; the constitution of a Court of Arbitration for the solution of international questions and disputes; and lastly, for the prevention of infractions, the establishment of a universal boycott."[33]

The pope, his secretary of state, and his nuncio to Bavaria all welcomed the fourteenth point in Wilson's peace proposal, which called for the establishment of a general association of nations for the purpose of providing mutual guarantees of political independence and territorial integrity for great and small states alike. Later Pacelli supported the League's successor, the United Nations. Unfortunately the League's performance did not fulfill its promise which contributed to Benedict's depression and death at the beginning of 1922. With the continued support of Cardinal Gasparri, Pacelli's diplomatic career would advance during the stormy pontificate of Achille Ratti, who became Pope Pius XI in 1922, the same year that Benito Mussolini became prime minister of Italy.

33. Cardinal Gasparri to the archbishop of Sens, October 7, 1917, in Koenig, *Principles for Peace*, 238–39.

FOUR

In Germany, 1917–1929

Soon after becoming Pope, Pacelli told a group of pilgrims from Germany: "We have always loved Germany where We were able to spend many years of Our life, and We love Germany even more today. We rejoice in Germany's greatness, rise, and well-being and it would be false to assert that We do not desire a flourishing, great, and strong Germany."

The German foreign minister von Ribbentrop, following a meeting with Pius XII, said, "the Pope *has always his heart in Germany* and a great and lasting desire to reach a firm and lasting understanding with Hitler."

IN 1917 PACELLI WAS dispatched by Pope Benedict XV to Bavaria as nuncio, and entrusted with the delicate and difficult task of gaining German support for the papal peace effort.[1] It was a surprising, indeed extraordinary appointment. Pacelli, despite his enormous self-confidence and extraordinary intellectual ability, had limited international experience, with the exception of his drafting the white book on the rupture of diplomatic relations with France and his earlier mission to Austria-

---

Epigraphs are from George O. Kent, "Pope Pius XII and Germany: Some Aspects of German-Vatican Relations, 1933–1943," *American Historical Review* 70, no. 1 (October 1964): 65; and Pierre Blet et al., eds., *The Holy See and the War in Europe, March 1939–August 1940* (London: Herder, 1965), 359.

1. See ASV, Archivio della Nunziatura Apostolica in Monaco, Monsignor Eugenio Pacelli (nunzio, 1917–1925) buste, or folders, 307–415; and Segretaria di Stato, Rapporti con gli stati, Archivio Storico, Affari Ecclesiastiche Straordinari, Baviera, posizione 190, fascicolo 29; posizione 198, fascoli 40–53.

74

Hungary in 1915.[2] His visits to London were ceremonial rather than substantive, the white book he drafted in 1905 was more legal than diplomatic, the concordat he signed with Serbia in 1914 was criticized for the unfortunate consequences it allegedly produced, while his visit to Vienna in 1915 proved brief and unsuccessful. This history did not elude the Germans, who commented on his lack of experience in foreign service and international affairs.[3] His appointment as nuncio and peace emissary entailed far greater responsibility and prestige than any of his previous assignments, explaining his consecration as an archbishop. It was an honor bestowed for diplomatic rather than pastoral purposes.

This assignment proved more important for Pacelli than the peace process. For the newly minted archbishop it was virtually transformative.

His long residence in the Reich played a key role in confirming him as a Germanophile. He was stationed in Munich from 1917 to 1925, and in Berlin from 1925 to 1929. In June 1920 he was accredited as apostolic nuncio to the Weimar Republic, presenting his credentials to Friedrich Ebert, its president, at the end of the month. The first years of his tenure as nuncio were crucial ones in Europe and witnessed the end of the First World War; the Bolshevik Revolution in Russia, which inspired revolutions in Central Europe and Germany; the Treaty of Versailles; and the tormented birth of the federal Weimar Republic from the ashes of the German Empire. Economic dislocation combined with political dissatisfaction to create an explosive situation over much of the Continent, while the Bolshevik threat from Russia compounded the confusion.

In the "new Germany," a federal republic with seventeen states and as many governments, Pacelli witnessed firsthand the

2. Fattorini, *Germania e Santa Sede*, 17.
3. Stewart A. Stehlin, *Weimar and the Vatican, 1919–1933: German-Vatican Relations in the Interwar Years* (Princeton, N.J.: Princeton University Press, 1983), 13.

problems of a troubled country he came to love and the chaos of a divided continent. During his long stay in Germany he sympathized with the plight of the population whose virtues, scientific skills and technological innovations, and culture he soon admired and whose language he liked to speak. Some, such as the journalist John Cornwell, have charged that the nuncio's correspondence from Munich reveals that Pacelli also came to adopt some German vices, including anti-Semitism.

In *Hitler's Pope*, Cornwell charges this is revealed in his refusal to support the request of Rabbi Werner to have the Vatican intervene with the Italian government to permit the export of palm branches, needed for their celebration of the Feast of Tabernacles.[4] If anything, it reflected the anti-Judaism which indeed persisted in certain quarters of the pre-Vatican II Church and curia, and opposed the Jews on a religious rather than a racial basis. Though different in origin from anti-Semitism, it proved discriminatory and detrimental to the well-being of Jews in Italy and abroad. Pacelli, over the course of some four decades, might have imbibed from this well or perhaps simply pandered to those in the Church infected by it. This religious discrimination, rather than racial stereotyping, would have influenced his and the Vatican's reservations about assisting the Jews conduct their religious services.

Apparently the nuncio recognized that it would be insensitive and unwise to reveal the Holy See's reluctance to assist the Jews conduct their religious services. Thus his formal and diplomatic rejection claimed the Holy See could not fulfill the Jewish plea because it did not have diplomatic relations with the Kingdom of Italy, and therefore did not have the means to secure the request.[5] One might also question Cornwell's contention that

---

4. Cornwell, *Hitler's Pope*, 70–71
5. Pacelli to Gasparri, September 4, 1917, and Gasparri to Pacelli, September 18, 1917, Archivio Segreto del Vaticano, Segreteria di Stato, Germania, fascicolo 852, ff 2–4.

the nuncio's description of the negative features and boorish behavior of the Jewish revolutionaries in Bavaria in 1918 was representative of "stereotypical anti-Semitic contempt," intimating once again that Pacelli was an anti-Semite.

Unfortunately, recourse to such language and stereotypical descriptions were all too common at the turn of the century but were not always consciously reflective of racist sentiments. In fact, Pacelli had used similar derogatory language in his description of Chancellor Theobald von Bethmann-Hollweg—who was not Jewish. Furthermore, the memo Cornwell cites was written by Pacelli's assistant Monsignor Lorenzo Schioppa—although most likely approved by Pacelli—and the original in Italian is somewhat more descriptive and less derogatory. Perhaps the frequent references to the Russian nationality and Jewish religion of the revolutionaries was meant to convey the political and religious threat the Church in Germany confronted by appealing to the anti-Bolshevik and anti-Judaic sentiment that prevailed in certain curial circles. To be sure there were anti-Semites in the Church, as some have noted,[6] but this persuasion was personal rather than institutional and there is no indication that Pacelli was a member of that small group who violated the Christian principle that salvation was available to all races and peoples.

A more accurate accusation was launched by the Allies who charged that the Vatican was sympathetic to the Austro-Hungarian state and its German ally, sentiments which Pacelli clearly shared. Some suspected that he also sympathized with the German hierarchy, including Monsignor and future cardinal Michael Faulhaber, who believed the war against France was a just one. Word of Pacelli's meetings with the German chancellor and the kaiser in 1917 confirmed the Allies' suspicion that the pope's projected peace plan was inspired by the Central Pow-

6. In this regard, see David Kertzer, *The Popes against the Jews: The Vatican's Role in the Rise of Modern Anti-Semitism* (New York: Knopf, 2001).

ers. This was not so, even though the kaiser in his memoirs later claimed he played a crucial role in its elaboration. German input in Benedict's proposal seems unlikely since the German authorities in general, and their military in particular, did not believe that Benedict's proposal reflected the military reality. Both camps therefore rejected papal mediation. The intervention of the United States led them to accept Woodrow Wilson's fourteen points as a basis for the peace.

Pope Benedict, his secretary of state, and his nuncio to Bavaria all supported the American proposal in the hope and expectation it would provide the basis for a lasting peace. Striving to preserve his impartiality, Benedict indicated that the well-being of the troubled continent rested on a fair treatment of Germany and a just peace. Pacelli shared this conviction. At the same time the pope urged the Allies to end their blockade, which burdened civilians, and to abandon their plans to condemn the kaiser and his leading officials as war criminals. In fact, the papal secretary of state, Pietro Gasparri, warned that if Germany were not given a reasonable peace, it would become a Bolshevik ally and imitate Russia. His prediction proved prophetic for in 1918 and 1919 a series of communist-inspired uprisings erupted in Germany. These outbursts, it was believed, flowed from the fact that papal pleas for a just peace were not heeded and many of Wilson's points were violated during the peacemaking at Paris. To add insult to injury, the Germans were constrained to acknowledge their responsibility for provoking the conflict in the "war guilt clause" (231), while article 227 of the treaty sought the trial of the kaiser and his officials. These developments set the stage for the reparations commission's determination that Germany would have to pay a total of 132 billion gold marks.

These burdensome terms along with the financial instability stoked by the prospect of a huge reparation bill each year contributed to the revolutionary agitation that gripped much of postwar Germany. Pacelli, like Benedict, sympathized with the German people, questioned the wisdom of the harsh terms of Versailles, and deplored the violations of the commitments the Allies had made to end the war. Upset by the terms he considered grossly unfair, the usually discreet and diplomatic Pacelli branded the treaty an "international absurdity." This judgment was shared by Gasparri. "We now count ourselves as lucky not to have been invited and not to have participated in this work," he asserted, warning that the proposed "peace" terms would "result not in one but in ten wars."[7] Similar sentiments were expressed in the *Osservatore Romano* and the *Civiltà Cattolica*, which reflected the Vatican's viewpoint.

On the other hand, neither the Catholic press nor the nuncio in Munich approved of the violent left-wing reaction and the chaotic revolutionary agitation in the Reich provoked by the "betrayal" of the Allies. Pacelli, who remained in Bavaria, favored the parties of order following the fall of the Wittelsbach dynasty and deplored the Spartacist revolution in Bavaria led by Kurt Eisner. He described the leader of the revolution to Gasparri as an "atheist, radical socialist, propagandist and intimate associate of Russian nihilists," adding "what's more a Galician Jew."[8] Within this context Pacelli included Eisner's religion within his catalogue of complaints against the revolutionaries, but it is not clear whether this was simply a reflection of his own thought or an appeal to the Secretariat of State which some claim was anti-Judaic if not anti-Semitic.

It did reveal Pacelli's strong and determined opposition to this communist revolution and the "democratic social republic" it created.[9] For a series of reasons Pacelli continued to avoid all

7. Stehlin, *Weimar and the Vatican*, 71.
8. Pacelli to Gasparri, November 15, 1918, ASV, AAES, Nunziatura Apostolica Baviera, n. 10856
9. Pacelli to Gasparri, November 8 and 10, 1918, ASV, Archivio della Nunziatura Apostolica in Monaco, posizione 397, fascicolo 1, folios 2r, 3r.

contact with its leader, Eisner, but did not specifically list his Jewish background for this boycott. He explained his rationale to Gasparri. First, his government was only provisional; second, it was composed of atheists, radical socialists, and friends of the nihilists, while its leader had been arrested many times for his political crimes. He therefore deemed Eisner a figure with whom an apostolic nuncio should not, and could not, have any respectable relationship. Furthermore, he continued, any association or meeting with him would provide this revolutionary renegade a certain legitimacy while having a deplorable impact on Catholics and all those who championed order.[10]

As chaos and violence escalated in Munich, the nuncio alerted the Vatican to the gravity of the situation.[11] Pacelli feared for the security of the nunciature as well as his own personal safety and with Gasparri's permission left for Switzerland at the end of November 1918. He wrote the secretary of state that he did not want to be a representative to a communist regime or provide it any legitimacy.[12] Following the elections of January 12, 1919, for the Bavarian Landtag, which awarded the parties of order a substantial majority, Pacelli returned to Munich, despite the warnings of his friend Monsignor Faulhaber. Indeed, when he returned at the close of 1919, the situation in Munich remained precarious and the nuncio's concerns were compounded. His fears were not mitigated by the new and provisional Bavarian constitution which introduced a separation of Church and state which Pacelli believed sought to undermine the privileged position of the Church in Bavaria. He was particularly alarmed by article 15 of the constitution of this revolutionary regime, which

10. Pacelli to Gasparri, November 20, 1918, ASV, Archivio della Nunziatura Apostolica in Monaco, posizione 397, fascicolo 1, folios 22r–24r.

11. Pacelli to Gasparri, November 20, 1918, ASV, Affari Ecclesiastici Straordinari, 42.

12. Pacelli to Gasparri, November 15, 1918, ASV, Affari Ecclesiastici Straordinari, Baviera, posizione 129, n. 10856.

specified that the school curriculum would be determined only by the state, which in Pacelli's perspective called into question the Church's right to require religious instruction in the schools of Catholic Bavaria.[13]

Pacelli believed that in postwar Bavaria and Germany two sorts of regimes might emerge: a democratic and parliamentary one, or a dictatorship of a minority. Although he perceived weaknesses in both, he preferred the first over the latter.[14] The course of events confirmed him in this conviction. The assassination of Kurt Eisner on February 21, 1919, led to the creation of a more radical and revolutionary regime which imprisoned its critics and confiscated property. Pacelli denounced its leader Max Levien as "dirty," a "Russian Jew" and "repulsive"—but not as "a repulsive, dirty Jew." His "bossy" comrade and companion Pacelli found equally disagreeable, describing her as a "divorcee" and likewise a "Russian Jew."[15] In the post-Holocaust era such descriptions and usage would immediately and quite rightly be deemed anti-Semitic. However, in the context of the period and during the course of its revolutionary events, such unfortunate descriptions used by some clerics and part of the laity reflected the anti-Judaism which still prevailed in the Church.

Apparently Pacelli shared some of these sentiments as he seemed to tie the religious background of the revolutionaries with the attacks upon Catholicism and the Church. He reported that these Jewish figures, directing a radical and socialist mob, exploited the fact that Eisner's assassin was a Catholic to commence a campaign against the Church and its clergy, thereby creating a more dangerous situation in Bavaria than the earlier rev-

---

13. Provisional Constitution of Bavarian Republic, January 7, 1919, ASV, Archivio della Sacra Congregazione per gli Affari Ecclesiastiici Straordinari (AAES), Baviera, posizione 129.

14. Chenaux, *Pie XII*, 132.

15. Pacelli to Gasparri, April 18, 1919, ASV, AAES, Germania, Nunziatura Apostolica Baviera, n. 12572, included in appendix of Fattorini, *Germania e Santa Sede*, 322–25.

olution of November 7, 1918.¹⁶ The distressed nuncio informed the papal secretary of state that a dictatorship of the proletariat had been established in Bavaria, emulating those in Russia and Hungary, and feared the consequences.¹⁷

Pacelli catalogued the abuses of the "red rabble" led by the Jewish couple, reporting that in their rampage, they sent troops into the residence of the archbishop, invaded two legations, and at the end of April attempted to seize the automobile of the nunciature, thereby dismissing and violating its extraterritoriality. When the representatives of the various legations met with the provisional revolutionary government to secure their right of extraterritoriality, Pacelli refused to meet with its leaders and dispatched his assistant Lorenzo Schioppa. The head of the government, Max Levien, who Pacelli once again noted was Jewish, and his foreign minister, Hermann Dietrich, promised Schioppa that their government would recognize their rights so long as they did not make any attempt against the revolutionary regime and its ministers, adding that they intended to separate Church and state.¹⁸ Pacelli deplored this and other decisions taken by the Jewish leaders of the "Bolshevik" government, convinced that they aimed to undermine the position of the Church in Bavaria.¹⁹

The nuncio complained that the promises made by the revolutionary regime to respect the Church's rights were not kept, but repeatedly violated. On the evening of May 3, 1919, the palace of the nunciature came under gunfire by government troops, and when this barrage ceased, three officials accompanied by some twenty troops, heavily armed with hand grenades, rifles,

---

16. For the significance of and problems flowing from the second Bavarian revolution, see AAES, Baviera, posizione 129.
17. Pacelli to Gasparri, April 7, 1919, AAES, Baviera, posizione 129.
18. Pacelli to Gasparri, April 18, 1919, Achivio della Nunziatura Apostolica in Monaco, posizone 397, fascicolo 2, folios 154r–55v.
19. Pacelli to Gasparri, June 19, 1919, Achivio della Nunziatura Apostolica in Monaco, posizione 397, fascicolo 3, folios 3–11.

and revolvers, pounded on their door. Charging that shots had been fired from the nunciature upon their soldiers, killing four of them, the officials demanded to search the premises. Pacelli, whose constant self-diagnoses and health concerns led him to fear that he might be stricken by a series of ailments, was once again at a clinic that evening. In his absence, Monsignor Schioppa accompanied the revolutionary officials and armed troops who scoured the various rooms of the residence as well as the rooftop. Even after the investigation produced no evidence of shots fired, the officials sought to remain in the building but finally settled upon leaving two sentinels to keep watch.[20] The damage they inflicted was not only physical—holes in the wall, broken windows, and the like—but also psychological. Indeed, some believe that the psychological trauma on Pacelli persisted, leaving him not only an anticommunist but also an anti-Semite—since many of the leaders of this revolutionary experiment were Jewish. Although delighted by the collapse of the Red Regime in Bavaria, the nuncio never forgot the Judeo-Bolshevik threat posed to the Church in Bavaria, Germany, and Europe as a whole.[21]

There were those who looked primarily to the parties, particularly the Catholic Center Party, to guarantee the rights of the Church in Bavaria and Germany but neither the Vatican nor Pacelli shared this sentiment. Still, they could not ignore the fact that during the war Matthias Erzberger, the Center Party leader, had collected money for the Vatican and urged the establishment of a Vatican State to assure papal independence. Furthermore, in the elections of 1919 the Center Party collected some 6 million votes and won 91 of the Reichstag's 421 seats, second only to the Social Democrats who had received over 11 million votes and won 163 seats. Given this political distribu-

20. Pacelli to Gasparri, May 5, 1919, AAES, Baviera, posizione 124, and ANM, posizione 379, fascicolo 3.
21. Pacelli to Gasparri, May 3, 1919, ANM, posizione 397, fascicolo 2, folios 105r–11v.

tion, collaboration between the two parties made perfect sense to the nuncio who at this juncture again displayed a degree of pragmatism, despite the opposition of the Vatican to an "alliance" of the Center Party with a socialist party.

Pacelli acknowledged that many in the curia opposed such a partnership, instead hoping for the formation of a government composed of bourgeois and conservative parties. However, the nuncio realistically noted that the prospect of such a coalition then faced insurmountable obstacles given the distribution of assembly seats. He concluded that under the circumstances the Center Party's decision to ally with the socialists was both understandable and necessary, warning that in its absence a more dangerous coalition might have emerged. Finally, he argued that it was wrong to conclude that the formation of the coalition implied that the Center Catholic Party had abandoned its principles and program.[22] Thus despite the criticism of conservatives in the curia, at this point the nuncio supported the decision of the Center Party to join the coalition government with the parties of the left. As Pacelli advanced in the Vatican hierarchy, he would eventually abandon this practical stance for one that was increasingly ideologically driven and more in harmony with curia sentiments he sought to placate.

Pacelli cited the advantages which accrued to the Church as a result of the Center Party's participation in the government as he had proposed. Among the provisions the Center Party included in the government's program were liberty of conscience and freedom of religion and the press. Pacelli also appreciated the role and impact of the Center Party in the drafting of the Weimar Constitution, which he believed provided enormous advantages to the Church. An important innovation introduced at the urging of the Center Party, eliminated all state intervention in the assignment of ecclesiastical posts. Another concession was pro-

---

22. Pacelli to Gasparri, Febuary 20, 1919, AAES, Germania, posizione 442.

vided by article 124, which guaranteed the right to all Germans to form and join associations—which Pacelli believed would be welcomed by the religious congregations, while article 119 offered special state protection for the institution of marriage—which the Church deemed a sacrament. In turn, articles 135 and 136 provided that individuals were free to enter public careers regardless of their religious affiliation, rendering it illegal to discriminate against the Catholic minority in the Reich, while article 137 prohibited the establishment of any state religion.[23]

Pleased with these provisions, Pacelli had also sought the inclusion of freedom to teach, but the Center Party did not succeed in overcoming Protestant and provincial opposition to this measure.[24] The nuncio, following instructions from the curia, attempted to provide for this right in the concordat he sought with the central government, and as early as 1919 opened talks with Berlin to discuss possible terms for such an agreement.[25] The Germans seemed amenable, recognizing and appreciating the moral and diplomatic support the Vatican had provided them in its search for a just peace. In September 1919 they sought to further improve relations with Rome by appointing a minister to the Holy See. Pacelli was pleased by their announcement that the Prussian legation in Rome was to be transformed into a German embassy, and Diego von Bergen, who had served as Prussian minister to the Vatican, would become the first German ambassador. This Protestant of Spanish ancestry, appointed in 1920, was well liked by the Italians in the curia and would remain the German representative to the Holy See for over two decades. In 1920, Pacelli also learned that his mother was seriously ill and with Gasparri's permission left Munich for Rome,

23. Relations between Church and state under the new constitution of Germany, August 18, 1919, AAESS, Germania, posizione 464.
24. Pacelli to Gasparri, March 15, 1919, AAES, Baviera, posizione 442.
25. Gerhard Besier, *The Holy See and Hitler's Germany*, translated by W. R. Ward (New York: Palgrave/Macmillan, 2007), 56.

but to Pacelli's dismay she died before he arrived home, thrusting him into a deep and prolonged depression.

The distraught nuncio found some solace in the advent of full diplomatic relations with Berlin which displeased the Bavarians, who suspected that this formed part of the centralization campaign of the Weimar government to monopolize not only foreign relations but representation to the Vatican. Despite their vocal opposition, in 1920 the cardinal secretary of state reported that he would send a nuncio to Berlin and that Pacelli would fill the office, but in the interim he would continue to represent Bavaria and would commute between Munich and Berlin as circumstances warranted. Deeming Germany vitally important as a bulwark against Russian communism, Pacelli favored the Berlin nunciature which would bring it into closer contact with the Vatican. However, from the first he insisted that the Bavarian nunciature not be abandoned, supporting the stance of Baron Otto von Ritter who had represented Bavaria in Rome since 1909.[26] He also sought the permission of the Holy Father to continue to reside in Munich, a request that was rejected. However, he would be permitted to remain in Munich until the concordat with Bavaria was concluded.[27] In the interim Pacelli refused to accept a delegate to represent him in Berlin during his absence, doubting that anyone could negotiate as effectively as he could. The self-confidence of the youthful Pacelli remained very much intact despite the string of setbacks he had endured.

Two major official considerations determined the decision to delay Pacelli's transfer from Munich to Berlin: the first, to allay the fears and concerns of the Bavarians; the second, to allow Pacelli the opportunity to complete the sensitive negotiations for the conclusion of the Bavarian concordat. There was a third, unspoken but real consideration, which stemmed from the fact

26. Pacelli to Gasparri, October 6, 1919, AAES, Baviera, posizione 62, fascicolo 40, folios 78r–92v.
27. Gasparri to Pacelli, May 26, 1918, ASV, AAES, Germania, 387.

that Pacelli had grown accustomed to Munich, which he considered his second home, and preferred living there rather than Berlin, especially after the death of his beloved mother. These considerations combined to permit Pacelli to remain in Munich for some five years following his appointment to Berlin.

When Pacelli presented his credentials to the Weimar government in June 1920, he was the first diplomat to do so, and thus became the dean of the diplomatic community in Berlin. On this occasion Pacelli promised President Friedrich Ebert that he would devote all his energy to cultivating and strengthening the relations between the Holy See and Germany,[28] and remained true to his promise. In the years from 1920 to 1924 he continued the delicate concordat discussions with Bavaria, as well as dealing with the internal and international consequences of the French occupation of the Ruhr in January 1923. Some, noting that Pacelli remained aloof from the Vatican's strong protest of the Franco-Belgian occupation of the Ruhr, exonerated him from the Holy See's departure from impartiality or neutrality, by favoring Germany vis-à-vis France. In fact, Pacelli may have unwittingly encouraged the Vatican's strong response by repeating and reporting back home the unsubstantiated and racist accusations of the German bishops citing the alleged abuses and lack of all restraint shown by black troops in the French military against German girls and women during the occupation.

It was not the function of the nuncio to Germany to issue a protest to the French, but the responsibility of the secretary of state who was pushed by the confrontational pope to do so. Pacelli, who continued to favor conciliation, officially noted that since the Vatican had never criticized the German invasion of Belgium, logic and impartiality dictated that it should not condemn the Franco-Belgian occupation of the Ruhr. However he was discreet in expressing this opinion since Gasparri, follow-

28. Fattorini, *Germania e Santa Sede*, 196.

ing the command of the new pope, Pius XI (1922–1939), felt constrained to issue a protest. Meanwhile Secretary of State Gasparri supported the Genoa Conference called in 1922 to deal with the reparations issue and the Continent's economic problems, to which both Germany and the Soviet Union were invited. To Gasparri's dismay little progress was made on either fiscal or economic issues, although the Germans and the Soviets concluded the Treaty of Rapallo during the course of the conference. This ended Soviet and German ostracism and isolation by restoring diplomatic relations between the two, providing the basis for future economic cooperation between the former pariahs who were in the process of being transformed into increasingly important powers.

Pacelli regarded this treaty, as well as others, of great importance. A student of civil and canon law, he placed great emphasis on remaining within the confines of both. His legalism was a key factor in his call for the conclusion of concordats which he believed would provide the Church and the faith with guarantees transcending the shifting world of party politics. These sentiments were in part shared by Achille Ratti, who became Pope Pius XI in 1922, following the unexpected death of Benedict XV after a short illness. The new pope attained the tiara the same year that Mussolini came to power in Italy and proved willing to work with the Duce even after he assumed dictatorial control of the peninsula. However, from the issuance of his first encyclical, *Ubi arcano*, in December 1922, Pius XI stressed the unity of humanity. A firm believer in the Kingship of Christ as outlined in his *Quas Primas* of 1925, he continued the international policy of Benedict XV and kept Gasparri as his secretary of state.[29] The retention of his mentor in a position of power pleased Pacelli for political, philosophical, and personal reasons.

29. Emma Fattorini, *Pio XI, Hitler e Mussolini. La solitudine di un papa* (Turin: Einaudi, 2007), 20.

The Germans, on the other hand, had hoped for the election of Gasparri, who along with Pacelli had been an advocate of their cause for some time, but got Ratti instead. While some noted the new pope's shrewdness and tenacity, others commented on his stubbornness and inflexibility. Like Pacelli he knew the German language, but he was not seen to be as sympathetic to the German cause as were Gasparri and Pacelli. Suspicious of socialism and communism, he was likewise critical of extreme nationalism and the risk of tying it to Catholicism. Pius XI personally favored monarchical structures, but recognized that the Church could not remake the world in its own image and had to adjust to a variety of political entities, finding the concordat the most efficient means of doing so. For these reasons both he and Pacelli appreciated the delicate task of signing agreements with both the Bavarians, who had a long, close, and special relationship with the Holy See, and the Berlin government, which sought to monopolize relations with the Vatican by eliminating the representation that Bavaria had long enjoyed with the Holy See.[30]

Immersed in these delicate operations and determined to impress the new pope, Pacelli paid little attention to the Hitler Putsch of November 8–9, 1923, in Munich, which did not arouse in him the same antagonism provoked by the earlier "red revolution." This has led some to conclude that the nuncio was more opposed to Bolshevism than Nazism because the first opposed Christians while the Nazis' principal target was the Jews. Actually Pacelli's relatively muted response to the Hitler putsch was due to his preoccupation in negotiating the concordat with Bavaria as well as the fact that the attempted Nazi revolution did not succeed, and therefore it had little, if any, impact on most in Bavaria. However, in response to the secretary of state's inquiry about the event, on November 14, 1923, Pacelli reported to Gas-

---

30. Pacelli to Gasparri, December 4, 1921, AAES, Baviera, posizione 148.

parri on the putsch and noted the anti-Catholic nature of the National Socialist movement and its leader, Adolf Hitler.[31]

In a second report on the movement, Pacelli related that the Nazis were against the Church and Catholics as well as against the Jews. The nuncio described the violent, vicious, and vulgar campaign of the folkish or racist press which he likewise condemned.[32] He also reported on the wave of anti-Catholicism unleashed during the course of the Ludendorff trial in which the general was acquitted.[33] Pacelli warned Gasparri that the excessive nationalism which emerged was the most dangerous heresy of the epoch.[34] These reports alarmed Pius XI more than Gasparri, leading the pope to condemn the emerging totalitarianism and the notion that the state was an end in itself.

The more pragmatic Gasparri reminded the nuncio that it was the Holy See's policy of impartiality not to interfere or become embroiled in the internal political affairs of any country.[35] The application of impartiality to domestic affairs was a course Gasparri along with Pacelli espoused. Indeed, Pacelli adhered to it while nuncio (1917–1929), secretary of state (1930–1939), and pope (1939–1958). The more impulsive and interventionist Pius XI, on the other hand, had serious reservations about Gasparri's mandate of impartiality for the Holy See in internal and international affairs—even though it assumed the status of a dogma in the Secretariat of State.

From the first days of his pontificate Pius XI refused to hold his tongue when he believed a religious or ethical issue such as racism was involved in international affairs or in the internal

31. Pacelli to Gasparri, November 14, 1923, AESS, Baviera, posizione 396, fascicolo 7, folio 6.

32. Pacelli to Gasparri, April 24, 1924, AAES, Baviera, posizione 396, fascicolo 7, folio 6f.

33. Pacelli to Gasparri, March 3, 1924, ASV, ANM, Baviera, posizione 396, fascicolo 7, folios 9r–19v.

34. Chenaux, *Pie XII*, 141.

35. Gasparri to Pacelli, February 14, 1920, AAES, Baviera, n. 2435, included in appendix of Fattorini, *Germania e Santa Sede*, 342–43.

policy of a state. Despite the anti-Judaism prevalent in Church circles, which the Holy See often tolerated if it did not sanction,[36] Pius XI early on assumed a public opposition to racism, denouncing it in the first year of his pontificate by emphasizing that "Christian charity extends to all men whatsoever without distinction of race."[37] Later he censured Charles Maurras's anti-Semitic Action Francaise,[38] and in 1928 condemned anti-Semitism when the Holy Office, with his approval, suppressed the Friends of Israel.[39] He was alarmed by the anti-Semitism of the National Socialists in Germany, but so long as Hitler and his cohorts were a fringe group, he did not feel the need to speak out against them. It is true that in 1929 Pius XI concluded an agreement with Mussolini's Italy, but at the time anti-Semitism was not a feature of the regime, and the Duce proudly proclaimed himself a firm Catholic believer.[40]

In light of racist currents on the right, and the anticlerical ones on the left, in postwar Bavaria and Germany, the pope and Pacelli sought guarantees for the Church in Germany. Pacelli viewed such agreements as the best means of assuring the liberty of the Church. He remained convinced of the need for concordats to assure the future of the Church, especially in Central Europe which after the war was a graveyard of the dynasties the Vatican had formerly relied upon. As a consequence some forty concordats were signed in the interwar period.

The negotiations with Bavaria lasted half a decade for a number of reasons, including the turmoil in the state. In March 1924 Pacelli finally succeeded in signing a concordat with Bavaria, which was ratified by its Landtag at the opening of the follow-

36. In this regard, see Coppa, *The Papacy, the Jews, and the Holocaust*.
37. *Cum Tertio*, September 17, 1922, in Koenig, *Principles for Peace*, 329.
38. Consistorial Allocution of December 20, 1926, in *Discorsi di Pio XI*, ed. Domenico Bertetto (Turin: Società Editrice Internazionale, 1959), 1.647.
39. *Decretum De Conosciatione Vulgo, "Amici Israel" Abolenda*, March 25, 1928, AAS, 20.103–4; Passelecq and Suchecky, *The Hidden Encyclical of Pius XI*, 144.
40. Mussolini's declaration to the apostolic nuncio in Italy, August 1930, ASV, AAES, Italia, posizione 739, fascicolo 241, folio 76.

ing year. It proved extremely advantageous to the Church and the Vatican and would remain in effect until 1966.[41] Under its provisions the state by and large adhered to the new code of canon law that Pacelli had helped elaborate, granting the Church broad power over the educational system and assuring the continuation of religious instruction in the schools. In fact, half of the agreement's sixteen articles concerned the Church's rights in education. Among other things, the continuation of Catholic theological faculties in the universities was preserved and assurances provided that at least one professor of philosophy and one of history teaching at each school would have a thorough Catholic training and background. Pacelli considered the concordat with Bavaria his greatest achievement while nuncio in Germany, and in some ways his assessment was accurate. It was certainly more favorable to the Church than the agreements he concluded with either Latvia (1922) or Poland (1925).

However, he was not allowed much time to celebrate his success in Bavaria. Having completed his concordat assignment, the last obstacle that prevented Pacelli from moving from Munich to Berlin was removed, and Pacelli soon learned that unlike Benedict XV, Pius XI had thrust aside all of his delaying tactics and expected, indeed demanded, immediate compliance. The pope insisted that the nuncio, who had been assigned to Berlin in 1920, finally assume his post there. Recognizing that Pius would tolerate no further excuses, the reluctant Pacelli complied and left Munich for Berlin on July 14, 1925.[42] His residence there was in the parklike setting of 21 Rauchstrasse—later renamed the Pacellistrasse. With the passage of time Pacelli, who surrounded himself with an entourage of familiar figures, adjusted to living in Berlin

Pius XI, who did not share Pacelli's proclivity for the Germans, assigned his nuncio in Berlin three major tasks: two were

41. For the terms of the agreement, see AAS, 17 (1925), 41–54.
42. Pacelli to Pizzardo, December 8, 1925, ASV, AAES, Germania, posizione 511, fascicolo 24, folios 95r–96r.

public and one secret. The public duties entailed the negotiation of concordats with the state of Prussia and the central German government. The secret one was to negotiate an agreement with the Soviet ambassador in Berlin, Nikolai Krestinski, to resolve differences between the Vatican and the Soviet Union, with which the papacy since 1917 had sought a modus vivendi. Regarding this last assignment, Pacelli very much favored some agreement to guarantee the rights of the Church in the Soviet Union, but did not believe the time was ripe for its conclusion.[43] However, having heard that this pope was determined to pursue these negotiations, Pacelli prudently did not reveal his pessimism regarding a successful conclusion to renewed talks.

Pacelli's reservations about negotiating with the Soviet Union were both pragmatic and philosophical. Although ideologically opposed to communism, he had some experience in negotiating with the Soviet Union and was painfully aware of the problems its leaders posed. As early as the summer of 1918 the Holy See had commissioned him to negotiate an agreement with the Soviets that would allow the Vatican to provide asylum for the imprisoned Tsar Nicholas and his family. However, before the talks could be finalized, on the evening of July 16–17, 1918, the tsar and his family were executed, rendering further discussion superfluous. Subsequently, in March 1922 Pacelli was involved in the conclusion of an agreement with the Soviets for the Vatican to provide humanitarian assistance to its suffering population. The thirteen-point secret agreement, ironed out by Pacelli and Waclaw Worowaski, head of the Soviet commercial commission in Rome, was facilitated by the German ambassador to Moscow, Count Ulrich von Brokdorff-Rantzau. Its terms proved restrictive for the Church, which was prohibited from sending either pastors or missionaries to the Soviet state, while its activity was limited to providing charitable assistance. From the first Pius XI boldly—the Soviets

43. Pacelli to Gasparri, June 16, 1924, ASV, Nunziatura di Berlino, 30.

charged blatantly—ignored these restrictions and proceeded to establish dioceses and a hierarchical structure that extended from the Ukraine to Vladivostok, much to the displeasure of Lenin and the other Soviet leaders.

Hoping to regularize its activities, early in July 1922, again with the assistance of the German ambassador to the Soviet Union, Pacelli met with Maximilan Litvinov of the Russian foreign ministry in Berlin and proposed concluding an agreement that would provide Vatican recognition of the Soviet state in return for concessions for the Church in Russia. Although the papacy heard reports of continued persecution of its clergy in the Soviet Union, it pragmatically allowed the secret negotiations to continue. These talks were a major reason for the papal insistence that Pacelli stay in Berlin. Pius XI felt that more could be accomplished if his nuncio remained in the German capital, where the Soviets had a presence, rather than shuffling back and forth from Munich.

Despite the nuncio's best efforts, his negotiations with the Soviets did not go well, as reservations persisted on both sides. Pacelli encountered difficulties not only in his secret negotiations with the Soviets but also in his public talks with the Germans. Despite his pro-German behind-the-scenes stance on the future of Silesia—which helped Germany win 60 percent of the March 1921 vote there—he proved unable to convince the Prussian and the central government to make concessions such as Bavaria earlier had made. Pacelli was not surprised by the Prussian refusal and realized that the Protestant state would not, and perhaps could not, make concessions similar to those granted by Catholic Bavaria. In fact, he personally did not believe a concordat with Prussia was necessary because the Weimar Constitution provided for religious liberty—and that was the most he felt Prussia would concede. Since the curia sought broader concessions, however, Pacelli obediently followed their instructions without informing them of his own conclusion that their expectations were highly unrealistic and not readily attainable. Not wishing to be the bearer of bad news or being branded a pessimist, he once again failed to speak out and provide his own assessment of the situation. As in the past, he sought to avoid a possible confrontation with his superiors.

Privately Pacelli noted the Prussian government questioned the very name of any accord, preferring "solemn agreement" or "convention" to "concordat." It soon became apparent, as Pacelli had privately predicted, that the Prussian government refused to grant most of the conditions and concessions sought by the Vatican in the negotiations opened in 1926. Among other things it balked at issuing the guarantees the curia wanted regarding the Church's rights in education and assurances that the pope could appoint Prussian bishops without any governmental input. They refused both demands, and in order to get an accord Pacelli was constrained to compromise, convinced that a weak agreement was better than none at all as a means of avoiding the charge that he had failed once again. Sibling rivalry might have also played a part in Eugenio's decision to sign the agreement because his older brother Francesco was exacting major concessions from Fascist Italy and concluded the Lateran Accords with Mussolini on February 11, 1929. With some reservations, Pacelli agreed to the fourteen articles of the concordat/solemn agreement with Prussia on June 14, 1929, which was ratified by the Prussian Landtag on August 14, 1929.[44] It provided less than many in the curia expected, and proved disappointing except for the creation of two new dioceses: Aix-la-Chapelle and Berlin.

The negotiations for a Reich concordat proved even more difficult for Pacelli as deep divisions emerged between Berlin and Rome over educational issues, compounded by mutual suspicions of one another's motives and aims. On the one hand, the curia would not conclude any agreement with the Weimar Republic

44. For the terms of the Prussian concordat, see AAS 21 (1929), 521–41.

that did not provide contractual protection for its confessional schools, a concession the republic was unwilling and unprepared to make. This rendered signing a concordat with Berlin virtually impossible for even the most capable and experienced diplomat—and at this juncture Pacelli was neither.

He proved unwilling to place the blame on the curia for the impasse, where it belonged, for this would have jeopardized his career, which Gasparri later charged was paramount for Pacelli.[45] Seeking an explanation that would not challenge his superiors or assume the responsibility for the failure, Pacelli tended to blame the Catholic Center Party. Abandoning his earlier positive assessment of this party and praise for its substantial achievements on behalf of the Church, he now claimed it did not have a sufficient commitment to ecclesiastical interests. In his determination to place much of the responsibility for the failure on the Center Party, Pacelli increasingly sided with the more conservative element in the party, discounting the obvious constraints the party confronted.

Pacelli could not blame the Center Party for the difficulties he encountered during his secret negotiations with the Soviet Union, which proved even more troublesome than those with the Weimar Republic. This time he more accurately blamed the Soviets, alerting the pope and the curia that the Kremlin's demands for any agreement were excessive, asking much and offering little in return. Among other things the Soviets insisted that the papacy cease its campaign against Bolshevism and recognize the legitimacy of the Soviet state, while insisting that the Church accept a series of state and party restrictions including the separation of Church and state, in return for its readmission to Russia. This meant that the Church did not have the right to intervene in state affairs—but the state could interject itself

---

45. Carlo M. Fiorentino, *All'Ombra di Pietro. La Chiesa Cattolica e lo spionaggio fascista in Vaticano 1929–1939* (Florence: Editrice Le Lettere, 1999), 57–58.

in Church and clerical matters. Resisting papal centralization, the Soviets insisted that the newly formed Catholic congregations be allowed to select their priests and bishops without any outside intervention. The hard line assumed by the Soviets reflected the fact that their diplomatic situation had dramatically improved in light of the recognition they received from Weimar Germany in 1922, followed by their recognition by Fascist Italy and Great Britain in 1924. The Soviet Union was now no longer an isolated pariah desperate for the recognition of the papacy.

Pius XI, alerted to the demands posed by the Soviets, grew increasingly skeptical that they desired an agreement with the Holy See. When he heard that they were posed to execute a Catholic priest of Polish background, he ordered Pacelli to temporarily close the secret talks. However, Pius XI did not abandon his Russian mission, but assumed a different course. In February 1926 he decided to send the French Jesuit Michel d'Herbigny to the U.S.S.R. to consecrate bishops secretly and establish an apostolic succession there. Pius involved Pacelli in his plan by having the nuncio consecrate d'Herbigny as bishop before his departure for the Soviet Union. The newly minted bishop managed to enter the Soviet Union, but in the face of the brutal Soviet repression he and the men he consecrated had perforce to remain underground. This led Pius XI once again to press for a negotiated solution and he ordered Pacelli to reopen his dialogue with the Soviet representatives in Berlin. The nuncio followed the papal instructions without comment or complaint but once more privately expressed doubts that there could be any agreement with the existing Soviet regime, which he accurately claimed was determined to eliminate religion within its borders. Pius XI, on the other hand, continued to press for some understanding with the Soviets until 1929, when Josef Stalin introduced his state-sponsored program to eradicate religion in the Soviet Union.

Stalin's program substantiated what Pacelli had long suspected, that it was difficult, if not impossible, for the Vatican to reach even a minimal understanding with the Soviet state. He had negotiated with the Soviets not out of conviction but at the behest of his superiors. This did not spare the nuncio from criticism, which led some to focus on the fact that Pacelli had failed in two of the three assignments Pius XI had given to him. Critics harped upon his inability to secure agreements with the Weimar Republic and the Soviet Union, and deemed his "success" in concluding the Prussian concordat as problematic at best, for he had not acquired the concessions sought by the curia. Some clerical competitors even blamed him for the earlier failure of Benedict's peace mission and questioned his diplomatic ability. Although much of this criticism was manifestly unfair, it created consternation for the sensitive nuncio.

It has been suggested that Pacelli had mixed feelings in 1929 when he heard that he was going to be recalled home and learned that his mentor and patron had resigned.[46] His concerns were somewhat alleviated when he learned he was to receive the red hat at the end of 1929 and was to replace Gasparri as cardinal secretary of state at the opening of 1930. The old cardinal was convinced that Eugenio had connived with his brother Francesco, and the Jesuits, to push him out of the office he had occupied for a decade and a half.[47] Pacelli denied the accusation and looked forward to returning home and assuming his new post.

"My mission in Germany has come to an end," he said at the reception in his honor on the eve of his departure from the Weimar Republic, adding, "A greater, more embracing task in the heart of the Universal Church now begins."[48] Although he appreciated the importance of his new assignment and relished the thought of returning to Rome, at this juncture he was somewhat saddened

---

46. Camille M. Cianfara, *The War and the Vatican* (London: Burns, Oates and Washbourne, 1945), 78.
47. Fiorentino, *All'Ombra di Pietro*, 52–58.
48. Smit, *Angelic Sheperd*, 49.

to leave Germany, whose language, people, and culture he had come to admire; he left the country a confessed Germanophile. He bought a bit of the Reich back with him in the persons of his housekeeper, Sister Pascalina Lehnert; his private secretary, Father Robert Leiber; Monsignor Ludwig Kaas of the Center Party; and his Jesuit confessor, Father Augustine Bea. Some believe that his love of Germany blinded him to certain unfortunate realities in the Reich. In fact, in the early 1920s Pacelli was taken in by the German propaganda campaign against the use of "black" French forces in the occupation of the Rhineland, relating the charge that they proved unable to show any sexual restraint. Although Pacelli opposed launching a protest to the French, his report played a part in the futile Vatican effort to have these "violent" and "rapacious" "black troops" replaced by "white" ones.[49] The French ambassador to the Holy See responded that he knew that racism was widespread but was shocked that "such a prejudice could find an echo among the representatives of the Catholic Church which teaches the fraternity of races and the equality of souls."[50]

The French and others were disturbed by the nuncio's partiality toward the Germans, with some convinced this influenced his policy toward the Nazi regime. Others observed that while the nuncio had come to love the Germans he apparently despised the Nazis, but as in so many other instances he kept his feelings to himself and did not let them know. Unfortunately, his persuasive performance fooled not only many Nazis but a good number of their enemies as well and has played a part in his historical assessment.

There is no reliable evidence of any pro-Nazi sentiments on Pacelli's part, but evidence abounds for his concern for the future of Catholicism in Germany, which shaped and motivated much of his conduct toward the Reich. At the end of his ten-

49. Pacelli to Gasparri, April 26, 1920, in Fattorini, *Germania e Santa Sede*, 406–7.
50. The French ambassador to the Holy See to Cardinal Gasparri, January 16, 1921, in Fattorini, *Germania e Santa Sede*, 409.

ure as nuncio, he was clearly worried about the future of the Catholic Church in the country he was leaving. Pacelli revealed his concerns in a forty-five-page report on *The Situation of the Catholic Church in Germany*. Mainly statistical and descriptive, his account did shed some light on his views of ecclesiastical and political events, as he complained of the communist campaign to draw the faithful from mother Church and the lack of vigor on the part of the German clergy, which he found too accommodating in political and ecclesiastical matters. Providing an essentially traditionalist and conservative critique, he particularly deplored the clerical tendency to grant dispensations allowing too many "mixed marriages" and denounced the liberal sentiments prevailing in their seminaries. While Pacelli admired the German literary and musical contribution and its leadership in science and technology, he found its religious life wanting

During more than a decade in Germany, he had grown increasingly critical of the Catholic Center Party, which he feared did not have the preservation of the faith as its main objective, accusing some of its members of believing one could be a Catholic and a socialist. Although he would leave Germany and return to Rome, he remained concerned about the future of the faith in the Reich during his years as secretary of state and subsequently during his pontificate. Some suspect that his perception of the problems confronting German Catholicism and his desire to spare the Church in the Reich from persecution, later contributed to his conciliatory course toward the Nazi regime. His assessment of the fragile nature of the Church in Germany, coupled to his fear of the Nazi response to a public papal protest, and the inevitable retribution he feared would be imposed upon Catholics as well as Jews, in large measure accounts for his cautious reaction to the Holocaust. He said as much on numerous occasions. One can question the wisdom and even the morality of his decision—but there is no evidence to attribute it to anti-Semitism.

FIVE

Secretary of State to Pius XI, 1930–1939

The recent opening of the papers of Pius XI reveal the growing chasm between the Pope and his Secretary of State on how to respond to German and Italian anti-Semitism and what the Vatican could, or should, endure to retain the concordat of 1929 with Fascist Italy, and that of 1933 with Nazi Germany. The Pope's confrontational response clearly conflicted with the conciliatory course of Cardinal Pacelli, who saw to it that the Pope's speech critical of the fascist regimes was not released.

PIUS XI'S DECISION to make Eugenio Pacelli a cardinal and his new secretary of state in Februrary 1930 surprised some but not all Vatican observers. This flowed from the fact that some were unaware of the conflict between the pope and Pietro Gasparri on the policy to pursue toward the fascist dictatorship's boisterous claims. The pope proved critical of Mussolini's all-embracing totalitarian assertions in his speech of May 13, 1929, on the Lateran Accords, and favored a strong response to the

> Epigraph draws on Appunti di Monsignor Domenico Tardini, ASV, AES, pos. 576, fascicolo 607. Tardini on February 15, 1939, notes receiving a telephone call from Montini conveying the instructions of Pacelli to retrieve the pope's last critical discourse on the dictatorial regimes from the Vatican printing office and prevent its publication. See Appunti di Monsignor Domenico Tardini, ASV, AAES, posizione. 576, fascicolo 607. Once pope, Pacelli also shelved the encyclical Pius XI had secretly commissioned against anti-Semitism.

dictator's claims. In turn, some liberal opponents of the regime criticized Pius for concluding the agreement with the Duce in the first place. Pius responded that to save even a single soul he "would find the courage to deal even with the devil himself"—but this did not mean he was willing to let him win.[1] Nor would Pius XI allow his secretary of state Gasparri to pursue a policy or course that contradicted his own. When he did, the infuriated pope fired him. He did so despite Gasparri's crucial role in the negotiation for and conclusion of the Lateran Accords.

For a series of reasons the conflict between the pope and his secretary of state was not widely known even in the Secretariat of State over which he had long presided, especially since Pius continued to praise Gasparri and bestow favors and honors on his aged minister. Small wonder that most believed that the eighty-year-"old" and "tired" Gasparri, who had dominated the Secretariat of State for a decade and a half, had resigned. Supposedly, Pius XI had reluctantly accepted his decision. Many also believed that the pope, Gasparri, and Pacelli all supported the policy of impartiality and shunned involvement in internal political conflicts and international disputes. In fact, Pius XI often and strongly disagreed with Gasparri's call for impartiality and nonintervention in politics but this disagreement was not made public. When the old cardinal supposedly resigned, it seemed logical that the pope would replace the mentor with his pupil Pacelli. Those who made these assumptions also maintained that Pius XI and Pacelli, who collaborated for the greater part of the tumultuous decade from 1930 to 1939, saw eye to eye on most political and diplomatic issues. Finally, many were convinced that the pope, who made Pacelli *camerlengo*, or chamberlain, who directs events in the Vatican from the death of a pope until the election of another, as well as secretary of state, later sought his election as successor to the papal throne.

1. Wolf, *Pope and Devil*, 1.

Most of these assumptions have been increasingly questioned during the last decade as additional documents and memoirs have become available. These recently opened sources confirm what others had suspected—that Pius XI, on the one hand, and Gasparri and Pacelli, on the other, disagreed on a number of issues. Among other things, Pius XI and Gasparri clashed over the question of how best to respond to the abuses of Fascism and Nazism, with the pope determined to confront and condemn features of these dictatorships that conflicted with the tenets of the faith. His secretary of state, on the other hand, assumed a more diplomatic, less confrontational course. Convinced that neither Fascism nor Nazism would survive more than two or three decades, the pragmatic secretary of state argued that unless vital Church interests were clearly threatened the Vatican should remain politically impartial, avoiding a direct and costly clash with the fascist regimes that could wreak havoc upon the Church. This was also the prevailing sentiment in the curia as well as the Secretariat of State—which Gasparri had fashioned in his own image during his long tenure there. It was adopted by Pacelli and utilized by him during the course of his own pontificate. In many respects, Pius XI found himself virtually isolated.[2]

Although Pius XI was enraged by his secretary of state's "disobedience" and "arrogance," he curbed his temper and tongue in order not to jeopardize the delicate negotiations with Mussolini's Italy conducted by Gasparri, retaining him for the better part of a decade. The pope forced him to resign following its successful conclusion when Pius XI and his minister disagreed on how to respond to the Fascist violations of the agreement.[3] In the words of one historian "Gasparri ... had to give way so that Pius XI could exercise his sovereignty undisturbed."[4]

Unrepentant, Gasparri continued to call for appeasement

2. In this regard, see Fattorini, *Pio XI, Hitler e Mussolini*.
3. Chenaux, *Pie XII*, 171; Fiorentino, *All' Ombra di Pietro*, 41–83.
4. Besier, *The Holy See and Hitler's Germany*, 70, 227, n. 247.

even when forced out of office, urging the papacy to refrain from condemning Hitler's party so long as it did not wage war on the Holy See or the hierarchy in Germany.[5] Pacelli, who feared subjecting the Church in Germany to Nazi retaliation, concurred with his patron and mentor and appreciated the need to temper moral outrage with diplomatic pragmatism. However, he was far more cautious, diplomatic, and less outspoken than Gasparri in pursuing a policy he had learned the pope considered nothing short of mistaken and which he deemed inappropriate for the Vicar of Christ. Pacelli privately disagreed with the pope on this issue, but remained publicly silent.

This, in part, explains why Pius XI chose the younger, less assertive, and more respectful Eugenio Pacelli to succeed as secretary of state. He did so knowing Pacelli had been out of the country for some two decades and therefore Pius was convinced that he did not have the overwhelming support in the curia and the Secretariat of State to challenge the pope and pursue an independent course, as Gasparri had attempted to do. Furthermore, although Pacelli shared the practical approach of his patron and mentor, the younger prelate was far more diplomatic and deferential to his superiors than the blunt cardinal. Additionally, Pacelli did not broadcast his sentiments, so in 1929 Pius XI did not know how deeply committed Pacelli was to compromise and to the course Gasparri had charted. Once again silence had bought advantages for Pacelli. Finally, the pope believed his selection of Gasparri's protégé would soothe the legion of supporters of the old cardinal entrenched in the Secretariat of State, which Gasparri had shaped from 1914 to 1930. By choosing Pacelli, Pius hoped to avoid the difficulties that most other candidates would inevitably confront and thus avoid needless dissension. Not all the papal expectations materialized.

5. "Pietro Gasparri's Memorandum of June 1933," ASV, Archivio della Nunziatura Apostolica in Monaco, posizione 396, fascicolo 7, folios 75–76.

The Vatican was divided on the policy to pursue toward the fascist dictatorships, and contrary to popular belief the Holy See's policy was not determined solely by the pope. Furthermore, relations between Pius XI and his new secretary of state Pacelli were not as harmonious as some have suggested. To be sure there were similarities between the two for both were solitary figures and voracious readers, were accustomed to getting their way, were fluent in many languages, and devoted to their mothers. Additionally, the two had become staunchly anticommunist while serving as nuncios, Ratti in Poland and Pacelli in Bavaria, and both sought to assure the position of the Church by means of concordats. However, there is increasing evidence and a growing realization that Pope Pius XI and his secretary of state, from 1930 to 1939, differed in a number of ways.

The two varied in style as well as substance, in physical features—Ratti was athletic while Pacelli was frail—as well as temperament and personality. In a sense the pope and his secretary of state complemented rather than mirrored one another.[6] While Ratti was spontaneous, outgoing, outspoken, and openly assertive, Pacelli was studied, aloof, and cautious and indirect in speech as well as diplomatic in action. While the pope did not hesitate to resort to confrontation, his secretary of state preferred conciliation. The two had different agendas as well as different personalities. Not surprisingly, they often disagreed on the path to pursue, reflecting not only their own differences but the deep divisions prevailing in the curia and Vatican circles. Both opposed the anti-Semitism of Hitler's Germany, later copied by Mussolini's Italy, recognizing that the Nazi mania for racial purity violated Christian principles and Catholicism's universal ministry.[7] They disagreed on how to respond to those who violated

---

6. Fattorini, *Pio XI, Hitler e Mussolini*, 54.
7. Gene Bernardini, "The Origins and Development of Racial Anti-Semitism in Fascist Italy," *Journal of Modern History* 49, no. 3 (1977): 434; John S. Conway, "The

these principles, and the pope eventually realized that his secretary of state, like most in the curia, did not share his intransigent opposition to the fascist regimes. The differences between the two are subtly but unmistakably manifest in the reports Pacelli made of his meetings with the pope from 1930 to 1938.[8]

Despite their substantial differences, there was little conflict or dissension between the two. Such was the case because Pacelli was not prone to openly and directly challenge a superior—least of all the pope. Instead, he quickly and obediently followed Pius XI's orders—even when he disagreed with them—before they were forcefully expressed. He did so not only because he believed in the need to respect authority but also because he knew that Pius XI had dismissed Gasparri, at a time when his reputation had reached a high point after decades of distinguished service, because of his disagreement with papal policy. This increased the caution of an already prudent Pacelli. Despite his differences with Pius XI, Pacelli was careful to moderate his opposition to the pope, whose influence ironically he had strengthened by his revision of the canon law.

Pius XI, who was used to giving orders and being immediately obeyed, was irritated by Pacelli's hesitation and circuitous language, which he correctly surmised cloaked his disagreement. He concluded that this was responsible for many of his tentative and indecisive, diplomatic responses on various issues. Disturbed by this cautious approach and Pacelli's passive resistance, the pope urged him to provide his opinion freely and to openly express his views even when he disagreed with the pope, who would make the final decision.[9] Actually, Pius was willing to listen to other views and was prepared to modify his actions when convinced the suggestions made sense and did not violate

---

Vatican, Germany and the Holocaust," in *Papal Diplomacy in the Modern Age*, edited by Peter Kent and John Pollard (London: Praeger, 1994), 106.

8. See *I fogli di udienza del Cardinale Eugenio Pacelli*.
9. Chenaux, *Pie XII*, 169.

Catholic principles or his own beliefs. However, there were matters on which this pope would not be silenced such as racism.

Despite the anti-Judaism prevalent in certain Church circles, which the Holy See often tolerated if it did not openly sanction, Pius XI was convinced that the Vicar of Christ had a moral responsibility to denounce racism which was manifestly contrary to the faith. Thus he did not hesitate to censure Charles Maurras's anti-Semitic *Action Française*[10] or to suppress the Friends of Israel, which sought to convert the Jews.[11] After Pius XI approved the terms of the Lateran Accords with Fascist Italy, he resented the Fascist violations of the agreement, straining relations between Mussolini's Italy and the Vatican.

Pacelli determined to avoid his mentor's fate by refusing to openly challenge Pius XI's opposition to the racism of the fascist regimes, and other matters. He knew that the pope was especially sensitive to Fascist infringement on the Catholic organizations grouped under Catholic Action, and could not prevent him from accusing the Fascists of launching false charges and violating the solemn agreement they had signed. Although he shared Gasparri's reservations about endangering the Lateran Accords by pursuing a confrontational course, Pacelli cooperated in drafting the critical encyclical *Non abbiamo bisogno* of June 1931. According to papal wishes, the letter denounced Fascist attempts to dominate all citizen organizations and youth groups, while explicitly condemning Fascist theories and the "heathenish deification of the state." Inspired by Pius XI, it was drafted by Pacelli at the pope's behest. At this stage Pacelli was not prepared to openly challenge the pope who made it clear that he would forfeit neither the bodies nor the souls of the younger generation to the fascist regime. During the decade he served

10. "Consistorial Allocution of 20 December 1926," in Domenico Bertetto, ed., *Discorsi di Pio XI* (Turin: Società Editrice Internazionale, 1959), 1.647.

11. *Decretum De Conosciatione Vulgo, "Amici Israel" Abolenda*, March 25, 1928, *AAS*, 20.103–4; Passelecq and Suchecky, *The Hidden Encyclical of Pius XI*, 144.

as secretary of state, Pacelli found it difficult to assert himself against the strong-willed and authoritarian pontiff, but as in the past he had recourse to passive resistance.

Pius XI was even less likely to accept the call for reconciliation with the ultranationalists in Germany than with the Fascists in Italy. His suspicions of the Nazi movement were confirmed in March 1931 when the bishops of the Cologne Church province deemed the errors of National Socialism similar to those of the Action Française, earlier condemned by Pius XI. In April 1931, Hitler, hoping to reconcile the papacy to his party, sent Hermann Göring to Rome, where the Nazi deputy sought to meet with Pacelli. Pius decided otherwise and Pacelli obediently complied. Determined to avoid the fate of Gasparri, Pacelli generally followed the pope's lead in opposing Fascist and Nazi errors, but pursued a more independent course in the conclusion of the concordat of 1932 with Baden. More prudent than the volatile pontiff he served, Pacelli was most likely responsible for the Vatican's cautious response to Hitler's appointment on January 30, 1933, carefully avoiding any hint of papal displeasure.[12] Likewise, in mid-March 1933, the Vatican simply noted that the Fuehrer had assumed police powers after his electoral victory.[13] Following the advice of a cautious Secretariat of State, the Vatican passed no judgment on the formation of the Nazi dictatorship.

Familiar with German developments as a result of his decade-long residence in Munich and Berlin, Pacelli quickly emerged as Pius XI's principal advisor on Reich matters. The pope, a native of Desio in Lombardy, which had endured Austrian control and repression, had no special love for the Germans in general and was particularly distrustful of the Nazis. He did not deem an agreement with their regime possible. His secretary of state dip-

---

12. Thomas E. Hachey, ed., *Anglo-Vatican Relations 1914–1939: Confidential Reports of the British Minister to the Holy See* (Boston: G. K. Hall, 1972), 250.
13. "Cronaca Contemporanea," March 10–13, 1933, *Civiltà Cattolica*, anno 84 (1933), 2.205–6.

lomatically disagreed and concurred with the German hierarchy and the nuncio in Berlin that once the Nazis were in power the Church should modify its hostile stance toward them.[14]

The Nazis, hoping to curtail the opposition of the volatile pope, assumed the initiative in proposing an agreement between Church and state that Pacelli had sought but failed to attain during his tenure in Germany as nuncio. To facilitate the accord Hitler assured a delegation of German bishops of his high regard for the Catholic Church, claiming his state was based on Christian principles.[15] Pius found the Fuehrer's assertions unbelievable and recalled Pio Nono's response to Italian abuses during the Risorgimento: "belle parole, ma brutti fatti," or "nice words, but ugly deeds." In the spring of 1933, the Catholic vice-chancellor of Nazi Germany, Franz von Papen, ventured to Rome and suggested an accord between the Vatican and the Nazi state, asserting that such an agreement would prove beneficial for both.[16] From the first Pacelli supported the conclusion of a concordat with the Nazi state, but the pope remained less than enthusiastic about the prospect. Pius XI distrusted Nazism's pagan ideology and its anti-Semitic principles and practices, which he denounced as anti-Catholic, anti-Christian, and antihuman.

Pius XI reluctantly reconsidered his position following Nazi harassment of the organizational Church.[17] Scandalized by the dismantling of Catholic unions, *Civiltà Cattolica* branded the Nazi system "totalitarianism in action."[18] Determined to preserve Catholic youth organizations in Germany and to safeguard

14. Orsenigo to Pacelli, April 6, 1933, ASV, AAES, Germania, posizione 643, fascicolo,159.
15. Orsenigo to Pacelli, May 8, 1933, ASV, AAES, Germania, posizione 643, fascicolo 157.
16. "Cronaca Contemporanea," April 7–12, 1933, *Civiltà Cattolica*, anno 84 (1933), 2.301.
17. Hachey, *Anglo-Vatican Relations, 1914–1939*, 250; "Concordat of the Holy See and Germany," *Catholic World*, August 1933, vol. 137.
18. "Cronaca Contemporanea," June 23–July 6, 1933, *Civiltà Cattolica*, anno 84 (1933), 3.203–5.

religious and educational freedom, and strongly encouraged by his secretary of state, Pius XI finally succumbed and sanctioned negotiations.[19] In light of Pacelli's broad background in German affairs, numerous attempts to conclude a concordat with the Reich since 1920, and recognized expertise in concordat diplomacy, Pius XI relied on him to negotiate for the Vatican, as he had earlier trusted Gasparri to negotiate with Fascist Italy.

Although out of office for three years, Gasparri remained a force to reckon with and still exercised considerable influence in the Secretariat of State he had long shaped and dominated. In 1933, following the Nazi assumption of power, when the prospect of a concordat materialized, Gasparri quickly drafted a memorandum in favor of such an agreement with the Third Reich. To ensure a successful conclusion he advised the Church to cease its criticism of the Hitler regime and comply with some of its wishes. Among other things he advised that should the Nazis seek the dissolution of the Catholic Center Party—which he claimed did precious little to assist the papacy—the Vatican should comply without hesitation. Finally, he proposed that the Holy See and the hierarchy remove the restrictions upon Catholics from joining the Nazi Party, which Gasparri believed reflected genuine national sentiments and desires.[20] Consequently, he ignored the first wave of anti-Semitic violence in April 1933, but the pope did not, describing the "German persecution of the Jews" as "an offence not only against morality but against civilization."[21] Most of the hierarchy in the Reich, like Pacelli, did not openly contest the pope's position and at this juncture supported the papal anti-Nazi stance.

However, once Hitler was installed as chancellor, the pope

19. Hachey, *Anglo-Vatican Relations, 1914–1939*, 250.
20. Gasparri's memorandum of June 1933, ASV, AAES, Germania, posizione 645, fascicolo 163.
21. Peter Godman, *Hitler and the Vatican: Inside the Secret Archives That Reveal the New Story of the Nazis and the Church* (New York: Free Press, 2004), 8.

could no longer count upon the support of the German hierarchy to support his opposition to the Nazis. Indeed, the German bishops withdrew their declaration of August 1932 forbidding the faithful from joining the Nazi Party. Pacelli, for his part, quietly concurred with the actions of the German bishops, supporting both the negotiation of a concordat and the adoption of a more conciliatory Vatican policy toward the Third Reich—even though the Nazis had commenced their campaign against the Jews and the disabled. The papal secretary of state proved accommodating to the Nazi state in order to protect vital Church interests in the Reich. A similar rationale was employed by Cardinal Faulhaber of Munich, a friend of Pacelli, who argued that the Church should not intervene on behalf of the Jews, for the battle against them would degenerate into a war against Catholics. In fact when the German journal *Der Blitz* reported in mid-November 1934 that Cardinal von Faulhaber had defended the Jews in one of his sermons, the cardinal vehemently "denied the charge."[22]

Assured of the support of most of the German hierarchy, along with a solid majority in the Secretariat of State, in the summer of 1933 Pacelli was instrumental in concluding the controversial concordat with the Third Reich.[23] Although Pacelli, like the British foreign secretary, John Simon, did not believe that Hitler could be trusted, he still sought an agreement with him, convinced that some protection was better than none. Deemed an "ignoble bargain" by some, critics accused the Vatican of negotiating with a monster for ecclesiastical advantages, and for providing a moral sanction for the odious Nazi regime. Neither the pope nor Pacelli believed such was the case. In fact, Vatican officials made it clear that their ratification of the Reich

22. ASV, AAES, Germania, 1933–137, posizione 650, n. 3863.34.
23. Cardinal Gasparri congratulates Cardinal Pacedlli on the conclusion of the Reich Concordat, 24 July 1933, ASV, Secreteriadi Stato, Rapporti con gli stati, Archivio Storico, AAES, Germania, 1922–1939, posizione 645, fasicolo 165.

Concordat in September 1933 did not imply that they sympathized with Hitler's Reich,[24] or that the agreement legitimized or approved of the Nazi government.

Despite these protestations, conclusion of this accord did provide the Hitler regime with a degree of legitimacy—to the chagrin of Pius XI. Pacelli favored the negotiation of a concordat with Nazi Germany because he was convinced it represented the sole means of preventing the destruction of the Catholic Church and its various organizations in Germany.[25] In fact, all sorts of concessions were accorded the Church by the concordat but few of them were honored by the Nazis, as the pope quickly observed.

Pacelli's rationale for the concordat with Nazi Germany was undermined, in the pope's eyes, by their immediate violation of the agreement. Pacelli countered that without the concordat things would have been even more difficult for the Church, and defended it even after the collapse of Nazi Germany.[26] Pius XI disagreed and divisions between the pope and his secretary of state arose once again on how best to respond to the flagrant violations of the "contracts" by the dictatorial regimes. The combative pope remained determined to energetically protest every breach, while his secretary of state proved more willing to hold his tongue as Gasparri had earlier suggested. Pacelli privately acknowledged that he and the pope had their differences on how to respond to the Nazi violations of the concordat.

The pope grew increasingly disenchanted with the Reich concordat as his initial suspicion that the Nazis could not be trusted to adhere to the agreement was daily confirmed. Throughout much of 1933 and 1934 there was conflict between the German government and the Holy See in interpreting the terms and the

24. *Concordato fra la Santa Sede ed il Reich Germanico*, July 20, 1933, *AAS*, 25.389–408.

25. Mr. Kirkpatrick (the Vatican) to Sir R. Vansittart, August 19, 1933, *Documents on British Foreign Policy*, pp. 524–25n324; *L'Osservatore Romano*, September 11–12, 1933; "Cronaca Contemporanea," September 7–26, 1933, *Civiltà Cattolica*, anno 84 (1933), 4.89.

26. Pius XII, "La Chiesa e il nazionalsocialismo," *AAS*, 37 (1945), 161.

meaning of the various articles of the concordat.[27] In response to the Vatican's complaint about an anti-Catholic article in *National Zeitung* of September 7, 1933, the Reich government proclaimed it had nothing to do with its appearance—even though it was the official organ of Goering and protected by the regime.[28]

Troubled by Nazism's neopagan policies, Pius XI felt constrained to protest the Reich's sterilization legislation, which he complained was against divine law.[29] Pacelli, on the other hand, considered such protests "inopportune." There were other disagreements, for Pius rejected the Nazi contention that the Jewish question was an internal racial issue rather than a religious one, and therefore not subject to papal scrutiny or commentary.[30] This stance was openly embraced by Gasparri, quietly supported by Pacelli, but flatly rejected by Pius XI. He also rejected Hitler's claim that his restrictions on the "pernicious" Jews worked for the benefit of the Church as well as the state.[31] Like the American Jesuit John La Farge, who had condemned racism in a series of publications, the pope deemed racism immoral, sinful, and intolerable. His motto "Christ's Peace in Christ's Kingdom" revealed his firm conviction that the Church had to be involved in world affairs and pursued an interventionist course when state policy infringed upon the faith, unlike Gasparri and Pacelli who favored impartiality and nonintervention in the state's "political" affairs.

The Nazi's blatant violations of the Reich Concordat and persecution of the Church in Germany continued throughout most of 1934. In October, while Pacelli was the papal representative to the Eucharistic Congress in Buenos Aires, the pope again ex-

27. ASV, AAES, Germania, 1933–1945, posizione 647, fascicolo 191.
28. ASV, AAES, Germania, 1933–1945, posizione 647, fascicolo 191.
29. For the papal reaction to the Reich's sterilization legislation, see Segreteria di Stato, Rapporti con gli stati, archvio storico, ASV, AAES, Germania, 1922–1939, posizione 32, fasciclo 150–52.
30. Hachey, *Anglo-Vatican Relations, 1914–1939*, 253–54; Cianfarra, *The War and the Vatican*, 96; *Documents on German Foreign Policy*, Series C, vol. 30, 793–94.
31. ASV, SS, AAES, Germania, posizioni 641–43.

pressed his deep dissatisfaction with Nazi policy to the German ambassador to the Holy See, Diego von Bergen. The ambassador worried that without the moderating influence of Pacelli, the pope would make disastrous decisions. In fact, Pius XI, who had serious misgivings about concluding the agreement with Nazi Germany in the first place, considered renouncing it but was dissuaded from doing so by his secretary of state, who feared this would threaten the position of millions of German Catholics. Pacelli frankly acknowledged his role in its retention.

Yes, Pius XI was so indignant about what was happening in Germany that he once said to me, "How can the Holy See continue to keep a Nuncio there? It conflicts with our honor." The Holy Father feared that the world would not understand how we could continue diplomatic relations with a regime which treated the Church in such a manner. So I replied to him, "Your Holiness, what good would that do us? If we withdraw the Nuncio how can we maintain contact with the German bishops?"[32]

Both the pope and his secretary of state found Nazi policy and practices reprehensible, and came to view Hitler as an evil if not a demonic figure. They disagreed on how to respond to the regime, with the pope favoring confrontation and his secretary of state conciliation. Convinced of the futility of a policy of intransigence as practiced by Pio Nono, and supported by his own nonno or grandfather, Pacelli stressed the need for diplomacy in order to preserve the concordat and protect the Church. Pius XI was not persuaded by the arguments of his secretary of state in favor of a conciliatory course toward these "pagan regimes." Between 1933 and 1937 Pius XI wrote over fifty notes protesting Nazi action regarding Church doctrines. Most of these were ignored by the German government, arousing the anger of Pius XI, who concluded that Pacelli's reliance on private protests had failed miserably. Pacelli, for his part, continued to believe that his diplomacy

32. Rhodes, *The Vatican in an Age of Dictators*, 228–29.

and impartiality would spare the Church from the full wrath of the Fuehrer and far greater Nazi abuse of the faith, and should be preserved. There was some truth in Pacelli's assessment, which was supported by the greater part of the Church hierarchy, but for Pius XI the moral price for such an arrangement was too costly for the Church and the faith.

The pope, sensing an inevitable confrontation with the Nazi regime, sought to bolster the international position of the Holy See by sending his secretary of state on missions to South America (1934), the United States (1936), France (1935, 1937), and Hungary (1938). Some suspected he also wanted to be free from the pressure of the conciliatory Pacelli, whom he hesitated firing to avoid a rebellion from the members of the Secretariat of State and the greater part of the Church hierarchy who supported his cautious and conciliatory stance. Toward the end of his pontificate Pius found himself increasingly isolated and alone.[33]

Discounting Pacelli's and Gasparri's optimism that the Nazi regime would collapse before it waged war on the Church, Pius XI believed that the Nazis, who pretended to defend Western civilization, really sought to subvert its Christian heritage, replacing it with a pagan philosophy. Unlike his secretary of state who followed the Gasparri doctrine of doing everything possible to avoid a rupture of relations with this dictatorial regime, Pius XI believed the dignity of the Holy See required him to denounce the Nazi outrages, confident that the Church would survive the persecution.[34] He therefore refused to moderate, much less discontinue, his denunciations of these pagan regimes.[35] Following the remilitarization of the Rhineland, Pius XI did not hesitate

33. In this regard, see Fattorini, *Pio XI, Hitler e Mussolini*, and Peter Kent, "A Tale of Two Popes: Pius XII and the Rome-Berlin Axis," *Journal of Contemporary History* 23, no. 4 (October 1988): 589–608.
34. "Ai giovani Cattolici di Germania," August 8, 1934, in Bertetto, *Discorsi di Pio XI*, 3.188; Passelecq and Suchecky, *The Hidden Encyclical of Pius XI*, 93.
35. "Ai Giovani Cattolici Tedeschi," October 8, 1934, in Bertetto, *Discorsi di Pio XI*, 3.218.

to openly reveal his anti-Nazi sentiments to the French ambassador.[36]

Pius XI resented Nazi actions and laws which violated Church teachings and basic human rights, complaining to the German ambassador that he was "deeply grieved and gravely displeased." Diego Von Bergen reported that Pacelli was upset by the pope's anti-Nazi outbursts, but was not prepared to question, much less challenge, the pope.[37] Pacelli avoided openly clashing with Pius XI. Thus he was seen by some to be incapable of curbing the impulsive pontiff, who fell seriously ill at the end of 1936 and was bedridden for weeks—but remained lucid and determined.[38]

Casting aside the conciliatory course advocated by his secretary of state, Pius XI continued his "crusade" against racism and anti-Semitism. His opposition to the doctrine of blood and race was also reflected in the critical articles that appeared in *L'Osservatore Romano* and *Civiltà Cattolica*. One of these articles in *Civiltà Cattolica* claimed that the Church had always opposed persecution of the Jews.[39] While far from accurate, it expressed the papal desire to disassociate clerical anti-Judaism, which still persisted in the Church, from the pagan anti-Semitism of the Nazis. The papal denunciations of racism earned Pius XI respect in the Western capitals, but condemnation in Berlin. The continued attacks on the Church and its doctrines led Pius XI to speak out despite the subtle restraining influence of his secretary of state. In March 1937 he issued the encyclical *Mit brennender Sorge*, which he managed to have read from all the Catholic pulpits in Germany on Palm Sunday. "With deep anxiety and increasing dismay," Pius wrote, he had witnessed the "progressive oppression of the

---

36. Francois Charles-Roux, *Huit ans au Vatican* (Paris: Flammarion, 1947), 106.

37. *Documents on Germany Foreign Policy*, Series C, 4n482; Rhodes, *The Vatican in an Age of Dictators*, 199.

38. Emma Fattorini, *Hitler, Mussolini and the Vatican: Pope Pius XI and the Speech That Was Never Made* (Cambridge: Polity Press, 2011), 7.

39. "La Questione Giudaica," *La Civiltà Cattolica* (1936), anno 87, vol. 4, p. 45.

faithful." Denouncing the abuses and aberrations of the Hitler regime, the pope catalogued the articles of faith trampled upon by the Nazis including the adulation of race and the state. He concluded by urging the clergy to unmask and refute Nazism's errors whatever their form or disguise.[40] Although Pacelli, under papal order, played a part in drafting this critical encyclical, he quietly continued his efforts to prevent a break between Berlin and the Vatican. Pacelli's overriding determination to preserve the contacts between the Holy See and the German Church was a preoccupation that would persist during his own pontificate.

In June 1938, when Mussolini's Italy followed Hitler's Germany and embraced anti-Semitism, an enraged Pius XI let the Duce know that this action made him ashamed of being Italian.[41] While Pacelli avoided commentary on the papal action in his minutes of the meeting of September 9, 1938, when the matter was discussed, he repeatedly warned the pope of the adverse consequences that would flow from a disruption of relations with Fascist Italy and the Third Reich. These admonitions, along with earlier ones issued by Pacelli, apparently convinced Pius XI that he could not rely on his secretary of state for the unequivocal condemnation of racism and anti-Semitism he was determined to issue. For this reason in June 1938 he asked to see the American Jesuit John La Farge, whose books and articles denounced racism. Skirting his conciliatory Secretariat of State and its head, who seemed to prefer appeasement to war, the pope secretly commissioned La Farge to draft an encyclical demonstrating the incompatibility of Catholicism and racism. He did so without informing Pacelli of his intentions.[42]

40. "Lettera enciclica sulla situazione della Chiesa Cattolica nel Reich Germanico," *AAS*, 29 (1937), 168, 182, 185–86.
41. Pacelli's minutes of audience of September 9, 1938, *Fogli di udienza*, ASV, AAES, Italia, posizione 1054, fascicolo 727.
42. Robert A. Hecht, *An Unordinary Man: A Life of Father John La Farge, SJ* (Lanham, Md.: Scarecrow Press, 1996), 114–15.

Gustav Gundlach, who collaborated with La Farge in producing the encyclical *Humani Generis Unitas* (The Unity of the Human Race), was convinced that the secretary of state was not informed of their project. Indeed, Pacelli later acknowledged as much.[43] Since the projected encyclical would have led to a deterioration in the Vatican's relations with the Axis powers, and probably would have torpedoed the concordats, it is telling that the pope did not inform his secretary of state of his intentions. Apparently Pius XI suspected that Pacelli and his allies in the Vatican and the Secretariat of State would oppose the encyclical, and attempt to frustrate its issuance. It was an accurate assessment on the part of the pontiff.

Pius XI's insistence on secrecy was prompted by his determination to curtail the opposition he knew such an encyclical would provoke both inside and outside the Vatican. Ignoring the subtle but nonetheless persistent opposition of his secretary of state to any steps that would arouse the Fuehrer, Pius XI made it clear that he intended to continue his condemnation of racism, which he believed to be contrary to the faith, and by extension felt the need to condemn those regimes that flaunted it.[44] The three Jesuits who drafted the encyclical—the American John La Farge, the Frenchman Gustave Desbuquois, and the German Gustav Gundlach—perforce had to inform the head of their order of their assignment and in late September 1938, following protocol, placed a draft of the encyclical denouncing anti-Semitism tentatively titled "The Unity of the Human Race" in the hands of the general of the Jesuits, Vladimir Ledochowski, for transmission to the pope. Their expectation that this would be done quickly was undermined not only by the personal reservations of Ledochowski, but also by the opposition to such a step in the Vatican, where rumors abounded of the impending death of the "intransigent" pope.

---

43. Georges Passelecq and Bernard Suchecky, *L'Encyclique cachée de Pie XI. Une occasion manquée de l'Église face à l'antisémitisme* (Paris: La Decouverte, 1995), 124–26.

44. Fattorini, *Pio XI, Hitler e Mussolini*, 176.

The pope's determined opposition to Nazi racism and his collision course with the Hitler regime aroused great concern in the Secretariat of State that continued to adhere to Gasparri's pacific policy—which Pacelli admittedly shared. Ignoring the appeasement suggested by Pacelli, the pope's public denunciation of racialism worried Pacelli, who like his predecessor Gasparri diligently and consistently sought to prevent a break between the Vatican and Berlin.[45] Nonetheless, his cautious call for a moderate papal response to the Axis powers did not sway Pius XI, who was uncomfortable with the racism of the Berlin government. Its adoption by Fascist Italy only increased his anxiety and anger. Meanwhile, La Farge wondered when Pius would issue the encyclical drafted at his behest, while his collaborator, Gundlach, questioned whether the pope had received it. His suspicions were soon confirmed.

Father Heinrich Bacht, who translated the draft into Latin, reported that Ledochowski found La Farge's draft "too strong and provoking" and like Pacelli deemed it unwise to stumble into a head-on confrontation with Rome and Berlin. He therefore sought to tone down the draft, which reflected the sentiments and convictions of the pope.[46] We do not know if Pacelli or the Secretariat of State played any part in keeping the projected encyclical from the pope and called for its "moderation." We do know that both were determined to avoid antagonizing Fascist Italy and Nazi Germany, which would undoubtedly have occurred if *Humani Generis Unitas* had been released.

The long encyclical openly and clearly condemned anti-Semitism as reprehensible and "did not permit the Catholic to remain silent" in its presence.[47] Perhaps most disconcerting to those like

---

45. William M. Harrigan, "Pius XII's Efforts to Effect a Detente in German-Vatican Relations, 1939," *Catholic Historical Review* 49 (July 1963): 177.
46. "Jesuit Says Pius XI Asked for Draft," *National Catholic Reporter*, December 22, 1972, p. 4.
47. Galleys of La Farge's copy of the encyclical *Humani Generis Unitas*, p. 33, para.

Pacelli, the encyclical called for, indeed mandated, ecclesiastical action against racism. "It is the task and duty of the Church, the dignity and responsibility of the Chief Shepherd and of his brother Shepherds whom the Holy Ghost has placed to rule the Church of God, that they should point out to mankind the true course to be followed, the eternal divine order in the changing circumstances of the times," the projected encyclical read. This opinion was shared by Pius XI, who deplored the racist and anti-Semitic policies which Fascist Italy adopted as it moved closer to Nazi Germany. Discounting diplomatic niceties, he believed that the Vicar of Christ had the moral obligation to condemn these errors—and could not be dissuaded from doing so.[48]

Some in the Vatican feared that Pius XI's rift in relations with Fascist Italy and Nazi Germany would have disastrous consequences for the Church, and called for a more diplomatic course.[49] This current counted upon the election of a more conciliatory successor to Pius XI, and was responsible for the conclusion of an agreement with Fascist Italy on the racial issue. According to Father Angelo Martini, who was granted access to these Vatican documents, the "pact" of August 16, 1938, provided that in return for Fascist consideration of papal sensibilities on Catholic groups and organizations organized under Catholic Action in Italy, the papacy was to leave the "Jewish Question" entirely to the regime.[50] It represented a tactic favored by the

---

131, and p. 36b, para. 147; Passelecq and Suchecky, *L'Encyclique cachée de Pie XI*, 283–84, 292–93.

48. The encyclical against racism and anti-Semitism, *Humani Generis Unitas*, commissioned by Pius XI but shelved by his successor, Pius XII, was to be published in the *Catholic Mind* in 1973 but did not appear. The galleys of the encyclical were discovered by Professor Robert A. Hecht of the City University of New York, who graciously sent them to me. Later, in 1996, another copy of this "hidden encyclical" was published by Georges Passelecq and Bernard Suchecky (see note 43). My reference is to the galleys of the encyclical for the *Catholic Mind*, 33, para. 36b, and Passelecq and Suchecky, *L'Encyclique cachée de Pie XI*, 283–84, 292–93, 296.

49. Giovanni Miccoli, "Santa Sede e Chiesa Italiana di Fronte alle Leggi Antiebraiche del 1938," *Studi Storici*, anno 29, no. 4 (October–December 1988), 881.

50. Angelo Martini, "L'Ultima battaglia di Pio XI," in *Studi sulla questione romana e la conciliazione* (Rome: Cinque Lune, 1963), 186–87.

Secretariat of State but denounced by the pope. It is inconceivable that Pius XI would have concluded or adhered to such a pact, which violated his convictions—and he did not! It was apparently concocted behind his back, in the expectation that the gravely ill pope would soon be dead.

Despite his failing health, the pope made his opposition to racism clear in early September, announcing that the Vicar of Christ could not remain silent in the face of grave errors and the violation of human rights.[51] Italy's racist legislation represented an attack on the Church's teachings. On November 10, 1938, Mussolini published a decree forbidding marriage between Italian Aryans with persons of "another race." Pius responded by writing both the king and Mussolini that this was a violation of the Lateran Accords. He made public his displeasure in his Christmas address.[52] In light of the Vatican's campaign of increased opposition to totalitarian racism, the path was paved for issuing La Farge's encyclical which echoed the pope's sentiments, but there was no word or hint of its release.

There was little opportunity for the authors of the antiracist encyclical to explore the lack of response to their draft by the ailing pope, whose schedule was severely curtailed, especially after his two heart attacks on Thursday, November 25, 1938.[53] Even public audiences with diplomats were now limited to five minutes because of his grave condition and concern that he might further disrupt relations with the dangerous Fascist regimes. Consequently, the authors of the encyclical did not have ready access to the pope's person. Given the hierarchical structure of the Church and the quasi-military discipline of their order, an appeal to the pope over the heads of their superior was no trivial

---

51. "Ad Insegnanti di Azione Cattolica," September 6, 1938, in Bertetto, *Discorsi di Pio XI*, 3.796.
52. "Con grande," December 24, 1938, in Koenig, *Principles for Peace*, 549–51; *New York Times*, December 25, 1938.
53. Desmond O'Grady, "Pius XI—Complex and Imperious," *National Catholic Reporter*, December 15, 1972, p. 15.

matter. Nonetheless, Father Gundlach convinced La Farge to write directly to Pius XI, who had charged him with the assignment of drafting the encyclical. Once informed that the encyclical had been signed and delivered, the seriously ill pope demanded to have it immediately sent to him, which prompted the reluctant Ledochowski to comply.

Father Walter Abbot reports that the Vatican received the document on January 21, 1939, but is not certain if the pope saw or read it before his death.[54] Most likely he did not, even though the dying Pius XI was working on a speech to be presented to the bishops cataloging Fascist abuses and errors. He died on February 10, 1939, at 5:31 in the morning, before he could deliver it.[55] Some suspected foul play; Cardinal Eugene Tisserant, prefect of the Vatican Library, even launched the charge that the Duce, aroused by the pope's opposition, had him murdered! Although Mussolini looked forward to the election of a "less contentious pope," as did the conciliatory contingent in the Vatican, there is no evidence to suggest that the seriously ill pope did not die from natural causes.

The death of Pius XI led to the "death" of the encyclical against anti-Semitism and racism. The draft of encyclical, with an attached note from Monsignor Domenico Tardini, indicating that Pius XI wanted it without delay,[56] was found on the desk of the deceased pope.[57] The critical address Pius XI planned to present to the Italian bishops on the tenth anniversary of the Lateran Accords, was also there. Not surprisingly, Eugenio Pacelli, who became Pope Pius XII on March 2, 1939, decided to shelve both. Indeed, Domenico Tardini reports in documents recently opened in the Secret Vatican Archive, that in a memorandum of

54. "Jesuit Says Pius XI Asked for Draft," p. 3.
55. *AAS*, 31 (1939), 33; PP, 2.114.
56. "Jesuit Says Pius XI Asked for Draft," p. 4.
57. Jim Castelli, "Unpublished Encyclical Attacked Anti-Semitism," *National Catholic Reporter*, December 15, 1972, pp. 13–14.

February 15, 1939, Secretary of State Pacelli ordered the Vatican printing house to destroy all evidence of the papal speech which he feared would widen the rift with Mussolini's Italy and his Nazi ally. The draft of the "secret encyclical" was returned to its authors. These steps were symptomatic of the new conciliatory course that Pacelli as Pius XII would pursue toward Fascist Italy and Nazi Germany.

SIX

Confronting the Second World War

A diplomat must see many things and hold his peace ...
Whoever wants to help must not provoke Hitler
If we keep silent ... We do so also
Ad maioram mala vitanda.

ALTHOUGH A LITERARY rather than a historical work, *The Deputy*, which admittedly launched some outrageous and unsubstantiated charges against Papa Pacelli and the Vatican, nonetheless arrived at a few perceptive conclusions such as the one cited above. Avoiding greater evil provides a coherent explanation of papal conduct during the war and the Holocaust. Hochhuth also recognized the divergence between Pius XI and his secretary of state who succeeded him as Pius XII, noting that it was Pacelli rather than the pope who sought conciliation with the Reich and was responsible for the quick conclusion of the concordat with Nazi Germany.[1] Some historians, on the other hand, tend to see a solidarity between the two.

Despite assertions of solidarity, after 1937 Pius XI's confrontational course toward the fascist dictators clashed with the con-

---

In the epigraph, the character of Pope Pius XII is commenting on Nazi atrocities and the genocide of the Jews, from Rolf Hochhuth, *The Deputy* (New York: Grove Press, 1964), Act 4, 200.

1. Hochhuth, "Sidelights on History," *The Deputy*, 296.

ciliatory one pursued by his secretary of state, Cardinal Eugenio Pacelli. Although Pacelli's tone was more moderate than that of his mentor, the conflict reflected the pope's earlier battle with Cardinal Pietro Gasparri.² Pacelli continued to adhere to the cautious stance toward the fascist regimes followed by Gasparri, while the pope called for stronger action against these "odious dictatorships" and their un-Christian philosophies and practices. This led him to commission the encyclical condemning Nazi and fascist racism without informing Pacelli. Although Pacelli, and the Secretariat of State over which he presided, catalogued the dangers inherent in alienating the fascist regimes, Pius XI determined to forge ahead with his "crusade" against racism and anti-Semitism.

Pacelli's call for reconciliation with the fascist states was but one of many problems Papa Ratti confronted as he challenged the totalitarian claims and racist policies of the Rome and Berlin governments. Suffering from diabetes and heart disease, he found it increasingly difficult to overcome the strong pacifist sentiment in the curia, the Secretariat of State, and other Vatican circles. As his health deteriorated, Pius XI witnessed the active and passive resistance to his program increase dramatically. Hoping that the diplomatic community would be more alert to the danger these dictatorships posed than the conciliarists in the Vatican, he was disappointed by the lack of resolve he found in Neville Chamberlain and Lord Halifax when the British prime minister and foreign minister visited him in mid-January 1939.³ To his dismay he learned that the two shared the call for appeasement that prevailed in his own Secretariat of State.

Determined to avoid the wrath of the dictatorial regimes, the pacifist element in the Vatican was far from passive and took

---

2. Fiorentino, *All'Ombra di Pietro*, 42–45; also see Fattorini, *Pio XI, Hitler e Mussolini*, and Alessandro Duce, *La Santa Sede e la questione ebraica (1933–1945)* (Rome: Studium, 2007).

3. Padellaro, *Portrait of Pius XII*, 132.

the extraordinary step of concluding a pact with Mussolini's Italy behind the sick pope's back. It promised to allow the Duce to pursue his racial policy without Vatican interference in return for Fascist assurances to be granted to Catholic groups and activities in the peninsula, collectively known as Catholic Action.[4] Aware that this agreement violated the pope's principles and challenged precepts of the faith, they concluded it knowing that Papa Ratti was seriously ill and near death, and planned for a successor who would implement their pact. Its authors must have realized that Mussolini's racism, like that of the Nazis, was in violation of Catholic universalism, but tolerated it *Ad maiora mala vitandato*—to avoid greater evil.[5] This policy based on expediency rather than morality enraged the pope, who though near death was not senile. Although unaware of the pact, he sensed the opposition to his approach, and became furious when alerted to the fact that the "secret encyclical" he had commissioned had been delivered but deliberately kept from him. He demanded its immediate release, which belatedly triggered its transmission. It has been established by figures close to the pope that he died before he could read or release it.

Following his death on February 10, 1939, the conclave of early March to select a successor met as Hitler was on the verge of making new demands and the clouds of war thickened. In light of the differences between the former pope and his secretary of state, the widespread notion that Pius XI sought Pacelli as his successor is questionable. The prospect of Pacelli's selection was further undermined by the long-standing tradition that the conclave seldom named the last secretary of state as successor. For these and other reasons, the archbishop of Milan, Cardinal Ildefons Schuster, did not expect Pacelli, who entered the conclave

---

4. See Angelo Martini, "L'Ultima battaglia di Pio XI," 175–230.

5. P. Blett, et al., *Actes et documents du Saint Siège relatifs à la seconde guerrre mondiale (ADSS)* (Rome: Liberia Editrice Vaticana, 1965–1981), vol. 2, n. 105.

as secretary of state and papal chamberlain, to be elected as successor, a view shared by a number of other cardinals in the college. However, a majority of the cardinal electors sought a diplomatic pope to deal with the impending crisis such as Leo XIII or Benedict XV, rather than a pastoral one such as Pius X, much less a confrontational one the likes of Pius XI. The thought of a destructive conflict created consternation in the Vatican, but the possibility that the Church, its members and hierarchy, and the Holy See itself might become a target and victim of the dictatorial regimes created even greater alarm.

The cardinals in conclave, some 90 percent of whom hailed from Europe, were aware and appreciative of Pacelli's persistent efforts to mitigate the confrontational course of the past pope which they feared provoked the dictatorial regimes and endangered the Church and the faithful in Fascist Italy and Nazi Germany. They quickly decided that Pacelli was the figure best able to calm the dictators and spare the Church their revenge. Thus, it appears that Pacelli was not elected to continue the confrontational policies of his predecessor as is widely accepted, but elected to reverse the confrontational course of his predecessor. He was seen to possess both the temperament and diplomatic expertise to do so. He had served as nuncio to Germany in the 1920s, secretary of state from 1930 to 1939, knew Germany well, had visited France, and even traveled to North and South America. Thus on March 2, 1939, Pacelli's birthday, in the shortest conclave since 1623, the Roman Pacelli was elected pope in less than twenty-four hours, on the third ballot. He took the name Pius XII—the first Roman to occupy the chair of Peter in two hundred years and the first secretary of state to immediately don the tiara since Clement IX (1667–1669). He was crowned on March 12 in the Vatican Basilica in the presence of representatives from thirty-five nations, including Joseph Kennedy of the United States.

Although he styled himself Pius XII, and many assumed he took the name to honor Pius XI, the record reveals that from the first Pacelli avoided his predecessor's argumentative and confrontational course. He was convinced that Pius XI's combative policies endangered relations with Mussolini and Hitler, threatened the concordats with Italy and Germany, making matters worse for the institutional Church in both countries while placing Vatican City in jeopardy. Some suspected he was also concerned about his own personal safety, but this is speculation. What is known is that the quiet and aloof Pacelli had long shared Gasparri's concerns about the consequences flowing from the confrontational policies of Pius XI toward the fascist regimes and diplomatically discouraged papal opposition. First as nuncio, then as secretary of state, and finally as pope, Pacelli worked tirelessly to prevent a break between Berlin and the Vatican which was appreciated by many in the Reich. He did so not because he admired the Nazi Party or the Third Reich, but because he feared its irrational and irresponsible leader and the havoc he might heap upon the Church and its clergy if he felt provoked.

The German cardinals regarded the Germanophile Pacelli as their special protector, and even the Nazis appeared to approve his election. Following his selection Josef Goebbels's newspaper, *Der Angriff*, commented that the new pope was "a good judge of the present times,"[6] while Heinrich Himmler, who headed the police in Nazi Germany, praised Pacelli's tact and prudence. Hitler himself later admitted that he was pleased that the Holy Father spoke German.[7] In Italy both the Duce and his son-in-law and foreign minister Count Ciano applauded Pacelli's election. In fact, the Duce indicated he was prepared to offer Pacelli

---

6. *AAS*, 31.125, 146, 151.

7. P. Blett et al., *Records and Documents of the Holy See Relating to the Second World War: The Holy See and the War in Europe*, trans. Gerard Noel (Washington, D.C.: Corpus Books, 1968) (RDHSWW), 122, 166.

advice on how best to conduct papal affairs.⁸ The efficacy of his diplomatic skill and tact was attested to by the fact that the Germans and Italians as well as the French and English considered him the best candidate to succeed Pius XI.

When he became pope, Pacelli personally contrasted his conciliatory approach with the confrontational one of his predecessor, explaining how he had restrained him.⁹ This was well known in the conciliatory circles that supported his election, and he did not disappoint them. Shortly after his accession as Pius XII, the German ambassador noted the relaxation of tensions between the Vatican and Berlin. One of the new pope's first actions was to call together the German cardinals, Theodore Innitzer of Vienna, Michael Faulhaber of Munich, Karl Josef Schulte of Cologne, and Adolf Bertram of Breslau, indicating his intention of dispatching a personal letter to the Fuehrer announcing his accession.¹⁰ Hitler, still smarting from the policies pursued by Pius XI, did not respond, and Germany was the only major power that did not dispatch a representative to the pope's coronation. Nonetheless, the pope was cordial and conciliatory when he met Diego von Bergen, German ambassador to the Holy See, a few days later, assuring him that relations would be improved with the Reich during his pontificate.

Pacelli also revealed his intention of pursuing a more conciliatory policy toward Germany to the Italian foreign minister, Count Galeazzo Ciano, certain that the message would be transmitted to Berlin—and it was! The Fascist government welcomed Papa Pacelli's "new course." These initial actions of the new pope led the Italian minister to believe that they could "get along well with this Pope."¹¹ The directors of the right-wing Action Fran-

---

8. Galeazzo Ciano, *The Ciano Diaries, 1939–1943*, ed. H. Gibson (Garden City, N.Y.: Doubleday, 1945), 36.

9. Rhodes, *The Vatican in the Age of Dictators*, 228–29

10. Hanjakob Stehle, *Eastern Politics of the Vatican*, trans. Sandra Smith (Athens: Ohio University Press, 1981), 67.

11. Ciano, *The Ciano Diaries*, 36, 47.

çaise also found Pius XII more accommodating than Pius XI and therefore more acceptable. They petitioned the new pope and had the ban imposed by his predecessor lifted.[12] Francisco Franco also found Papa Pacelli less "intransigent" and more accommodating than Papa Ratti and welcomed the change in pontificates.

The conciliatory tone of Pius XII also pleased the Nazis who had deeply resented the course pursued by Pius XI. They appreciated the fact that the new pope chose the accommodating Cardinal Luigi Maglione as his secretary of state.[13] Pius, for his part, continued his campaign to achieve a rapprochement with the Axis powers his predecessor had alienated. Speaking to German visitors in April 1939, Pacelli openly revealed his love and sympathy for Germany. Paradoxically, he added "We love Germany even more today."[14] Perhaps he meant to reassure the Nazis in order to protect Catholic interests in Germany, but in retrospect his choice of words was unfortunate and led some to conclude that he favored the Nazis. In fact he was an admirer of Germany, which he often acknowledged, but Pius XII was no friend of the Nazis. His pro-German proclivities were reflected in the company he kept—his housekeeper, private secretary, and confessor all hailed from the Reich. These relationships led others to suspect that Pacelli's Germanophile sentiments and anticommunism translated into support for Hitler and the Nazis. There is no evidence suggesting that he was sympathetic to either, but substantial sources indicating he was suspicious of both. The most reliable evidence indicates that his conciliatory course towards the Nazi regime was driven more by fear than love.

By nature shy and gentle, the new pope lacked the fighting spirit of his combative predecessor, reported Monsignor Domenico Tardini, secretary of the Congregation of Extraordinary

---

12. *AAS*, vol. 31 (1939), 303–17.

13. "Nomine Pontificie," *AAS*, vol. 31 (1939), 136.

14. George O. Kent, "Pope Pius XII and Germany: Some Aspects of German-Vatican Relations, 1933–1943," *American Historical Review* 70 (October 1964): 65.

Ecclesiastical Affairs, who was in close, often daily, contact with Pius XII. The new pope differed from Pius XI in his estimation of how much the Church could or should endure to preserve the Reich Concordat, and the best means of securing Nazi compliance with it. Criticism increased when Hitler violated the Munich Agreement and occupied Prague and what remained of Czech territory, without provoking a Vatican protest. Instead, the nuncio in Berlin, Cesare Orsenigo, attributed this action to the "nationalist fanaticism of the new generation,"[15] without any direct condemnation of Nazi action and aggression. The prospect of war loomed large as the Nazis increased their demands on Poland, prompting their ambassador to the Holy See to urge it to condemn the belligerent actions contemplated by the Nazi regime. Pius XII, however, refused to intervene as the Nazis pressured the Catholic Poles for a series of concessions, maintaining a strict impartiality between aggressor and aggrieved.[16] Sanctioning a degree of pacifism that some branded appeasement, Pius proposed that Catholic Poland make concessions to the pagan Nazi state to avoid war and urged the British, French, and Italians to support his suggestion.[17] Following Benedict XV, he insisted that the papal position was not one of neutrality, which might imply indifference to evil, but impartiality, which justified papal public and political inaction against such evil. It was a distinction contrived to balance the papacy's moral responsibility and its cautious and neutral political role. It did not succeed and deemed sophistry in the allied camp.

The pope, seeking to prevent the outbreak of war and assure the security of the Church and its leadership, felt the need to communicate with the Germans as well as the Poles, French, and British. He steadfastly refused to allot responsibility for the

---

15. *RDHSWW*, 95.
16. Ibid., 93–96, 146; Koenig, *Principles for Peace*, 569–70.
17. "Nuntius Radiophonicus," *AAS*, vol. 31 (1939), 335–36.

impending conflict, maintaining good relations with both camps in order to avoid retribution and protect the faithful and institutions of the Church. Some later charged that in his persistent pursuit of peace Papa Pacelli sacrificed principle—an accusation others challenged. What is certain is that from the first days of his pontificate his major objectives were to preserve the peace and protect the Church, two considerations which determined his policy. He expressed his concerns about the preservation of the peace in his Easter Message of April 9, 1939, but adhering to his impartiality would not assign responsibility nor indicate who threatened it.[18]

In April 1939 Pius XII avoided antagonizing Nazi Germany and Fascist Italy by refusing to support President Franklin Roosevelt's message urging them not to attack some thirty-one nations. Instead, in May, Pius invited Britain, Germany, France, Italy, and Poland to a conference at the Vatican to consider the Polish-German dispute over Danzig and help resolve the difficulties between Italy and France, hoping to avert another war. The Soviet Union was conspicuously excluded. The Duce, who knew Italy was not prepared for war, favored the initiative, but the Fuehrer rejected it, as did the Allied Powers. At this juncture British public opinion questioned making further concessions to Nazi Germany as Rome suggested.

For his part, the astute pontiff must have known that the appeased dictator could not be trusted to preserve the peace and when one concession was made, demanded another. Apparently Pius XII sought time, reassured by Gasparri's earlier pronouncement that these dictatorial regimes would not last long and should be appeased in the interim to avoid their wrath while waiting for their inevitable collapse. The British no longer shared the optimism of the Vatican. Popular opinion in England was disillusioned by Hitler's repudiation of the Four Power Agreement

18. *RDHSWW*, 92, 100.

reached at Munich, which did not bring peace in their time but only whetted the appetite of the Nazis for more.

The French followed the English lead in rejecting another international conference. "A Pope's word on the moral issue would be more helpful than a Five Power Conference," noted the French ambassador to the Holy See, François Charles Roux, who found Pius XII's impartiality and continued conciliation of the dictatorial regimes inexplicable and reprehensible. "We cannot be put on the same level as the others as far as peaceful intentions, moral issues, and the uprightness of our attitude are concerned," he noted in response to the papal invitation. He added that "the countries that should be stopped from sliding into war are in the other camp, that is Germany and Italy. He added that it was these two states that placed peace in danger, the one by raising claims on Danzig, the other by supporting them."[19] Privately, Pius XII concurred, but publicly he preserved his impartiality, hoping thus to avert the furious wrath of Nazi Germany.

The pope refused to abandon his quest to preserve the peace. The rejection of his call for a conference led him to propose another means of resolving differences between the powers, suggesting papal mediation of the rival claims of Germany and Poland on the one hand, France and Italy on the other. The Germans rejected the papal offer to mediate their differences with Poland, while the French rejected the offer of papal mediation between themselves and the Italians. Paris resented the Holy See's "impartial" suggestion that concessions had to be made by all in the interest of peace, denouncing it as a dangerous policy of appeasement. However, what other alternative did the Vatican have at this juncture? Perhaps silence would have been more appropriate, but this probably would have been criticized as indifference! After Munich the British proved increasingly skeptical of appeasement, letting it be known that they would

19. Ibid., 145–46, 210.

defend the Poles if they were attacked by Nazi Germany. Some found it ironic that Protestant England was prepared to resort to military means to defend Catholic Poland, but the Vicar of Christ proved unwilling publicly to lend even moral support to the Catholic Poles. These critics fail to mention that Britain was a great power protected by the Channel and her navy, while the tiny Vatican state was at the mercy of the Fascist regimes. Clearly neither anti-Judaism or anti-Semitism played a part in the papal recourse to impartiality as the Nazis contemplated aggression against Catholic Poland.

Although Britain had assumed the initiative in the Allied camp by abandoning appeasement, ideologically driven clerical circles tended to blame republican France for the alleged "Allied intransigence." The French Republic's dissatisfaction with papal generalizations and insistence on impartiality led the nuncio to France, Valerio Valeri, to dubious conclusions. He suspected that French dissatisfaction with the papal proposal flowed from the fact that Protestants in France worried about the increase in the Holy See's prestige should it be able to preserve the peace. He also claimed that the criticism of the papacy stemmed "from the secret powers of Freemasonry in France and of the extremist currents, still very potent in the country."[20] This paranoia was shared by a number of others in the curia and reflected the influence of the Action Française of Charles Maurras, which had been condemned by Pius XI. Nonetheless, its attitude prevailed in certain clerical circles, especially after Pius XII lifted the ban on membership and reading its newspaper.

Both the nuncio and the papal secretary of state, Maglione, refused to accept any complaint against the papal policy of impartiality which treated perpetrator and victim alike. "The Holy Father cannot suppose that the desire for peace exists only in one nation," Maglione responded to the Allied criticism of the

---

20. Ibid., 138–39, 172.

papal position, adding that in appealing for peace the pope "cannot and he must not make distinctions."[21] Both curia and pope rejected the French charge of irresponsible papal indifference and Pius XII continued to pursue the "impartial" course Gasparri had originated during World War I.

In his radio message "To Those in Power and Their Peoples" of August 24, 1939, Pius XII, who some already hailed as the "Pope of Peace," while others condemned him as an "apostle of appeasement," invoked peace among families, rulers, and nations based on justice and charity. He warned that the "horrible catastrophe" of another conflict loomed ever larger, adding, "Nothing is lost by peace, but everything may be lost by war."[22] His plea in 1939 reached a broad audience for by this time some forty states sent diplomatic representatives of one sort or another to the Holy See, more than double the foreign powers accredited to it on the eve of the First World War.[23] Furthermore, the new pope quickly made it known that he would employ all the mechanisms of the communications revolution to make his voice heard. Determined to attune the Church to twentieth-century technology, Pius, like Roosevelt, had frequent recourse to the radio, and during his tenure Vatican Radio broadcast in some twenty different languages. Both the American president and the pope faced a difficult and deteriorating diplomatic situation. One of the few positive international developments, from the papal perspective, was the triumph over the Spanish Republic of Francisco Franco, who Pius XII congratulated in mid-April 1939. Here, too, Pius XII departed from the stance of his predecessor. While Pius XI had opposed Franco's actions and was suspicious of his exploitation of Catholicism to achieve his political ends, his successor acclaimed

21. Ibid., 145–46
22. Charles Rankin, ed., *The Pope Speaks: The Words of Pius XII* (New York: Harcourt, Brace and Co., 1940), 146.
23. Great Britain, *British Documents on the Origin of the War, 1898–1914* (London: His Majesty's Stationary Office, 1926), 400.

Franco's victory as a defense of the faith and Christian civilization against those who championed atheism. Subsequently, he hailed the veterans of Franco's "crusade" as "defenders of the faith."[24] In applauding Franco's victory he abandoned the impartiality he cited in dealing with Nazi Germany.

Pius XII dared not abandon his impartiality nor alienate or antagonize the Third Reich and continued his steps to maintain cordial relations with its evil leader. Among other things he did not release Pius XI's encyclical condemning racism and anti-Semitism. Pius XI's critique of Fascist violations of the Lateran Accord was likewise scuttled. However, the new pope did permit Gundlach to incorporate sections of the "Hidden Encyclical" into his own first encyclical, *Summi Pontificatus* (On the Limitations of the Authority of the State), of October 20, 1939. In it the pope acknowledged that his office obliged him to teach that in Christ there is neither Gentile nor Jew, while rejecting the claims of the absolute or totalitarian state.[25] However, Pius XII chose to abandon the explicit condemnation of anti-Semitism in Pius XI's planned encyclical, which he knew would arouse Hitler and the Nazis.[26] While some acclaimed his effort to preserve the peace by curbing his tongue, others disagreed with the notion that the best words were those that were not said. Instead, they charged that he allowed political expediency to triumph over ethical principles.

Prior to the controversy over Pius XII's "silence" during the Holocaust there were complaints by a few individuals inside and outside the Church that he craved peace at any price, even at the cost of compromising his moral mission. Those threatened by Nazi aggression resented this pope's "detachment," "appease-

24. *New York Times*, June 12, 1939.
25. Ethel Mary Tinnemann, "The Silence of Pope Pius XII," *Journal of Church and State* 21, no. 1 (Winter 1979): 265.
26. *AAS*, 31 (1939), 413–53; Gordan Zahn, "The Unpublished Encyclical: 'An Opportunity Missed,'" *National Catholic Reporter*, December 15, 1972, p. 9.

ment," and recourse to generalities in the face of the approaching Nazi whirlwind. French Catholics were upset that the pontiff had not raised his voice when Albania had been bombed by the Italians on Good Friday, 1939. Even as Nazi Germany threatened the peace of Europe, the pope in April 1939 expressed his sympathy for the Reich and its people.[27] German diplomats were led to understand that Pius XII favored a public truce, so long as vital Church institutions were not threatened.[28] Now that Pacelli was pope he could pursue Gasparri's conciliatory course as he sought to preserve the impartiality of the Holy See and thus protect the Church in Germany.

In pursuit of peace, the Holy Father implored the faithful in both camps to commence a crusade of prayer for a peaceful resolution of all disputes. However, the European situation remained troubled, aggravated by the conclusion of the military alliance between Fascist Italy and Nazi Germany on May 22, 1939, dubbed the "Pact of Steel" by the Duce. It bound Fascist Italy to support Nazi Germany without condition. Undaunted by the failure of his initial diplomatic efforts, Pius XII followed the path blazed by Benedict XV by continuing his peace efforts. On August 19, he urged a group of pilgrims from Venice to pray for peace in Italy, Europe, and the world. On August 24, 1939, the day after the world was shocked by the news of the Nazi-Soviet pact, Pius XII issued a radio appeal to the heads of nations, politicians, writers, and public leaders to do all within their means to avert another catastrophe. Preserving his impartiality in this instance, the pope insisted that the Holy See had perforce to remain above all public disputes. The nuncio to Paris, Cardinal Valerio Valeri, explained that while the Holy See endeavored to improve relations among nations, it could not compromise its impartiality, which would

---

27. Kent, "Pope Pius XII and Germany," 65.
28. Harrigan, "Pius XII's Efforts to Effect a Detente in German-Vatican Relations," 184.

jeopardize its mediation efforts. While the papal position won support in the Axis camp, the French were furious with the "diplomatic dance" conducted by the Vatican, which seemed shielded by the armor of indifference. Charles Roux made it clear that the French were terribly disappointed that Pius XII had virtually abandoned the principles pursued by his predecessor Pius XI.[29]

A number of factors determined Pius XII's diplomacy toward Nazi Germany including a deep affection for that nation and its people; an unwillingness to place German Catholics in a position where they would be constrained to choose between their religion and their state; a strong commitment to the preservation of the Reich Concordat of 1933; an overriding opposition to communism; and above all fear of the wrath of an enraged Hitler assisted by Fascist Italy, which surrounded the Vatican.[30] This fear was generated by the papal concern that publicly ranging itself alongside the Allies would violate the neutrality it had pledged in the Lateran Accords. Pius XII also feared that abandoning his impartiality would traumatize German Catholics, subject them to Nazi persecution, and jeopardize the unity of the universal Church. Perhaps he also shared the concern expressed by the nuncio in Berlin that if German Catholics were constrained to choose between their patria and their faith, they might choose the former over the latter.[31] Thus, though Pius selected the alleged Francophile Cardinal Luigi Maglione, former nuncio to Paris, as his secretary of state, his first priority remained the determination to conciliate or appease Nazi Germany, ending the criticism of the Reich initiated by the former

29. *RDHSWW*, 169.
30. In this regard, see the correspondence between Pacelli and Orsenigo in the ASV, S di S, Rapport con gli stati, ASV, AES, Germannia, 1922–1939, as well as Michael Feldkamp, *Pius XII und Deutschland* (Goffingen: Vandenhoeck and Ruprecht, 2000).
31. See the letters of March 7, 1933, and May 2, 1933, in which Orsenigo warns Pacelli that German Catholics should not be made to choose between the new regime and their Catholic faith; ASV, S di S, Rapporti con gli stati, AS, AES, Germania, posizione. 641–43, f. 157 and posizione 643, f. 159.

pope. He did so to protect Church interests and activities in the Reich, as well as the German Catholic clergy.

At the same time, the Holy Father seconded President Franklin Delano Roosevelt's nonpartisan diplomatic initiatives as he again called upon the faithful in both camps to pray for peace.[32] Early in June, Pius, who sought solace in Scripture and prayer, issued another appeal without referring to specific issues, territorial disputes, or differentiating aggressor from aggrieved. The nuncio to France defended Pius' position by asserting that the Holy See had to preserve its contacts with the two blocs, alienating neither. The French ambassador to the Holy See responded that the Holy See could fulfill its mission by relying on politics and diplomacy, or by asserting and standing by the principles which the Church cherished, and which were completely contrary to the fascist doctrines. The second seemed the more appropriate for the French, but Pius XII was seen to rely on his fund of diplomatic experience. Reportedly, he would not allow Father Martin Gillet, master general of the Dominicans, to plead with the totalitarian governments to renounce the use of violence in international relations, fearing such a declaration would violate the Vatican's impartiality and unleash adverse consequences for the faith and the faithful.

As the diplomatic situation deteriorated, the Holy See received identical communications from the Berlin and Rome embassies asking the pope to submit a proposal for Allied consideration. It called for a thirty-day truce to organize a conference of the foreign ministers of France, Great Britain, Italy, and Germany which would resolve the Danzig question by mutual agreement, without Polish participation. Subsequently, the British government would submit the proposed solution for Polish acceptance.[33] Neither London nor Paris was willing to coerce Warsaw into what seemed "a second Munich," certain to alien-

32. Koenig, *Principles for Peace*, 565–66.
33. *RDHSWW*, 203.

ate public opinion at home and undermine resistance to Nazi aggression. Undaunted by this failure, Pius continued his efforts on behalf of peace as war loomed. Preserving his public impartiality, the pope insisted that the Holy See remain above public disputes and spoke only in the name of God. On August 31, 1939, Pius again pleaded for peace.[34] Inviting the representatives of Britain, France, Germany, Italy, and Poland, along with the American ambassador to Italy, to the Vatican, he urged them to communicate with their governments to do all within their power to prevent the outbreak of a new war. This attempt at mediation by Pius XII proved no more successful than his earlier efforts.

On September 1, 1939, when the German army invaded Poland, sparking the Second World War, Pius refused to condemn the aggression. After Britain and France declared war on Germany on September 3, Pius revealed his determination to remain neutral to a group of visiting German pilgrims, telling them, "For a priest, it is now more than ever before, imperative to be wholly above all political and national passion."[35] His determination to preserve the Vatican's "impartiality" in the Anglo-French confrontation with Nazi Germany flowed from a number of factors including the example set by Benedict XV and Cardinal Gasparri during the First World War, as well as his perception of article 24 of the Treaty of the Lateran Accords, in which the Holy See pledged to remain apart from temporal disputes between states. Furthermore, the pope did not wish to offend the Catholic faithful who were found in both belligerent camps, and like the German hierarchy he dreaded the consequences that might follow a rupture with the Axis powers that surrounded the Vatican.

Although publicly preserving the strictest political neutral-

---

34. Ibid., 183–84; *PP*, 1.116; Koenig, *Principles for Peace*, 584–57.
35. *RDHSWW*, 293.

ity that his impartiality required, Pius XII's Vatican secretly informed the Western Allies at the end of 1939 and early in 1940 that a group of German generals were prepared to overthrow the Nazi regime, if they could be assured a just and honorable peace. On January 11, 1940, Pius XII met with Francis D'Arcy Osborne, the British representative to the Vatican, to acquaint him with the scheme of part of the German military to oust the Fuehrer and seek a peace settlement that would include the restoration of Poland and Czechoslovakia but would not challenge the union of Germany and Austria. The message was transmitted to London, which responded that it could not proceed on this "nebulous proposition." In April when the Nazis invaded Denmark and Norway the Vatican's *L'Osservatore Romano* deplored this extension of the conflict, arousing Mussolini who threatened its circulation and existence. This led Pius XII, who feared Fascist retaliation, to impose additional restrictions on the journal. Despite these public papal concessions to the Axis, the Vatican once again privately revealed its pro-Allied bias when it quietly alerted them to the impending Nazi invasion of France and the Low Countries. However, the pope, acting on behalf of what he believed to be in the best interest of the Church and Catholicism in the Reich, refused to publicly reveal his inner sentiments.

The pope, who was primate of Italy and bishop of Rome, sought to keep Italy from entering the conflict as Benedict and Gasparri had in 1914. He indicated as much to the new Italian ambassador to the Holy See, Dino Alfieri. The pope repeated this message during the visit of King Victor Emmanuel III and Queen Elena to the Vatican on December 21, 1939. During their meeting, Pius XII sought to convince the king to restrain Mussolini from dragging Italy into the conflict. He reiterated this appeal the following week, when he returned the royal visit by going to the Quirinal Palace to see the Italian king and queen. President Franklin Delano Roosevelt, who had met Pacelli when as secretary of state he had visited the United States, appreciated his attempt to contain the conflict and mitigate its consequences. The American president pondered the prospect of opening some form of diplomatic relations with the Vatican, despite the anti-Catholicism still widespread in the United States.

Roosevelt, like Pius, sought to limit the war and endeavored to bring it to a speedy conclusion in conjunction with the intricate network of international representation which he was convinced had the Vatican at its disposal. To coordinate papal and American efforts, the American president decided to dispatch the businessman, industrialist, and philanthropist Myron C. Taylor to the pope as his personal representative at the end of December 1939. Seeking to avoid the negative Protestant reaction that a formal confirmation would inevitably provoke, the status of the Episcopalian Taylor was not specified, nor was funding for his mission requested. The Holy See, for its part, however, quickly granted him ambassador status.

The American initiative pleased Pius, who subsequently felt a little less isolated and rather more secure in the "Europe of the dictators." "This is a Christmas Message which could not have been more welcome to Us," wrote the pope, "since it represents on the part of the eminent head of a great and powerful nation, a strong and promising contribution to Our desire for the attainment of a just and honorable peace and for a more effective and wider effort to alleviate the sufferings of the victims of war." During this perilous period, when Nazi Germany, on the one hand, and the Soviet Union, on the other, threatened the future of the Church, Pius XII was somewhat reassured by the presence of Roosevelt's representative.[36]

The reticent pope revealed some of his thoughts and convictions while adhering to his impartial policy in his five-point pro-

36. Myron C. Taylor, ed., *Wartime Correspondence between President Roosevelt and Pope Pius XII* (New York: Macmillan, 1947), 22–23, 33.

gram invoking the Christian reconstitution of the human family. It called for the right of nations large and small to independence; general disarmament; the revival of international institutions; an objective analysis of the needs of people, nations, and racial minorities; and finally, a sense of responsibility among people and their rulers. The more moderate Nazis found these lofty generalizations nonthreatening and led the German foreign minister, Joachim von Ribbentrop, to declare, "This is a real Pope."[37] Von Ribbentrop concluded that "the Pope has always had his heart in Germany," claiming that he sought a lasting understanding with Hitler. Heinrich Himmler likewise revealed his appreciation of Pius XII's tact and prudence.[38] The diplomats of the Axis were not troubled by his veiled critique of totalitarianism and apparently appreciated his 1939 message to Hitler expressing his "deep satisfaction" that the Fuehrer had escaped an assassination attempt.[39] While some saw the message as pro forma, others deemed it an unfortunate accommodation with a satanic figure. Papal critics charged that this was an instance in which "silence" would have been appropriate.

Pius XII expressed disapproval of the "calculated act of aggression against a small, industrious, and peaceful nation," but responding to later Fascist and Nazi complaints assured the German foreign minister von Ribbentrop, who ventured to the Vatican in 1940, that the small nation he had alluded to was Finland, the victim of Soviet aggression.[40] This exchange revealed both the advantages and disadvantages of Pius XII's recourse to generalizations. These vague statements represented a compromise between the Vatican's need to assume a moral stance and its determination not to jeopardize its public impartiality and face

37. *ADSS*, 1.387.
38. *RDHSWW*, 166, 359.
39. José M. Sánchez, "The Enigma of Pope Pius XII," *America*, September 14, 1996, p. 19.
40. Stehle, *Eastern Politics of the Vatican*, 197.

the fury of fascist reaction. Later, in mid-May 1940, Domenico Tardini, undersecretary of state, drafted a condemnation of the German invasion of Belgium, Holland, and Luxemburg, but the pope refused to release it. Instead he chose to dispatch messages of sympathy to their rulers, which were printed in *L'Osservatore Romano* and represented the strongest but still indirect papal protest against German aggression. Nonetheless, the publication of these letters provoked Mussolini, who threatened the continuation of the Vatican journal and the very existence of Vatican City. These threats proved successful and the *L'Osservatore*, following a papal directive, subsequently refrained from launching even indirect criticism of the fascist regimes.

Some resented Pius XII's recourse to a cautious criticism of the aggressors, while others understood and applauded this expedient to avoid Nazi retaliation. Father Gundlach, one of the authors of *Humani Generis Unitas*, which condemned Nazi racism, recognized the difficult position of Pius XII. He was also aware of the fact that Papa Pacelli, like his predecessor, had to answer to a large and influential faction in the Vatican and the curia who called for caution, promoted "silence," and insisted on impartiality.[41] Gundlach's contemporary assessment of the motivation for Pius XII's cautious policy is one of the most objective and accurate ones to emerge. Nonetheless, the wisdom, and morality of pursuing this conciliatory course toward the Hitler regime remains in contention.

Despite the sustained efforts of Washington and the Vatican to contain the conflict, the war expanded in 1941. In June of that year Nazi Germany attacked the Soviet Union, and at the end of the year the Japanese attacked Pearl Harbor and brought the United States into the conflict. The Americans hoped that the Vatican would denounce the "unprovoked" attack on its territory, but the Holy Father did not condemn the Japanese aggres-

---

41. Passelecq and Suchecky, *The Hidden Encyclical of Pius XI*, 91.

sion. To make matters worse from the American perspective, the Vatican, still pursuing its impartiality, opened diplomatic relations with Japan in the spring of 1942 by receiving M. Harada as minister to the Holy See. The Allies hoped that the pope would denounce Nazi aggression and atrocities, but Pius XII's long-awaited Christmas message of December 1942 provided only indirect criticism without specifically citing the Nazi abuses. The pope steadfastly refused to abandon his impartial stance and condemn Axis aggression to the dismay of the Allies, the Poles, and the Americans. In turn, the pope explained why he would not, and could not, condemn the Nazis.

First, there are over forty million German-speaking Catholics. If I should denounce the Nazis by name as you desire and Germany should lose the war, Germans everywhere would feel that I had contributed to the defeat, not only of the Nazis but Germany herself; for the German population not to be able to make the distinction between the Nazis and the fatherland would only be human in the confusion and distress of defeat. I cannot risk alienating so many of the faithful. One of my predecessors, Pope Benedict XV in the First World War, through an unfortunate public statement of the type you now wish me to make, did just this and the interests of the Church in Germany suffered as a result. Second, if I denounce the Nazis by name I must in all justice do the same as regards the Bolsheviks whose principles are strikingly similar; you would not wish me to say such things about an ally of yours.[42]

At this juncture Pius did not mention three other concerns that led him to adhere to a strict public impartiality. First, he shared Gasparri's fear that the Nazis and Fascists would retaliate against the organizational Church. Second, to denounce the Nazis would work to the advantage of the Bolsheviks of the Soviet Union whom this pope found more reprehensible than the Fascists or the Nazis. Finally, the Duce might consider any partisan remarks of the pope a violation of the Lateran Accords and

42. Tittmann III, *Inside the Vatican of Pius XII*, 124–25.

occupy the Vatican in retaliation. After Italy entered the war in 1940, shortly before the French agreed to an armistice, Pius sought to have Rome proclaimed an "open city," fearing it might otherwise be decimated by aerial bombardment, but encountered resistance in both camps. For its part the Vatican rejected Allied suggestions that the pope excommunicate either Mussolini or Hitler. Critics complained that rather than seeing the struggle as one between the forces of good versus evil, Pius XII seemed to perceive it as conflict between brothers of the same faith. Like Benedict during the First World War, Pius scrupulously preserved papal impartiality during the Second World War, even though the situations were dramatically different. In 1940 and 1941, despite repeated reports of Nazi atrocities culminating in genocide, Pius adhered to this public position.

All sorts of stories have been circulated about the pope's friendliness towards Nazi Germany as it commenced its plan to eliminate the Jews, including one that claims that the young Saul Friedländer in 1962 discovered a papal telegram inviting the Berlin Opera to perform selections from Wagner at the Vatican even as these horrific events were occurring. "It shocked me; I was astonished," Friedländer supposedly said, adding that he "decided then and there ... to study the history of the event, the Holocaust, so no one would ever forget it."[43] If he is quoted accurately Friedländer apparently has forgotten what he wrote about the incident in his 1966 volume. There he quotes a memorandum written by Montini and corrected and revised by Pius XII which relates a quite different account.

His Holiness wishes to make it clear that the facts in the matter are very different. He had received through Father Grisar a letter from the parish priest of one of the artists, with a recommendation from the archbishop. In this letter, an audience was requested for some Catholic

---

43. "Saul Friedlander: Holocaust Historian Seeks the Whole Story," *Los Angeles Times*, July 15, 2007, p. 1.; History News Network, http://hnn.us/roundup/entries/40972.html (accessed November 11, 2009).

performers who would be joined by a few Protestants. At this audience they proposed in addition to perform some small item of music, presented on a limited basis, and they mentioned the last scene of *Parsifal* or of a "Stabat Mater." The Holy Father sent a reply to the effect that he would be glad to grant the audience; as for the musical performance, he would prefer a passage from the St. Matthew's Passion by Bach, which would be more in keeping with the prevailing Lenten season. It is, therefore inaccurate to say that the Holy Father took the initiative in the matter and that he suggested the Wagner segment indicated above.[44]

While it is true that while Pius XII deplored war in general, he dared not say who provoked this specific conflict. President Roosevelt pressed the pope to support Great Britain and the Soviet Union against the Nazis, urging the Vatican to moderate its anticommunist stance. On September 9, 1941, Pius received a letter from the American president, claiming the Soviets were preparing to introduce religious freedom in their territories and asserting that the survival of Russia would prove less dangerous to religious life than the Nazi dictatorship. The pope remained skeptical of the alleged Soviet conversion and both he and the curia continued to fear the spread of communism. Despite this prevailing suspicion of communism inside the Vatican, Pius sought to accommodate the Americans regarding the Soviet Union, drawing a distinction between communism, which his predecessor had condemned in *Divini redemptoris* (On Atheistic Communism), and the suffering people of Russia. Nonetheless, at this juncture Pius XII was still preoccupied by the communist menace, and told the Spanish ambassador that he had "nothing against" Germany, which he "loved and admired," nor against the Hitler regime, although he acknowledged that some of its measures caused him profound sadness.[45] In his rather

44. Saul Friedlander, *Pius and the Third Reich: A Documentation*, trans. Charles Fullman (New York: Knopf, 1966), 69.
45. José M. Sánchez, "The Popes and Nazi Germany: The View from Madrid," *Journal of Church and State* 38 (Spring 1996): 374.

mild criticism of the notorious Nazi regime, the pope refused to say precisely what he found disturbing in its policies, convinced that his words would reach the Fuehrer whom he sought to placate rather than provoke. Only at the war's end, when a defeated Nazi Germany was no longer a threat to the Church and the Vatican, did he denounce this regime as satanic.

Despite his unwillingness to publicly differentiate aggressor and aggrieved, Pius XII was not indifferent to the plight of the persecuted as some have suggested. Drawing upon his experience in assisting the casualties of conflict during the First World War, he established the Vatican Information Service in 1939. Covering all theaters of the war and paralleling the work of the Red Cross, it succeeded in putting relatives in touch with prisoners of war, missing persons, and refugees while monitoring and mitigating the suffering and separations provoked by the conflict. This service was asked to learn the fate of millions of these displaced and incarcerated people and report back to their families—and it did so with considerable efficiency.[46] Vatican Radio transmitted hundreds of thousands of messages, while the Pontifical Relief Commission provided material assistance to the needy in those countries where it was allowed to function and fulfilled a wide range of needs. Relief in the form of food and medical supplies was provided to France, Belgium, Holland, Greece, Finland, Norway, Ethiopia, Malaya, and the Philippine islands, among others.[47] Pius quietly instructed the Church and clergy to provide discreet aid to both Christians and Jews—which saved many lives. For some, the Vatican effort was the sole avenue of information and assistance, but others complained that the Holy See should and could have done more.

In turn, aspects of the Allied position disturbed Vatican

46. The files of this Vatican Information Service are now open in the Vatican Archives. Its holdings are catalogued in the two-volume *Inter Arma Caritas: Uffizio Informazioni Vaticano per I prigionieri di guerra istituito da Pio XII (1939–1947)* (Vatican City: Archivio Segreto Vaticano, 2004).
47. Padellaro, *Portrait of Pius XII*, 195.

circles, as Pius questioned the "unconditional surrender" policy which Churchill and Roosevelt had agreed upon during the Casablanca Conference of January 1943. The pope deemed this neither prudent nor practical, fearing it would drive the Germans to prolong the war and benefit the Soviet Union, which would push its way into Eastern Europe. On the other hand, neither he nor the curia could provide a viable alternative. In light of the Nazi atrocities, Pius XII dared not propose negotiations with the Hitler regime. In May 1943, Taylor informed the Vatican that the United States was prepared to negotiate with a successor government to Mussolini's regime, suggesting that this message be transmitted to those in a position to depose the Duce. This prospect apparently struck a responsive chord in the Vatican, which once more abandoned its public impartiality by secretly conveying the message to King Victor Emmanuel III, who proved noncommittal. However, the Vatican later learned that the king was involved in the conspiracy that overthrew Mussolini.

The Axis threat to the Vatican increased following the Allied invasion of Sicily, the fall of Mussolini, and the Nazi occupation of much of the peninsula, including Rome in September 1943. Rumor circulated in the Eternal City of a Nazi plot to smash into the Vatican, kidnap the pope, and hold him hostage—as the French had done in the revolutionary and Napoleonic age. In fact, in September 1943, Hitler allegedly favored the seizure of the pope, but was supposedly dissuaded by his subordinates. These rumors assured that the pope would continue his cautious and impartial approach to avoid provoking Nazi retaliation against the Church, the papacy, and his person. During the Nazi occupation of the Eternal City which lasted until the entry of Anglo-American forces in June 1944, Pius privately protested against any violence contemplated against the Vicar of Christ.[48] Following the attack on a group of S.S. police in Rome, killing

48. Smit, *Angelic Shepherd*, 234.

over thirty of them, an infuriated Hitler retaliated by having ten Italians executed for each of his men killed. Three hundred and thirty-five perished. The pope, who had protested the partisan attack on the S.S. police, did not dare to protest the savage Nazi reprisal in the Ardeatine Cave massacre. Papal impartiality, which still prevailed, determined the Vatican's careful response.

The precarious position of the papacy improved as Allied troops pushed toward Rome and the German forces under Field Marshal Albert Konrad Kesselring withdrew from the Eternal City. The relieved pope issued an address reviewing the afflictions of the Church and the city. On June 4, 1944, the Allies entered Rome, and some one-half million Romans flocked to St. Peter's, cheering the pope they deemed *Defensor Civitatis*, "Defender of the City." Preserving his impartiality, Pius told the assembled Romans that thanks to the mutual collaboration of both contending parties, the Eternal City has been preserved. Once again he publicly equated the two belligerent camps, refusing to publicly pass judgment on either. He did so knowing that the problems of the papacy were far from over. In the postwar period Pacelli would have to confront the physical and psychological ravages of the war (1939–1945), the problems of reconstruction, the threat of Soviet and communist expansion, and, most frightening of all, the prospect of nuclear annihilation.

Fearing the consequences that might flow from abandoning his impartiality, this pope refused to name any perpetrator or victim during the course of the conflict. His failure to publicly protest the roundup of Jews in Rome in 1943, "under his very windows," would later contribute to the controversy over his legacy. Clearly, Pius XII aimed to appease rather than arouse the dangerous dictatorial regimes as he sought peace for the Church and the world. He was thus both pope of peace and apostle of appeasement, hoping to attain the first through the latter. This led to his impartiality during the Second World War, which was commended by some but condemned by others. Those who have supported his course note that his prudent policy averted open warfare between Catholicism and Nazism, which would have taken a terrible toll upon the faithful, while possibly making the plight of the victims worse. Critics complained that his quest for peace at any cost compromised his moral mission and that Pius XII allowed expediency to triumph over ethics. The debate intensified over the issue of his "silence" during the Holocaust, which should be seen and interpreted within the broader context of his impartiality.

SEVEN

The "Silence" during the Holocaust

> The Pope at times cannot remain silent. Governments only consider political and military issues, intentionally disregarding moral and legal issues in which, on the other hand, the Pope is primarily interested and cannot ignore. His Holiness said regarding this point ... that God would subject him to the most stringent judgment if he did not react to evil or did not do what he thought was his duty.

IN THE PERIOD LEADING to the outbreak of the Second World War, and during the conflict itself, a number of voices were raised against the papal recourse to the policy of impartiality, which grew louder as news leaked out of Nazi atrocities against civilians and the genocide of the Jews. Pius XII's secretary of state, Cardinal Luigi Maglione, responded to the outcry by claiming that the Vatican's sensitive and precarious position constrained it to adhere to a political policy of impartiality, and therefore it could not publicly condemn particular atrocities but could and did denounce atrocities in general.[1] This explanation satisfied few papal critics during the war and the dissatisfaction

---

Epigraph is from Report of Monsignor Montini on Pius XII's remarks to Dino Alfieri, Italian ambassador to the Holy See, on May 13, 1940, in Blett et al., *Records and Documents of the Holy See Relating to the Second World War*, 423.

1. David S. Wyman, *The Abandonment of the Jews: America and the Holocaust, 1941–1945* (New York: Pantheon Books, 1984), 75.

increased in the 1960s following the Eichmann trial (1961) and the performance and publication of *The Deputy* (1963). At this juncture Pius XII was accused of not speaking out against the genocide perpetrated by the Nazis, and of doing little, if anything, to help millions of its Jewish victims. Compounding the criticism, in the postwar period the Vatican of Pius XII was seen to help Nazi criminals escape the arm of justice by providing them with diplomatic assistance, passports, and financial aid. The accusations launched against Pope Pius XII, his policies, and politics prompted an angry and aggressive defensive reaction by others, leading to the "Pius War."[2]

The controversy was further fueled by the discovery in the 1990s of the encyclical his predecessor Pius XI (1922–1939) had commissioned denouncing the anti-Semitism of the fascist regimes, which Pius XII decided not to release. Some accused him not only of public silence but indifference during the genocide, citing his refusal to sign the Allied Declaration condemning the Nazi extermination of the Jews or release his own public condemnation. Later this led Isaac Herzog, the Israeli minister of social affairs, to charge that although the Vatican was fully aware that the Jews were being slaughtered by the tens of thousands, "the Pope kept silent—and perhaps even worse."[3] Finally, Papa Pacelli was accused of initiating as well as implementing the "unfortunate policy" of impartiality, which invoked, sanctioned, and indeed required a degree of public papal silence.

Despite the continuing controversy surrounding Pius XII's "silence" and the numerous books and articles that focus on this topic, neither critics nor supporters have clearly defined or concurred on what it entailed. For some this papal "silence" implied

2. See Joseph Bottum and David G. Dalin, eds., *The Pius War* (New York: Lexington Books, 2004), and Frank J. Coppa, *The Policies and Politics of Pope Pius XII: Between Diplomacy and Morality* (New York: Peter Lang, 2011).
3. Justin Ewers, "Sainthood on Hold: The Wartime Record of Pope Pius XII Roils Catholic-Jewish Relations," *U.S. News & World Report*, November 17/20, 2008, p. 44.

the Holy See's unwillingness to address and condemn Nazi atrocities; for others "silence" represented the failure to do so publicly; and for still others it entailed the failure to promote such a condemnation of Nazi abuses so that it would reach a broad audience. The reasons or rationale for the papal recourse to this "silence" is a separate issue, as is the question of the results and consequences of this policy. Finally, little is known and even less objectively written about its use during the Holocaust, and its relationship to the papal policy of impartiality. The latter, all too often simply identified with neutrality, remains an enigma for the broad public, and surprisingly for a large part of the scholarly community as well. Although Pius XII played a part in the formulation of the notion of impartiality, and had recourse to it during his pontificate, he did not originate the policy which emerged during the course of the First World War, inspired, outlined, and fully developed by Cardinal Gasparri and implemented by Pope Benedict XV (1914–1922). It specified that the pope, as Vicar of Christ, could and should condemn policies that violated principles of the faith, without naming those who violated these principles and thus assuring papal political neutrality. Pius XII adopted it during the course of the Second World War when the Nazi regime committed horrible transgressions that culminated in genocide. Recognizing the need to condemn such abuses, but fearful of antagonizing Hitler, it proved a useful construct.

Pius XII had recourse to it because he shared the view of a widespread and vocal faction within the Vatican, which opposed openly condemning the policies of the Nazi state, fearing it would endanger the Reich Concordat and place the Church, and the Catholic population in the Reich, in peril. He thus reflected the opinions of the majority in the Secretariat of State, the curia, and the College of Cardinals, who dreaded the cost and consequences of the contentious course earlier pursued by Pius XI, and following his death in February 1939 sought a more "diplomatic pope" and a less confrontational policy. For this reason it turned to Eugenio Pacelli, a disciple of the pragmatic Pietro Gasparri. The newly elected pope, who favored conciliation over confrontation, quickly concluded that the publication of his predecessor's antiracist encyclical would enrage both Mussolini and Hitler and decided to shelve it and pursue the more diplomatic course he had long championed.

Hitler and the Nazis initially assumed that Pacelli's selection of the name Pius, as well as his association with the former outspoken pope, indicated that he would continue his predecessor's confrontational policies. Very likely this is why Berlin at first had reservations about his election,[4] leading Berlin's *Morgenpost* to express its disapproval of his selection on March 3, 1939, the day after the conclave. Nazi concerns proved premature, for the new pope was convinced that his predecessor's contentious course had been counterproductive and dangerous, and determined to change direction. Consequently, those in Berlin and Rome who had feared that Pius XII would continue the opposition of Pius XI to their policies were pleasantly surprised by Pacelli's new conciliatory course. German reservations regarding the new pope were soon dispelled as Pius XII made a sustained effort to improve relations with the Nazi state, early on confiding to the Italian foreign minister, Count Galeazzo Ciano, that he intended to pursue a more conciliatory policy toward the Reich—and he did so. Count Ciano, Mussolini's son-in-law as well as his foreign minister, expressed his satisfaction with Pius XII and wrote in his diary, "I believe that we can get along with this Pope."[5] Berlin was equally enthusiastic, as Nazi officials were convinced that they could achieve a modus vivendi with Pius XII. Not surprisingly, Pacelli's pacific policy also found favor in the curia and the Vatican's Secre-

---

4. *RDHSWW*, 4; Oscar Halecki, *Eugenio Pacelli: Pope of Peace* (New York: Ferrar, Strauss and Young, 1951), 138.
5. Ciano, *The Ciano Diaries, 1939–1943*, 50.

tariat of State for it promised to provide security for Vatican City, the Church, and the hierarchy, clergy, and Catholic groups in the Reich.

Once pope, Pacelli moved quickly to fulfill his promises to improve relations with the Reich—no simple task, for this program had negative as well as positive consequences. Among other things it required a degree of papal toleration for the Hitler regime, which showed itself increasingly anti-Catholic, anti-Semitic, as well as contentious and aggressive. In fact, Pius believed that Hitler was possessed by the devil and attempted a number of "long-distance exorcisms" to drive Satan out of him—all to no avail.[6] Nazi hostility toward Catholicism as well as Judaism was recognized by Pius XII, who was not "Hitler's Pope" but rather sought to avoid becoming the prime enemy of this satanic figure. To ensure that the Church was not Hitler's main target, the newly elected pope made it clear that he intended to chart a new, and much more conciliatory course. While Pius XII denounced the violation of treaties and the preparation for war in his Easter Message of April 1939 and his radio appeal of August 24, 1939, he did so without abandoning his impartiality by naming those responsible for the impending conflict. Likewise, Pius XII's first encyclical, *Summi Pontificatus*, condemned forgetfulness of the law of human solidarity,[7] but it did not include an explicit condemnation of Nazi racism or anti-Semitism, or their aggressive intentions of territorial revision.

Pius XII's problems were compounded when war erupted on September 1, 1939, and even more so when Mussolini entered the conflict on June 10, 1940. The Vatican was now encircled by Hitler's ally. To avoid any pretext for fascist intervention and reprisal, Pius restricted the representatives of France, Britain, Poland, and Belgium to the Vatican City and forbade any kind

---

6. Wolf, *Pope and Devil*, 10.
7. *AAS*, 31 (1939), 413–53.

of political discussion in public. At the same time he apparently recognized the moral imperative of speaking out against the immoral actions and atrocities of the Nazi regime which were reported to him. Quoting St. Catherine's warning to an earlier pope, he feared "that God would subject him to the most stringent judgment if he did not react to evil or did not do what he thought was his duty." Referring to the European situation of 1940, Pius asked, "How could the Pope, in the present circumstances, be guilty of such a serious omission as that of remaining a disinterested spectator of such heinous acts, while all the world was waiting for his word?"[8] Many others later raised the same question, finding impartiality in the face of evil immoral.

The pope recognized the need to speak out against criminal conduct but found it was no easy matter or simple task to fulfill his moral responsibility to denounce the evil embraced by the fascist regimes without arousing the dictatorships at the Vatican's doorstep that threatened the Church as well as the Holy See. His solution was to have recourse to the construct of impartiality which relied on circuitous language and broad generalizations that he hoped fulfilled his moral obligations as Vicar of Christ but were not so plain as to provoke the retaliation of the Rome-Berlin Axis. Another expedient initially employed was to allow the *Civiltà Cattolica* and *L'Osservatore Romano* to report on, and Vatican Radio to broadcast, things Pius XII dared not speak.[9] Initially few, but later many more, denounced this silence of the Holy See as immoral, citing the failure of the Vicar of Christ to alert the flock to the evil these regimes represented that should have been shunned rather than supported.

Nonetheless, it would be unfair and inaccurate to claim that the pope said or did nothing in response to Nazi abuses. In a

---

8. *RDHSWW*, 1.423.
9. Memoirs of a prisoner of Dachau sent to the Vatican in 1940, ASV, SS, AAES, Germania, 1922–1939, posizione 670–73, fascicolo 233, n. 1572/40.

series of encyclicals, addresses, and talks Pius XII did condemn many of the principles espoused by the fascist regimes. For example, in his Easter message of 1941, he lamented the evils afflicting not only fighters but entire populations: the old, the innocent, the peace-loving, and those bereft of all defense. "To the powers occupying territories during the war, We say with all due consideration: let your conscience guide in dealing justly, humanely ... with the peoples of occupied territories," Pius advised, "Do not impose upon them burdens which you, in similar circumstances, have felt or would feel to be unjust."[10] Thus Pius XII was not totally silent and his condemnations were available to the public who could read Latin and thus elude the Nazi net of censorship. It is true that here and elsewhere during the genocide, Pius XII did not speak of the Jews as a distinct group of victims.[11] Critics assume this flowed from his alleged anti-Judaism or anti-Semitism, but more likely Pius XII's cautious approach was sparked by his desire not to arouse the vindictive Nazi regime.

The Allies and the Americans hoped that the pope would say more and openly denounce the notorious Nazi violations of the moral and natural law, but Pius XII did not heed their advice. In fairness, it is important to recognize that this pope likewise rejected the "requests" of the Axis powers for papal approval. Pius continued his diplomatic course following the German invasion of the Soviet Union in June 1941, which he refused to support as he adhered to his impartiality. Privately, however, Pius recognized that he should be saying more, especially on the Jewish issue. When he met with his apostolic delegate to Greece and Turkey, Giuseppe Angelo Roncalli (the future Pope John XXIII), in October 1941 he clearly worried about how his "inaction" was per-

---

10. Smit, *Angelic Shepherd*, 224–25.

11. Martin Rhonheimer, "The Holocaust: What Was Not Said," *First Things* 137 (November 2003): 18–28; O Shea, *A Cross Too Heavy*, 18.

THE "SILENCE" DURING THE HOLOCAUST 159

ceived abroad and inquired whether his silence on Nazi behavior and mistreatment of the Jews was judged badly.[12] Unfortunately, John does not indicate in his diary entry if he responded to the papal question, and if he did address the issue, how he responded to the query and how his response was received by the pope.

A historical analysis of the dichotomy between Pius XII's moral code and pragmatic policies vis-à-vis Nazi Germany, dramatically expressed by the Swiss playwright Rolf Hochhuth, has been explored by José Sánchez with greater objectivity if less literary flair than the playwright. This historian concludes that Pius XII was torn between two roles: diplomat and pastor. It was diplomatic finesse rather than moral sentiment that led the pope to tell the Spanish ambassador at the end of 1941 that he had a "special love" for the Germans, adding that he had "nothing against" Germany, which he "loved and admired," nor against the Hitler regime, although he acknowledged he was saddened by some of its measures.[13] This was a rather mild critique of the outrageous crimes of this notorious regime. This unfortunate choice of words by Pius XII was uttered because the pope was aware of the close relationship between Franco, Mussolini, and Hitler, and believed his words would reach all three fascist dictators rather than the general public. It must therefore be seen as part of Pope Pius's plan to placate rather than provoke Hitler, and spare the faithful in the Reich from his wrath and revenge.

At the opening of the new year in January 1942, the fifteen attendees at the Wannsee Conference charged with the task of genocide made preparations for the "final solution." The Vatican soon learned of their diabolical intention. During the course of 1942 a series of reports reached it of Hitler's genocidal practices

---

12. Angelo Giuseppe Roncali, *I Diari di Giovanni XXIII. La mia vita in Oriente. Agende del delegato apostolico: 1940–1944* (*My Life in the Orient: Memoranda of the Apostolic Delegate, 1940–1944*, edited by Valeria Martano (Bologna: Istituto per le scienze religiose, 2008), 290–91.

13. Sánchez, "The Popes and Nazi Germany," 374, 376.

and executions of the feeble-minded and inmates of insane asylums and hospitals. The Allies hoped that the pope would openly denounce these atrocities and say something specifically and publicly. Pius XII proved unwilling to do so or to abandon his public impartiality. Thus his long-awaited Christmas message of December 1942 provided only general statements and indirect criticism, without citing the gross Nazi violations of human rights or mentioning the perpetrators or the victims of the abuses. It did express Vatican concern for those "who without fault on their part, sometimes only because of race or nationality, have been consigned to death or to a slow decline."[14] Some deemed this as "too little, too late" but what he said was more than most governments and statesmen had uttered. The *New York Times* praised his effort and deemed his a lonely voice crying in the silence of the Continent.[15] At that time few publicly contested the *Times*'s assertion.

During the Holocaust the pope was alerted by various means that the German regime was committing the most horrible crimes against the Jews and others. In May 1942, Pius was told of the mass extermination *(uccisioni in massa)* of Jews from Germany, Poland, and the Ukraine. The undersecretary of state, Giovanni Battista Montini, who later became Pope Paul VI (1963–1978), concluded that the massacre of Jews had assumed frightening proportions. Meanwhile, the military chaplain Father Pirro Scavizzi personally reported to Pius XII that the elimination of Jews through mass murder was almost total, without regard for children or even infants.[16] More than two million had already perished and he feared they would be followed by millions more. Some passionately believed such evil required a response and a clear denunciation from the papacy, but Pacelli, seeking to preserve his impartiality

---

14. Koenig, *Principles for Peace*, 804.
15. *New York Times*, December 25, 1942, p. 16.
16. Stehle, *Eastern Politics of the Vatican*, 214–20.

and fearful of the consequences, proved cautious in his reaction.[17] This caution upset the British minister to the Holy See, Sir Francis D'Arcy Osborne. "A policy of silence in regard to such offenses against the conscience of the world," he wrote Foreign Secretary Anthony Eden, in October 1942, "must necessarily involve a renunciation of moral leadership." Later he noted his disappointment in his diary. "The more I think of it, the more I am revolted by Hitler's massacre of the Jewish race," he wrote, and "the Vatican's apparently exclusive preoccupation with the effects of the war on Italy and the possibilities of the bombardment of Rome."[18] This is an emotional though hardly an objective assessment.

Although Pius did not make a specific public pronouncement against Nazi abuses, as noted, his encyclicals indirectly revealed the Church's opposition to their policies. In his *Mystici Corporis Christi* of June 1943, he once more stressed that the Church embraced all peoples "whatever their nationality or race," commenting that the Catholic Church was not confined by boundaries of race or territory. At the same time he decried those who "return to the teachings, customs, and practices of paganism," indicating that there must be love of one's neighbors rather than persecution. He found it impossible to claim to love the redeemer if we hate those who he has saved by means of his precious blood.[19] He indirectly criticized Nazi racism by noting that the Church embraced the whole human race without exception. He found it unfortunate that there were "some who extoll enmity, hatred, and spite as if they enhanced the dignity and worth of man." Pius XII confessed, "We look with sorrow on the disastrous consequences of this teaching."[20] He also indicated in this encyclical that "from the very beginning of Our pontificate, we

17. O'Shea, *A Cross Too Heavy*, 27.
18. Robert S. Wistrich, *Hitler and the Holocaust* (New York: Modern Library, 2001), 139.
19. *Mystici Corporis Christi*, June 29, 1943, in *PE*, 5.37–38.
20. Ibid., 5.57.

have committed to the protection and guidance of heaven those who do not belong to the visible Body of the Catholic Church," adding, "We desire nothing more ardently than that they may have life and have it more abundantly."[21] Subsequently, in his encyclical of September 30, 1943, he deplored the fact that in a number of nations there "has been extinguished the sense not only of Christian moderation and charity, but also of humanity itself."[22] Unquestionably a number of his encyclicals were critical of Nazi theories and policies, but most never reached the German public—and those that did were often not understood.

Clearly, Pius was not silent, though he was reluctant to say more publicly or to protest loudly the Nazi crimes culminating in the Holocaust, fearing the Nazi reaction to his abandonment of political neutrality. His carefully crafted criticism of Nazi abuses, tucked away in long encyclicals, was designed to achieve two contradictory objectives: first and foremost, to ease the conscience of the pontiff who recognized, and often stated, that as Vicar of Christ he had the responsibility of alerting the faithful to the evils prevailing in state and society; second, his need not to unduly arouse Hitler and the Nazi regime, which he feared would very likely take revenge by additional punitive measure against the Church, the hierarchy, and the faithful in the Reich. In a sense both objectives were partially achieved because Pius believed—perhaps because he wanted to believe—that he had spoken out and fulfilled his responsibility as Vicar of Christ without provoking the wrath of Nazi Germany with which the Vatican preserved diplomatic relations. However, his critical messages in little read, long encyclicals did not reach the broad masses. Pacelli sought to conciliate rather than confront the dangerous dictatorial regimes in order to avoid exposing the Church and Catholics in Germany to Hitler's wrath. Critics complained that under this policy Jews were perceived as "lesser victims."

21. Ibid., 5.58
22. *Divino Afflante Spiritu*, in PE, 4.76.

Privately and inwardly, Pius XII continued to question whether he had chosen the proper path—more so than many of those who later defended his policies. He knew that his veiled accusations and generalizations did not reach or influence the German masses. One had to search for these critiques as critics of the regime abroad and Allied newspaper reporters were prone to do, but he realized that such scrutiny was impossible within the Nazi state with its repressive censorship. This helps to explain the paradox that neither critics nor champions of Pius XII have resolved: why contemporary reporters from abroad found papal objections to the Nazi regime and praised Pius for these criticisms of Nazi Germany. They found them because they were looking for some critique of this odious order and focused on and publicized what they found. Unfortunately, most of these reports never reached the German masses—and in one sense they were never meant to. Apparently Pius XII was convinced that Nazi censorship would not have permitted a more open criticism to reach the German population and would have done little to help the victims of Nazism.

The Church, however, would have paid a heavy price for his pursuit of such a confrontational course. Furthermore, since a good part of the Catholic minority joined the Protestant majority in supporting Hitler and the Nazis, Pius feared that his criticism of the Nazi regime might provide the pretext for them to leave the Church. This was all the more upsetting because he questioned whether his words would prove able to stop the genocide. He revealed as much in response to the pleas of Bishop Konrad von Preysing to help the Jews of Berlin, when Pius XII responded that he could not impose "useless sacrifices on German Catholics, who are already so oppressed for the sake of their faith."[23]

Some have charged that the Pope was indifferent to the

---

23. Wistrich, *Hitler and the Holocaust*, 144.

plight and suffering of the Jews because of the anti-Semitism or at least the anti-Judaism that prevailed in the leadership of the Church. This is challenged by the fact that Pius XII was also reluctant to name aggressor and aggrieved during the course of the war and insisted on preserving his "impartiality"—and none but the most partisan could trace this "silence" to either anti-Semitism or anti-Judaism. Furthermore, there were two earlier genocides during the conflict: one of the Catholic Poles and the other of the orthodox Serbs, during which Pius likewise preserved his diplomatic silence. Indeed, he followed the lead of Pope Benedict XV who did not publicly condemn the genocide of the Armenians—and this earlier silence, too, had nothing to do with either anti-Judaism or anti-Semitism. Finally, all the available evidence indicates that Pius XII was not insensitive to the suffering of either Jews or Christians. In fact, the bewildered pontiff pondered what he could, and should, do, to provide assistance to the victims without contributing to the creation of new ones. His diplomatic plea to the Vichy government on behalf of Jewish expatriates residing there in the summer of 1942 was ignored as foreign Jews were arrested and deported to Eastern Europe as the Germans demanded.[24]

Representatives from Catholic Brazil, Poland, and Belgium, as well as those from the United Kingdom and the United States all urged Pius to speak out publicly against the Nazi oppression of Jews and Poles. Their pleas upset Vatican officials who defended Papa Pacelli's determination to preserve his impartiality by avoiding the dangerous consequences of a more partisan and direct intervention in international affairs. "There is constant pressure on the Holy See from the Axis powers to denounce alleged Allied atrocities and, because of its silence, the Holy See is very often accused of being pro-ally," he responded, adding that "[t]he Holy See could not very well, therefore, condemn

---

24. "Vichy France Rounds Up Foreign Jews," *Washington Post*, August 27, 1942.

Nazi atrocities on the one hand without saying something, for instance, about Russian cruelties on the other."[25]

Some complained that Roosevelt and Churchill, who had the means to do more for the victims of the genocide, did not exercise this option and did little beyond issuing words of denunciation and condemnation. Pius XII's cautious approach and lack of public protest, which might be deemed his "silence," did not mean papal inactivity. Pius XII provided assistance to the Jews of Slovakia, Romania, Hungary, and Turkey among others. When the government of Slovakia promulgated its anti-Semitic Jewish Code in 1941, Pius had his secretary of state issue an official protest to its government. When Monsignor Tiso, its president, indicated that he perceived no conflict between Nazi principles and Catholic doctrine, the Vatican threatened to strike him from the list of monsignori if he did not retract.[26] It was only the repeated Vatican protests against the deportation of Jews and their annihilation that led Slovakia in 1943 to discontinue its contribution to the "final solution."[27] Documentation from the Vatican Archive suggests that Pius XII's assistance to the Jews of Europe was substantial and provoked protests in a number of Catholic countries. Bishop Agostino Pacha of Romania wrote that some of the faithful accused the Holy See of exercising a "preference for Jews," which they resented. The chief rabbi of Romania, instead, wrote to express his deep appreciation of what the pontiff had done for the Jews of Romania and Transylvania, promising that "[t]hese deeds will never be forgotten."[28] He was mistaken, for

---

25. George Kent, "Pope Pius XII and Germany," *American Historical Review* 70 (October 1964): 71.

26. For the efforts made by Pius XII on behalf of the Jews of Slovakia, see *Actes et Documents du Sant Siège*, 5, n. 123, and Richard J. Wolff, "The Catholic Church and the Dictatorships in Slovakia and Croatia, 1939–1945," *Records of the American Catholic Historical Society of Philadelphia*, 1978.

27. Jorg K. Hoensch, "Slovakia: 'One God, One People, One Party,'" in *Catholics, the State and the European Radical Right, 1919–1945*, edited by R. J. Wolff and J. Hoensch (New York: Columbia University Press, 1987), 177.

28. *Civiltà Cattolica*, 1961, 3.462.

some have not only forgotten but discounted or denigrated this and other contributions made by Pius XII.

Some members of the diplomatic community and the Church pressed the pope to do more, urging him to follow in the footsteps of Pius XI and denounce the Nazi persecution, citing the danger his continued public "silence" posed to papal moral leadership. Even Sister Pascalina, the pope's housekeeper, cook, and the closest thing to a companion and confidant, claims she advised the pope to take a stronger stance against Nazi inhumanities. "The Holy See must aid the Jewish people to the best of our ability," Pius XII reportedly responded, "But everything we do must be done with caution. Otherwise the Church and the Jews themselves will suffer great retaliation."[29] "They deplore the fact that the Pope does not speak," he told the Jesuit rector of the Gregorian University in December 1942, adding, "But the Pope cannot speak. If he spoke, things would be worse."[30] Here and elsewhere, he revealed his fear of Nazi retaliation. In addition, Vatican officials diplomatically argued that the Holy See had to pursue a balanced political policy and could not condemn Nazi atrocities without criticizing Soviet ones; that the charges would have to be investigated, and the difficulties in assembling impartial and accurate evidence would be enormous; that the pope had already condemned major offenses against morality in wartime, to which was added the voice of the hierarchy, who spoke on his behalf; and finally, a condemnation of Nazi abuses would further undermine the position of Catholics in these areas.[31]

Other considerations contributed to Pius XII's "silence." According to German reports, the Vatican's principal preoccupation was the bolshevization of Europe and it feared the task

29. Paul L. Murphy with Rene Arlington, *La Popessa* (New York: Warner Books, 1983), 197.
30. José M. Sánchez, *Pius XII and the Holocaust: Understanding the Controversy* (Washington, D.C.: The Catholic University of America Press, 2002), 115.
31. Kent, "Pope Pius XII and Germany 71–72.

of defending the Continent against this danger would exceed German resources. While the Holy See had few illusions about National Socialism, it had absolutely none about Bolshevism. The first persecuted the Church; the second prohibited its existence within its borders. Consequently, Pius hesitated to condemn the first, lest it redound to the advantage of the latter. For this, among other reasons, he was reluctant to speak out against Germany's brutal conduct in Catholic Poland even though its president in exile pleaded, "may the voice of the Holy Father ... finally break [through] the silence of death."[32]

In April 1943 Pius responded to the bishop of Berlin's plea on behalf of the persecuted Jews, claiming his Christmas message of December 1942 referred to what was being done to the non-Aryans under German occupation.[33] "We have spoken briefly but we have been well understood," wrote the pope. He promised to do more on their behalf if circumstances permitted. There was disagreement by a minority in the Vatican with this cautious and conservative approach. "I am afraid history will reproach the Holy See for following a policy of convenience for itself, and not much more," complained Cardinal Eugene Tisserant, prefect of the Congregation of the Eastern Church, adding that this was "extremely sad, above all for those who lived under Pius XI."[34] On the other hand, others appreciated the papacy's diplomatic impartiality, which allowed the Church to provide refuge for the dispossessed and persecuted within many Catholic institutions.

Pius clung to his impartiality during the Allied invasion of Sicily in July 1943. This paved the way for the dismissal of the Duce on July 25, 1943, followed by Italy's surrender in September. This prompted a German drive into the peninsula, leading

---

32. John Lukacs, "The Diplomacy of the Holy See during World War II," *Catholic Historical Review* 60 (July 1974): 277.

33. Radio message of December 24, 1942, *AAS*, 35.23.

34. Karl Otmar von Aretin, *The Papacy and the Modern World*, trans. Roland Hill (New York: McGraw-Hill, 1970), 213.

to the occupation of Rome on September 10. The Vatican was now subject to increased Nazi pressure during Rome's longest winter.[35] "I'll go into the Vatican when I like," Hitler allegedly threatened. "You think the Vatican worries me? We'll just grab it.... After the war there won't be any more Concordats. The time is coming when I will settle my accounts with the Church."[36] Rumors abounded of a Nazi plot to seize the Vatican and kidnap the pope. Whether this was Hitler's intention is not known, but the kidnapping never occurred. Nonetheless, the papal presence did not deter the roundup of some thirteen hundred Jews in occupied Rome on October 16, 1943. While the Vatican managed to secure the release of some two hundred, another one thousand were transported to concentration camps, where more than eight hundred were slaughtered.

While publicly silent, Pius once again was not inactive or unmoved by the Nazi actions in Rome and elsewhere. In response to the arrest and deportation of Rome's Jews, he had Bishop Alois Hudal, the rector of Santa Maria dell' Anima, complain to the German commander general Rainer Stahel, while the papal secretary of state, Cardinal Luigi Maglione, protested to the German ambassador, quietly securing the release of some two hundred baptized Jews. Furthermore, it is believed that the papacy's behind-the-scenes efforts and protests saved many Italian Jews, with a good number housed in the extraterritorial religious houses, including the Seminario Romano and the basilica di San Paolo fuori le Mura, which enjoyed diplomatic immunity. Dipping into the coffers of the Church, Pius XII provided shelter for some four thousand Jews. Vatican pressure was placed on a number of Latin American countries to provide passports for the persecuted Jews and documents were provided for emigration to

---

35. Andrea Riccardi, *L'Inverno più lungo: 1943–44: Pio XII, gli ebrei e nazisti a Roma* (Bari: Laterza, 2008).

36. Peter Hebblethwaite, *Paul VI: The First Modern Pope* (New York: Paulist Press, 1993), 187.

Palestine. Defenders of Pius XII also note that his prudence during the war and the Holocaust quietly saved tens of thousands of lives. Others have disputed the claim, concluding that by his failure to publicly protest the Nazi actions Pius XII substituted "immoral silence" for the "moral leadership" of Pius XI, and his quest for security compromised the moral mission of the Church. The discussion and dissension continues.

Despite the contentious debate, some facts have been established. The record reveals that Pius XII did not personally and publicly protest the roundup of Jews for extermination "under his very windows," preserving his diplomatic approach and impartiality during the arrest of Jews in the Eternal City. During this incident, the Germans themselves commented on the differences between the approaches of Pius XI and Pius XII.[37] However, an objective assessment of the available sources suggests that pragmatism and recourse to diplomacy rather than anti-Semitism or anti-Judaism determined the conduct of Pius XII. This is also revealed by the fact that subsequently he did not protest the massacre of 335 Italians in the Ardeantine Caves on March 24, 1944.

Nonetheless, the papacy paid a price for its impartial approach, which Pius XII himself worried about and suspected might occur. As early as 1940, he privately acknowledged his doubts, fearing his caution would be perceived as anti-Semitism—as indeed it was by some. These doubts were also expressed to the Italian ambassador Dino Alfieri in May 1940, according to notes taken by Monsignor Giovanni Montini, subsequently Pope Paul VI.[38] Later, in March 1944, Pius confided to the archbishop of Cologne that it was "painfully difficult to decide whether reticence and cautious silence are called for, or frank speech and strong action."[39]

---

37. John F. Morley, *Vatican Diplomacy and the Jews during the Holocaust, 1939–1943* (New York: KTAV Publishing House, 1980); Raul Hilberg, *The Destruction of the European Jews* (Chicago: Quadrangle Books, 1961), 430.
38. *RDHSWW*, 1.423.
39. Stehle, *Eastern Politics of the Vatican*, 213.

Although the times and circumstances of the two pontificates differed, Pius XI was more prone to resort to frank speech and strong action, whereas Pius XII more often relied on diplomatic reticence and public silence. The opening of the Vatican archive for the pontificate of Pius XI confirms the differences between the two. Critics proved more judgmental of this policy shift, charging that the "ethical" course pursued by Pius XI was abandoned in favor of the more "expedient" one of Pius XII. This policy change does not substantiate the charge that Pius XII was indifferent to the plight of the Jews. In fact, Pope Pius XII not only permitted, but also apparently quietly encouraged, Catholic religious to rescue Jews and ecclesiastical institutions, including Vatican properties, to shelter them.

Furthermore, his nuncios in Slovakia, Bulgaria, Rumania, and Hungary made strenuous and repeated efforts to stop the deportation of Jews to the death camps. The pope's personal appeal to Admiral Miklós Horthy on behalf of Jews in 1944 was instrumental in stopping the deportation of Hungarian Jews. During the war the papal representative in Hungary, Gennaro Verolini, provided papers that protected thousands of Jews. In his encyclical of April 15, 1945, appealing for prayers for peace, Pius XII called upon the faithful to pray for those who had been banished from their homeland and those in captivity still awaiting liberation. He revealed his sentiments and his strategy to a group of visiting Jewish refugees ("La vostra presenza") in November 1945, after the war, confiding that the ideal of brotherhood did not permit racial distinctions.[40]

Despite the numerous clandestine papal efforts on behalf of the persecuted during the war and the genocide, when millions were massacred, Pius XII publicly adhered to his impartial stance and cautious diplomacy. The documents he issued alluded to this human tragedy in an oblique manner, in indirect terms,

---

40. *PP*, 1.123.

and in a legalistic fashion rather than in the language of outraged conscience as had those released by his predecessor, Pius XI. He failed to publicly denounce German aggression, Nazi atrocities, and Hitler's Holocaust and did not prohibit Catholics from joining the party he later described as satanic. Even following the German occupation of Rome and the roundup of Jews for extermination, the pope did not publicly protest the crime perpetrated "under his very windows." In this fashion the bishop of Rome, primate of Italy, and Vicar of Christ proved more cautious than many in the hierarchy, the common clergy, and the Catholic laity. On the other hand, his responsibility for the Church and faithful was also greater, and this undoubtedly in part accounts for his cautious response. This papal policy toward the persecution, and later the extermination, of the Jews was governed by Pius XII's recourse to broad diplomatic measures rather than specific moral condemnations to achieve Catholic objectives. In the eyes of some this pragmatic diplomatic approach achieved positive results for the persecuted. For others, it represented the triumph of diplomacy over morality.[41]

Over the years critics have deplored the fact that Pius XII did not respond to the plight of the Jews with a sense of urgency and moral outrage, failing to raise an authoritative public voice on their behalf. Others have launched more serious charges against him including anti-Semitism and Machiavellianism. In turn, his defenders contend that public protests would have made matters worse and proven detrimental to all. The debate and the plethora of publications continues. We do not know, and cannot know, what impact more spirited and public papal protests of the Holocaust would have had on the Nazi genocide. Many are convinced, however, that it would have better preserved the moral integrity of the papacy and the reputation of Pius XII.

41. Frank J. Coppa, "Between Morality and Diplomacy: The Vatican's "Silence" during the Holocaust," *Journal of Church and State* 50 (Summer 2008): 566.

Jacques Maritain, named French ambassador to the Holy See after World War II (April 1945–June 1948), was profoundly troubled by the persistent anti-Semitic current in Western society and the anti-Judaism in the Church. He urged Pius XII to condemn anti-Judaism and anti-Semitism. The French philosopher and ambassador appreciated the pope's reluctance to speak out directly on behalf of the Jews during the horrific events "in order not to make the persecution even worse and not to create insurmountable obstacles in the way of the rescue he was pursuing." However, once Nazism had been overthrown, he begged Pius "to make his voice heard." Pius XII granted him an audience, during the course of which Maritain was deeply disappointed by the reaction of the pope, disturbed by the discursive language and what he deemed the evasive tone of his remarks. Although he had spoken to the pope about the Jews and anti-Semitism, Pius in his response referred to neither. Nor did Maritain understand why the pope refused to acknowledge the unfortunate role played by contempt for the Jews flowing from part of the Christian theological heritage. The Frenchman deemed Pius XII's postwar "silence" much more damning that his wartime reticence—an issue that many defenders of Pius XII have not addressed. Writing a friend, Maritain discerned an absence of papal leadership on the Jewish question.[42]

Dissatisfaction with Pius XII's postwar stance on the Jewish issue was one of the reasons Maritain resigned as French ambassador to the Holy See. Nonetheless, his critique of Pius XII's Jewish policy remained private, in contrast to the public one unleashed by Hochhuth. During the postwar period Pius XII did not initiate efforts for Catholic-Jewish reconciliation, and despite the enormity of the Holocaust apparently saw no reason for such a reconciliation. In the mid-1950s Pius did direct that in

---

42. *Jacques Maritain and the Jews*, ed. Robert Royal (South Bend, Ind.: University of Notre Dame Press, 1994), 2.

the prayer for the Jews, *Pro Perfidis Judaeis* no longer be translated as "perfidious" but "unbelievers" or "unfaithful,"[43] a small but important step. Some were disappointed he did not say or do more.

Was what he said enough? Were there good or valid reasons for the pope's refusal to say more? Did this pope as Vicar of Christ fulfill his moral obligations? Would it have helped the victims if he had said more? Could a critical public papal message penetrate the tight Nazi censorship to reach the German masses? Would it have proven detrimental to the Catholic minority in Germany? Would it have undermined the Nazi regime or forced it to halt its genocide? Might open warfare between Rome and the Reich have stopped the genocide or broadened it? Was Pius XII's response to the war, the Holocaust, and other Nazi atrocities, saintly? These and other difficult questions remain at the heart of the "Pius War," which to date has not produced many answers and over the years has shed more heat than light. Praised by some for his tact and diplomacy and concern for the protection of the Church, he has been denounced by others for his relative public silence during the Holocaust. In 1965 Pope Paul VI, who had worked closely with Pius XII, proposed that Papa Pacelli be considered for sainthood—at the same time that the controversy over his alleged silence was at its peak. Bestowing sainthood often has political implications and consequences, and this has been the case with the cause of Pius XII. In fact, the controversy surrounding Pius XII intensified following the proposal for his beatification at the dawn of the twenty-first century. The debate on Pius XII's beatification and response to the Holocaust continues, as does discussion of the impact of his cautious diplomacy upon his moral mission.

43. Cardinal William Keeler, "The Catholic Church and the Jewish People," p. 6, available at http://www.bc.edu/research/cjl/meta-elements/texts/articles/keeler_ICCJ_2003.htm.

EIGHT

On Palestine and Israel

> But although the actual fighting is over, tranquility or order in Palestine is still very far from having been restored. For We are still receiving complaints from those who have every right to deplore the profanation of sacred buildings, images, charitable institutions, as well as the destruction of peaceful homes of religious communities. Piteous appeals still reach Us from numerous refugees of every age and condition who have been forced by this disastrous war to emigrate and even live in exile in concentration camps, the prey to destitution, contagious disease and perils of every sort.

P IUS XII, like his predecessor, Pius XI, did not believe, perhaps did not want to believe, that the Church's attitude toward the Jews—based on religious considerations—contributed to Nazism's racism and the anti-Semitism which culminated in the Holocaust. Acknowledging no responsibility for the Nazi genocide, he did not perceive the need to apologize, reexamine, or reassess the Church's relationship to its elder brothers or its qualified attitude toward Jewish emigration to Palestine. As regards the papal position concerning Palestine, this pope did not originate the Vatican policy toward the Holy Land which had been set by his predecessors following the birth of Zionism at the end of the nineteenth century and the creation of the Palestine

Epigraph is from *Redemptoris Nostri Cruciatus* (Encyclical of Pope Pius XII on the Holy Places in Palestine), April 15, 1949, in *PE*, 5.163.

Mandate under British direction following World War I. While the situation of European Jewry had changed dramatically in the ensuing decades, and international support for a Jewish state had increased exponentially following the Holocaust, Pius XII perceived no need to question, much less challenge or change, the existing papal policy opposing Jewish control of the Holy Land as well as placing it in the hands of any other religious rival.

Although the papers of the Archivio della Delegazioine Apostolica in Gerusalemme e Palestina in the ASV still remain largely closed, other sources reveal that Pius XII's position toward Palestine followed that of his predecessors going back to Pius X, and was motivated first and foremost by the need to protect the position of the faith there. A wide range of sources confirm that the papal stance toward Palestine, to which Pius XII clung tenaciously, was crafted to protect the interests of Catholicism in the Holy Land. Vatican concern for the future of Palestine opposed the Jewish territorial aspirations expressed at the first Zionist Congress held in Basle, Switzerland, in May 1897.[1] Having lost Rome during the course of the Risorgimento and Jerusalem centuries earlier, the popes at the turn of the century were determined to preserve the rights they retained in locations they deemed crucial for the faith, such as Jerusalem.

Pius X (1903–1914) was no exception in his commitment to preserving the Church's position in the Holy Land. Despite the limited financial resources of the Vatican, he supported some thirty orders and associations there, some twenty convents and monasteries, and eighteen hospices as well as five hospitals. Funds were also provided for the upkeep of the Christian shrines over which the various denominations had been accorded certain rights and responsibilities by the Muslim Turks through the centuries.

1. In this regard, see Livia Rocach, *The Catholic Church and the Question of Palestine* (London: Saqi Books, 1987).

Catholicism was not alone in its determination to protect its rights in the Holy Land. Conflict over control of the holy places had created tension between the various Christian denominations and their national protectors which at the end of the nineteenth century was compounded by the call for a Jewish state in Palestine. In 1853 Christian rivalries provided the pretext for the opening of the Crimean War as France and Russia clashed over Catholic versus Orthodox protection and supervision of the Christian shrines in Palestine. Subsequently, the emergence of a Zionist movement under Theodore Herzl (1860–1904) created new and pressing problems for the Church's future in Jerusalem.

Pius X, who had been forewarned of Jewish territorial aspirations and claims to the Holy Land, sought to assess Jewish plans for the area. He gained considerable information from Theodor Herzl himself, who sought papal support for the establishment of a Jewish state in Palestine. In response to his plea for papal assistance, the pope made it clear that the head of the Church could not second this endeavor. Pius confessed that the papacy could not stop the Jews from settling in Palestine, but added that it did not favor the creation of a Jewish state there. Later his secretary of state Cardinal Rafael Merry dal Val elaborated the Vatican's position and policy regarding the Jewish presence in the Holy Land. Like the pope, he specified that if the Jews only wished to establish agricultural colonies in Palestine, Rome would deem it a humanitarian effort and would not impede the endeavor. However, it soon became apparent that the first president of the World Zionist Organization wanted more than the papacy was willing to concede.

During the pontificate of Pius X's successor, Benedict XV (1914–1922), the future of Palestine emerged from the realm of theory to reality following the British invasion and liberation of the Holy Land from the Turks by General Edmund Henry Allenby (1861–1936) at the end of 1917. Abandoning the impartial public stance Benedict's Vatican's had adopted and scrupulously clung to during the First World War, Cardinal Pietro Gasparri dispatched his congratulations to the British envoy on December 16, 1917. In turn, *L'Osservatore Romano*, delighted that centuries of Turkish and Muslim control had come to an end, proclaimed the liberation of the Holy Land a "victory for Christian civilization." The celebration in the Vatican proved short-lived. Benedict XV was distressed by the "British Declaration of Sympathy with Zionist Aspirations" issued by London's foreign secretary, Lord Arthur James Balfour, on November 2, 1917. The promise to provide the Jews territorial rights in the Holy Land clashed with papal plans and aspirations for the future of Jerusalem.

Pope Benedict, like his predecessor, was deeply concerned about the Holy Land, He met with the Zionist leader Nahum Sokolov in 1917 after he had been questioned by Eugenio Pacelli —the future Pope Pius XII—and the secretary of state, Gasparri. Both the secretary of state and his major disciple proved suspicious of Zionist goals and apparently transmitted their concerns and reservations to Sokolov, who was made to understand that the Vatican would not, indeed could not, support Jewish territorial aspirations in the Holy Land. Consequently, when Benedict XV met Sokolov later in 1917, the pope provided a warm welcome largely because Sokolov—having gleaned the Vatican's stance on Palestine from Gasparri and Pacelli—did not plead for papal support for a national homeland for the Jews there.[2] This did not mean—as Pope Benedict seemed to believe at that moment—that the Zionists had abandoned their determination to establish a Jewish homeland in Palestine.

Under the illusion that the secretary general of the World Zionist Organization sought only agricultural settlements far

2. Richard P. Stevens, "The Vatican, the Catholic Church and Jerusalem," *Journal of Palestine Studies* 19, no. 3 (Spring 1981): 103.

from the sacred sites, Benedict concluded the interview by saying, "I think we shall be good neighbors."[3] In fact, Benedict regarded the return of individual Jews to Palestine as "providential" and "consonant with God's will."[4] However, having only recently witnessed the liberation of the Holy Land from Muslim control, he, like Pacelli and Gasparri, did not wish to see it placed under a jurisdiction that might question, challenge, or restrict the rights and privileges the Church had acquired there over the centuries. To preserve its position in the Holy Land, the Vatican continued to oppose the dream of establishing a Jewish state in the Holy Land.[5] In mid- December 1917, Gasparri related the rationale for the Vatican's opposition to "the transformation of Palestine into a Jewish state." He claimed this would not only endanger the holy places and damage the feelings of all Christians, "it would also be very harmful for the country itself."[6] The Vatican was aware of the Palestinians' opposition to the creation of a Jewish state on territory they considered their homeland, and early on predicted it would lead to conflict and chaos, endangering the holy sites dear to Catholics.

For these and other reasons, the prospect of a Jewish state in Palestine, exercising control over the Christian shrines and a resentful native population, alarmed the Vatican. In fact, it led the pope and his secretary of state to have a change of heart regarding their support of Jewish emigration to Palestine, fearful that an increased Jewish presence there would bolster the fulfillment of the British promises to the Zionists, quite possibly at the expense of the Church's rights and Palestinian interests. The

3. Andrew M. Canapa, "Zionism, Israel and the Vatican," in *Encyclopedia of the Vatican and Papacy*, edited by F. J. Coppa (Westport, Conn.: Greenwood Press, 1997), 458.
4. Howard M. Sachar, *Israel and Europe: An Appraisal in History* (New York: Knopf, 1999), 196.
5. In this regard, see Sergio Minerbi, *The Vatican and Zionism* (New York: Oxford University Press, 1990).
6. Sergio Minerbi, "Pius XII: A Reappraisal," in *Pope Pius XII and the Holocaust*, edited by Carol Rittner and John K. Roth (Leicester: Leicester University Press, 2002), 98.

Vatican outlined its opposition to the Balfour Declaration of November 1917, which promised a Jewish homeland in Palestine, and the subsequent steps to implement it.[7] At the end of 1917 Pope Benedict revealed his concern to the British representative to the Vatican, fearing that the British government would turn Palestine over to the Jews "to the detriment of Christian interests."[8] Distressed by the possibility of Jewish or Muslim control over the Holy Land, Benedict confided in a secret Vatican consistory on March 10, 1919, "it would be for us and all Christians a bitter grief if the unChurched were ... placed in a privileged and prominent position."[9]

Benedict, Gasparri, and Pacelli sought to ensure that this transformation did not occur and the "inalienable rights" and established position of the Church in Palestine be preserved and protected from Jews, Muslims, and Protestants. In an allocution of June 13, 1921, he proclaimed, "We do not wish to deprive the Jews of their rights; we want, nevertheless, that they be not in any way preferred to the just rights of the Christians."[10] That same year Gasparri confessed that "[t]he danger we most fear is the establishment of a Jewish state in Palestine."[11] Long before the pontificate of Pius XII, the Vatican took steps to prevent this from happening.

In 1922 the Vatican initiated a major diplomatic effort to prevent the implementation of the Balfour Declaration. It dispatched a memorandum to the secretary-general of the League of Nations criticizing a number of the articles in the draft of the British mandate for Palestine, concluding that those provisions that sought to implement the Balfour Declaration of 1917 violated the

7. Fréderic Yerly, "La Saint-Siège et l'État d'Israel au Moyen-Orient," *Vingtième Siècle Revue "Histoire"* 51 (July–September 1996): 6.
8. Minerbi, *The Vatican and Zionism*, 120.
9. Ibid., 197.
10. *The Tablet* (Brooklyn), June 25, 1921.
11. Minerbi, "Pope Pius XII and the Holocaust," 99.

Covenant of the League.¹² Although sympathetic to the plight of the Jews, Benedict opposed granting them political control of Palestine, the home of three world religions, as did Achille Ratti once he became Pope Pius XI (1922–1939). "The Roman Catholic Church is a powerful world organization with a permanent interest in the historic see of Christianity where it maintains numerous monasteries, Churches and schools," one writer indicated in 1926. He noted that during the pontificate of Pius XI it had kept up a lively propaganda effort in the East, gaining predominance among Eastern Christians after Soviet Russia withdrew its support and protection from the Orthodox Church.¹³

The Catholic press during Ratti's pontificate proved more critical of Zionism than the pope, often resorting to anti-Judaism in its critique of the establishment of a Jewish homeland in Palestine. In 1929, *L'Osservatore Romano* denounced "[t]he Jewish Danger Threatening the Entire World," while the Jesuit-run *Civiltà Cattolica* proclaimed that "the Jews constitute a serious and permanent danger to Christianity."¹⁴ This anti-Judaic conviction at times degenerated into the anti-Semitic rhetoric that prevailed in certain Catholic quarters.

Despite the attempts of some of Pacelli's adversaries to blame him for the Vatican's opposition to a Jewish state in the Holy Land, the documentary evidence indicates he inherited a policy the Vatican had long pursued. Thus the Vatican's opposition to turning over Palestine to the Jews was set before the opening of his pontificate. Like his predecessor, Papa Pacelli expressed concern about the Middle East and especially Jerusalem, which became embroiled in the cold war, the Arab-Jewish struggle, great

---

12. Anrej Kreutz, "The Vatican and the Palestinians: A Historical Overview," in *Papal Diplomacy in the Modern Age*, edited by Peter C. Kent and John F. Pollard (London: Praeger, 1994), 171.

13. Quincy Wright, "The Palestine Problem," *Political Science Quarterly* 41, no. 3 (September 1926): 384.

14. Sachar, *Israel and Europe*, 197.

power diplomacy, as well as the religious rivalry among the various Christian denominations. Following in the footsteps of the former popes harking back to Pius X, Pius XII did not favor the creation of a Jewish state, fearing it would not respect Catholics privileges and the rights of its religious communities there. Furthermore, he also worried that the emergence of such a Jewish state on lands long occupied by the Arabs would undoubtedly arouse their enmity and very likely spark a war that would engulf the region, endanger the sacred sites, and possibly embroil the entire world.

Like his predecessors Pius XII also worried about the supervision of the holy places in Palestine. These sites, sacred to Jews, Christians, and Moslems, had been under Moslem rule for thirteen centuries when the Turkish Ottoman Empire disintegrated at the end of the First World War. During the course of Ottoman rule, the rights and privileges of the non-Moslems had been gradually ensured by the sultans, who by and large had proven respectful of the religious interests of the other faiths within their empire. Dissension had arisen primarily among the Christian communities that struggled for control and administration of the holy places. Their conflicting claims led to international tension as Russia supported the Orthodox Christians and their religious orders until the Bolshevik revolution, while France upheld those of Roman Catholics.[15] These disputes were compounded and complicated by the increased Jewish immigration in the postwar period and the Zionist desire and determination to establish a Jewish state, which aroused the Palestinian Arabs as well as the papacy.

Confronted with their conflicting claims, in July 1937 the Palestine Royal Commission's Report, also known as the Peel

15. A number of attempts were made in the nineteenth century to settle the conflicting Christian claims by establishing their rights, such as those assigned in the early 1850s. This provision was included in the articles of the Congress of Berlin in 1878 but failed to end the dissension.

Report, proposed the partition of Palestine into Jewish and Arab sectors. This division found little support in England and even less abroad. David Lloyd George denounced it as "a deplorable ending to one of the most imaginative and promising experiments which the Great War made possible."[16] In his eyes partition was a lamentable admission that Britain had failed to fulfill the mission entrusted to it. To make matters worse, the Zionists, whom the plan's creators thought would be ecstatic because it provided for the creation of their long-sought state, gave it only lukewarm support because of their wider territorial ambitions. The Arabs, on the other hand, strongly and unequivocally opposed the partition, as did the Vatican.

In 1943 Pius XII's secretary of state, Cardinal Luigi Maglione, following Pius XII's directive, wrote the apostolic delegate in the United States, Amleto Cicognani, to apprise Washington of the Vatican's opposition to the establishment of a Jewish state in Palestine. Hoping to garner American support, he wrote, "the Catholics of the entire world could not but feel wounded in their religious sentiment if Palestine were to be given over in preponderance to the Jews."[17] He warned that the creation of such a Jewish state would enrage the Muslim population and endanger peace and stability in the region.[18] America technically remained noncommittal, but its governing class proved supportive of Jewish claims in the Middle East. This led Pius XII's Vatican to reiterate in the strongest language its opposition to Jewish control over Palestine. There were those who believed that the anti-Judaism in the Church was behind the Vatican's opposition to such a Jewish state. Cardinal Johann Willebrands of Holland explained the rationale for this policy, which he personally opposed. Convinced that the Jews as a people were collectively re-

---

16. Aaron Klieman, "In the Public Domain: The Controversy over Partition for Palestine," *Jewish Social Studies* 4, no. 2 (Spring 1980): 149.
17. Canepa, "Zionism, Israel and the Vatican," 459.
18. Sachar, *Israel and Europe*, 197.

sponsible for the death of Christ, they were condemned "to eternal pilgrimage across the world outside of Israel."[19] Very likely some in the Vatican shared this sentiment, but there is no indication that Pope Pius XII, who during the war helped to facilitate the transfer of thousands of Jewish children from Bulgaria to Palestine, was among them.

Despite the contentions of responsible theologians as well as historians, and the more lurid insinuations of the polemical "biographers," the best available evidence suggests that Pius XII's primary objection to a Jewish state, like that of his patron Gasparri, flowed from his determination to protect and preserve Catholic interests in the Holy Land. This concern also led the Holy See to oppose Arab Muslim domination there.[20] "The Vatican would have preferred," noted the British minister to the Holy See, "that neither Jews nor Arabs, but a Third Power should have control of the Holy Land."[21] When the British refused to remain saddled with this responsibility, the Vatican of Pius XII concluded that the best solution for all was the internationalization of Jerusalem. It further proposed that the city along with its environs be placed under the auspices and supervision of the newly formed United Nations, just as Danzig and Memel had been internationalized under the League of Nations.[22] This was an unfortunate comparison because the League's effort regarding Danzig had failed miserably. Some in the Church, and some outside it, sought other solutions. Although the Catholic Church was most vocal in its opposition to placing Jerusalem under the political control of any competing religious denomination, it was not the only Christian

19. Michael Phayer, *The Catholic Church and the Holocaust* (Bloomington: Indiana University Press, 2000), 176.
20. Silvio Ferrari, "The Vatican, Israel and the Jerusalem Question (1943–1984)," *Middle East Journal* 39, no. 2 (Spring 1985): 316–17.
21. Silvio Ferrari, "The Holy See and the Postwar Palestine Issue: The Internationalization of Jerusalem and the Protection of the Holy Places," *International Affairs* 60, no. 2 (Spring 1984): 261.
22. Stevens, "The Vatican, the Catholic Church and Jerusalem," 105.

Church to reveal concern about the future of Palestine in general, and Jerusalem in particular.[23]

Practical as well as theoretical considerations rendered necessary a solution to the puzzle of Palestine as violence soon erupted between Jews, Muslims, and Christians, as well as against the British. For the latter, who had exercised the League of Nations's mandate over the region since the end of the First World War, Palestine proved an onerous and costly responsibility. Indeed, after 1945 the British increasingly had to resort to military force to subdue the constant clashes between Arabs and Jews—a task complicated by the conflicting diplomatic initiatives they had to confront. A diplomat by inclination, training, and background, Pius XII opposed violent means to achieve even legitimate ends. "We disapprove of any recourse to violence and force wherever it may come from," he told a visiting Palestinian delegation in 1946. "We have condemned in the past on various occasions the persecution which a fanatic anti-Semitism has waged against the Hebrew people."[24] Pius XII hoped and believed that the conflict over the future of Jerusalem, as well as other disputes, could be resolved diplomatically. On April 10, 1945, he received Moshe Sharett, head of the Jewish agency's Political Department and subsequently Israel's foreign minister, in private audience. Although there is no record of their specific conversation, some believe that an agreement and settlement of sorts was outlined that promised that in return for Vatican support of a Jewish homeland in Palestine, Catholics would be assured of a place in the new state.[25] If such an agreement was discussed or made, it was not implemented.

Some continued to see a link between the Church's anti-

---

23. In this regard, see Duncan L.Clarke and Eric Flohr, "Christian Churches and the Palestinian Question," *Journal of Palestine Studies* 21, no. 4 (Summer 1992): 67–79.

24. Pinchas Lapide, *Three Popes and the Jews* (New York: Hawthorn Books, 1967), 278.

25. Ibid., 281.

Judaism and its opposition to a Jewish state in Palestine. Among their ranks was Jacques Maritain, who in the postwar period became the new French ambassador to the Holy See. He sought to persuade Pius XII to issue some statement on Catholic anti-Judaism and to favor a homeland in Palestine for the masses that had survived the Holocaust. He failed in both these efforts and concluded that Pope Pius XII seemed more preoccupied with the present threat of communism in Italy and Europe than with the past threat of Nazi anti-Semitism.[26] Some complained that when the pope met with generals Dwight Eisenhower and Mark Clark in September 1945, he focused on the means of protecting the West against godless communism rather than addressing the future of Palestine. This was neither surprising nor Machiavellian, for containing communism was the American mission and to have expected the pope to change their agenda was highly unrealistic. The two American military men had something to say about the defense of Europe, but had no particular competence on matters of the Middle East in general, or on Palestine in particular.

Others complained that the Vatican's preoccupation with communism became a virtual mania that marginalized other issues and problems. In Germany Gertrud Luckner, who perceived anti-Semitism as a greater threat than communism, sought to persuade her fellow Catholics that neither "theological considerations nor biblical teachings would justify a negative position among Christians toward the establishment of a Jewish state in Palestine."[27] She angered a number of members of the Holy Office, who charged that some who favored a Jewish state in Palestine were flirting with indifferentism—the belief that one religion was as good as another.[28] This was a notion that the Vatican would not accept.

26. Phayer, *The Catholic Church and the Holocaust*, 79–182.
27. Ibid., 177.   28. Ibid.

Personally Pius sought to remain above the fray, preserving his "impartiality" in the Palestinian conflict as he had during the course of the Second World War, relying on others to defend the Vatican opposition to Jewish control over the area. He related his position to a group of Jewish refugees who visited him in November 1945. Very likely expecting this Jewish group to ask him to lend support for a Palestinian homeland, Pius immediately but indirectly explained why he could not. The Church remains aloof from political problems and territorial issues, he related, referring once again to papal impartiality, but added that it "lays foundations for their solution."[29] In saying so he conveniently ignored the current massive papal intervention in Italian political life. In fact this ambiguous assertion, like so many of his other statements, provided no clue regarding the solution he favored. Pius proved no more explicit in the encyclical he issued in 1948 following the outbreak of the Arab-Israeli war, claiming that impartiality "was imposed by Our apostolic duty, which places Us above the conflicts which agitate human society."[30] Prior to the outbreak of this war, Pius XII was able to avoid issuing any statement regarding territorial issues in Palestine. In fact his recourse to "impartiality" in this instance was more apparent than real.

The pope was soon constrained to review his position, as were the British. The latter confronted colonial rebellions, disputes, and difficulties elsewhere, and anxious to protect their own colonies, turned the thorny problem of Jerusalem over to the successor of the League of Nations, the newly formed United Nations, in early 1947. If the British were determined to withdraw from Palestine, the Vatican believed that the next best solution was to have its administration perpetually entrusted to the United Nations rather than to those who championed a rival religion. This prospect posed a series of problems, as the administrative history of its pre-

29. "La Vostra Presenza," in *PP*, 1.123.
30. *In Multiplicibus curis*, October 24, 1948, in *PE*, 5.161.

decessor, the League of Nations, revealed. In light of this record, the U.N. Special Committee on Palestine (UNSCOP) sought to limit its responsibility, recommending the partition of Palestine and the internationalization of Jerusalem.[31] The resolution of the General Assembly of November 29, 1947, which followed, provided that the city of Jerusalem and its immediate environs would be governed as a *corpus separatum* under an international regime administered by the United Nations. This restricted the role and responsibility of the U.N. although its administration would still cover some 100 square miles of territory and a population of over 200,000, and would encompass Bethlehem and the other suburbs of Jerusalem.[32]

Pius XII's Vatican tacitly accepted United Nation's Resolution 181 even though it had reservations about the partition of the Holy Land into a Jewish and an Arab state. However, the partition was rendered minimally palatable for the pope by the proposed internationalization of Jerusalem and Bethlehem—a central concern of both pope and curia. In retrospect, the Vatican's approval of the plan was reflected in the support it received from the Catholic countries of Latin America and other Catholic countries such as Belgium, France, and the Philippines, all protective of Church interests.[33] Zionists, less than happy with this solution, believed that a number of Latin American states had been pressured by the Vatican to favor the internationalization of Jerusalem.[34] Whether outright pressure or subtle solicitation was employed, Vatican diplomacy clearly played a part in securing Catholic support for this measure.

Following the General Assembly's approval of the partition

31. Ferrari, "The Holy See and the Postwar Palestine," 262–63
32. Evan M. Wilson, "The Internationalization of Jerusalem," *Middle East Journal* 223, no. 1 (Winter 1969): 5.
33. Ferrari, "The Vatican, Israel and the Jerusalem Question," 319.
34. Edward B. Glick, "The Vatican, Latin America, and Jerusalem," *International Organization* 11, no. 2 (Spring 1957): 213.

plan rejected by the Arabs, the prospect of war loomed large. In April 1948 the Holy See communicated its profound anxiety to the Americans and the British fearing the outbreak of armed conflict, and urging them to protect the Holy City and its sacred sites. The Vatican's concerns and warnings did not prevent the British from withdrawing from Palestine as planned on May 15, 1948, and that very day at 12:00 P.M. the Polish-born David Ben-Gurion announced the creation of the state of Israel. He would serve as premier from that moment until 1963—with only one short interruption. The British-born Chaim Weizmann, who had been instrumental in securing the Balfour Declaration, became provisional president. The two faced an immediate challenge as the Vatican questioned the legality of the new state diplomatically, while the surrounding Arab countries attacked it militarily. Jerusalem, in turn, fell under the control of the Israelis and the Jordanians.

Although Pius XII once again proclaimed his impartiality, he was clearly troubled by developments in the armed conflict in the Holy Land.[35] The outbreak and consequences of the war rendered both the partition and internationalization proposed by the United Nations problematic. At the end of May 1948, the Latin patriarch of Jerusalem accused the Israelis of violating the sanctity of churches, convents, and other Church institutions and sought redress. Pope Pius XII, accepting the accusations without investigating them, was outraged and shocked that "the Christian world would allow the devastation of the Holy Places."[36] Perhaps it was this papal stance that prompted the *Civiltà Cattolica* to support the Arab cause throughout the 1948 war.

Confronted with the prospect of a long-range control of the Holy Land and its sacred sites by the Israelis and Jordanians, Pius XII felt constrained to modify his hitherto personal silence

---

35. Camille M. Cianfarra, "Pope Is Troubled by Palestinian War," *New York Times*, May 16, 1948, p. 6.
36. Sachar, *Israel and Europe*, 198.

and impartiality to make his position clear to all. On October 24, 1948, he released the encyclical *In Multiplicibus curis*, which added his own voice to those who proposed placing Jerusalem under international control. "It would be opportune," he wrote, "to give Jerusalem and its outskirts, where are found so many and such precious memories of the life and death of the Savior, an international character."[37] This encyclical marked a decisive turning point in the policy of the Holy See in that the pope himself called for internationalization of Jerusalem, rather than having this desire voiced by his subordinates. In addition to invoking protection for the sacred sites, Pius championed the cause of the Muslim and Catholic refugees, some 800,000 of whom were either ejected or escaped from the territory now controlled by Israel.

Ecclesiastical estimates indicated that some 75 percent of Christian Arabs had fled or had been pushed out of the territory presently under Israeli control and Rome believed that all—Muslim and Christian alike—should be allowed to return. This papal call for the repatriation of exiled Palestinians, and the strong and consistent Israeli resistance to this demand, created another obstacle between the Vatican and the Jewish state.[38] To his dismay, Pius XII witnessed the United States and the Soviet Union compete in a race to recognize the Israeli state, which the Vatican opposed. The United States would remain committed to the preservation and protection of Israel, whereas the Soviet Union would soon turn away from it and, by a strange coincidence, during the cold war find itself momentarily ranged alongside the Vatican in opposing Israeli actions and policies.

To make matters worse from the papal perspective, the Israeli victory ensured a larger territory for the Jewish state, which felt

---

37. *PE*, 5.162.
38. Ghazi Falah, "The 1948 Israeli-Palestinian War and Its Aftermath," *Annals of the Association of American Geographers* 86, no. 2 (June 1996): 256; Ferrari, "The Holy See and the Postwar Palestine," 271.

sufficiently strong to resist the internationalization of Jerusalem sought by the Vatican and approved by the United Nations. In early May 1948, Pius issued the encyclical *Auspicia Quaedam*, which invoked prayers for peace in Palestine and the protection of the holy sites.[39] "If there exists any place that ought to be most dear to every cultured person," the pope proclaimed, "surely it is Palestine,"[40] revealing that the danger to these sites brought anxiety and affliction to his heart, which ached for a solution. At this juncture he did not specify the solution sought or how this might be achieved. Subsequently an editorial in *L'Osservatore Romano* in mid-May 1948 charged that modern Zionism represented a secular state and therefore the Holy Land and its sacred sites belonged to Christianity, the true Israel.[41] Although Pius XII never personally issued such a claim, he was very much concerned about the future of the sacred sites and after the 1948 war continued to favor the internationalization of Jerusalem. In a speech of November 10, 1949, Pius called upon "all who glory in the name of Christian" to intensify efforts toward achieving a just and permanent peace in Palestine.[42] This was easier said than done.

The new Jewish state survived both the Arab military campaign and the diplomatic initiatives and opposition of the Vatican. The emergence of Israel disturbed Pius XII for two reasons: first, he feared that the rights of the Church would not be recognized and respected as they had been in the past, and second, he worried that Arab dissatisfaction with Western "imperialism" would turn them toward the Soviet Union for assistance. It was well known that the Palestinians and other Arabs looked upon Zionism as a manifestation of Western and especially British

39. These included the Basilica of the Holy Sepulchre, the Sanctuary of the Ascension, the Tomb of the Virgin, the Basilica of the Nativity at Bethlehem, and the Field of the Shepherds at Bethlehem, among others.
40. *Auspicia Quaedam*, May 1, 1948, in *PE*, 5.158.
41. *PE*, 5.282.
42. "New Palestinian Peace Effort Urged by Pope," *Washington Post*, November 11, 1949, p. 4.

imperialism.[43] Pius XII feared that frustrated Arab nationalism might provide the opportunity for a Soviet intrusion into the Middle East and complement its domination of Eastern Europe. "The Vatican, it was pointed out, had scrupulously abstained from taking sides in the Palestinian question, despite repeated attempts by both Arabs and Jews to enlist its support." The papacy let it be known that it "would warmly support any conciliatory proposal that would halt the conflict, although it is realized that the attitude of intransigence of both groups rendered the achievement of a permanent solution extremely difficult at present."[44]

To guarantee the rights of the Church in the sacred city, Pius XII continued to insist on the internationalization of Jerusalem, which a number of Catholic states publicly supported. Following his suggestion and diplomatic efforts, at the end of 1949 the United Nations General Assembly adopted a resolution for such an internationalization, backed by almost all the Catholic powers in the assembly as well as the Soviet bloc but opposed by Israel, the United States, and Great Britain. Despite the vocal opposition of the latter, the assembly voted to place Jerusalem under a permanent international regime to be administered by the United Nations for a decade. With the assistance and support of the Vatican, a constitution was drafted for the city and a commissioner appointed for its implementation. However, neither Israel nor Jordan, who jointly occupied the city, accepted the resolution. Instead, the Israelis voted to move their government to Jerusalem and proposed a limited international or functional supervision over the holy places, which Pius XII had originally rejected as insufficient. In turn, King Abdullah of Jordan issued a decree conferring Jordanian citizenship on the inhabitants of the West Bank, including Jerusalem. The events of the 1948 war, mean-

43. Kjell-Ake Nordquist, "Contradicting Peace Proposals in the Palestine Conflict," *Journal of Peace Research* 22, no. 2 (June 1985): 168.
44. Cianfarra, "Pope Is Troubled by Palestinian War," p. 6.

while, left some of the holy places inside Israel and others inside Jordan. Rejecting this situation, Pius XII continued to insist on the internationalization of Jerusalem, which remained a bone of contention in his dealings with Israel. The war continued until an armistice was signed in the spring of 1949, one clause of which provided for the formulation of arrangements for securing free access to the holy places and assurances for Catholic cultural institutions. It too remained a dead letter to the increasingly loud and public dissatisfaction of Christians, Jews, and Muslims—and Pius XII.

Pius XII refused to accept the fait accompli or abandon the long-established papal policy toward the Holy Land. James G. McDonald, the special American representative to the provisional Israeli government, claimed Pius XII opposed Israeli control of Jerusalem because he did not trust it would respect the rights of the Christians therein. Pope Pius XII said as much on numerous occasions. Apparently this message was transmitted to the Israelis, and in 1948 Rabbi Jacob Herzog of the Israeli Ministry for Religious Affairs ventured to Rome to reassure the Vatican in this regard. However, Herzog was not received by either Montini or Tardini, the two papal undersecretaries of state, let alone by Pope Pius XII, who deplored the evacuation and displacement of a good part of the Palestinian population, including many Christians, from the Holy Land.

In his encyclical *In Multiplicibus curis* of October 1948, issued while the war still raged, Pius XII decried the suffering of the Palestinian people, the blood being shed in the Holy Land, and the resulting damage and destruction of the sacred sites. He called once again for prayers for peace along with international guarantees, free access to the Holy Places scattered throughout Palestine, as well as freedom of worship and respect for the customs and religious traditions of all.[45] Following the conclusion

---

45. *In Multiplicibus curis*, October 24, 1948, in *PE*, 5.161–62.

of the armistice in mid-April 1949, Pius XII issued *Redemptoris Nostri Cruciatus*, reminding people of the danger facing the holy places in Palestine, including their possible desecration and destruction as well as the plight of the Palestinian refugees. It also insisted that "all rights to the Holy Places, which Catholics during many centuries have acquired" and defended, "should be preserved inviolate."[46]

Pius XII focused on two issues: the call for Catholic institutions to continue their educational mission and other efforts in the Holy Land without impediment, and the recognition and preservation of the rights the Church had secured in Palestine, including Christian custody of the sacred sites. As regards the call for internationalization, Monsignor Domenico Tardini, undersecretary of state, explained that "the Vatican had no particular preference with regard to any specific manner whereby Jerusalem and its environs would be placed under international control, provided such control would effectively protect Catholic interests."[47] Pius XII, in turn, called upon the members of the United Nations meeting in New York to resolve the problems of the Middle East and do so by respecting the rights of Christians, Jews, and Muslims.[48] Partly in response to these papal pleas, at the end of 1949 the General Assembly reaffirmed its intention of internationalizing Jerusalem but once again proved unable to fulfill this commitment, to the increasing dismay and frustration of Pius XII.

The distraught pope did not easily abandon this objective but continued to press the United Nations to implement the internationalization of Jerusalem, as well as a string of its earlier resolutions on Palestine. When he encountered delay and opposition, Pius XII supported the plans of the Arab League to raise

46. *Redemptoris nostri cruciatus*, April 15, 1949, in *PE*, 5.164.
47. Ferrari, "The Holy See and the Postwar Palestine," 269.
48. "New Palestine Peace Effort Urged by Pope," *Washington Post*, November 11, 1949, p. 1.

the issue during the 1950 fall meeting of the General Assembly, encouraging the largely Catholic Latin American states to vote for the Arab resolution. In the interim, the assembly approved the compromise proposal on internationalization submitted by Holland and Sweden, which recognized the partition of Jerusalem between Israel and Jordan, and created an international commission to protect the interests of the religious communities therein and guarantee free access to the holy places. Pius rejected this compromise, which he believed was encouraged by the United States, as a poor substitute for true internationalization, leading to tension between the Vatican and Washington. All sorts of conjectures, some quite fantastic if not bizarre, were fabricated to explain Pius XII's insistence on the internationalization of Jerusalem, including the notion that if Italy had gone communist in the postwar period, as many in the Church feared, the pope intended to establish a new Vatican City in Jerusalem!

Meanwhile, the relationship between Rome and Washington remained somewhat strained early in 1950 when Truman submitted the appointment of General Mark Clark to the Senate for confirmation as ambassador to the Holy See. The National Council of Churches, representing the major Protestant denominations, protested what it claimed was a gross violation of the separation of Church and state.[49] Protestant opposition and anti-Catholicism combined to torpedo Clark's appointment, contributing to the growing dissidence between Washington and the Vatican. It was primarily the anticommunism shared by Pius XII and President Truman that prevented any further widening of the rift between the two. Consequently, the papal refusal to recognize Israel, which the Americans clearly sought, did not interfere with their cooperation elsewhere. Nonetheless, Pius XII sought to improve the Vatican's diplomatic position in

---

49. Gerald Fogarty, SJ, "The United States and the Vatican," in Kent and Pollard, *Papal Diplomacy in the Modern Age*, 233.

the Middle East and the Islamic world by establishing relations with Syria and Iran in 1953, while preserving the friendship of Jordan and Egypt. In 1953, despite its close cooperation with the United States and the Western European powers in the cold war against the Soviet Union, Pius once again proclaimed papal "impartiality" and freedom from any political alliance or bloc.[50] By these and other measures, such as the creation of the Pontifical Mission for Palestine (PMFP) in 1949, Pius XII was the first modern pope to open serious and sustained relations with the Muslim world. Some saw this as the fulfillment of the proverb, "Necessity is the mother of invention."

The PMFP was essentially a humanitarian effort on the part of Pius to provide Palestinian refugees with food supplies, housing, and essential services, a resurgence of sorts of his wartime "Crusade of Charity." Although in the postwar period Pius XII questioned a large-scale Jewish emigration to Palestine, Jewish visitors to Rome, such as Rabbi Philip Bernstein, advisor to the United States European theater commander on Jewish affairs, reported that Pius was not insensitive to the plight of Holocaust survivors and helped feed and house them prior to their emigration to Africa or America. His massive relief effort for all the victims of the Israeli-Palestinian war commenced prior to that of the United Nations Relief Work Agency (UNRWA), which soon followed suit.[51] The success of this papal mission led to the creation of mission committees for East and West Jordan, Egypt, Gaza, Israel, and Syria. His efforts were appreciated in the Arab and Muslim world. In 1949 Egypt became the first Muslim state to establish formal diplomatic relations with the Holy See. Jordan also appreciated the Vatican's massive relief effort; at the end of 1950 Pius received the "warmest Christmas

---

50. "Nous nous réjouissons," in *PP*, 1.150.

51. George Emile Irani, "The Holy See and the Israeli-Palestinian Conflict," in *The Vatican, Islam and the Middle East*, edited by K. C. Ellis (Syracuse, N.Y.: Syracus University Press, 1987), 133.

greetings" from Abdullah, its king.[52] Willing, indeed anxious, to provide assistance for those in need, Pope Pius deplored certain developments in the region, including the Israeli move to make Jerusalem their capital in 1953, and the Soviet entry into the political affairs of the Middle East.

"There is no change whatsoever in the Vatican's position" lamented Israeli foreign minister Moshe Sharett in his diary entry of November 10, 1953, as he contemplated the policy of Pius XII toward Palestine and Jerusalem.[53] Pius, indeed, remained dissatisfied with Israeli policy and the course it pursued, and did not seem to recognize that what had been the Zionist dream for a few had become the pressing need for a homeland for many. Some charged that his policy concerning Israel reflected the guardian of Church and clerical interests rather than the voice of the Vicar of Christ. Almost all concur that he was consistent in his search for peace. Toward the end of 1955 he expressed grave concern over the growing tension between Israel and the Arab countries, making a special plea to those who planned aggression to desist from doing so both for the sake of the local population and the security of the holy places. He implored the rulers of nations to make every effort to prevent "new bloodshed, new mourning, new useless massacres" for "the sake of justice and charity,"[54] invoking special prayers for the peaceful resolution of Israeli-Egyptian differences.[55] As in the Second World War era, his impartiality prevented him from naming aggressor or aggrieved as he prayed for peace.

Pius XII's fears of renewed conflict and a broader conflagration in the Middle East materialized in 1956 when Gamal Abdel Nasser nationalized the Suez Canal, precipitating a crisis

52. Joseph L. Ryan, "The Holy See and Jordan," in *The Vatican, Islam and the Middle East*, edited by K. C. Ellis (Syracuse, N.Y.: Syracuse University Press, 1987).
53. Sachar, *Israel and Europe*, 201.
54. "Pope Asks Rulers to Prevent War," *New York Times*, November 7, 1955, p. 2.
55. "Laetamur admodum," November 1, 1956, PP, 1.180.

that culminated in the joint attack on Egypt by Israel, France, and Great Britain, threatening to usher in the destabilization of the Middle East that the Vatican had long predicted. Pius XII watched the conflict with deep concern not only because of the damage and suffering that it would likely inflict in the region but also because of the prospect that it would spread to other areas of the world. During the war the pope once again had recourse to impartiality, prompted by the desire to preserve good relations with France and Great Britain without alienating the Arab world. In order to maintain some balance in 1956 he condemned both the Soviet suppression of the Hungarian revolution and those nations that had destroyed peace in the Middle East. Despite American pressure, Pius XII refused to establish diplomatic relations with Israel, although it was hinted that de jure recognition might be granted if "minimally functional internationalization" or international control over the sacred sites was granted. Since this was not accorded, Pius XII continued to oppose the recognition of Israel. This did not stop him from receiving Jewish groups such as the American Jewish Committee, which he met on June 25, 1957. However, in this, and other audiences, he did not discuss the Israeli-Palestinian issue or the overall Vatican stance on the affairs of the Middle East.

Piux XII did not live long enough to witness the outbreak of the third Arab-Israeli war (1967), during which Israel captured East Jerusalem, including the Old City—of special interest to Christians, Jews, and Muslims. The long-held and determined opposition of Pope Pius XII to the recognition of Israel continued. His refusal to grant recognition was motivated by the Israeli refusal to adhere to the United Nations resolutions on the internationalization of Jerusalem; the Jewish state's unwillingness to permit the return of displaced Palestinians to their homes; and the unilateral proclamation of Jerusalem as their capital, without permitting any international protection for the adherents of non-Jewish religions. Referring to this catalogue of complaints, Pius XII resisted the pressure of the United States to recognize this "American ally." Consequently Pope Pius found himself in opposition to American policy in the Middle East from the founding of Israel to his death in 1958. The many differences separating the Vatican and Washington regarding Israel may have played a part in bringing about changes in Pope Pius XII's broader "alliance" with the United States and the Western bloc in the cold war.

NINE

The Cold War

PIUS XII FINDS HIS VOICE

Addressing the Crowd in St. Peter's Square on February 20, 1949, Pius XII condemned the Communist regimes which demanded silence from the Church asking the crowd if they could envision: "a Church that is silent when it should preach ... a Church that does not oppose the violation of conscience ... a Church that, with a dishonorable, slavish mentality closes itself within the four walls of its temples.... Can you imagine a successor to Peter who would bow to such demands?"

D URING THE Second World War, when President Franklin Delano Roosevelt sought to bolster the Soviet Union against the Nazi onslaught, he urged the Vatican to moderate its anticommunist campaign, suggesting that the Stalinist regime had adopted a more conciliatory stance toward religion and the churches. This American optimism was countered by the long-standing papal opposition to communism. Nineteenth-century popes from Gregory XVI (1831–1846) to Leo XIII (1878–1903) had vehemently and frequently denounced this ideology and

---

Epigraph quote is from Hansjakob Stehle, *Eastern Politics of the Vatican* (Athens: Ohio University Press, 1981), 270–71.

Pius did not—and was mindful of the Confiteor at the opening of the Mass: "I confess to almighty God / and to you my brothers and sisters / that I have greatly sinned / in my thoughts and in my words, / in what I have done / and in what I have failed to do."

its "misguided adherents." Following the Bolshevik Revolution, when the ideology was transformed into a political and military reality, the Holy See opposed both the militant atheism of the Soviet state and its subversion of the social, political, economic, and religious orders. It quickly perceived the Soviet system and its adherents as a real peril to Western Christian civilization as well as a threat to the Church, its clergy, and the faithful.

Following the revolution of 1917, Pope Benedict XV (1914–1922) opposed the resulting Soviet state that favored universal revolution, preached atheism, and waged war upon organized religion and traditional society. Papal successors followed suit, concerned about the aims and aspirations of the movement and the state that advanced them. Catholic fears of this ideology and its advocates was revealed in the apparitions of Fatima of 1917, where Mary was said to have appeared and invoked prayers for the conversion of Russia—the very day Benedict XV consecrated Pacelli as archbishop. Vatican opposition to the Soviet Union increased following the failure of negotiations to reach some accommodation with Moscow in the 1920s. Later papal concerns were cataloged in Pius XI's 1937 encyclical *Divini Redemptoris*, which condemned atheistic communism.[1]

Papa Ratti's successor, Eugenio Pacelli, who became Pius XII on the eve of the Second World War, proved even more suspicious of the communists than his predecessors. He had nourished a fear of Bolshevism since witnessing the excesses of the Spartacist rising of 1919 and the reign of terror it unleashed in Munich during his tenure as nuncio there. Subsequently, Pius XI had commissioned him to negotiate with the Soviet representatives in Berlin, which he did to no avail. Once pope, his "denunciation" of totalitarianism in his first encyclical *Summi Pontificatus* (On the Limitations of the Authority of the State)[2] was directed

---

1. "*Divini Redemptoris* on Atheistic Communism," in Koenig, *Principles for Peace*, 510–35.
2. *AAS*, October 28, 1939, vol. 31 (1939), 413–45.

against Stalin's Russia as well as Hitler's Germany. Not surprisingly, he remained dubious of the alleged communist conversion vis-à-vis religion in general, and Catholicism in particular, that President Roosevelt had miraculously witnessed from North America. Indeed, some believe that his overriding fear of Bolshevism led Pius XII to mitigate his criticism of Nazism, which he reportedly perceived as the lesser of two evils.

Although a self-acknowledged Germanophile, Pius XII had no love for the Nazis. As secretary of state from 1930 to 1939 he had received at firsthand the reports of the Nazi abuses against Christians as well as Jews and certainly knew that the Vatican's relations with Hitler's Germany had been troubled from the first. Indeed, he was often called upon to respond to the repeated Nazi violations of the concordat of 1933, which he had negotiated. Nonetheless, it appears that Pacelli judged the prevailing Soviet attacks upon the Church and clergy more detrimental for the faith than the Nazi onslaught.

As pope he noted that the Nazis, despite their pagan beliefs and racist ideology, unlike the Bolsheviks, had not outlawed religion, closed churches, or suppressed the faith, and therefore represented less of an immediate threat than Bolshevist Russia for the institutional Church. However, he harbored no illusion about Nazism's future plans. These convictions were hardly unique to Papa Pacelli, having been enunciated earlier by his pragmatic mentor Gasparri, and this perspective permeated a good part of the Secretariat of State. Furthermore, Pius XII noted that if Stalin found it expedient during the Nazi invasion to provide some relief for the Russian Orthodox Church to pacify its congregants, this change in policy was not extended to the Catholic Church. The Church, Pius lamented, remained subject to persecution as the Soviets sought to merge the Ukrainian Catholic Church with the Russian Orthodox Church.

Pius XII decried the fact that members of the hierarchy who

resisted the abusive conditions imposed by the Soviets were imprisoned, along with the other clergy or lay faithful who dared question the communist schemes. He was both saddened and outraged by reports of seminaries, schools, publishing houses, and charitable foundations and institutions that were either confiscated and closed, or turned over to the Russian Orthodox Church. For these and other reasons, the pope and the curia appeared to fear the spread of communism more than the threat of Nazism. The latter permitted the Church and its hierarchy to exist if not flourish in Germany, the Soviets did not do so in Russia. To make matters worse, the Soviets tended to depict Pius XII, whose housekeeper, confessor and private secretary were all German, as a crypto-Nazi and the Church as the advocate and agent of right-wing resistance to social justice.

Some within the Church, such as the pro-Nazi bishop Alois Hudal, sought to use the fascists to combat the communists. Hudal formed the Austrian Office supposedly to aid Nazi victims but it helped some Nazi war criminals to elude justice. Their escape route to Latin America was termed "the ratline." Whether this was known by the Pontifical Commission of Assistance under which Hudal's group operated remains questionable—although the Vatican apparently funneled money to the organization.[3] "Pope Pius kept the ratlines going," one author has claimed, until "the United States joined in the effort to use fascists to fight communism."[4] Critics charged that Pius XII used not only fascists but all means at his disposal to combat communism—whose program and actions he found reprehensible. Furthermore, he deplored the Soviet Union's invasion of Poland; its attack on Finland; its absorption of Latvia, Lithuania, and Estonia; and its obvious designs on Eastern Europe. He deeply resented Stalin's continued persecution of the Catholic Church, which saw its property

3. Phayer, *Pius XII, the Holocaust and the Cold War*, 201.
4. Ibid., 250.

nationalized, its hierarchy shattered by deportations, arrests, exile and executions, and its churches closed. The persecution had been so thorough that by the end of the 1930s the Catholic Church had been virtually eliminated from the Soviet state.

To make matters worse from the papal perspective, once Soviet forces occupied eastern Poland and the Baltic states, the persecution was extended to them. Religious instruction in the schools was terminated, monasteries suppressed, and an aggressive program to impose atheism introduced. Likewise in Lithuania, whose population was 80 percent Catholic, the Church was brutalized by the Soviet occupation. Despite this reality, which contradicted Roosevelt's optimistic appraisal of communist policies, during the war Pius XII prudently recognized the need to accommodate the Americans, who would undoubtedly play a crucial role in the conflict and the peace settlement that would follow. Furthermore, his insistence on preserving papal impartiality prevented him from venting his opprobrium of the Stalinist regime while he remained relatively silent about the horrendous Nazi atrocities. For these and other reasons the Vatican determined not to oppose American aid to the Soviets.

Clinging to its public stance of impartiality—which it continued to differentiate from neutrality—the Vatican proved unable to support the Nazi invasion of Russia or to denounce Bolshevik atrocities without explaining why it had not condemned the Nazi aggression and genocide during the course of the war as well. Privately some in the Vatican perceived Nazism and Bolshevism as two devils in conflict, and hoped they would destroy one another.[5] Committed to his diplomatic approach,[6] Pius rejected the fascist suggestion that he provide moral support for Hitler's war against the Soviet Union or satisfy the Allied call

---

5. Stehle, *Eastern Politics of the Vatican*, 209.
6. See Frank J. Coppa, "Between Morality and Diplomacy: The Vatican's 'Silence' during the Holocaust," *Journal of Church and State* 50 (Summer 2008): 541–68.

for him to denounce Nazi atrocities. The pope let it be known that were he to denounce Bolshevik abuses he would be constrained to condemn those of the Nazis as well, threatening that if he spoke out one day he would say everything![7] In this fashion Pius personally provided a tacit acknowledgment that he did not speak out publicly and clearly against either Nazi or Bolshevik atrocities during the Second World War. He would only change course and act otherwise in the postwar period, when conditions had dramatically changed.

Following the liberation of Rome in June 1944, the pope shuddered at the news of the Soviet forces advancing into Eastern Europe, deeming their coming more of a curse than a blessing. Pius XII feared for the fate of Europe and the threat posed by the Soviet Union and its communist ideology. As the war ground to a halt, Pius XII did not hesitate to abandon impartiality and publicly proclaim his political position. Unlike the Americans, who initially saw communism as an essentially internal problem, Pius XII from the first perceived it as a European and international dilemma. He was not surprised that the Soviets sought to reap the harvest of the protracted conflict and uneasy peace by imposing their imperium and ideology on Eastern Europe. Marx had denounced religion as the opium of the people, Lenin had preached against it on the basis of class struggle, while Stalin had brutally implemented what he proclaimed as communist goals. Rome knew that this ideology called for a universal transformation, providing a convenient pretext for Russian expansion. In light of the social, economic, and political disruption in the war-torn continent and the steady military progress of the Russian armed forces, the triumph of Russian communism appeared a frightening possibility. Pope and curia trembled at the prospect of a Russian hegemony in Europe, fear-

---

7. Bernardo Attolico to Count Galeazzo Ciano, September 16, 1941, in *I Documenti Diplomatici Italiani*, 9th series, 1939–1943 (Rome: Libreria dello Stato, 1959), 7.580–81.

ing it would lead to a rapid diffusion of communism throughout the greater part of the war-stricken population.[8]

As the Russian forces marched inexorably westward, the pope brooded about the fate of Europe and the Church, alarmed by the expansionism of the Soviet Union and the danger presented by its subversive ideology. For Pius XII this was the realization of his recurring nightmares and worst fears, explaining why he had opposed the unconditional surrender the Allies decided to impose upon Germany at the Casablanca conference. The curia shared his concerns. Before his death Cardinal Luigi Maglione warned of the grave danger of Russian hegemony in Europe. His apprehension was echoed by Monsignor Domenico Tardini, undersecretary of state, who predicted the war would end with a predominant Russian victory in Europe, leading to the spread of communism to the detriment of European civilization and Christian culture.[9] Even if the Allied armies remained in Europe, Tardini foresaw the onset of a cold war, predicting that the uneasy peace would only rest on mutual fear. In his Christmas message of 1944, the pope partially abandoned his customary reserve and cautious impartiality to condemn totalitarianism and dictatorship, while favoring democracy.[10] His concerns were compounded when Soviet forces smashed into Eastern Europe at war's end, foreshadowing their domination of the area. Within the next decade, the Vatican contributed to both the campaign against communism and the waging of the cold war.

Pius reacted swiftly and publicly to the dangers he perceived would inevitably flow from Soviet expansionism, abandoning his impartiality and employing the "spiritual weapons" at his dis-

---

8. Stehle, *Eastern Politics of the Vatican*, 238–39.
9. Notes of Monsignor Tardini on German Peace Proposal, February 20, 1945, in *ADSS*, 11.692.
10. "Pius XII: Christmas Message of 1944,"*Catholic Mind*, 63.66–67.

posal to frustrate communist objectives. His September 1944 radio address insisted that Christians could not admit a social order that denied the right to own, or rendered impossible, the possession of private property.[11] Pius now found his voice, as he called for the banishment of atheism and the indestructibility of spiritual values in the political struggle against communism. He protested developments in Stalin-dominated Eastern Europe, when the dictator's cronies initiated a brutal repression against the Church and clergy of the region. Churches and other ecclesiastical properties were nationalized, schools taken over by the state, religion eliminated from the curriculum, monasteries and seminaries closed, and the Catholic clergy either arrested or deported. Pius XII denounced the persecution of the Church, the antireligious campaign, as well as the brutal attempts to eliminate the Uniate Church, launching a counterattack on the "unbelievers" whom he charged sought to subvert the faith.

To the surprise of many, the formerly cautious pontiff who avoided confrontation and favored conciliation during the war years, in the postwar world minced no words in his condemnation of communism. To stem its tide from inundating Italy and Germany, Pius jettisoned his impartiality along with his discreet pronouncements to openly endorse a policy critical of communism and publicly call for its containment. During the thirteen years of his pontificate following the close of the Second World War (1945–1958), Pius refused to remain either impartial or silent. Instead he called for the banishment of atheism and the indestructibility of spiritual values in the political struggle against communism and the Soviet Union.

Interestingly enough, he now deemed papal public silence on moral issues impossible. "Can, may the Pope be silent?" Pius asked the assembled crowd in St. Peter's Square on February 20, 1949, adding, "Can you imagine a successor to Peter who would

---

11. "Oggi, al compiersi," in *PP*, 1.121.

bow to such demands?" The crowd shouted an unequivocal, "No!"[12] The response pleased the pope, who relied on the support of the faithful for his policy of condemnation and containment of the Soviet Union. Eventually, his position was endorsed by the United States.[13] This policy was accelerated by Russian actions, and subsequently by the outbreak of the Korean conflict in 1950.

It has been suggested that Pius XII's frequent and public condemnations of Soviet abuses, along with his precipitous abandonment of impartiality, reflected the fact that he was unconcerned with the earlier Nazi crimes and its genocide of the Jews, and only concerned about attacks on the institutional Church. These voices fail to recognize that the later papal condemnations of the Soviet regime were rendered possible because the Soviets did not surround the Vatican the way the Fascist dictatorships had during the course of the Second World War. Furthermore, the pope and curia knew they would be shielded from Stalin's fury by the Americans in the postwar period and did not have to fear a Soviet intrusion into Vatican City as they had worried about a Nazi or Fascist incursion. Furthermore, the Nazis had not openly attacked the institutional Church and threatened its future in the territories they occupied, and the Vatican hoped that its discreet response to their regime would avoid greater harm. Since the Soviets had already decimated the Church in the Soviet Union, and were in the process of doing likewise in the occupied areas of Eastern Europe, Pius did not have to be concerned about the consequences his denunciations might provoke. The aggressive Soviet action in the postwar period led the pope to assume the initiative in the condemnation of communism.

In fact, Pope Pius XII mobilized Catholic forces to combat

12. Stehle, *Eastern Politics of the Vatican*, 270–71.
13. George Kennan, *Memoirs, 1925–1940* (Boston: Little Brown, 1967), 90–91.

communism before the Western Allies recognized the threat of Soviet expansion, before the Truman Doctrine (1947), and before the formation of the North Atlantic Treaty Organization (NATO, 1949). Assisted by conservative clerics who shared his concern, early on this pope initiated a global campaign against Bolshevism in general, and the Soviet Union in particular, contributing to the opening of the cold war. Both the religious and political aspects of Pius XII's anticommunist policy are important, as well as the means he employed in his struggle against communism. Although the Vatican did not participate in the formation of the United Nations, it approved of its general aims. Pius XII supported the successor to the League of Nations and the initial steps toward European economic integration as means to restore European prosperity and thus block communist subversion.

Early in 1946, a Vatican pronouncement (*Orientales Omnes Ecclesias*)[14] denounced the forced assimilation of the Catholic United Church into the Russian Orthodox one.[15] However, while pope and curia catalogued the perils of the cold war, they differentiated the danger stemming from the ideology and the state that adopted and exploited it. A 1947 editorial in *L'Osservatore Romano* reported that in Stalin's Russia state power prevailed over Marxist convictions, concluding that so long as Stalin did not deem war profitable, he would not wage it.[16] This observation helps to explain Pius's abandonment of impartiality in favor of the policy of containment that the Vatican originated, and a variant of which the United States subsequently adopted. While Rome had some reservations about the American version of containment, it was deemed preferable to Soviet expansion. Pius warned that unless the West upheld democratic regimes in

---

14. *AAS*, January 25, 1946, vol. 38 (1946), 33–63.
15. Dennis J. Dunn, "Stalinism and the Catholic Church during the Era of World War II," *Catholic Historical Review* 59, no. 3 (October 1973): 404.
16. Giuseppe della Torre, "Is War Inevitable?" *L'Osservatore Romano*, June 14, 1947.

Eastern Europe, the Russians would impose Soviet ones. Consequently, he welcomed the European Recovery Program that George C. Marshall announced at Harvard in June 1947 to reconstruct the faltering European economy and thus diminish the allure of communism to the economically distressed and psychologically depressed masses.

Following the communist putsch in Czechoslovakia, the communists drafted a new constitution that allowed them to dominate the country and took steps to subordinate the role of the Church therein. Among other things, they introduced obligatory civil marriage, followed by legislation which extended the prohibition against reading episcopal messages and papal encyclicals from church pulpits. Pius called the Czech bishops to Rome, encouraging them to defend the fundamental rights of the Church in their state. Nonetheless, throughout these dark days, the pope did not abandon the hope of securing a negotiated settlement. Early in 1949 the Vatican sought an agreement with the Czech communist government, but the talks failed, leading the regime to establish a national Catholic Church free from papal control. Its "Karlsbad Protocol" provided for the elimination of the papal-directed Roman Catholic Church in Czechoslovakia. The Vatican responded by excommunicating the communists and all those who supported them.[17]

Abandoning conciliation, Pius refused to bow to the regime's pressure and in 1951 urged the persecuted Catholics of Czechoslovakia to remain firm in their faith, praising them for their courage and constancy in the face of repression. At the same time the pope deplored Peking's disruption of relations between Rome and the Chinese hierarchy, and its heavy-handed attempt to create an alternative to the traditional faith—the Chinese Catholic Patriotic Association. In 1952 he publicly rebuked the

17. Ludik Nemec, "Stepan Cardinal Trochta: A Steadfast Defender of the Church in Czechoslovakia," *Catholic Historical Review* 64, no. 4 (October 1978): 652–54.

"unjust Chinese attack" upon the Church and its hierarchy. His encyclical *Cupimus imprimis* expressed his concern for Chinese Catholics and provided encouragement both to the clergy and the laity, urging them to trust in Christ.[18] During the course of the year he likewise sought to reassure the Romanians, who were experiencing a similar persecution, predicting their ultimate victory. He even reached out to the people of Russia, regretting the tribulations they endured, asserting that the communists could not erase the thousand years of Christian history in Russia. Despite the pope's certitude of ultimate victory, there was little immediate improvement for the faithful in these communist-controlled countries.

Rome's relations with Tito's Yugoslavia proved to be no better than those with the other countries of Eastern Europe and communist China. Controversy emerged over the conduct of Archbishop Alois Stepinac of Zagreb, who was arrested for allegedly supporting the Croat oppression of the Serbs. When Pius refused Tito's request that he be recalled to Rome, the archbishop was put on trial in October 1946 and found guilty of sanctioning the forced conversion of Orthodox Serbs into the Catholic Church. Once again Pius XII responded by launching a series of excommunications. Like the Czech regime, Tito's government responded by encouraging the formation of a Church free from episcopal control. This structure was immediately condemned by the Yugoslav hierarchy, who appealed to Rome for support. Pius XII, for his part, provided moral support and encouraged them to oppose "the heavy threat represented by the priests' organizations," which were created to replace the hierarchy. His message was accidentally leaked, leading the Tito government to complain early in November 1952 of the Vatican's "unwarrantable interference" in Yugoslavia's internal affairs. To make matters worse, Pius honored Stepinac by naming him a cardinal

---

18. *AAS*, 44 (1952), 153ff.

and, adding insult to injury, did so on November 29, Yugoslavia's national holiday.[19] This dual affront, as well as other perceived papal provocations, prompted Tito's government to sever diplomatic relations with the Vatican in mid-December 1952.[20]

Pius XII responded in an encyclical to the Catholic Churches of the East at the end of 1952, reaffirming Rome's desire for unity and deploring the exclusion of God from their lives. In combating the communist persecution in the East, Pius increasingly relied on the states of the West, and particularly their leader, the United States. On January 7, 1953, in his State of the Union message, President Truman reported that the United States had developed a hydrogen bomb, which proved a double-edged sword for the Vatican. On the one hand, the bomb would hopefully restrain the Russians and contain communism, but on the other hand, the potential for global destruction and human annihilation was exponentially increased. The pacifism of Pius increasingly led him to oppose all wars. He especially worried about the devastating consequences of a third world war so that when and where possible, he still preferred negotiation to confrontation. Among other things he invoked a form of passive resistance he had found useful since childhood. The summer of 1953, on the seventh centenary of the canonization of Saint Stanislaus, Pacelli focused on the life and martyrdom of this bishop of Krakow, asking the Poles to remain united and firm in resisting the Soviet-directed dechristianization campaign.[21]

In June 1953, Pius XII dispatched a pastoral letter to the three imprisoned archbishops of Eastern Europe, Stepinac of Zagreb, Mindszenty of Budapest, and Beran of Prague, urg-

19. Ibid., 45 (1953), 69, series 2, annus 45, 20, p. 69.
20. Stella Alexander, "Yugoslavia and the Vatican, 1919–1929," in *Papal Diplomacy in the Modern Age*, edited by Peter Kent and John Pollard (Westport, Conn.: Praeger, 1994), 158–61.
21. Frank J. Coppa, "Pope Pius XII and the Cold War: The Postwar Confrontation between Catholicism and Communism," in *Religion and the Cold War*, edited by Dianne Kirby (London: Palgrave, 2003), 59.

ing them and their followers not to despair, remaining secure in the knowledge that they would eventually prevail.[22] The following year, Pius vigorously refuted the "false accusations" and "scurrilous" charges launched against those Chinese Catholics who remained loyal to Rome. Addressing the clergy and people of China, whose persecution he deplored, the pope protested against the Chinese communist defamation of the Holy See, the propaganda campaign against the Church, and the arbitrary expulsion of the nuncio. He once again refused recognition for the Chinese communist establishment of an independent "Catholic Church" separate from the Holy See.[23] Influenced by Soviet intransigence, Pius abandoned papal neutrality by approving the American-led North Atlantic Treaty Organization designed to thwart Moscow's diplomatic coercion and military threats. Papal support for this military alliance proved crucial for its expansion. It enabled Alcide De Gasperi and his Christian Democrats to overcome left-wing opposition and secure Italian ratification of the treaty in April 1949, and also helped the Christian Democrats under Konrad Adenauer bring West Germany into NATO in 1955.

In addition to supporting military measures to stop the spread of communism, the Vatican did not hesitate to dip into its arsenal of spiritual weapons. In 1949 Pius issued a decree attacking the Soviet Union's totalitarianism and authorizing the Holy Office to prescribe excommunication for those who voted for, joined, or collaborated with the communists and their allies—a stance it had never assumed against either the nearby Fascists or the Nazis. In 1952, two years after the outbreak of the Korean War, Pius expressed his consolation for, and provided encouragement to, the clergy and people of China, urging Catholics there to suffer for Christ and trust in Him. To stem the

---

22. Alexander, "Yugoslavia and the Vatican, 1919–1929," 162.
23. "Ad Sinarum gentum," *AAS*, 47 (1955), 5ff.

advance of communism, the Vatican closely allied itself to the United States in the cold war between East and West.

Fearful of a communist takeover of Italy, Pius, who had long preferred to ensure Church rights by concordat rather than political action, now looked to the independent Christian Democratic Party, whose role and activity he had earlier questioned. To block a potential Bolshevik triumph in the Italian peninsula, he urged the three million members of Catholic Action groups to intervene in the parliamentary elections of 1948. In the postwar peninsula Pius, confronted by the threat posed by the Italian Communist Party (PCI), openly and publicly eschewed all traces of impartiality and embroiled himself in political life and public affairs. He did so by galvanizing the numerous groups in the Catholic Action Movement. Under the leadership of Professor Luigi Gedda and the supervision of the bishops, these organizations of the laity responded positively to the papal pleas. They opposed the parties of the left, supporting conservative ones and upholding Catholic policies in Italy. In postwar Italy, the pope who had long opposed the Church's becoming embroiled in partisan politics and stressed papal impartiality involved the Vatican in Italian politics to prevent the communists from attaining power.

Pius XII, the primate of Italy and bishop of Rome, proved determined and energetic in opposing a communist takeover so close to home. He encouraged the Vatican journal *L'Osservatore Romano* to warn the faithful that one could not be a Catholic and a communist simultaneously.[24] "Communism is a very grave and imminent danger for the Italian people," the pope reported, complaining that it would jeopardize the Holy See "if it were surrounded by a restless, agitated and extremist population."[25]

---

24. *L'Osservatore Romano*, July 23, 1944.
25. Notes drafted by Secretariat of State for the pope to discuss with Churchill during his visit of August 23, 1944, *ADSS*, 11, 505–6.

After members of the PCI entered the government following the liberation of Rome, Pius became greatly alarmed and had recourse to various expedients to curb their influence. The Vatican paid close attention and sought to micromanage developments in Italy.[26] In the postwar period it even sought to determine who would distribute American aid in the peninsula, calling for committees composed of "Catholics" and "honest" citizens to do so, rather than socialists or communists. In March 1946, in a first salvo, the pope alerted the Italian clergy that it was their duty to instruct the faithful to combat anti-Christian forces in politics and society—a mandate clearly directed against the extreme left. The Americans shared the papal perspective and appreciated Pius XII's determination to prevent the communists from assuming political control of the peninsula they had liberated.

While the Americans utilized economic measures and subtle political pressure to influence Italian events, the Vatican had recourse to spiritual means. In mid-July 1949 the Holy See made public a decree issued earlier by the Congregation of the Holy Office. It indicated that it was not permissible for the faithful to join or support the Communist Party because it was materialistic and anti-Christian, while its directors, both in theory and practice, proved hostile to God, religion, and the Church of Christ. Second, Catholics could not publish, disseminate, or even read books, periodicals, or other literature that upheld such doctrines. It further stipulated that those who violated these first two prohibitions should not be admitted to the sacraments. In fact the decree proclaimed that those who affirmed these doctrines and practices automatically fell under excommunication as apostates of the Catholic faith. On July 1, 1949, the decree was promulgated in the *Acta Apostolicae Sedis*,[27] providing papal sup-

26. In this regard, see Italo Garzia, "Pope Pius XII, Italy and the Second World War," in Kent and Pollard, *Papal Diplomacy in the Modern Age*, 121–36.
27. Sandro Magister, *La politica vaticana e l'Italia, 1943–1978* (Rome: Reuniti, 1979), 132–33.

port for a condemnation and excommunication that had never been launched against Nazism. Many of the accusations hurled by Pius XII against communism were equally applicable to Nazism, which likewise violated the basic teachings of the faith, but he pragmatically chose not to unleash such charges against it or its adherents from 1939 to 1945, fearing the consequences. However, in the postwar period Pius proved openly critical of Nazism, which was now a spent force, as well as communism, as he moved closer to the Western Allies in his campaign against Stalin's Russia.

There were those in the Vatican who characterized the postwar struggle in Italy and Europe as one between Moscow and Rome. Perceiving the elections of 1948, the first of the Italian Republic, as a crusade of Catholic values against Bolshevik ones, Pius helped Alcide de Gasperi's Christian Democrats win a majority of seats in the Chamber of Deputies. Unquestionably, the Church's involvement in the peninsula's electoral process in 1948 proved massive and unprecedented and played a major role in ensuring the Christian Democrats 48 percent of the vote, to the 31 percent garnered by the left-wing Popular Democratic Front.[28] In light of the crucial role of the Church in the Christian Democrats' electoral victory, Pius expected them to follow his wishes, which some perceived as dictates. He was disappointed when De Gasperi formed a multiparty government rather than accepting the one-party rule that the Vatican made known it preferred, resisting Vatican and clerical pressure to outlaw the Communist Party in Italy. Later, in 1952, during heated municipal elections in Rome, the pope was believed to favor a Christian Democratic coalition with the right-wing parties to prevent a Marxist electoral victory in the Eternal City. Once again De Gasperi refused to comply with the alleged papal wish, and this was seen by some

28. Elisa Carrillo, "The Italian Catholic Church and Communism, 1943–1963," *Catholic Historical Review* 77, no. 4 (October 1991): 650.

to widen the rift between the Vatican and the Christian Democratic leader.

Although Pius was particularly concerned about developments in Rome and Italy, his anticommunism transcended the peninsula and even the European continent. Mobilizing Catholic forces against Bolshevism, he initiated a global campaign against communism in general, and the Soviet Union in particular. Throughout most of the thirteen years of his pontificate following the close of the Second World War, Pius pursued this anticommunist course. A number of observers considered his entire postwar pontificate defensive, claiming he attempted to preserve Catholic civilization in a world shaken by militant Bolshevism. Pius did in fact employ the moral weight of Catholic preaching against the U.S.S.R. and its allies, while moving closer to the West. He was especially reassured by the promise of American aid to Italy, and Washington's determination to maintain a military presence in Europe. Indeed, the common interests of the United States and Vatican multiplied following Roosevelt's death, during the increasingly hostile reaction of the Truman administration toward the Soviet Union. Charging that the totalitarian, antireligious state demanded the silence and acquiescence of the Church, Pius XII rejected these conditions. "What was in the opinion of many a duty of the Church, and what they demanded of her in an unseemly[!] way," he protested, 'is today ... a crime in their eyes and a forbidden interference in domestic affairs of the state: namely resistance against unjust restraint of conscience by totalitarian systems and their condemnation all over the world."[29] Repeatedly setting forth the tenets of the faith contradicted by communist doctrines and policies, Pius XII fought Soviet political designs in Italy, Europe, and abroad.

The papal message was echoed across the Atlantic by Bish-

---

29. Stehle, *Eastern Politics of the Vatican*, 268.

op Fulton Sheen, the "television priest," who branded communism the Antichrist, and led many American Catholics to press Washington to join with Christ and Mary in their war against "Satan and his Communist allies." The Holy See's anticommunism, which garnered the moral and material support of the Western alliance during the course of the cold war, played a part in the decision of the American president to propose opening normal diplomatic relations with Rome in 1950. As noted this aroused the latent but still widespread anti-Catholic sentiment in the United States, forcing President Truman to withdraw the nomination to "the Pope of the Atlantic alliance." Despite this rebuff, the pope continued to preach against "godless" communism, remaining a virtual if not a formal ally of the Western bloc. In 1956, he denounced the Soviet invasion of Hungary. Two years later, he issued yet another condemnation of Chinese persecution of the Church.[30] The Vatican's "alliance" with the Western bloc, which contributed to the triumph of Christian Democracy in Italy and Germany as well as to the containment of the Soviet Union, compromised papal neutrality, revealing a certain selectivity in its recourse to "impartiality." Pius XII apparently recognized as much once the communist threat had somewhat diminished and never lost hope for a diplomatic rather than a military solution.

While the pope still supported the efforts of the Europeans and the Americans against the march of communism, he recognized the danger of the cold war and the "coexistence of fear" that prevailed on the Continent. Emphasizing the opposition of the Church to wars, except those of a strictly defensive nature, the pope relied on prayer and the intercession of Mary to overcome the difficult dilemma facing the Church in Eastern Europe and the Far East. Pius, who had early on predicted the opening

30. "Ad Apostolarum Principis," *AAS*, 50 (1958), 601–4.

of the cold war, looked forward to its conclusion. The death of Stalin in March 1953 did not end the Soviet threat, but facilitated a sort of rapprochement between the Vatican and Moscow. Returning to his conciliatory course, Pius XII's Christmas message of December 1954 called for a "coexistence in truth" to replace the "climate of fear."[31]

Anxious for a restoration of some tranquility in a divided continent, Pius contributed to this development by distinguishing once again between the "suffering" Russian people and the "odious" communist system. Nonetheless, in the interest of peace, he offered hints that an accord with this regime might be necessary and possible.[32] During the course of 1955 the pope further elaborated his call for coexistence between East and West. "The true Christian westerner nourishes thoughts of love and peace toward the peoples of the east, who live within the sphere of influence of a materialistic *Weltanschauung* supported by state power," the pope proclaimed. "If the question of coexistence continues to move the spirit: faithful westerners pray together with those on the other side of the iron curtain who are still stretching out their hands to God."[33] Thus though Pius XII openly fought communism in the postwar years, he never totally abandoned the diplomatic option in dealing with the Soviet regime and others who he felt persecuted the Church.

Pius XII made it clear in December 1956 that while he waged war against the communist ideology, he did not launch a Christian crusade against the Soviet Union. In fact this "Pope of the Atlantic Alliance" warned the West against an indiscriminate opposition to any sort of coexistence. As a consequence, papal diplomacy did reach some accommodations with the communist regimes of Eastern Europe, contributing to a cease-fire of sorts

---

31. *L'Osservatore Romano*, January 3, 1955.
32. Ibid.
33. Stehle, *Eastern Politics of the Vatican*, 287.

in the cold war. Although he protested the Soviet intervention in Hungary in 1956, Pius hinted that Vatican-Soviet relations could improve if the Church were accorded freedom to proclaim Christ's message. These Vatican signals were received by Moscow, which recognized that despite ideological differences there might be "useful" and perhaps even "official" relations between their party and the papacy.[34] Thus, at the end of Pius XII's pontificate in 1958, the Vatican sought a tentative accord with the Soviet system allowing it to reach an understanding with communist but still Catholic Poland, as well as one with Tito's Yugoslavia. As a consequence, the pope who had assumed a leading role in the opening of the cold war now joined forces with those who called for its conclusion.

Despite his campaign for coexistence, Pius XII could not be dubbed "Moscow's favorite pope." Indeed, some believe that for political purposes the Kremlin sought to discredit and denigrate him. This is the claim made by Lieutenant General Ion Mihai Pacepa, the former head of Romanian Intelligence, who indicated that Moscow enlisted the playwright Rolf Hochhuth in its defamation campaign against the image of Pius XII and the Church during the course of the cold war.[35] He reports that Hochhuth was instructed "to smear the Vatican" and portray Pius XII as a "coldhearted Nazi sympathizer," as well as "an anti-Semite who had encouraged Hitler's Holocaust." Although Pacepa's accusations have been disputed and in the eyes of some discredited, Hochhuth's play *The Deputy: A Christian Tragedy* (published in German in 1963 and in English in 1964) launched a series of charges against this pope that found an audience that accepted its contentions that Pius was indifferent to the genocide and failed to raise an authoritative public voice on behalf of

---

34. Ibid, 299.
35. Ion Mihai Pacepa's article "Moscow's Assault on the Vatican" appeared in *National Review Online* (January 25, 2007).

the persecuted. Father Peter Gumpel, the Jesuit coordinator of the cause of Pius XII's sainthood, notes that while there is ample evidence that the Soviets sought to discredit Pope Pius and used *The Deputy* to undermine the papacy during the course of the cold war, there is no evidence that Hochhuth was commissioned to write the play to do so. The controversies about this and other aspects of Pius XII's pontificate continue.

TEN

Traditionalism and Modernity

> But let us leave the past and turn our eyes towards that future which, according to the promises of the powerful ones of this world, is to consist, once the bloody conflicts of today have ceased, in a new order founded on justice and on prosperity.

THE CONTROVERSIES surrounding Pius XII's impartiality during the Second World War, his "silence" during the Holocaust, and his outspoken stance during the cold war have dominated his image following his death. However, they are not the only issues that continue to swirl about this pope and his pontificate. Some have seen him as a conservative figure and have stressed his rigid adherence to past practice and tradition, criticizing him as a pope who looked backward rather than ahead. Others have focused on the reformism of his policies and the modernity of his interests and outlook, hailing him as the "first modern pope," attuned to the world of science, technology, and innovation. These diverse views have contributed to the confusion and controversy about Pius XII and his pontificate. This debate continues and to date there is no clear consensus on his reformism versus his traditionalism.

Epigraph is from "Summi Pontificatus" of Pius XII, October 20, 1939, in *PE*, 5.15.

This divergence was not breached but broadened during the pontificate of his successor John XXIII (1958–1963), who convoked the Second Vatican Council (1962–1965). As preparations commenced for its opening, word spread that Pius XII had quietly—some said secretly—pondered convoking such a body, provoking speculation whether he planned for a council of restoration or one of reform. Not surprisingly, those who perceived Pius XII as a staunch traditionalist were convinced that Pope Pius planned to convoke a second Council of Trent (1545–1563) or First Vatican Council (1869–1870)—both of which were called to reaffirm traditional doctrine and reassert the primacy of the pope. Others, however, believe that Pius provided the initiative for the changes introduced by John XXIII and Pope Paul VI (1963–1978), and would probably have introduced many more modifications with the backing of the bishops during the course of a council. The nature of the council Pius XII planned forms one part of the broader debate on his traditionalism versus his reformism.

This debate, like so much else about him and his pontificate, assumed a partisan tone following his death. Those who perceive Pius XII as an essentially conservative traditionalist have charged that he shared the authoritarianism of Pius IX (1846–1878), whose name he adopted along with his belief in papal infallibility. Both were seen to reveal a certain insensitivity to Jewish concerns, prompted by their alleged support of the baptism of Jewish children without parental permission. Pius IX was embroiled in the Mortara affair of 1858 and Pius XII has been associated with the Finaly affair that dragged on from 1945 to 1953. In the first case a Christian domestic in a Jewish household in Bologna secretly baptized the young Edgardo Levi Mortara, and when the papal police found out, they entered the home and seized the boy. Despite international pressure to return the child to his parents, Pius IX would not relent and insisted on keeping him within a

Christian environment. He prevailed in doing so and eventually Mortara became a Catholic priest.[1]

Papal action in the Finaly affair is somewhat more obscure, and the role of Pius XII therein less than certain. The Finalys fled Nazi-occupied Austria in 1939, the year that Pacelli became pope, settling in a suburb of Grenoble, France, where their two sons were born in 1941 and 1942. Fearing for the safety of their children during the German occupation, they turned them over to a Catholic nursery, placed them in a municipal school, and eventually entrusted them to the nuns of Our Lady of Zion. Following the orders of the Nazi occupiers, the Finalys were transported to Auschwitz, where they found not work but death. Their boys were baptized and after the war those responsible for their security and education resisted the requests of surviving family members for their release and return. When a court in Grenoble ruled that the boys should be turned over to their relatives, they were smuggled into Spain in 1953—a move that the pope allegedly approved.[2] Supposedly Pius XII indicated an unwillingness to see the boys returned to their Jewish relatives without guarantees that their Catholic education would be continued and their faith preserved.[3] If such sentiments were held by Pius XII they were never expressed publicly in written or verbal form. We know that Pius XII did not protest when the boys were returned to their Jewish relatives in June 1953; this was a "silence" few criticized.

It is true that Pius XII fully matched Pius IX in his devotion to the Virgin Mary and encouraged the study of Mariology. Pius IX proclaimed the Immaculate Conception (1854) of Mary, who was declared free of original sin. Nearly a century later

1. In this regard, see David Kertzer, *The Kidnapping of Edgardo Mortara* (New York: Knopf, 1997).
2. Catherine Poujol, *Les Enfants cachés. L'Affaire Finaly* (Paris: Berg, 2006), 189.
3. Joyce Block Lazarus, *In the Shadow of Vichy: The Finaly Affair* (New York: Peter Lang, 2008), 50–52.

Pius XII, having recourse to the infallibility favored and promoted by Pius IX, pronounced the doctrine of the Assumption in 1950. He asserted in *Munificentissimus Deus* that Mary was taken body and soul into heaven after the completion of her earthly life.[4] Papa Pacelli's pronouncement remains the only one to date issued under the provision of infallibility. Some perceived Pius XII's action as papal arrogance, neglecting to mention that in his 1946 encyclical *Deiparae Virginis Mariae* he had sought episcopal approval for the definition of the dogma—and received it. For some reason, still not known, the letter dated May 1, 1946, did not appear in printed form in the *AAS* until November 1950![5] Having attained episcopal endorsement, Pius continued his campaign to honor Mary, to whom he had been devoted since childhood. His 1951 encyclical on the rosary once again invoked the "powerful protection" of the Mother of God,[6] while his 1953 encyclical *Fulgens Corona* designated 1954 a Marian year to commemorate the centenary of Pio Nono's definition of the dogma of the Immaculate Conception.[7] In October 1954 his encyclical *Ad Caeli Reginam* proclaimed the Queenship of Mary, describing her as "above all other creatures in dignity and, after her son, possessing primacy over all."[8]

These doctrines were criticized by some who sought Christian unity, convinced that this Marian emphasis alienated many Protestants, including some who were otherwise close to Catholicism. Furthermore, both Pius IX and Pius XII were criticized for their political policies—the former for his lack of diplomacy and speaking too often and too publicly; the latter for being too diplomatic and not speaking more openly or forcefully against the Nazi evil that culminated in genocide. Both faced grave challenges. Pius IX had to endure revolutionary upheaval

4. *PP*, 1.138.
5. *AAS*, 42 (1950), 782–83.
6. *PE*, 5.213.
7. Ibid., 5.231–38.
8. Ibid., 5.275.

in Rome and temporary exile, the seizure of his state by the Italians and the Kulturkampf that persecuted the Catholic Church in Bismarck's Germany. Later, Pius XII had to confront the destructive Second World War, the abuses of the Nazi, Fascist, and Soviet regimes, the Holocaust and other atrocities, and in the postwar period, the cold war and the threat of nuclear extinction. Disagreement flows from the conflicting assessments of his responses to these challenges.

Those prone to depict Pius XII as a conservative and traditionalist point to his strict emphasis on Thomism, neo-Scholasticism, and the antimodernist position he assumed during the pontificate of Pius X (1903–1914). They also cite his collaboration with the ultraconservative Umberto Benigni, and his revision of the Code of Canon Law, which enhanced the position of the pope in the Church. Others complained of his alleged role in the subordination of women in state, Church, and society during his pontificate, and his emphasis on the family, which he described as "the primary and essential cell of society."[9] They also point to his insistence that a consummated marriage was by divine law indissoluble,[10] as well as his frank discouragement of marriage between Catholics and those outside the faith.[11] "Such marriages," he wrote, "are rarely happy and usually occasion grave loss to the Church." Among the vices of the day he cited the breakup of the family, birth control, the weakening of respect for authority, and divorce. The latter he deemed a plague that proved destructive to both Church and state.[12] His emphasis on the recitation of the rosary, the subject of his 1951 encyclical *Ingruentium Malorum*,[13]

9. Encyclical letter "On the Function of the State in the Modern World," October 20, 1939 (Washington, D.C.: National Catholic Welfare Conference [hereafter NCWC], 1939), 25.
10. "Già per la terza volta," in *PP*, 1.119.
11. *AAS*, 31 (1939), 303–4, 317, 650–51.
12. Encyclical letter of Pope Pius XII "To the Church in the United States," 1939 (Washington, D.C.: NCWC, 1939), 7–14.
13. *PE*, 5.213–16.

was seen by some as another sign of his traditionalism and "excessive" devotion to Mary. In fact, it also reflected his childhood family practice and the memory of his mother leading him and his siblings in reciting the rosary.

Others have complained about Pius XII's lifting the ban on the Action Française in 1939, and his delight at Franco's triumph during the Spanish Civil War. His critics have also denounced his conciliatory policy toward Fascist Italy and Nazi Germany, as well his "impartiality" during the Second World War. The catalogue of complaints compiled by liberals include this pope's censure of the priest-worker movement and the new theology in France. His *Humani Generis* (1950) was seen to halt new theological trends and supposedly exposed his conservative views on nature, grace, existentialism, and evolutionism among other things. This encyclical was also seen to reflect his suspicion of ecumenism and noted the importance and impact of papal encyclicals. Commemorating the hundred and fiftieth anniversary of the establishment of the hierarchy in the United States in 1939, Pius stressed "the unity and indissolubility of marriage," denouncing divorce as "the greatest harm to the prosperity of families and of States."[14]

In the political realm, and in Church-state relations, there was criticism of Pope Pius's continued reliance in the postwar period on concordats with dictatorial regimes such as Franco's Spain. On the other hand, he was seen to be totally committed to his anticommunist campaign, which was likened to a virtual crusade. Fearing a communist victory in the Italian elections of 1948, Pius, it is believed, sought to persuade the Christian Democrats to form an alliance with the right-wing and neofascist parties to block such an eventuality. The alleged attempt proved unsuccessful. We do know that in the postwar period Pius did not hesitate to excommunicate those who disagreed with what

---

14. *AAS*, 31 (1939), 651.

he deemed fundamental principles, such as Bishop Carlos Duarte Costa, a critic of clerical celibacy.

Although Pacelli pursued a number of conservative policies during his long clerical career one must recognize that he was far from close-minded in religious matters or an intransigent conservative in the political realm. An objective analysis of his record reveals a willingness to support a degree of reformism in both areas. Thus, unlike Pius IX, Pius XII did not wage war upon the modern world or lock himself in the Vatican. In his *Divino Afflante Spiritu* (With the Help of the Divine Spirit) of 1943, he sanctioned a limited use of critical historicism for biblical studies as he called for "the adoption of Scripture studies to the necessities of the day."[15] Among other reasons for such a reassessment, Pius noted that "what is the literal sense of a passage is not always as obvious in the speeches and writings of the ancient authors of the East, as it is to the works of the writers of our own time." Citing the contribution of "textual criticism" in the correction of profane writings, Pius believed it could be used in the case of sacred books, discussing the most opportune way to promote biblical study to cast new light upon Sacred Scripture.[16]

His *Mystici Corporis Christi* (Mystical Body of Christ) of the same year, sought to promote a more positive relationship between the Church and nonbelievers. "True love of the Church therefore requires not only that we should be solicitous one for another," Pius XII wrote, adding, "we should recognize in other men, although they are not yet joined to us in the Body of the Church, our brothers in Christ."[17] On numerous occasions he expressed his conviction that the Church strives and prays for all.[18] At the same time he emphasized that the Church embraces

15. *Divino Afflante Spiritu*, September 30, 1943, in PE, 5.77.
16. Encyclical letter of Pope Pius XII "On the Most Opportune Way to Promote Biblical Studies," September 30, 1943 (Washington, D.C.: NCWC, 1943), 18.
17. "*Mystici Corporis Christi*," June 29, 1943, in PE, 5.57.
18. "*In questo giorno*," June 2, 1939, in PP, 1.116.

and cares for the whole of humanity and looked forward to seeing those outside the fold return home. However, Pius recognized that "this must be done of their own free will, for no one believes unless he wills to believe."[19] This assertion contradicts and therefore calls into question the stance he supposedly assumed during the Finaly affair and the baptism of Jewish children without parental consent.

Even some critics of Pius XII acknowledge that his *Mediator Dei* (Mediator of God) of 1946 furthered liturgical reform. "The Church is without question a living organism," as is her liturgy, Pius explained, seeking to reassure those who feared and opposed change in the Church. He added that "she grows, matures, develops, adopts and accommodates herself to temporal needs and circumstances, provided only that the integrity of her doctrine be safeguarded."[20] At the same time he warned against an exaggerated attachment to ancient rites and ceremonies.[21] In his encyclical letter on "The Sacred Liturgy" he deemed the use of the Latin language "a beautiful sign of unity" but added that "the use of the mother tongue in connection with several of the rites may be of much advantage to the people."[22] In this encyclical Pius again revealed his willingness to accept change. "As circumstances and the needs of Christians warrant," he wrote, "public worship is organized, developed and enriched by new rites, ceremonies, and regulations."[23] These and similar assertions support the contention that Pius XII in many religious, political, and social matters often favored reform rather than reaction.

On more than one occasion Pius denounced the exaggerated and indiscriminate attachment to the ancient rites extolled by

---

19. "*Mystici Corporis Christi,*" June 29, 1943, in *PE,* 5.58.
20. "*Mediator Dei,*" November 20, 1947, in *PE,* 5.130.
21. Ibid.
22. "Encyclical on the Sacred Liturgy," November 20, 1947 (Washington, D.C.: NCWC, 1947), 25.
23. "*Mediator Dei,*" November 20, 1947, in *PE,* 5.123.

certain conservatives and traditionalists, which he flatly rejected. He asserted that at times change was not only useful but necessary. "The Liturgy of the early ages is most certainly worthy of all veneration," he wrote, to reassure traditionalists. However, he was quick to add that "ancient usage must not be esteemed more suitable and proper, either in its own right or in its significance for later times and new situations, on the simple ground that it carries the savor and aroma of antiquity," while asserting that "the more recent liturgical rites likewise deserve reverence and respect." He concluded that it was "neither wise nor laudable to reduce everything to antiquity by every possible device."[24] His deeds followed his thought when at the end of 1945 he provided a new constitution for papal elections.[25]

Pius XII continued along the path of reformism by revising the liturgy to make evening masses possible. At the same time he urged the laity to participate more fully in the mass and other religious services,[26] introducing a series of changes in the Church that made this possible. To facilitate lay participation in the Eucharist, at the beginning of 1953 he issued the Apostolic Constitution *Christus Dominus*, "Concerning the Discipline to Be Observed with Respect to the Eucharistic Fast." Acknowledging the changed times and conditions, he modified the Eucharistic fast to enable Catholics to receive Holy Communion more frequently. Among the new provisions, the drinking of water was no longer deemed to break the fast; moreover, the sick were allowed to drink other nonalcoholic beverages as well as water before receiving the Eucharist. At the same time his revised rule permitted bishops to sanction evening masses where they were deemed useful. In 1957 Pius issued a decree that further liberalized the provisions on fasting and evening masses.

---

24. Ibid.
25. "*Vacantis Apostolicae Sedis*," December 8, 1945, in *PP*, 1.123.
26. "*Mediator Dei*," November 20, 1947, in *PE*, 5.136.

Among other things it removed the restriction on the number of evening masses that could be allowed each year and reduced the period of fasting before communion to three hours.

Pius also invoked a greater role for the laity in setting goals for the faith and the salvation of souls.[27] To aid the faithful in understanding ecclesiastical developments and the positions assumed by the papacy, his pontificate was the first to publish papal speeches in the vernacular on a regular basis. Furthermore, while some in the Vatican opposed any form of birth control, Pius XII pragmatically affirmed the legitimacy of the regulation of offspring popularly dubbed the "rhythm method" for family planning. He also justified the use of pain killers for the terminally ill—even if this shortened life.[28] Nor did this pope shy from challenging and changing other Church practices and traditions.

In the postwar period he directed that in the prayers for the Jews, *Pro Perfidis Judaeis, perfidis* should no longer be translated as "perfidious" but as "unbelievers." Some deemed this a small change, apparently forgetting that the attempt of the Friends of Israel to eliminate the reference to "perfidious Jews" from the Good Friday prayer had precipitated the suppression of this organization in March 1928.[29] The record reveals that Pius XII did not tackle the anti-Judaism that still prevailed in certain Church circles. Like many others in the Church he did not believe, perhaps refused to believe, that anti-Judaism played any role in the abuses and crimes promoted by the racial anti-Semitism of Hitler's Germany. It is also worth noting that the two central figures in effecting a Catholic-Jewish reconciliation during the Second

---

27. "Se a temperare," September 4, 1940, in *PP,* 1.118.
28. Pius XII's Address to Family Front Congress, November 27, 1951, and his addresses to physicians of September 8, 1953, and that of January 8, 1956, in Michael Chinigo, ed., *The Pope Speaks: The Teachings of Pope Pius XII* (New York: Pantheon Books, 1957), 45.
29. *AAS,* 20 (1928), 103.

Vatican Council and its aftermath were devoted to Papa Pacelli and did not perceive him to be anti-Judaic, much less anti-Semitic. His confessor, Augustin Bea, and his undersecretary of state, Giovanni Montini, the future Pope Paul VI, did not believe they were going against the wishes of Pius XII in effecting their interfaith dialogue and reconciliation with Judaism but rather were absolutely convinced that they were continuing along the path of his reformism.

Pius XII also proved amenable to a transformation of the College of Cardinals, rendering it more universal. In his consistory of 1946, he bestowed the red hat on clergy from China, India, and the Middle East, making the Sacred College truly international and eliminating the long-standing Italian majority. For the first time in history the college had representatives from all the inhabited continents. This global vision was continued, indeed strengthened, following Pius XII's consistory of January 1953. In the postwar period Pius made an effort to bring younger candidates to the episcopacy, including in 1958 the thirty-eight-year-old Karol Wojtyla—who two decades later donned the papal mantle as John Paul II.

Although Pius continued to require long periods of quiet solitude, a need he had since early childhood, this was not out of disdain for the world around him. Rather it was inspired by his need to study and meditate upon it. Some believe that the pope's accommodation with the modern world was fostered by his attendance at a state school where he reportedly came to appreciate the need for change in state and society. The years of his secular education may have also played a part in sustaining his interest in science and technology, which was originally instilled by his broad range of readings. His interest in astronomy, in turn, was stimulated by Father Giuseppe Lais, an early model and mentor for Pacelli, who took him to a conference on astronomy held in Paris in 1896. His interest in the contribution of modern science was further nourished by his decade in Germany, where he witnessed firsthand a number of extraordinary technological innovations that left lasting impressions. His appreciation of the advances of German science very likely played a part in his positive assessment of the Reich. One must keep in mind that Pacelli admired Germany, not Nazism.

Pius XII's call for change was not restricted to the religious realm, where he sanctioned a series of modifications in the Church and its liturgy. The pope also saw the need for reform in the broader society. Long a champion of social justice, Pius XII repeatedly invoked social reform and like a number of his predecessors did not hesitate to condemn the abuses of a laissez-faire capitalism, driven solely by the profit motive. It is true that he favored capitalism over socialism or communism, but like Leo XIII (1878–1903) he insisted that capitalism be imbued with the need for equity, if not equality, ensuring all members of society a living wage rather than simply enriching a few, often at the expense of the majority. In the very first year of his pontificate he wrote the Americans that God did "not wish that some have exaggerated riches while others are in such dire straits that they lack the bare necessities of life."[30] Peace, internally and internationally, he proclaimed in his Easter message of 1939, had to be based on "justice and charity."[31] He insisted "that the goods created by God for all men should in the same way reach all," "justice guiding and charity helping," to assist the less fortunate. In his commemoration of the fiftieth anniversary of Leo XIII's *Rerum novarum*, he reaffirmed the right of all to use the material goods of the earth.[32] Like Leo, he continued to call for a wider distribution of goods and favored social equity, internally and internationally.[33] During the war, Pius sponsored a "crusade of charity" to assist victims of the conflict and continued

30. *AAS*, 31 (1939), 654.
31. "Quoniam Paschalia Sollemnia," April 9, 1939, in *PP*, 1.115.
32. "La solemnità della Pentecoste," June 1, 1941, in *PP*, 1.118.
33. "Oggi, al compiersi," September 1, 1944, in *PP*, 1.121.

his charitable campaign in the postwar period. In his encyclical *Quemadmodum* at the beginning of 1946, he made a passionate plea on behalf of the world's destitute children.[34]

Pius returned to the need for a fair distribution of goods in his encyclical of June 1951, *Evangelii Praecones*, on the promotion of Catholic missions along with the need for social reform in the technologically advanced countries of the world. While continuing his condemnation of the various forms of Marxist socialism as fallacious and subversive, the pope acknowledged that in some capitalist countries workers were exploited. Pius insisted that this abuse required correction, again demanding that the goods of the earth be enjoyed by all, as the Savior intended. Christians and especially priests should not, and could not, remain deaf to the cries of the downtrodden and exploited and had the obligation to denounce this departure from God's plan. Failure to do so by remaining silent, the pope insisted, "would be culpable and unjustified before God."[35]

After the war, Pius XII championed economic and political reform along with social justice as a means of alleviating the widespread suffering in so many parts of the world. He also supported changes in the European state system along with a revision in international relations. Confronted by the destruction and dislocation of the Second World War, Pius XII, who stressed the transnational nature of the Church,[36] believed transcending state sovereignty might also prove useful for the European world and was in the forefront of promoting the continent's integration. He also championed a degree of European unity as a means of eliminating conflict by effecting a reconciliation between victors and vanquished. He thus hoped to ease the suffering of so many souls, as well as to stop Soviet expansion into Western Europe. Much of his vision was shared by the Christian

34. "*Quemadmodum*," in *PE*, 5.105–7.
35. *PE*, 5.197.
36. "Ad Sinarum gentum," Ocober 7, 1954, in *PE*, 5.265–69.

Democratic leaders who emerged after the war, including Robert Schuman of France, Konrad Adenauer of West Germany, and Alcide de Gasperi of Italy. These men, and the parties they led, seconded the papal calls for social justice, economic reform, and European integration, as well as his call for defending Western Europe against the Soviet Union and the "free" capitalist economy against the communist alternative. Economic realities, the emergence of the cold war, and American advice—all contributed to the pope's call for some form of supranational and intergovernmental European organization.

During the postwar decades American pressure reinforced the papal initiative for European integration. In fact, the first steps in that direction followed the American insistence in 1947 on the need for a European entity to distribute United States aid under its European Recovery Program (ERP) or Marshall Plan. This led to the formation of the Organization for European Economic Cooperation (OEEC) by seventeen Western European nations. Two years later, in 1949, a Council of Europe was established to promote European integration. Its task proved difficult as the Eastern European states, pressured by Stalin, refused to participate and a number of Western European states, particularly Great Britain, fearing infringement of their sovereignty, offered only a limited commitment. Pope Pius XII was not upset by Stalin's refusal to join, but regretted the obstacles placed in the path of union in Western Europe. In his Christmas message of December 1948 he once more rejected the dogma of absolute state sovereignty that had prevailed since the Peace of Westphalia of 1648 and invoked an alternative.

The resistance to political integration and the fierce determination of a number of states to protect their national sovereignty led Europeanists such as the French foreign minister, Robert Schuman, and the economist Jean Monnet to call for economic integration. They commenced by proposing the pooling of the continent's coal and steel resources and production. In May 1950, they proposed placing Franco-German coal and steel production under a common authority, while making provision to have other European states join this economic entity. The Treaty of Paris was signed in April 1951, and in 1952 six countries, France, Germany, Italy, and the Benelux countries (Belgium, the Netherlands, and Luxemburg) established the European Coal and Steel Community (ECSC). Supporting this newly established community, Pius expressed concern about the physical, psychological and spiritual needs of the miners—many of whom were immigrants. Britain, still concerned about the infringement of its sovereignty, initially refused to join—but economic constraints and the failure of the European Free Trade Association (EFTA) convinced them to do so later.

The French continued to call for further economic integration, proposing the establishment of a European Economic Community (EEC). This was created by the Rome Treaties of 1957, supported by the Vatican, which abolished tariffs between members and made provision for a common tariff upon goods entering from non-EEC countries. The objectives of the EEC were applauded by Pius XII in the summer of 1957. He catalogued the advantages provided by the European organization in the fall of that same year, calling for a closer political union as well—citing the crucial role of Christian values in their efforts for consolidation. Indeed, from the first, Pius XII perceived the European Union as a Christian community.

Although Pacelli's aloof personality and physical appearance projected an other-worldly and detached image, which some claimed he cultivated to impress his audiences, others noted that this façade did not reflect the personality behind it. During his pontificate and throughout his life, he remained deeply interested and closely attuned to contemporary developments. For one thing, as an adult he continued the study habits he had developed as a child, spending many hours reading every day on a wide range of subjects, including political, economic, social, and cultural issues as well as philosophical, religious, and theological questions. This gave him knowledge of all sorts of matters from advances in telecommunications, atomic energy, entertainment—radio, television, the movies—to developments in the medical field and innovations in science and technology. He was fascinated by the prospect of travel in space and was aware of the advances in rocketry made in Germany and the United States. Pius XII kept abreast of developments in the social sciences as well as the physical sciences and remained very interested in studies of the mind and personality. He indicated as much in his Address to the Rome Congress of the International Association of Applied Psychology delivered in April 1958, the last year of his life. Some claimed that the breadth of his knowledge was greater than its depth, but in fact both were extraordinary, as was his determination to utilize this knowledge to attain positive ends for both the Church and society

Throughout his diplomatic career and pontificate, Pius XII kept abreast of the wave of discoveries that characterized the twentieth century, appreciating the contribution that physics, chemistry, geology, biology, and psychology—among others—could make to the Church as well as to state and society.[37] He was convinced that their findings could be utilized for the common good of humanity.[38] Fascinated by the march of science and technology during his pontificate, he found much in contemporary society pleasing and did not perceive any conflict between science and religion, maintaining that the former supported the latter. During his pontificate, as throughout his life, he affirmed that "true science discovers God in an ever-increasing degree—as

---

37. However, he was fully aware of the danger that would flow from their misuse.
38. Leo J. Haigerty, *Pius XII and Technology* (Milwaukee: Bruce Publishing, 1982), 196–97.

though God is waiting behind every door opened by science."[39]

He confided as much early on in his message to the Americans in 1939, in which he expressed the desire "that scientific progress in all branches be ever more universally affirmed."[40] He saw in science not only the means to achieve technical results and improvements but a mechanism for a better understanding of the world of nature.[41] Like Max Planck, who was not Catholic, Pius believed that the study of the atom led one to believe in God.[42] The pope was convinced that since technological progress came from God, it could, should, and would lead to an enhanced awareness of the Creator. For this and other reasons he stressed the role of the Church in the march of science and technology. Thus unlike some evangelical conservatives, he was even prepared to acknowledge the evolution of human beings—but not their souls.[43]

Pius XII's lifelong dedication to science and technology has been largely ignored by many, overshadowed by the focus on the pope's "silence" during the Holocaust and his impartiality during the Second World War. The volume compiled by Leo J. Haigerty, *Pius XII and Technology* (1982), which concentrates on Pope Pius's numerous discourses on the impact and importance of science and his acceptance of the cultural and religious implications of the technological explosion in the modern world, is very much the exception rather than the rule. Likewise, little is known and written about his early assessment of the promise, as well as the problems, posed by atomic power. Those aware of this strong papal interest in and appreciation of science and technology have argued that Pius could more accurately be dubbed the

39. Pius XII's Address of November 22, 1951, to the Pontifical Academy of Sciences (Washington, D.C.: NCWC, 1951), 3.
40. Encyclical letter of Pope Pius XII "To the Church in the United States," 1939 (Washington, D.C.: NCWC, 1939), 15.
41. In this regard, see his Address of April 24, 1955, to the Pontifical Academy of Sciences (Washington, D.C.: NCWC, 1955).
42. Haigerty, *Pius XII and Technology*, 45.
43. Pius XII's *Humani Generis* of August 12, 1950, in *PE*, 5.181.

"Pope of science and technology" than the "Pope of Silence." In 1941 he named Saint Albert the Great patron of the natural sciences.

Pius XII's interest in the advances of scientific knowledge and technological innovation was both personal and practical as well as theoretical and philosophical, for he welcomed and had recourse to contemporary technological innovations. He frequently used his typewriter both to preserve his privacy and to be better able to read his notes and commentary; he often had problems in deciphering his own small and shaky script. The grandson of the founder of the *L'Osservatore Romano* was acutely aware of the impact of instruments of communications and immediately recognized the importance of new developments such as the radio, the cinema, and television. He embraced rather than denounced the communications revolution, which he hoped to put at the service of the Faith.

Long appreciative of the impact of radio, which he described as a "marvelous invention,"[44] he was the first pope to use it extensively to broadcast his messages—a characteristic he shared with his contemporary President Franklin Delano Roosevelt. In fact, he made greater use of the radio than Roosevelt and utilized it to broadcast his first speech to the Catholic world. He understood the role both radio and television could play in educating the masses and fostering unity.[45] Following the path of his grandfather Marcantonio, Papa Pacelli likewise appreciated the importance of the press. Subsequently, he embraced the motion picture and television as marvelous mechanisms for spreading truth and educating the masses. Indeed, he was the first pope to make an appearance on television. Quick to recognize the importance of telecommunications for the internationalization of Church and society, in the early 1950s he brought the

---

44. *AAS*, 31 (1939), 652.
45. Pius XII on radio and television in Rankin, "The Pope Speaks," 175–80.

Vatican into the International Union of Telecommunications, while proclaiming the Archangel Gabriel the patron of telecommunications. In 1954 he inaugurated a television network—later christened Eurovision—among eight European states.[46] In his exhortation "I rapidi progressi" of that same year, he focused on television's potential for the dispersion of the Faith. The following year he established a papal commission for cinematography, radio, and television to coordinate Catholic principles and policies in a number of states.

In 1957 Pius issued the encyclical *Miranda Prorsus* on the impact of the communication revolution and the role of motion pictures, radio, and television, whose discoveries and proper use the Church welcomed. Noting the remarkable progress made by each and the promise they collectively offered humanity, the pope also expressed concern about potential problems they might pose. Among the latter he listed their attempt to impose political or economic goals for the benefit of a small minority, and the belief that they had a right to present whatever they wanted, including immoral material.[47] Pius considered this an improper role for the media, urging instead the dissemination of information and the extension of education. "They should serve the spread of truth so that the bonds between peoples will be made closer so that men will have better mutual understanding and will help one another in time of crisis," he wrote. Finally, he looked to the media to increase cooperation between individual citizens and public authority.[48] With considerable insight, Pius recognized the increasing influence of these media to provide news for the masses and in 1958 proclaimed Saint Clare of Assisi the patron saint of television.

Himself the product of an earlier generation, Pius XII con-

---

46. "8 nation TV Network in Europe Opened by the Pope," *New York Times*, June 7, 1954.
47. PE, 5.350–51.   48. Ibid., 351.

tinued to rely on the print media for much of his own information. Years before the first successful reaction of atomic fission and the launching of the first satellite into space, Pius had predicted these developments and assessed the consequent promise and problems they presented. Fully aware that modern technologies could be abused, he preached that put to proper use they could prove a boon to humanity. Thus, he adamantly and frequently denied the charge that the Church or the papacy opposed technological innovation. Unlike many heads of state who had little or no knowledge of atomic power, Pius XII early on was aware of its emergence and pondered its consequences. In his 1941 address to the Pontifical Academy of Sciences, Pius proclaimed that the Church was deeply interested in probing the physical and moral results of atomic power, which he perceived as an inevitable prospect. At the start of 1943, despite his wartime preoccupations, Pius noted the extraordinary progress in the nuclear field and urged the responsible control of its power, and he was among the very first to champion "atoms for peace."[49] The pope's support of atomic energy was a key feature of his postwar pontificate. Recognizing the limitations of the use of fossil fuels long before most of his contemporaries, he appreciated the future importance of atomic energy. This was especially the case for countries like Italy, which had little coal and was therefore heavily dependent on oil and gas from abroad.

Adhering to his wartime impartiality and neutrality, Pius XII did not openly and publicly condemn the United States for dropping atomic bombs on the Japanese civilian populations of Hiroshima and Nagasaki in August 1945, resulting in hundreds of thousands of casualties of innocent civilians. Despite this "public silence" and failure to launch a clear and specific condemnation of the American action, the use of atomic power to kill and maim represented the realization of Pius XII's worst fears and night-

---

49. "In questa solenne adunza," February 21, 1943, in *PP*, 1.120.

mares. Consequently, the pope revealed in general terms that he deplored the use of atomic energy to create weapons of mass destruction, its potential to pollute the atmosphere, and the prospect that it would become a pathogenic menace for the whole of humanity.[50] In his speech of February 8, 1948, before the Pontifical Academy of Science, he warned of the disastrous consequences of the abuse of atomic power.[51] Acknowledging that atomic energy, when misused, represented a threat to all of mankind, the pope recognized that when properly employed it could serve humanity's needs. In fact, he dedicated himself to the task of utilizing atomic power for positive rather than destructive ends. To do so in the postwar period (1956), he brought the Vatican into the International Agency for Atomic Energy, and supported the program of "atoms for peace."[52] He urged scientists to join him and cooperate to achieve justice and peace. Despite certain traditional political and religious convictions, Pius XII, more than any of his predecessors, sought to harmonize the Catholic civilization of the Church with the evolving technological society. Favoring modernization, he was clearly a reformer, as he was in his call for a reorganization of international relations.

Pius XII, who assumed the papal tiara on the eve of the Second World War, like his predecessors questioned the prevailing international disorganization that had led to the outbreak of two destructive world wars in half a century and sought an alternative. Like Leo XIII and Benedict XV, he favored negotiation and arbitration to resolve international tensions and made his position known. In his first encyclical letter the pope decried the lack of morality in international relations and the deification

---

50. This pope's support for and reservations about atomic power can be read in his various speeches, allocutions, encyclicals, and broadcasts during his tenure. Some of these have been catalogued in the *Discorsi e Radio Messagi di Sua Santità Pio XII* and the *Acta Apostolicae Sedis*, which contains the laws, pronouncements, and various addresses and encyclicals of the Holy See.
51. Haigerty, *Pius XII and Technology*, 45.
52. *PP*, 1.120.

of the state.⁵³ In his letter to the new minister from Haiti, Pius returned to the need to reorganize international relations and, following Benedict XV, called for a fruitful global organization that would secure the reciprocal independence of small and large nations alike, while safeguarding the liberty of all.⁵⁴

He returned to this theme in his Christmas message of 1939, in which he announced the principles of a general settlement. In it, Pius invoked international institutions for preserving the peace, a call he repeated in his Christmas messages of 1940 and 1941, and those that followed.⁵⁵ In his Easter homily of March 24, 1940, he urged the nations of the world to settle their disputes not by violence but by truth, justice, and charity. In April 1940 he confided to the members of the Royal Academy of Santa Cecilia that he wished international relations could be as harmonious as their music. In June 1940 Pius pleaded with the belligerent nations to observe the principles of humanity and international law in their treatment of noncombatants and occupied countries—a strong though indirect critique of Nazi policies. In December 1940 Pius invoked a new world order, and at the end of 1941 he indicated that "to procure the re-birth of mutual trust, certain institutions must be established which will merit the respect of all."⁵⁶

In the call for a harmonious internationalism American and papal interests coincided. In 1942 President Roosevelt coined the term United Nations to refer to the twenty-six nations at war with the Axis, suggesting the creation of a new international organization to replace the League of Nations. The proposal immediately received papal endorsement. In June 1944 Pius XII praised

53. *AAS*, 31 (1939), 454–80.
54. Ibid., 661–62, 670–76, 703–7, 758.
55. E. E. Y. Hales, *The Catholic Church in the Modern World* (Garden City, N.Y.: Hanover House, 1958), 279; Edward J. Gratsch, *The Holy See and the United Nations, 1945–1995* (New York: Vantage Press, 1997), 60–61.
56. Koenig, *Principles for Peace*, 655–59, 758.

efforts to achieve an international reorganization and a new world order.[57] From August to October 1944, when delegates from the United States, Great Britain, the Soviet Union, and China met in Washington to outline plans for the successor to the League of Nations, Pius proved supportive.[58] In fact he deemed the formation of an organization for the preservation of the peace absolutely essential. No one could be more welcoming of such an organization than the papacy, he wrote, which had long challenged the notion that states could and should resolve differences by waging war.[59] When the United Nations officially came into existence in October 1945, Pius seconded its general aims, as Benedict had earlier approved those of the League of Nations.[60]

To be sure, the pope had reservations about its two-tier structure, which differentiated the great powers of the Security Council from the general membership in its Assembly—as well as the veto power accorded the Soviet Union. Nonetheless, in his Christmas message of 1948 Pius provided the doctrinal basis for papal support of the United Nations, asserting that the Church had long maintained that the nations of the world constituted a community, and once again rejected the notion of absolute state sovereignty.[61] He repeated this supportive stance in his Christmas message of 1951. That year, following the suggestion of Giovanni Montini (the future Paul VI), he appointed Angelo Roncalli (the future Pope John XXIII) as Vatican observer to UNESCO in Paris, but did not accept the permanent observer status that was accorded to any state that belonged to one or more of the United Nations specific agencies. In part, this hesitation to accept permanent observer status stemmed from the question of the nature of papal participation. This was only resolved by an exchange of letters between the Holy See and the secretary general of the U.N.

57. *E ormai passato un anno*, June 2, 1944, in *PP*, 1.121.
58. *AAS*, 37 (1945), 19.   59. Ibid.
60. Ibid., 166.   61. Ibid., 61 (1949), 10–12.

in September 1957, in which it was agreed that the papacy would be represented at the U.N. as the Holy See, rather than the Vatican "state."[62] Pius perceptively recognized that as the Holy See it would command far greater influence than it would have if represented as a minuscule state.

Pius XII continued to rely on negotiation and diplomacy to achieve what he perceived as the Church's objectives and in the process proved willing to compromise on a number of issues, as he had during the Second World War. In many questions affecting Church, state, and society he departed from traditionalism and the conservative agenda, assuming a more liberal and reformist course. Thus although he shared Pius IX's devotion to Mary and belief in papal infallibility, he was not the intransigent conservative that Pius IX became when he returned to Rome in 1850 following his forced exile at the end of 1848. Once the Italians seized Rome, in 1870, Pius IX locked himself in the Vatican and refused to recognize the Italian Law of Papal Guarantees or accept the funds the Italians offered. He made it clear that the Church could never conciliate itself with error and that the pope ought not, indeed could not, separate himself from the Church.[63] This was a stance the diplomatic Pius XII chose not to follow and, unlike Pio Nono, he sought conciliation rather than confrontation with a dangerous regime. Although some in the Vatican admired Pio Nono's consistency and perseverance, a number of popes who followed abandoned his intransigence to pursue a more diplomatic course, including Leo XIII, Benedict XV, and perhaps most notably Pius XII. Papa Pacelli sought to appease the Nazis not out of love but for fear of their satanic regime, and relied on a diplomacy which entailed impartiality and public silence to avoid greater harm. His decision to do so proved controversial, bringing the approval of some but the opprobrium of others.

62. Gratsch, *The Holy See and the United Nations*, 10.
63. Pasquale de Franciscis, ed., *Discorsi del Sommo Pontefice Pio IX Pronunziati in Vaticano ai Fedeli* (Rome: G. Aureli, 1972), 1.283–84.

Conclusion

History is one of the sciences that has a close relationship to the Catholic Church.... The judgments passed on her are extremely varied; they range from total acceptance to the most determined rejection. But whatever the final verdict of the historian may be, [his] ... task it is to see and to expound—as far as possible just as they happened—facts, events, and circumstances.

PIUS XII'S DEATH in his summer palace at Castel Gandolfo on October 9, 1958, for many seemed to mark an important transition for the papacy. Under his successor, John XXIII (1958–1963), who convoked the Second Vatican Council (1962–1965), the Church appeared to embark on a program of rapid and major transformation. Others, however, saw and stressed continuity rather than change. During the course of the council called by John, word surfaced that his predecessor—whose code of canon law exalted the papacy in the Church's legal structure—had seriously considered convoking a council, but for reasons still unknown did not do so. This provoked speculation concerning his intentions for the council and the Church, compounding the controversy surrounding the legacy of Pius XII. The widely divergent assessments of Pope Pius's principles, policies, and diplomatic and political actions vindicated his distrust of many historians to accurately assess past events.[1] Very likely Pius would not

Epigraph is from Address of Pius XII to the International Congress of Historical Sciences, September 7, 1955, in Rankin, *The Pope Speaks*, 361.

1. Chenaux, *Pie XII*, 11.

have been shocked to learn that after his death assessment of his person and pontificate was dramatically altered.

Pius, who was praised for his "heroic efforts" during the Second World War on behalf of the persecuted, within a decade after his death was denounced for his inaction during the genocide perpetrated by the Third Reich and depicted by vocal critics as indifferent to the suffering of the Jews and other victims of Nazi brutality. He was accused of being anti-Judaic if not anti-Semitic. The charge of "silence" launched by Hochhuth against Pius XII unleashed a torrent of criticism by a host of others who sought to assign responsibility for the atrocities perpetrated by the Third Reich. These critical, often biased accounts of his role during the Second World War, stimulated a defensive, in some cases hagiographic, historiography, leading to the so-called Pius War.[2] The conflict continues with some asking whether Pius acted as pope or Pilate,[3] Hitler's friend or foe; while others have depicted him as a moral coward if not an anti-Semite.[4] Those in the "Pius camp" have counterattacked, defending his cautious diplomacy and denouncing his opponents. Both groups contributed to making his "silence" during the Holocaust the central feature of his papacy—often to the exclusion of other crucial aspects of his life, career, and pontificate.

The storm surrounding the person and policies of Pius XII was reinforced by the Church's decision to beatify him along with John XXIII at the end of the twentieth century. There were those within and outside the Church who questioned Pope Pius's conciliatory course toward, and cooperation with, the "satanic" Nazi regime. They vociferously challenged his sanctity, as supposedly did some who served and admired him. Those who

---

2. Joseph Bottum and David G. Dalin, eds., *The Pius War: Responses to the Critics of Pius XII* (New York: Lexington Books, 2004).

3. James Murray, "Pope or Pilate?" *Western Australian*, February 15, 2003, p. 22.

4. Ben Macintyre, "Was Pope Pius a Moral Coward or a Saint?" *The Times* (London), October 23, 2008.

uphold the latter stance point to the fact that in the 1950s when seminarian Hans Küng asked Father Robert Leiber if Pius XII was a saint, the Jesuit—who had long and loyally served Pius—reportedly replied, "No no! Pius XII is not a saint. He is a great man of the Church."[5] Very likely Leiber was simply referring to the situation at that time, but his remarks were consciously misused to substantiate opposition to his sainthood on the part of his detractors.

Clearly there has been and there remains opposition, as well as support, for the proclamation of his sanctity. This may have contributed to the Vatican decision to postpone his beatification, advancing the cause of the conservative Pius IX (1846–1878) in 2000 to balance the more liberal John XXIII. Both critics and champions of the pontificate of Pius XII acknowledge his recourse to diplomacy, avoidance of confrontation, and appeasement of the Axis, but disagree in their assessment of the motivation for and the consequences flowing from this policy. While his adverseries cite the triumph of diplomacy over morality, his admirers point to the moral ends achieved by his cautious and pragmatic diplomacy.[6]

Schooled and experienced in law and diplomacy, the son and grandson of lawyers, it is not surprising that Pacelli's clerical career proved more diplomatic than pastoral. In fact, it is not widely known and even less cited that Pius was the only pope of the twentieth century who was never the bishop of an active diocese. His early life and family background provide a guide to the policies he would later pursue as pope, as does the fact that he was a protégé of the pragmatic and influential Cardinal Pietro Gasparri, who had served as secretary of state under Benedict XV (1914–1922)

5. David Gibson, "Pope Quiz: Is Every Pontiff a Saint?" *New York Times*, January 17, 2010, p. 4.
6. In this regard, see Frank J. Coppa, "Between Morality and Diplomacy: The Vatican's Silence during the Holocaust," *Journal of Church and State* 50, no. 3 (Summer 2008): 541–68.

and under his successor, Pius XI (1922–1930). The course Pacelli pursued as nuncio to Germany (1920–1929) and then as secretary of state (1930–1939) reveals the influence of Gasparri. This statesman believed it was dangerous and unwise for the Vatican to pursue a confrontational course toward the nearby Fascist and Nazi regimes, calling instead for a policy of accommodation to preserve the Church's rights in Italy and Germany. This conflicted with the stance of Pope Pius XI (1922–1939), who saw the need to publicly, clearly, and loudly denounce the pagan and racist policies of those regimes that violated the teaching of the Church. This disagreement between the pope and his secretary of state led Pius XI to dismiss the old cardinal. The fact that he replaced him with Pacelli would seem to suggest that Pius XI did not know how completely this taciturn figure and confirmed diplomat shared Gasparri's conciliatory approach toward the fascist regimes.

Almost a decade later, however, the members of the conclave to select Pius XI's successor were seemingly aware of Pacelli's call for conciliation rather than conflict with Fascism and Nazism. They apparently elected him pope in one day in March 1939 because they saw the need for a pope who possessed a cautious manner and diplomatic skills as the world teetered on the brink of another conflagration. Thus his mandate was not to continue but to discontinue the confrontational policy of his predecessor. The new pope did not disappoint those who sought conciliation rather than confrontation in dealing with the fascist regimes, and made a series of strenuous attempts to prevent the outbreak of another war. When he proved unable to stop the impending conflict, he determined to keep the Holy See from becoming embroiled in it and sought détente with Hitler to protect the Church's "vital interests" in Germany.[7]

To do so he resorted to the impartiality devised by Gasparri

---

7. Robert S. Wistrich, *Hitler and the Holocaust* (New York: Modern Library, 2001), 136.

for Benedict XV during the First World War. Their definition differentiated neutrality, which they opposed, from impartiality, which they accepted. Within this framework neutrality implied indifference or failure to pass judgment on principles in conflict; impartiality recognized the papacy's right and duty to pass judgment on principles and practices contrary to the faith, but discouraged the "father of all nations" from becoming embroiled in politics by favoring one side against another in conflict.[8]

The notion that one could evaluate differences in principles but not act upon them politically made more sense during the First World War than during the Second. This was recognized by Pius XII himself, who indicated that the pope at times should not and could not remain silent in the face of evil. The Vicar of Christ, he asserted, could not behave like purely political leaders who only considered political and military issues, ignoring the moral ones that each pope had to address.[9] Despite this conviction, the historical record reveals that Pius proved circumspect and cautious in his response to the abuses of Hitler's Reich. Apparently Pius XII believed that a clear and public indictment of Nazi crimes against both Jews and Christians would not have prevented the enraged Fuehrer from continuing his brutal campaign, but would have encouraged the deranged dictator to launch an attack upon the Church in Germany. He also feared that if a breach occurred between the Vatican and the Reich patriotic German Catholics might leave the Church. It was a risk and responsibility the new pope was reluctant to assume, and was strongly discouraged from doing so by Vatican circles.

Nonetheless, Pope Pius XII's conscience, sense of duty, and unavoidable responsibility did not permit him to remain totally silent when confronted with the evil inherent in the fascist re-

---

8. "Pope Eager to Convince the World at Large of His 'Absolute Impartiality' in the War," *New York Times*, July 24, 1916; Walter H. Peters, *The Life of Benedict XV* (Milwaukee: Bruce Publishing, 1959), 113.

9. *RDHSWW*, 169.

gimes. This led him to denounce the immorality inherent in totalitarianism as early as his first official documents. His initial encyclical, *Summi Pontificatus* (On the Unity of Human Society), issued on October 20, 1939, cataloged the "pernicious errors" of the day, placing the forgetfulness of the law of human solidarity and the equality of mankind at the top of his list. Thus without mentioning the anti-Semitism of Nazi Germany, the pope indicated that the Church rejected racism. Second, his encyclical denounced the deification of the state and the attempt to divorce civil authority from dependence on the Supreme Being. "To consider the State as something ultimate to which everything else should be subordinated and directed, cannot fail to harm the true and lasting prosperity of nations," he wrote, warning that this "can happen either when unrestricted dominion comes to be conferred on the State as having a mandate from the nation, people, or even a social order."[10]

The first two errors cataloged were clearly aimed at Mussolini's Italy and Hitler's Germany, while the third was obviously directed at Stalin's Russia. Pius was somewhat more explicit in his Christmas message of 1942, which pleaded on behalf of "the hundreds of thousands who, through no fault of their own, only because of their nationality or descent are condemned to death."[11] Although he did not directly cite or condemn the Nazi genocide of the Jews, his was seen as a lonely voice crying in the silence of the continent.[12] Since Pius did not, and perhaps could not, take steps to have this critique reach the German masses, he did not provoke the retaliation of the Reich, which he sought to elude while fulfilling his moral duty as Vicar of Christ.

Pius XII's cautious approach toward both Fascist Italy and Nazi Germany has been variously interpreted by his defenders

10. *Summi Pontificatus*, October 20, 1939, in *PE*, 5.13.
11. Pinchas E. Lapide, *Three Popes and the Jews* (New York: Hawthorn Books, 1967), 251.
12. *New York Times*, December 25, 1942.

and denigrators. A number in each of these opposing factions have concurred that any decision on the beatification and final evaluation of this pope should await the opening of the papers of his pontificate in the Secret Vatican Archives (ASV). This was suggested in the preliminary report in 2000 of the International Catholic-Jewish Historical Commission charged with examining the actions of Pius XII and the response of the Vatican to the Holocaust. It would be helpful if these papers were available to add to what we have learned from other sources including the eleven volumes of the *Actes et documents du Saint Siège relatifs à la seconde guerre mondiale* (Vatican City, 1965–1981), drawn from the papers of Pius XII. The opening of most of the papers of Pius XI dealing with Germany in the ASV, especially those of the Munich and Berlin nunciatures, where Pacelli served in the decade from 1920 to 1930, and those of the Secretariat of State, over which he presided from 1930 to 1939, have proven useful. Recently the first volume of Pacelli's notes on papal audiences has been published.[13] Finally, Pius XII left behind a wide range of encyclicals, radio messages, and other speeches and commentary that reveal considerable about what he thought, said, and did. Indeed, Pius believed, or perhaps more accurately hoped, they would stand as his spiritual testament.

Unfortunately, many of these available sources are either ignored or misused by both the partisan denigrators and committed defenders of the pope and his policies, who often consult them essentially to unearth material to bolster their pre-established and largely inflexible positions. Not surprisingly, there is little real dialogue between these advocates who launch pronouncements against their "adversaries" rather than talk to them, and whose commitment to their cause often degenerates into personal attacks upon those who hold conflicting views and

13. Pagano, Chappin, and Coco, *I fogli di udienza del Cardinale Eugenio Pacelli segretario di stato*.

are perceived and treated as enemies rather than fellow scholars. Thus after half a century of bickering these "combatants" in the "Pius War" have proven unable to agree upon a common definition of the "silence" attributed to Pius XII or to explore its roots and relationship to the "impartiality" the papacy employed in both world wars. Some include within their definition of silence papal indifference and inaction during the Holocaust. Others do not. Furthermore, there are few objective accounts of the rationale for Pius XII's conduct during the Second World War and the role that anti-Judaism within the Church may have played in determining his policies and its consequences. Despite the plethora of publications there has been little serious inquiry into why Pius XII abandoned impartiality in the postwar period during the course of the cold war, when he virtually shunned silence as shameful, or what this tells us about his earlier conduct. Finally, it seems obvious that one cannot understand Pope Pius's conciliatory conduct during the course of the Second World War and the Holocaust by limiting the study to the war years or even to his entire pontificate, as so many have done and continue to do.

As regards Pius XII's public "silence" this is part of the historical record—we know precisely what he said and when he said it, and does not require any further archival or alternative inquiry. It is also clear that Pius XII was very careful in launching criticism of the aggressors and the abuses they perpetrated and early on indicated he intended to replace the confrontational course of his predecessor toward Nazi Germany with a more conciliatory one. Likewise known is what Pius did to help the victims of the war, which was considerable and negates the notion that he was indifferent to their suffering and plight. We also know that like his predecessor, Pius XII deemed racism and anti-Semitism contrary to the faith and said so in a number of his encyclicals and messages. Consequently, the debate on his "silence" essentially centers on why Pius XII did not speak out more openly, clearly, and forcefully against the satanic Nazi principles and evil practices including the genocide during the course of the Second World War.

Some have seen anti-Semitism or anti-Judaism—which persisted in the Church—behind Pius XII's failure to take a stronger public stance against the genocide of the Jews. This supposition, which prevails in a broad section of the historiography, has been advanced by a number of Catholic authors as well as a number of non-Catholic writers. It is challenged by the fact that Pope Pius XII also refused to name aggressor and aggrieved during the Second World War—and no objective analysis could trace this silence to anti-Judaism. Furthermore, Pius also preserved his diplomatic "silence" during the genocide of the Catholic Poles and the Orthodox Serbs.[14] Thus he was not only "silent" about the brutalization of the Jews, but also about the Nazi aggression against Catholic Poland. Following the Nazi invasion of Poland, the Poles and French awaited the Holy Father's condemnation of Nazi aggression, violence, and cruelty,[15] but none was forthcoming.

Noting the absence of public support from the Vatican for the Catholic Poles, the historian Alessandro Duce has declared, "Can one expect someone who does not have the strength to protect 'his own flock' to save his 'neighbors?'"[16] In this fashion Duce has emphasized that papal silence not only impacted Jews but Catholics as well. One might well disagree with Pope Pius XII's recourse to impartiality during the Second World War and his conciliatory policy toward Nazi Germany, but there is no evidence that it was motivated by indifference or hostility toward the Jews.

The cautious papal approach was apparently prompted in part by the fear of Nazi Germany's retaliation against the Catho-

14. O'Shea, *A Cross Too Heavy*, 27.
15. *RDHSWW*, 281.
16. Alessandro Duce's interview with Zenit, Zenit online, November 7, 2006.

lics residing within the Third Reich and the possible dissolution of the Church within Germany as well as in Nazi-occupied Europe. Like Gasparri, Pius XII looked to the concordat and papal impartiality to provide temporary relief from the sinister anticlerical motives of National Socialism, which he hoped would collapse before it commenced its expected campaign against the Church. Furthermore, he feared that while public papal condemnations would arouse the regime and provoke its retaliation, the Nazi censorship would keep them from most of the German population and consequently do more harm than good. In one sense Pius XII's conciliatory policy toward the Nazi regime proved successful insofar as it served to allow the Catholic Church in the Reich and the occupied territories to survive. But was the price for this survival too high? It was a question that troubled the pontiff.

The conflict between realistic considerations and religious convictions burdened the pope, who pursued impartiality during the Holocaust. The available evidence and record of events reveal that he was not insensitive to the suffering of either Christian or Jew, but was painfully aware of the limited influence he could exercise over the pagan Nazi regime. It was essentially an accurate assessment. His diplomatic plea to the Vichy government in the summer of 1942 on behalf of Jewish expatriates residing there fell on deaf ears, and these Jews were arrested and deported to Eastern Europe as the Nazis demanded.[17] Apparently assessing the papacy's influence upon the course of events during the Second World War as limited, Pope Pius XII continued his policy of détente with Nazi Germany to avoid becoming the target of its volatile and dangerous leader. Poland was partitioned by both Nazi Germany and the Soviet Union in the East, and France partially occupied in the West; neither action evoked a papal protest.

17. "Vichy France Rounds Up Foreign Jews," *Washington Post*, August 27, 1942.

The Church, guided by Pius XII, condemned the principles of totalitarianism but remained politically neutral with the intent of avoiding greater evil. During the Second World War Pius XII followed the example of Pope Benedict XV during the First World War—even though the combatants and circumstances in the two conflicts were radically different. As the Nazis occupied much of Europe, the Vatican deemed it dangerous to condemn German actions. Recognizing that discretion is the better part of valor, Pope Pius XII carefully expressed his sentiment of impartiality within his papal encyclical on *The Internal Order of States and People*, delivered on Christmas Day of 1942:

> The Church would be untrue to herself, ceasing to be a mother, if she turned a deaf ear to her children's anguished cries, which reach her from every class of the human family. She does not intend to take sides for any of the particular forms in which the several peoples and States strive to solve the gigantic problems of domestic order or international collaboration, as long as these forms conform to the law of God. But on the other hand, as the "Pillar and Ground of Truth" and guardian, by the will of God and the mandate of Christ, of the natural and supernatural order, the Church cannot renounce her right to proclaim to her sons and to the whole world the unchanging basic laws, saving them from every perversion, frustration, corruption, false interpretation and error.[18]

The papal message directed against the Third Reich was not so clear, public, or provocative as to arouse the wrath of Hitler against the Church and precipitate additional persecution. Like so many of Pius XII's critiques it was a minimalist and a general condemnation which the pope believed, or wanted to believe, fulfilled his moral responsibilities without arousing the Nazis and endangering the Church. Adhering to his self-proclaimed duty to denounce principles that conflicted with the faith, Pius

---

18. "The Internal Order of States and People," Christmas message of 1942, in V. Yzermans, ed., *The Major Addresses of Pope Pius XII* (St. Paul, Minn.: North Central, 1961), 2.52.

refused to publicly take sides in the conflict between the Axis and Allied powers—his secret actions, however, reveal that that privately he favored the Western Allies.

Many have questioned why Pius XII, who was cautious and impartial in his approach to Nazi and Fascist abuses, later proved openly critical of Stalinism. Some have jumped to the conclusion that this change in approach flowed from the fact that he considered the communism of the Soviet Union more dangerous for the Church than the Nazism of Germany and responded accordingly. However, this would not explain his behavior and relative silence about Stalinism during the course of the Second World War. Chronology thus emerges as another factor in separating the more cautious papal action toward the two totalitarian states during the war, and the more outspoken criticism following its conclusion. Geography also played a part in permitting Pius to take a more fervent stance against the Soviet Union, which was hundreds of miles away, while Hitler's Germany was next door and its Italian ally virtually surrounded Vatican City. Following the fall of Mussolini, the Germans occupied Rome and Hitler reportedly considered capturing the pope and dragging him into exile—just as the French had seized Pius VI and Pius VII during the revolutionary and Napoleonic ages. At this juncture arousing the anger of Hitler would not only have proven dangerous for the Catholics of Germany but also threatened the safety of Vatican City, the position of the papacy, and the person of the pope himself. Was Pacelli's boyhood fear of martyrdom a factor in the papal decision?

Most objective observers recognize and acknowledge that a more forthright condemnation of Nazi abuses on the part of the pope would have endangered Catholics in the Reich and the future of the institutional Church therein. However, they ask how could this have made matters worse for Jews, who were clearly slated for slaughter? In truth, it could not have made matters much worse for those caught in the camps. However, it would have made life more tenuous for those Jews who were housed in Catholic institutions, religious houses, and Vatican City itself, and would have undermined the Church's ability to provide passports and baptismal certificates that saved the lives of many Jews. Impartial individuals such as Parsons J. Graham, assistant to the personal representative of the president of the United States to the pope, recognized that a more forthright papal condemnation carried great risk,[19] and played a key role in Papa Pacelli's cautious criticism of the Nazi genocide.

Whatever the motivation for his conciliatory course toward the Nazi regime, some deemed that this appeasement compromised the moral leadership of the papacy. Others have launched more serious charges against this pope, convinced that anti-Semitism or anti-Judaism—and many prove unwilling to recognize any difference between the two—led Pius XII to ignore the suffering and genocide of the Jews. Undeniably there was a degree of religious anti-Judaism in the Church and its hierarchy. However, anti-Judaism could not have played a part in Benedict XV's failure to denounce the Turkish genocide of the Armenians during the First World War. Nor could it have played a part in Pius XII's failure to denounce the genocidal policies the Nazis pursued in Catholic Poland, where the first to be brutalized were members of the faith.

In an interview given in 1964, Hochhuth acknowledged that his drama initially targeted the papal failure to denounce the aggression and abuses against the Catholic Poles and only later transferred his criticism to the papal failure to condemn the genocide of the Jews.[20] Did the Russians—who wanted to discredit the papacy—play a part in Hochhuth's decision? Hoch-

19. Interview of Parsons J. Graham, July 1, 1974, found in Truman Library.
20. Patricia Marx Ellsberg, "An Interview with Rolf Hochhuth," in *The Papacy and Totalitarianism between the Two World Wars*, edited by Charles F. Delzell (New York: Wiley and Sons, 1974), 118.

huth does not say. Finally one should note that Papa Pacelli did not originate the cautious policy that has been deemed "silence" but borrowed it from Benedict XV and Pietro Gasparri, who utilized it to bolster their diplomatic efforts during the course of the first world conflict. Pius XII also borrowed the related policy of "impartiality" during wartime from Benedict XV and Gasparri, who used it during the earlier war to rationalize their political neutrality while asserting the right and responsibility of the Holy Father to judge principles. Pacelli, who had collaborated with Gasparri and Pope Benedict in their diplomatic efforts, recalled the usefulness of impartiality in justifying papal policy, and balancing religious morality and political prudence. As pope, Pacelli had recourse to impartiality during the Second World War. He relied on it not only because of his close association with Gasparri and his diplomatic training, but also because it reflected the sentiments of the curia and the College of Cardinals, which did not wish to see the Church embroiled in a dangerous and destructive conflict with the nearby dictatorial regimes.

Rather than being Hitler's pope, Pius XII favored the Allies, as Cornwell himself subsequently acknowledged following the publication of his controversial book. In an interview half a decade later, Cornwell proved more appreciative of the difficulties and constraints the pope confronted and far less judgmental regarding the path Pius XII pursued during the war and the genocide.[21] A series of sources reveal that far from admiring the Nazi regime, Pius XII continued to distrust Hitler's Reich. He deplored its attempt to undermine Christianity and replace it with a pagan-like national faith, as well as many of its principles and practices, but would not say so plainly and publicly until the Nazis were defeated and signed an unconditional surrender in May 1945. In June of that year the pope finally branded Nazism

---

21. John Cornwell, "For God's Sake," *The Economist*, December 9, 2004.

as "satanic" and an "arrogant apostasy from Jesus Christ" as he denounced the regime that advocated a "cult of violence" and adhered to an "idolatry of race and blood."[22] Disagreement continues over whether Pius should have said this earlier and what impact this might have had on the Holocaust.

While Pius XII followed others in the molding of his wartime diplomacy and political policies, he revealed more originality in religious matters where he showed a greater degree of autonomy and a willingness to sanction a degree of reformism. Many of his critics and champions have largely ignored this aspect of his pontificate, in part because they focus on his "silence" during the Holocaust, in part because Papa Pacelli was not prone to reveal his inner sentiments—a trait he had nourished since childhood. Pope Pius XII was more complex than many realize, for as a diplomat, minister, and pope he retained the remote and solitary personality he had developed as a child and his most intimate contacts were his two canaries—one of which often sat on his shoulder.

In his policies as well as his personality he was something of an enigma, despite the publication of forty-one encyclicals and over one thousand speeches and messages on an extraordinarily wide range of subjects and issues. He pleased conservatives but upset liberals by suppressing the priest workers in France, but pleased liberals and upset conservatives by taking steps to revise the liturgy and making evening masses possible. Likewise, there was a mixed reaction from the left and the right to his denunciation of atomic weaponry and his 1956 establishment of the Latin American Episcopal Council. Finally, his emphasis on the importance of the laity in the Church and the need to reform the curia dismayed some conservatives, who questioned his commitment to tradition. Liberals and conservatives wondered what he

22. John S. Conway, *The Nazi Persecution of the Churches, 1933–1945* (London: Weidenfeld & Nicolson, 1968), 326.

would have fostered had he convoked the Church council that he had contemplated but did not call. Would he have championed change and liberal reform or would he have reinforced traditionalism? He did not condemn the anti-Judaism in the Church because he did not believe, nor want to believe, it contributed to or facilitated the Nazi racism and genocide. In Church-state relations, Pius continued to conclude concordats to ensure its pastoral and political ends—even with repressive regimes such as Franco's Spain in 1953 and Trujillo's Dominican Republic in 1954. However, since they did not threaten the Church as did Fascism and Nazism, he did not allow the postwar Church, much less the Vatican, to become subordinate to them—as exemplified by the excommunication of Juan Peron (1895–1974), dictator of Argentina, in 1955.

Pius XII's universal vision and his call for an international organization to resolve issues peacefully likewise has often been ignored. It, too, was an important part of his pontificate during which he virtually abandoned the political and diplomatic isolationism of Pius IX (1846–1878) and Pius X (1903–1914) to assume an increasingly internationalist stance, while providing support for the United Nations, which replaced the League of Nations. Often ignored as well is this pope's support of European economic and political integration as a means of easing the suffering of its people, while effecting a reconciliation between victors and vanquished. His vision of a supranational and intergovernmental European union was shared by the Christian Democratic leaders who emerged in the postwar period. In a sense the modern Vatican's adoption of the euro as its currency represents the continuation of a process commenced by Pope Pius XII.

Despite Pius XII's reformism and activity in the religious realm, his belief in technological innovation, adherence to the policy of containment of communism in the cold war, support for the United Nations, and contribution to European integration, the focus on his person and pontificate remains on his "silence" during the Holocaust. This accounts for the opposition of certain groups to his beatification and proposed sainthood. Others insist that the charges against Pius XII are unfounded and continue to press for his beatification and recognition as one of the Church's outstanding figures.

In 2006 the Vatican's Congregation for the Cause of Saints, which assesses a candidate's credentials for this honor, held its first meeting to assess Papa Pacelli's qualifications for beatification. It subsequently declared that Pius XII practiced all the virtues in heroic degree and should be declared venerable. The reaction to the pronouncement was mixed, with some annoyed at the slow pace in the pronouncement of his sainthood, while others complained of any movement in that direction. At the meeting held at the Lateran University, the eighty-nine-year-old Cardinal Fiorenzo Angelini, who knew Pius XII, declared, "Pius must be declared a saint. Admiration isn't enough. People must get moving."[23] On the other hand, the Israeli minister for social affairs, Isaac Herzog, has deemed sainthood for Pius unacceptable. Oded Ben-Hur, the Israeli ambassador to the Holy See, has likewise urged the Vatican to halt the process.[24] At the same time the Jewish-led "Pave the Way Foundation" nominated Pius to be listed among the righteous at the Yad Vashem Holocaust Memorial. To date the petition has not been fulfilled.

Others have invoked delay in the canonization of Pius XII, citing the need to examine all the relevant evidence—and particularly the Vatican archives for the period of the Second World War and the Holocaust, which remain closed. This was the request made to Pope Benedict XVI, by Abraham Lehrer, a Jewish community leader in Cologne.[25] In response a Vatican represen-

23. *Financial Times*, July 29, 2006.
24. "Vatican Urged to Halt Beatification of Pius XII," *The Times* (London), October 27, 2006.
25. *Financial Times*, July 29, 2006.

tative complained that at least fifteen Israeli archives containing references to Pius XII remain closed. In light of the polemic, Benedict XVI did not confirm the proclamation of venerable approved by the commission in 2007, in the hope that the controversy would subside. Even though it did not do so, at the end of 2009 Benedict confirmed the "heroic virtues" of Pius XII along with those of John Paul II. Not surprisingly various individuals and groups complained, including the American Gathering of Holocaust Survivors and Their Descendants who branded the decision on Pius XII "profoundly insensitive and thoughtless," seeing it as "an inevitable blow" to Jewish-Catholic relations.[26] A group of international scholars wrote Pope Benedict XVI urging him to delay Pius XI's beatification until the opening of the Vatican Archives for his pontificate.

In the hope of quieting the outcry, the Reverend Federico Lombardi, acting on behalf of the Vatican, issued a statement asserting that moving Pius closer to sainthood did not represent a hostile act against those who did not believe that Pius XII did enough to stop the Holocaust. Indeed, Father Lombardi sought to differentiate the Christian life of Pope Pius XII from "the historical impact of all his operative decisions,"[27] suggesting that the two were not intimately related. This attempt to separate the religious aspects of the pope's life from the historical consequences of his actions did not prove sufficiently persuasive to end the controversy, leading to the publication of a spate of new books on Pius XII and his policies.

The Vatican has taken a number of other steps to put an end to the polemic that continues to swirl about Pius XII, including the opening of its archives for the years from 1922 to 1939. These and other sources reveal that the pope's policy was not one of

26. Rachel Donadio, "The Pope Moves Two Predecessors Closer to Sainthood," *New York Times*, December 20, 2009, p. 13.
27. Rachel Donadio, "Vatican Defends Decision on Status of Wartime Pope." *New York Times*, December 24, 2009.

indifference to the suffering of the Jews and other victims of the Hitler regime, and that he took a series of steps to assist them. Adherence to impartiality allowed Pius to denounce the principles espoused by the Nazis and Fascists without citing them by name and invoking a retaliation, which would have punished the Church and rendered difficult, if not impossible, its "crusade of charity" on behalf of many of its victims. Thus the conciliatory papal policy toward the Hitler regime was not motivated by love of the Nazis but by fear that a more critical approach would have invoked a brutal response and made matters more difficult for Catholics as well as Jews. On a number of occasions Pius XII revealed that his conciliatory course toward Nazi Germany was designed to "avoid greater evil."

This inevitably leads to the question, "Does the end justify the means?" Pius IX did not believe so, and excommunicated those who united Italy and "stole" his state, refusing to negotiate with the usurpers—who were angelic in comparison to the "satanic" Nazis. Toward the end of 1871 Pio Nono proclaimed, "No, no sort of conciliation is ever possible between Christ and Belial, between light and darkness, between truth and lies, between justice and usurpation."[28] This intransigence, which Marcantonio Pacelli—Pius XII's paternal grandfather—supported, left the pope "a prisoner in the Vatican" and the papacy increasingly isolated. Conciliation and negotiation conducted by Pius XII's mentor Cardinal Pietro Gasparri and Pius XII's brother Francesco Pacelli concluded the Lateran Accords of 1929 which resolved the Roman Question. This and other experiences stretching back to his childhood led Eugenio Pacelli to favor conciliation rather than confrontation.

Professor John Conway has provided one of the few objective assessments of Pope Pius XII's development, noting that Pius was "[u]ndoubtedly a cautious and prudent man, but not the

---

28. Franciscis, *Discorsi del Sommo Pontefice Pio IX*, 1:283–84.

heartless monster of inhumanity portrayed by Hochhuth. It is true that more could have been done by the Catholic Church; it is not true to say that nothing was done."[29] Since the historian's task is to reconstruct and understand past events rather than predict what might have happened, we do not know and cannot know with any degree of certainty whether public papal protests would have helped the victims or made matters worse for them, the papacy, and the Church.[30] The debate continues about whether a more forthright condemnation would have proven more effective in saving lives. Most likely it would have led to a broader and more objective assessment of Pius XII and his pontificate.

29. John S. Conway, "The Holocaust and the Historians," *Annals of the American Academy of Political and Social Science* 450 (July 1980): 163.
30. José M. Sanchez has written an interesting fictional account of what might have happened if someone other than Pacelli had been elected pope in 1939. See his volume *Pope Gabriel: A Counterfactual History* (New York: iUniverse, 2006).

ENCYCLICALS OF POPE PIUS XII

Summi Pontificatus (On the Unity of Human Society), October 20, 1939
Sertum Laetitiae (On the 150th Anniversary of the Establishment of the Hierarchy in the United States), November 1, 1939
Saeculo Exeunte Octavo (On the Eighth Centenary of the Independence of Portugal), June 13, 1940
Mystici Corporis Christi (On the Mystical Body of Christ), June 29, 1943
Divino Afflante Spiritu (On Promoting Biblical Studies), September 30, 1943
Orientalis Ecclesiae (On St. Cyril, Patriarch of Alexandria), April 9, 1944
Communium Interpretes Dolorum (Appealing for Prayers for Peace), April 15, 1945
Orientales Omnes Ecclesias (On the 350th Annivesary of the Reunion of the Ruthenian Church with the Apostolic See), December 23, 1945
Quemadmodum (Pleading for the Care of the World's Destitute Children), January 6, 1946
Deiparae Virginis Mariae (On the Possibility of Defining the Assumption of the Virgin Mary as a Dogma of Faith), May 1, 1946
Fulgens Radiatur (On St. Benedict [of Nursia]), March 21, 1947
Mediator Dei (On the Sacred Liturgy), November 20, 1947
Optatissima Pax (On Prescribing Public Prayers for Social and World Peace), December 18, 1947
Auspicia Quaedam (On Public Prayers for World Peace and Solution of the Problem of Palestine), May 1, 1948
In Multiplicibus Curis (On Prayers for Peace in Palestine), October 24, 1948
Redemptoris Nostri Cruciatus (On the Holy Places in Palestine), April 15, 1949
Anni Sacri (On a Program for Combatting Atheistic Propaganda throughout the World), March 12, 1950
Summi Maeroris (On Public Prayers for Peace), July 19, 1950
Humani Generis (Concerning Some False Opinions Threatening to Undermine the Foundations of Catholic Doctrine), August 12, 1950
Mirabile Illud (On the Crusade of Prayer for Peace), December 6, 1950
Evangelii Praecones (On Promotion of Catholic Missions), June 2, 1951
Sempiternus Rex Christus (On the Council of Chalcedon), September 8, 1951

Ingruentium Malorum (On Reciting the Rosary), September 15, 1951
Orientales Ecclesias (On the Persecuted Eastern Church), December 15, 1952
Doctor Mellifluus (On St. Bernard of Clairvaux), May 24, 1953
Fulgens Corona (Proclaiming a Marian Year), September 8, 1953
Sacra Virginitas (On Consecrated Virginity), March 25, 1954
Ecclesiae Fastos (On St. Boniface), June 5, 1954
Ad Sinarum Gentem (On the Supranationality of the Church), October 7, 1954
Ad Caeli Reginam (On Proclaiming the Queenship of Mary), October 11, 1954
Musicae Sacrae (On Sacred Music), December 25, 1955
Haurietis Aquas (On Devotion to the Sacred Heart), May 15, 1956
Luctuosissimi Eventus (Urging Public Prayer for Peace and Freedom for the People of Hungary), October 28, 1956
Laetamur Admodum (Renewing Exhortation for Prayers for Peace for Poland, Hungary, and the Middle East), November 1, 1956
Datis Nuperrime (Lamenting the Sorrowful Events in Hungary and Condemning the Ruthless Use of Force), November 5, 1956
Fidei Donum (On the Present Condition of the Catholic Missions, especially in Africa), April 21, 1957
Invicti Athletae (On St. Andrew Bobola), May 16, 1957
La Pèlerinage de Lourdes (Warning against Materialism), July 2, 1957
Miranda Prorsus (On Motion Pictures, Radio, and Television), September 8, 1957
Ad Apostolorum Principis (On Communism and the Church in China), June 29, 1958
Meminisse Iuvat (On Prayers for the Persecuted Church), July 14, 1958

BIBLIOGRAPHY

NOTES ON SELECTED SOURCES

Archivio Centrale dello Stato, Roma Contains interesting reports on Vatican developments, including the reports of Fascist spies on events and activities in the Vatican.

Archivio di Stato di Roma A number of the files and papers of the State Archive of Rome, particularly the documents of the Consiglio di Stato and those of the Carte Miscellanea Politiche O Riservate, provide an important perspective on papal and Vatican developments.

Archivio Segreto del Vaticano, or the Secret Vatican Archives (ASV) This remains a crucial primary source for a study of the papacy and the political and diplomatic formation of Eugenio Pacelli, who became Pius XII in 1939. Deemed secret because the nucleus of this present collection originated in the *bibliotheca secreta* of Sixtus IV (1471–1484), it had earlier been open only to select scholars. Pope Leo XIII in 1880 opened it for general consultation. Although the documents made available were originally restricted to the early modern period, in 1967 the ASV was opened for the long pontificate of Pius IX (1846–1878)—which had a profound infuence on the grandfather of Eugenio, his son Filippo, and his grandchildren, including Eugenio who shared his apartment. Subsequently the ASV was opened for the pontificates of popes from Leo XIII (1878–1903) through Benedict XV (1914–1922). The papers of Leo XIII (1878–1903) and Pius X (1903–1914) shed light on Pacelli's early life and career, while those of Benedict XV (1914–1922) provide insights into the papacy's search for peace and Pacelli's mission to Austria-Hungary and the German Empire, which contributed to making him a Germanophile. At the dawn of the twenty-first century popes John Paul II (1978–2005) and Benedict XVI (2005–) opened most of the documents of Pope Pius XI (1922–1939), during which Eugenio Pacelli served as nuncio to Germany (1922–1929) and then secretary of state.

Acta Apostolicae Sedis, or *Acts of the Apostolic See (AAS)* This is the official journal of the Holy See containing laws, pronouncements, and addresses of the pope as well as the major documents issued by the various departments of the

267

Vatican. Following Pius X's constitution *Promulgandi* of September 29, 1908, the *AAS* has appeared since January 1909 as the official publication of the Holy See. It followed and replaced the *Acta Sanctae Sedis* (ASS), which served a similar function but did not enjoy its official character. Decisions and decrees published in it are officially promulgated, becoming effective three months from the date of issue.

Annuario Pontificio, or *Papal Yearbook,* or *Annual Papal Directory* Presently published by the Libreria Editrice Vaticana and printed by the Vatican Polyglot Press, some have traced the *Annuario* back to the compendium *Notizie,* first put out by the Holy See during the pontificate of Clement XI (1700–1721). During the pontificate of Pius IX (1846–1878) it was rechristened the *Annuario Pontificio,* and it was termed the *Annuaire pontifical catholique* in the later 1890s. Declared an official publication during the pontificate of Leo XIII (1878–1903), this reference source was ended in 1924, but it is still deemed essential for an understanding of yearly developments in the Church. It provides a wealth of statistical information regarding the Church, the biography and acts of the reigning pope, the cardinals and their sees, as well as biographical notes. At the same time, each yearly edition provides a list of members of the hierarchy and officials. Its articles are valuable for historical as well as ecclesiastical information.

Carlen, Sister M. Claudia, ed. *A Guide to the Encyclicals of the Roman Pontiffs from Leo XIII to the Present Day: 1878–1937.* New York: H.W.Wilson, 1939. This volume catalogues excerpts from the papal encyclicals from Pope Leo XIII through some of those of Pope Pius XI. Summaries of other papal encyclicals and pronouncements are found in Sister Carlen's two-volume work on papal pronouncements.

Carlen, Sister M. Claudia, ed. *The Papal Encyclicals.* 5 vols. Ann Arbor, Michigan: Pierian Press, 1981. (*PE*) In these five volumes, the editor has included the formal circular letters written by, or under the authority of, the modern popes from 1740 to 1981. Presently these encyclicals are almost exclusively papal documents. These letters and epistles are addressed explicitly to the patriarchs, primates, archbishops, and bishops of the universal Church in communion with the Holy See and thus to the faithful. Since the pontificate of John XXIII some of these letters have also been addressed to all persons of goodwill. By and large the epistles address a specific issue and often focus on a problem in a particular country. The letters generally have a broader audience. Sister Carlen also has produced a guide to the more recent encyclicals (see above).

Carlen, Sister M. Claudia, ed. *Papal Pronouncements. A Guide: 1740–1978.* Vol. 1, *Benedict XIV to Paul VI;* Vol. 2, *Paul VI to John Paul I.* Ann Arbor, Mich.: Pieran Press, 1990. (*PP*) These two volumes provide an authoritative guide not only to the encyclicals of the popes from the mid-eighteenth century to the present but also to many of their published allocutions—addresses delivered by the pope from the throne to the cardinals in secret consistory—as well as many sermons, *motu proprios* or papal decrees, and homilies and sermons, and even some radio messages. Listed in alpabetical order, the entries indicate the classification of the document, estimated length, and the occasion for its publication or its addressee, as well as an abstract of its contents. Within almost one thousand pages are included more than five thousand documents shedding light on the history of the modern papacy.

La Civiltà Cattolica This fortnightly review is a semiofficial journal of the Vatican under the direction of the Society of Jesus. Founded in Naples by Father Carlo M. Curci, assisted by Fathers Bresciani, Liberatore, and Zaparelli, with the blessing of Pius IX (1846–1878), it moved to Rome in 1853. Despite the tribulations of a stormy pontificate, the review maintained a continuous publication there from 1853 to 1870, moving to Florence at the end of 1870 to protest the Italian seizure of the Eternal City. The *Civiltà* returned to Rome in 1888, establishing its offices in the Via di Ripetta where it has remained. The articles in this review provide insights into papal thought and policy on social, religious, and politic issues, for the editors have remained consistently loyal to the Vatican.

Colección de enciclicas y otras cartas de los papas Gregorio XVI, Leon XIII, Pio X, Benedicto XV y Pio XI. Madrid: Ses hermanos, 1935. This collection makes available to a Spanish-speaking audience a series of encylicals and other papal papers and documents, including those of Gregory XVI (1831–1846), Leo XIII (1874–1903), Pius X (1903–1914), Benedict XV (1914–1922), and Pius XI (1922–1939).

Koenig, Harry C., ed. *Principles for Peace: Selections from Papal Documents from Leo XIII to Pius XII.* Washington, D.C.: National Catholic Welfare Conference, 1943. In the almost seven hundred pages of this volume, the editor has included papal documents and positions on many of the major contemporary religious, political, and social issues from the l870s through the pontificate of Pius XI (1922–1939).

L'Osservatore Romano The Roman Observer is considered the daily newspaper of the Holy See and has existed in its present form since 1861, when a group of laymen led by Marcantonio Pacelli, Eugenio's paternal grandfather, felt the need for its presence to protect the spiritual and temporal power of the papacy. It had predecessors in 1849 and 1851, but *L'Osservatore Romano* has only functioned as a daily since 1861. Since that time it has served as an important source of information on the activities and actions of the pontiff, justifying its position as the "official" newspaper of the papacy. Although begun as an independent organ, after 1870 it functioned as the authoritative, but unofficial organ of the Holy See, printing the texts of papal speeches along with official pronouncements and announcements. Its editors are appointed by the papal Secretariat of State. While it is printed in Italian every day of the week except Sunday, there are weekly editions in English, German, Spanish, French, and other languages, for a total of eight. An Italian Sunday edition is published separately, known as *L'Osservatore della Domenica*. It has been published in Vatican City since the Lateran Accords of 1929.

BIBLIOGRAPHY

Ufficio Informazioni Vaticano. *Prigionieri di Guerra* (1939–1947) The Vatican Information Service, which employed over five hundred individuals, provided news of, and in some cases contact with, prisoners in World War II. Its files, located in the ASV, provide some indication of papal efforts to assist the victims of the conflict.

ARCHIVES

Archives de Ministère des affaires Etrangerès, Paris.
Archivio Centrale dello Stato, Rome.
Archivio della Congregazione della Fede.
Archivio della Nunziatura Apostolica in Monaco.
Archivio della Sacra Cogregazione per gli Affari Ecclesiastici Straordinaari.
Archivio Segreto del Vaticano or the Secret Vatican Archives.
Archivio storico del Ministero degli affair esteri, Rome
Papers of James Grover McDonald in the Herbert Lehman Papers of the School of International Affairs, Columbia Univesity, New York.
Public Records Office, London.
U.S. Holocaust Museum Archives, Washington, D.C. A series of documents from the Vatican Archive, 1865–1939.

PUBLISHED PRIMARY SOURCES

Acta Apostolicae Sedis. Commentarium Officiale. Vol. 23 (1931) to vol. 40 (1948). Rome: Vatican Press, 1931–1948.
Acta Nuniature Polanae: Achilles Ratti (1918–1921). Rome: Institum Historicum Polonicum, 1995.
Acta Romana Societatis Iesu. Vol. 7 (1932–1934); vol. 9 (1938–1940). Rome: Vatican Press, 1933–1940.
Acta Sanctae Sedis (Compendium of Documents of the Holy See). 1865–1908.
Acta Synodalia Concilii Vaticani Secundi. Vatican City: Editrice Vaticani, 1965.
Acta Summi Pontificis Joannis XXIII. Vatican City: Typis Polyglottis, 1960, 1964.
Actes de Benoit XV: Encycliques, motu proprio, brefs. Paris: Bonne Presse, 1926–1934.
Actes de Leon XIII: Encycliques, motu proprio, brefs, allocutions, actes des dicastres. Paris: Bonne Presse, 1931–1937.
Actes di S.S. Pie XI: Encycliques, motu proprio, brefs, allocutions, actes des dicastres. Paris: Bonne Presse, 1932–1936.
Actes et documents de Saint Siège relatifs à la seconde guerrre mondiale. 11 vols. Edited by P. Blet et al. Rome: Liberia Editrice Vaticana, 1965–1981.
L'Action Francais.
Alfieri, Dino. *Dictators Face to Face.* Translated by David Moore. Westport, Conn.: Greenwood Press, 1978.
Angelini, Fiorenzo. *Pio XII, Discorsi Ai Medici.* Rome: Libreria Editrice Vaticana, 1959.

Annuario Pontificio, or *Papal Yearbook*, or *Annual Papal Directory*. Libreria Editrice Vaticana.

Appeals for Peace of Pope Benedict XV and Pope Pius XI. Washington, D.C.: Catholic Association for International Peace, 1931.

Belardo, Mario, ed. *Patti lateranensi, convenzioni e accordi successivi fra il Vaticano e l'Italia fino al 31 dicembre 1945*. Vatican City: Tipografia Poliglotta Vaticana, 1972.

Bellocchi, Ugo, ed. *Tutte le encicliche e i principali documenti Pontifici emanati dal 1740: 250 anni di storia visti dalla Santa Sede: Vol. 11. Pio XII (1939–1958), Parte prima 1939–1949*. Vatican City: Libreria Editrice Vaticana 2004.

Berenbaum, Michael, ed. *Witness to the Holocaust*. New York: Harper-Collins, 1997.

Bertetto, Domenico, ed. *Discorsi di Pio XI*. Turin: Società Editrice Internazionale, 1959.

———, ed. *Pio XII e l'umana sofferenza. Edizione italiana del magistero di Pio XII sul Dolore*. Rome: Edizioni paoline, 1961.

Bertone, Domenico, ed. *Discorsi di Pio XI*. Turin: Società Editrice Internazionale, 1959.

Beyrens, Eugene. *Quatre ans à Rome*. Paris: Plon, 1934.

Blet, Pierre, ed. *Lettres de Pie XII aux Eveques Allemands 1939–1944*. Vatican City: Libreria Editrice Vaticana, 1966.

———. *Pie XII et la Seconde Guerre Mondiale après les Archives du Vatican*. Paris: Perrin, 1997.

Blet, Pierre, Angelo Martini, and Burkhard Schneider, eds. *Records and Documents of the Holy See Relating to the Second World War*. Vol. 1, *The Holy See and the War in Europe March 1939–August 1940*. Translated by Gerard Noel. Washington, D.C.: Corpus Books, 1968.

Bondioli, P., ed. *Allocuzioni e messaggi natalizi di S.S. Pio XII (1939–1942)*. Milan, 1943.

Braga, Carlo. *La riforma liturgica di Pio XII. Documenti*. Vol. 1, *La "memoria sulla riforma liturgica."* Rome: Edizione Liturgiche, 2003.

Breitman, Richard, et al., eds. *Advocates for the Doomed: The Diaries and Papers of James G. McDonald*. Bloomington: Indiana University Press, 2007.

Bressan, Edoardo. "L'Osservatore Romano e le relazioni internazionali della Santa Sede (1917–1922)." In *Benedetto XV e la Pace—1918*, edited by G. Rumi, 233–53. Brescia: Morcelliana, 1990.

Brüning, Heinrich. *Memoiren, 1918–1934*. Stuttgart: Deutsche Verlags-Anstalt, 1970.

Capovilla, Loris, ed. *Giovanni XXIII, Lettere 1958–1963*. Rome: Edizioni di Storia e Letteratura, 1978.

Carlen, Sister Claudia, ed. *A Guide to the Encyclicals of Roman Pontiffs from Leo XIII to the Present Day, 1878–1937*. New York: H. W. Wilson, 1939.

———, ed. *Guide to the Documents of Pope Pius XII*. Westminster, Md., 1955.

———, ed. *The Papal Encyclicals*. Vol. 2, *1878–1903*; Vol. 3, *1903–1939*; Vol. 4, *1938–1958*. Ann Arbor, Mich.: Pierian Press, 1990.

———. ed. *Papal Pronouncements. A Guide: 1740–1978*. Vol. 1, *Benedict XIV*

to *Paul VI;* Vol. 2, *Paul VI to John Paul I.* Ann Arbor, Mich.: Pierian Press, 1990.
Casella, Mario. "La crisi del 1938 fra Stato e Chiesa nella documentazione dell' Archivio Storico Diplomatico degli Affari Esteri." *Rivista dei Storia della Chiesa,* in *Italia* 54 (January–June 2000): 91–186.
Cavagna, A., ed. *Pio XI e L'Azione cattolica. Documenti.* 3rd ed. Rome: Ferrari, 1933.
Cavalleri, Ottavio, and Germano Gualdo, eds. *L'Archivio de Mons. Achille Ratti Visitatore apostolico e nunzio a Varsavia (1918–1921).* Vatican City: Archivio Vaticano, 1990.
Caveterra, Emilio. *Processo a Pio XII. Intervista con P. Raimondo Spiazzi. Opinioni di De Felice, Del Noce, Valsecchi.* Milan: Pan, 1979.
Charles-Roux, François. *Huit ans au Vatican.* Paris: Flammarion, 1947.
Chinigo, Michael, ed. *The Pope Speaks: The Teachings of Pope Pius XII.* New York: Pantheon Books, 1957.
Cianfara, Camille M. *The War and the Vatican.* London: Burns, Oates and Washbourne, 1945.
Ciano, Galeazzo. *The Ciano Diaries, 1939–1943.* Edited by H. Gibson. Garden City, N.Y.: 1945.
———. *Diplomatic Papers.* London: Oldhams Press, 1948.
———. *L' Europa verso la catasrofe.* Verona: Mondadori, 1948.
———. *Diario.* Milan: Rizzoli, 1950.
———. *Hidden Diaries.* New York: Dutton and Co., 1953.
Ciprotti, Pio, and Anna Talamanca, eds. *I concordati di Pio XII (1939–1958) (Belgio, Germania, Portogallo, Spagna, Argentina, Bolivia, Colombia, Rep. Domenicana, Haiti).* Milan: Giuffrè, 1970.
La Civiltà Cattolica. 1850 to present.
Codex Iuris Canonici Pii X. Rome: Polyglottis Vaticana, 1947.
Collección de Enciclicas y Otras Cartas de los Papas Gregory XVI, Leon XIII, Pio X, Benedicto XV y Pio XI. Madrid: Ses Hermanos, 1935.
Collins, Joseph B., ed. *Catechetical Documents of Pope Pius X.* New York: Saint Anthony Guild Press, 1946.
———, ed. *Pius X: Catechical Documents of.* Paterson, N.J.: St. Anthony Guild Press, 1946.
Correspondence between President Roosevelt and Pope Pius XII. New York: Macmillan, 1947.
Correspondence between President Truman and Pope Pius XII. New York: n.p., 1952.
Crispolti, Filippo. *Pio IX, Leone XIII, Pio X, Benedetto XV. Ricordi personali.* Milan: Treves, 1932.
Dalla Torre, Giuseppe. *Memorie.* Milan: Mondadori, 1965.
De Gasperi, Alcide. *Lettere sul Concordato.* Brescia: Marcelina, 1979.
Di Ci, Pietro Elle, ed. *I papi e l'Europa. Documenti: Pio XII, Giovanni XXIII, Paolo VI.* Rome: Leumann, 1978.
Di Nolfo, Ennio. *Vaticano e Stati Uniti 1939–1952. Dalle carte di Myron C. Taylor.* Milan: Franco Angeli Editore, 1978.

Discorsi e Radio Messagi di Sua Santità Pio XII. 2 vols. Milan: Società Editrice "Vita e Pensiero," 1941.

Discorsi indirizzati dai sommi pontifeci Pio XI, Pio XII, Giovanni XXIII, Paolo I, Giovanni Paolo II alla Pontificia Accademia delle Scienze dal 1936 al 1986. Vatican City: Pontificiae Academiae, 1986.

Discorsi, messaggi, colloqui del Santo Padre Giovanni XXIII. 5 vols. Vatican City: Tipografia Poliglotta, 1961–1967.

Discourses of the Popes from Pius XI to John Paul II to the Pontifical Academy of Sciences, 1936–1986. Vatican City: Pontificia Academia Scientiarum, 1986.

Documentos Inéditos para la Historia del Generalisimo Franco. Madrid: Colección del Estudios Contemporáneos, 1991.

Documents Diplomatiques Français. Paris: Imprimerie Nationale, 1931–1939.

Documents on British Foreign Policy, series 2, vol. 5, no. 342. London: H.M.S.O., 1956.

Doenitz, Karl. *Memoirs: Ten Years and Twenty Days.* Westport, Conn.: Greenwood Press, 1959.

Doyle, Charles Hugo. *A Day with the Pope.* Garden City, N.Y.: Doubleday, 1950.

Dulles, Avery, and Leon Klenicki, eds. *Holocaust Never to Be Forgotten. Reflections on the Holy See's Document "We Remember."* New York: Paulist Press, 2001

Eade, Charles. *Winston Churchill's Secret Session Speeches.* New York: Simon & Schuster, 1946.

Enchiridion delle encicliche. Ediz. bilingue. Vol. 6: Pio XII (1939–1958). Bologna: Edizioni Dehoniane, 2003.

Faulhaber, Michael Von. *Judaism, Christianity and Germany.* Translated by George D. Smith. New York: Macmillan, 1934

Federzoni, Luigi. *Diario di un ministro del fascismo.* Edited by Adriana Macchi. Florence: Pasigli Editori, 1993.

Fontenelle, René, and Mary Elizabeth Fowler. *His Holiness Pope Pius XI.* London: Catholic Book Club, 1939.

Foundations for Peace: Letters of Pope Pius XII and President Roosevelt. London: Catholic Truth Society, 1941.

Fremantle, Anne, ed. *The Papal Encyclicals in Their Historical Context.* New York: G. P. Putnam's Sons, 1956.

Galeazzi-Lisi, Riccardo. *Dans l'ombre et la lumière de Pie XII.* Paris: Flammarion, 1960.

German Parliamentary Debates, 1848–1933. New York: Peter Lang, 2003.

Gilbert, G. M. *Nurenberg Diary.* New York: New American Library, 1961.

Giorani, Igino, ed. *Encicliche sociali dei papi.* Rome: Editrice Studium, 1942.

Giordano, Nicola, ed. *"Provida Mater" e "Primo feliciter" di Pio XII. Validità ed attualità degli istituti secolari.* Rome: Monopoli, 1997.

Giovanni Battisa Montini Giovane. Documenti indite e testimonianze. Turin: Marietta, 1979.

Goebbels, Joseph. *Goebbels Diaries: 1939–1941.* Translated by F. Taylor. New York: Putnam's Sons, 1983.

———. *Goebbels Diaries: 1942–1943*. Translated by Louis Lochner. Garden City: Doubleday, 1948.

Great Britain, Foreign Office. *British Documents on the Origins of the War, 1898–1914*. Edited by George P. Gooch and Harold Temperly. London: H.M.S.O., 1926.

Hachey, Thomas E., ed. *Anglo-Vatican Relations, 1914–1939: Confidential Reports of the British Minister to the Holy See*. Boston: G.K. Hall, 1972.

Haecker, Theodor. *Journal in the Night*. Translated by A. Dru. New York: Pantheon Books, 1950.

Haffner, Paul, ed. *Discourses of the Pope from Pius XI to John Paul II to the Pontifical Academy of Sciences*. Vatican City: Pontifical Academy of Sciences, 1986

Herzl, Theodor. *Diaries*. Translated by Marvin Lowental. New York: Dial Press, 1956.

Hilberg, Raul. *The Destruction of the European Jews*. Chicago: Quadrangle Books, 1961.

Hill, E., ed. *Die Weizsäcker Papiere, 1933–1950*. Frankfurt: Allstein, 1974.

Hill, Leonidas. "The Vatican Embassy of Ernst von Weizsacker, 1943–1945." *Journal of Modern History* 39 (1967): 138–59.

Hitler, Adoph. *Mein Kampf*. Translated by Ralph Manheim. Boston: Houghton-Mifflin, 1943.

———. *Hitler's Secret Conversations*. Translated N. Cameron and R. Stevens. New York: Farrar, Straus, and Cudahy, 1953.

Hlond, Cardinal H.E. *Persecution: The Catholic Church in German-Occupied Poland: Reports by H.E. Cardinal Hlond, Primate of Poland, to Pope Pius XII*. New York: Longmans, Green, 1941.

Hürten, Heinz. "Die Briefe Pius XII an die deutschen Bischöfe zur Kriegszeit. Ezentrale Quelle für seine Amtsauffassung." *Annali dell'Istituto Storico Italo-Germanico in Trento* 31 (2005): 355–65.

I Documenti Diplomatici Italiani, 9th series, 1939–1943. Rome: Libreria dello Stato, 1959.

Il magistero mariano di Pio XII. Edizione italiana di tutti i documenti mariani di Bertetto. Rome: Edizioni Paoline, 1960.

Inter Arma Caritas: Uffizio Informazioni Vaticano per I prigionieri di guerra istituito Pio XII (1939–1947). Vatican City: Archivio Segreto Vaticano, 2004.

International Catholic-Jewish Historical Commission. *The Vatican and the Holocaust: A Preliminary Report*. Submitted to the Holy See's Commission for Religious Relations with Jews, 2000. Printed in *Origins*, published by the Catholic News Service, November 9, 2000.

Katholische Kirche in Dritten Reich. Eine Aufsatzsammlung zum Verhältnis vom Papsttum, Episkopat, und deutschen Katoliken zum Nationalsozialismus 1933–1945. Mainz: Grünewald, 1976.

Kelp, Rosabelle, ed. *Sixteen Encyclicals of Pope Pius XI*. Washington, D.C.: National Catholic Welfare Conference, 1939.

Kennan, George. *Memoirs, 1925–1940*. Boston: Little Brown, 1967.

Kenzler, George, and V. Fabricus, eds. *Die Kirchen in dritten Reich*. Frankfurt: Fisher, 1984.

Kertesz, G. A., ed. *Documents in the Political History of the European Continent, 1815–1939*. Oxford: Clarendon Press, 1968.

Klemperer, Victor. *I Will Bear Witness: A Diary of the Nazi Years*. New York: Random House, 1999.

———. *The Lesser Evil: The Diaries of Victor Klemperer, 1945–1959*. London: Weidenfeld & Nicolson, 2003.

Koenig, Harry C., ed. *Principles for Peace: Selections from Papal Documents from Leo XIII to Pius XII*. Washington, D.C.: National Catholic Welfare Conference, 1943.

La Pira, Giorgio. *Beatissimo padre. Lettere a Pio XII*. Edited by Andrea Riccardi and Isabella Piersanti. Milan: Mondadori, 2004.

Lehnert, Pascalina. *Pio XII. Il prilegio di servivlo*. Milan: Rusconi, 1984.

———. *Ich durfte Ihm dienen, Erinneringen an Papst Pius XII*. Würzburg: Naumann, 1986.

Lettmann, Reinhard, and Heinrich Mussinghoff, eds. *Il Leone di Münster e Hitler. Clemens August Cardinale von Galen. La sua attività episcopale nel periodo della dittatura Nazionalsocialista in Germania*. Rome: Herder, 1996.

Lettres apostoliques de S.S. Pie X. Encycliques, motu proprio, brefs, allocutions, actes des dicastres. 8. vols. Paris: Bonne Press, 1930–1936.

Lieber, Robert, S.J. "Pius as I Knew Him." *The Catholic Mind* 57 (1959): 292–304.

———. "Pius XII," *Stimmen der Zeit* (Freiburg) 163 (1958–1959): 81 ff.

Lloyd George, David. *War Memoirs*. Vol 4. Boston: Little, Brown, 1937.

Löffler, Peter. *Bischof Clemens August Graf von Galen. Akten, Briefe und Predigten 1933–1946*. Vol. 1: *1933–1939*. Mainz: Grünewald, 1988.

Ludwig, Emil. *Talks with Mussolini*. Boston: Little, Brown, 1933.

Macmillan, Harold. *The Blast of War, 1939–1945*. New York: Harper & Row, 1968.

Malvezzi, N., ed. *Pio XI niei suoi sritti*. Milan: Treves, 1923.

Manhattan, Avro. *The Vatican in World Politics*. New York: GAER Associates, 1949.

Mariaux, W., ed. *Persecution: The Catholic Church in the Third Reich*. London: Burns & Oates, 1940.

McCormick, Anne O'Hare. *Vatican Journal, 1921–1954*. New York: Farrar, Straus, and Cudahy, 1957.

Mendelson, John. "The Holocaust: Rescue and Relief: Documentation in the National Archives." *Annals of the American Academy of Political and Social Science* 450 (July 1980): 237–49.

Merry del Val, Cardinal Raphael. *Memories of Pope Pius X*. Westminster, N.Y.: D. O'Conner Press, 1999.

Miccoli, Giovanni. *Chiesa e società in Italia dal concilio Vaticano I (1870) a pontificato di Giovanni XXIII: Vol. 1. Documenti*. Turin: Einaudi, 1973.

Migliorati, Vittorio. *Le chiese del silenzio. Testimonianze dirette*. Naples: La Nuova Cultura, 2003.

Momigliano, Eucardio, ed. *Tutte le encicliche dei sommi Pontefici.* Milan: dall' Oglio editore, 1959.
Montini, Giovanni Battista. "Pius XII and the Jews." *The Tablet* (London), July 6, 1963; reprinted in *Commonweal,* February 28, 1964, pp. 651–52.
Morgan, Thomas B. *A Reporter at the Papal Court: A Narrative of the Reign of Pope Pius XI.* New York: Longman, Green, 1937.
———. *The Listening Post: Eighteen Years on Vatican Hill.* New York: Putnam, 1944.
Mussolini, Benito. "Gli Accordi di Laterano." *Discorsi al Parlamento.* Rome: Litorio, 1929.
Napolitano, Matteo Luigi, and Andrea Tornielli. *Il Papa che salvò gli Ebrei. Dagli archive segreti vaticani tutta la verità su Pio XII.* Casale Monferrato: Piemme, 2004.
———. "Eugenio Pacelli diplomatico nell'archivio di famiglia." *Incipit* 1, no. 2 (July–August 2007): 39–43.
Official German Documents Relating to the World War. New York: Oxford University Press, 1923.
O'Reilly, Bernard. *Life of Leo XIII. From an Authentic Memoir Furnished by His Order.* New York: John Winston, 1903.
Pacelli, Eugenio. *La personalità e la territorialità delle leggi, specialmente del Diritto Canonico.* Vatican City: Poliglotta Vaticana, 1912.
———. *Discorsi e Panegirici.* Milan: Società editrice "Vita e Pensiero," 1939.
Pacelli, Filippo. *Sulla tutela del patrimonio artistico e scientifico.* Rome: n.p., 1891.
Pacelli, Francesco. *Diario della Conciliazione.* Vatican City: Libreria Editrice Vaticana, 1959.
Pagano, Sergio, Marcel Chappin, and Giovanni Coco, eds. *I fogli di udienza del Cardinale Eugenio Pacelli segretario di stato (1930).* Vatican City: Archivio Segreto del Vaticano, 2010.
Passelecq, Georges, and Bernard Suchecky. *The Hidden Encyclical of Pius XI.* Translated from the French by Steven Rendall. New York: Harcourt Brace, 1997.
Persecution of the Catholic Church in the Third Reich: Facts and Documents. London: Burns & Oates, 1940.
Picciotto Fargion, Liliana. *L'occupazione tedesca e gli ebrei di Roma. Documenti e fatti.* Rome: Carucci, 1979.
Pii X Pontificis Maximi Acta, or *Acta Pio X.* 5 vols. Rome: Typographia Vaticana, 1905–1914.
Pio XII. *La Allocuzione nel consistorio Segreto del 12 Gennaio 1953.* In *Pio XII, Discorsi e Radio Messagi di Sua Santita.* Vatican City, 1953.
———. *Discorsi e Radio Messaggi di Sua Santita Pio XII, 1939–1958.* 20 vols. Vatican City.
———. *Pio XII parla alla chiesa del silenzio.* Introduction by Jean Pierre Dubois-Dumée, edited by Alberto Giovannetti. Documenti pontifici 5. Milan: Biblioteca cattolica, 1958.
———. *Scritti e discorsi di S. Santità Pio XII nel 1958.* Siena: Cantagalli, 1959.

BIBLIOGRAPHY 277

Pio XII, vescovo di Roma, Pontificia Opera per la preservazione della fede e la costruzione di nuove chiese in Roma. Rome, 1958.

Pius XII. *Pope Speaks: The Words of Pius XII.* New York: Harcourt, Brace, 1940.

———. *Mind of Pius XII.* By Pius XII. New York: Crown Publishers, 1955.

———. *Guide for Living: An Approved Selection of Letters and Addresses of His Holiness Pope Pius XII.* New York: Longman, 1969.

Pius XII and Peace, 1939–1940. Washington, D.C.: National Catholic Welfare Conference, 1940.

The Pope and the People: Select Letters and Addresses on Social Questions by Pope Leo XII, Pope Pius X, Pope Benedict XV and Pope Pius XI. London: Catholic Truth Society, 1932.

Pope Pius and Poland: A Documentary Outline of Papal Pronouncements and Relief Efforts on Behalf of Poland, since March 1939. New York: American Press, 1942.

Raganella, L. *Diario di Roma in Guerra (1943–44).* Rome: Bulzoni, 1991.

Ratti, Achille. *Essays in History.* Freeport, N.Y.: Books for Libraries, 1967.

Rendtorff, R., and H. H. Henrix, eds. *Die Kirchen und das Judentum.* Paderborn: Bonifatius Press, 1988.

Riccardo, Andrea, ed. *Pio XII.* Rome-Bari: Laterza, 1984.

Rogari, Sandro. *Santa Sede e Fascismo. Con Documenti Inediti.* Correggio: Forni Editore, 1977.

Roncalli, Angelo. *Scritti e discorsi, 1953–1958.* 4 vols. Rome: Paoline, 1959–1962.

———. *La mia vita in Oriente, Agendo del delegato apostolico. Vol. 2: 1940–1944.* Bologna: Istituto per le Scienze Religiose, 2008.

Rosenberg, Alfred. *The Myth of theTwentieth Century.* Torrance, Calif.: Noontide Press, 1930.

Ryan, James H., ed. *Encyclicals of Pius XI.* London: Herder, 1927.

Sale, Giovanni. *Hitler, la Santa Sede e gli Ebrei. Con documenti dell'Archivio Segreto Vaticano.* Milan: Jaca Book, 2004.

Schaefer, Mary C. *A Papal Peace Mosaic, 1878–1936. Excerpts from the Messages of Popes Leo XIII, Pius X, Benedict XV, and Pius XI.* Washington, D.C.: Catholic Association for International Peace, 1936.

Schneider, Burkhard, ed. *Die briefe Pius XII an die Deutschen Bischofe 1939–1944.* Mainz: Gruenwald, 1966.

Scoppola, Pietro, ed. *La Chiesa e il Fascismo. Documenti e Interpretazioni.* Bari: Laterza, 1971.

Selected Documents of His Holiness Pope Pius XII: 1939–1958. Washington, D.C.:National Catholic Welfare Conference, n.d.

Selected Papal Encyclicals and Letters, 1928–1931. London: Catholic Truth Society,1932.

Shire, William L. *Berlin Diary: The Journal of a Foreign Correspondent, 1934–1941.* New York: Alfred A. Knopf, 1941.

Sonnino, Sidney. *Diario, 1914–1916.* Bari: Laterza, 1972.

Speer, Albert. *Inside the Third Reich.* New York: Avon Books, 1970.

Stasiewki, Bernhard, ed. *Akten deutscher Bischöfe über die Lage der Kirche, 1933–1945.* Mainz: Grünewald, 1968.

Tapia de Renedo, Benedicto. *Pio XII. ¿Inocente o culpable? Confrontacion de documentos secretos*. Madrid: Iberico, 1972.

Tardini, Domenico. "Diario inedito di Domenico Tardini (1933–1936)." In Carte di Tardini, ASV.

———. ed. *Pio XII*. Vatican City: Tipografia Poliglotta, 1960.

———. *Memories of Pius XII*. Westminister, Md.: Newman Press, 1961.

Taylor, Myron C., ed. *Wartime Correspondence between President Roosevelt and Pope Pius XII*. New York: Macmillan, 1947; reprinted New York: DaCapo, 1975.

Thierry, Jean Jacques. *Journal sans titre. Sur les écrits de Pie XII*. Paris: Juillard, 1970.

Tittman, Harold Jr. *Inside the Vatican of Pius XII. The Memoir of an American Diplomat during World War II*. New York: Doubleday, 2004.

Treaty and Concordat between the Holy See and Italy: Official Documents. Washington, D.C.: National Catholic Welfare Conference, 1929.

Unione giuristi cattolici italiani, ed. *Diritto e giustizia nel magistero pontificio. Da Pio XII a Giovanni Paolo II*. Rome: Studium, 1998.

U.S. Department of State. *Papers Relating to the Foreign Relations of the United States: The World War*. Washington, D.C., 1917–1918.

———. *Papers Relating to the Foreign Relations of the United States (1931–1939)*. Washington, D.C.: Government Printing Office.

Vatican Commission for Religious Relations with the Jews. "We Remember: A Reflection on the 'Shoah.'" *L'Osservatore Romano* (English edition), March 18, 1998.

Vatican Statement on Venerable Pius XII. Available at *http://www.zenit.org/article-27926?l=english*.

Velati, Maura, ed. *Diari di Angelo Giuseppe Roncalli/Giovanni XXIII. Pater amabilis. Agende del pontifice, 1958–1963*. Bologna: Istituto per le scienze religioso, 2007.

Volk, Ludwig, ed. *Akten Kardinal Michael von Faulhaber, 1917–1945*. Mainz: Grünewald, 1978.

Weisbraid, Robert G., and Wallace P. Sillanpoa. *The Chief Rabbi, the Pope, and the Holocaust: An Era of Vatican-Jewish Relations*. New Brunswick, N.J.: Transaction, 1992.

Wilk, Stanislavs. *Ed. Achille Ratti*. Vols 1–5. Rome: Institum Historicum Polonium Romae, 1995–1999.

Wiseman, Cardinal Nicholas Patrick. *Recollections of the Last Four Popes and of Rome in Their Times*. New York: Wagner, 1958.

Wynne, John J., ed. *The Great Encyclical Letters of Pope Leo XIII*. New York: Benziger Brothers, 1903.

Yzermans, Vincent A., ed. *All Things in Christ: Encyclicals and Selected Documents of Saint Pius X*. New York: Newman Press, 1954.

———, ed. *The Major Addresses of Pope Pius XII*. St. Paul, Minn.: North Central Publishing, 1961.

Zolli, Eugene. *Before the Dawn*. New York: Sheed & Ward, 1954.

BIBLIOGRAPHY

SECONDARY SOURCES

Aarons, Mark, and John Loftus. *Unholy Trinity: How the Vatican's Nazi Networks Betrayed Western Intelligence to the Soviets.* New York: St. Martins Press, 1991.

Acerbi, Antonio. "Pio XII e L'Ideologia dell'Occidente." In *Riccardi, Pio XII,* 149–78.

Adler, Joseph. "The Dreyfus Affair." *Midstream* 48, no. 1 (January 2002): 29–32.

Alberigo, Giuseppe, ed. Chiese italiane e Concilio. Esperienze pastorali nella Chiesa italiana tra Pio XII e Paolo VI. Genoa: Marietti, 1988.

———. "Pio XII: Uno sconosciuto." *Cristianesimo nella storia* 25 (2004): 987–94.

Alcover Valle, Manuel. *Pio XII, el Papa de la Paz.* Bilbao: Ediciones Paulinas, 1959.

Allessandrini, Raffaele. "Washington e Londra di fronte alla tragedia degli ebrei europei. Silenzi e omissioni al tempo della Shoah." *L'Osservatore Romano,* August 14, 2009.

Alexander, Edgar. *Hitler and the Pope: Pius XII and the Jews.* New York: Thomas Nelson, 1964.

Alexander, Stella. "Yugoslavia and the Vatican, 1919–1929." In *Papal Diplomacy in the Modern Age,* edited by Peter Kent and John Pollard. Westport, Conn.: Praeger, 1994.

Alvarez, David, and Robert A. Graham. *Nothing Sacred: Nazi Espionage against the Vatican, 1939–1945.* London: Frank Cass, 1997.

———. *Spies in the Vatican: Espionage and Intrigue from Napoleon to the Holocaust.* Lawrence: University of Kansas Press, 2002.

Anderson, Robin. *Between Two Wars: The Story of Pope Pius XI (Achille Ratti), 1922–1939.* Chicago: Franciscan Herald Press, 1977.

Andreotti, Giulio. *Pio XII.* Rome: Ed. Grafica, 1965.

Angell, Norman, Sir. *Peace with the Dictators.* New York and London: Harper, 1938.

Angelozzi, Gariboldi Giorgio. *Pio XII, Hitler e Mussolini. Il Vaticano fra le Dittature.* Milan: Mursia, 1988.

———. *Il Vaticano nella seconda guerra mondiale.* Milan: Mursia, 1992.

Aradi, Zsolt. *Pius XI: The Pope and the Man.* Garden City, N.Y.: Hanover House, 1958.

Arendt, Hannah. *Anti-Semitism.* New York: Harcourt, Brace and World, 1967.

Aretin, Karl Otmar von. *The Papacy and the Modern World.* Translated by Roland Hill. New York: McGraw-Hill, 1970.

Arlington, Paul L., with Rene Murphy. *La popessa.* New York: Warner Books, 1983.

Ascoli, Max. "The Roman Church and Political Action." *Foreign Affairs* 13 (April 1935): 441–51.

Askew, William C. "Italian Intervention in Spain: The Agreement of March 31, 1934, with the Spanish Monarchist Parties." *Journal of Modern History* 24, no. 2 (June 1952): 181–83.

Aubert, Roger, et al. *The Church in a Secularized Society*. New York: Paulist Press, 1978.

Avella, Steven M. "Pius XII." In *The New Dictionary of Catholic Social Thought*, edited by Judith A. Dwyer, 741–44. Collegeville, Minn.: Liturgical Press, 1994.

Balfour, R. E. "The Action Francaise Movement." *Cambridge Historical Journal* 3, no. 2 (1930): 182–205.

Bankier, David. *Probing the Depths of German Antisemitism*. New York: Berghahn Books, 1998.

Bard, Mitchell. *48 Hours of Kristallnacht: Night of Destruction/Dawn of the Holocaust*. New York: Lyons Press, 2008.

Bargellini, Piero. *Pius XII: The Angelic Shepherd*. New York: Good Shepherd Publications, 1950.

Bartlett, J. V. *The Popes: A Papal History*. Scottsdale, Ariz.: Sim Ridge Publisher, 1990.

Baum, Gregory. *Is the New Testament Anti-Semitic?* Glenn Rock, N.J.: Paulist Press, 1965.

Bayern, Konstantin von. *Papst Pius XII. Ein Lebensbild*. Stein am Rhein: Christiana Verlag, 1980.

Bea, Augustin Cardinal. *The Church and the Jewish People*. New York: Harper & Row, 1966.

Becker, Winfried. "Diplomats and Missionaries: The Role Played by German Embassies in Moscow and Rome in the Relations between Russia and the Vatican from 1921 to 1929." *Catholic Historical Review* 92, no. 1 (January 2006): 25–45.

Beecher, H. W. "Family." In *The New Dictionary of Thoughts*, edited by T. Edwards. New York: Standard Book, 1944.

Bendiscioli, Mario. *Germania religiosa e terzo Reich, Conflitti religiosi eculturali nella Germania nazista. Dalla testimonianza (1933–1945) alla storiografia (1946–1976)*. Brescia: Morcelliana, 1977.

Bently, Eric. *The Storm over "The Deputy."* New York: Grove Press, 1964.

Berenbaum, Michael. *The World Must Know: The History of the Holocaust as Told in the United States Holocaust Memorial Museum*. Boston: Little, Brown, 1993.

Bergen, Doris L. "An Easy Target: The Controversy about Pius XII and the Holocaust." In *Pope Pius XII and the Holocaust*, edited by Carol Rittner and John K. Roth, 105–19. Leicester, U.K.: Leicester University Press, 2002.

———. *Twisted Cross: The German Christian Movement in the Third Reich*. Chapel Hill: University of North Carolina Press, 1996.

Berliner, Abraham. *Storia degli Ebrei di Roma*. Milan: Ruscoi, 1992.

Bernabei, Domenico. *Orchestra nera. Militari, civili, preti cattolici, pastori, una rete contro Hitler. Che ruolo ebbe Pio XII?* Turin: ERI, 1991.

Bernardini, Gene. "The Origins and Development of Racial Anti-Semitism in Fascist Italy." *Journal of Modern History* 49, no. 3 (1977): 431–53.

Bertetto, D. *Pio XII e l'umana sofferenza*. Rome: Edizioni paoline, 1960.

Besier, Gerhard, with the collaboration of Francesca Piombo. *The Holy See and*

Hitler's Germany. Translated by W. R. Ward. New York: Palgrave/Macmillan, 2007.
Besse, Jean Pierre. *Pie XII, le pape outragé, suivi de Bonne nuit, très saint Père ... Petite histoire anecdotique de ce livre*. Grez-en-Bouère: Morin, 1988.
Biffi, Monica. *Cesare Orsenigo. Nunzio Apostolico in Germania, 1930–1946*. Milan: NED, 1997.
Binchy, D. A. *Church and State in Fascist Italy*. New York: Oxford University Press, 1941.
Bizzarri, Luigi. *Il principe di Dio. La vera storia di Pio XII*. Milan: Ancora, 2004.
Blet, Pierre. *Pius XII and the Second World War*. New York: Paulist Press, 1999.
Bokenkotter, Thomas. *A Concise History of the Catholic Church*. New York: Doubleday, 1966.
Borden, Sarah. *Edith Stein*. New York: Continuum, 2003.
Bottum, Joseph, and David G. Dalin, eds. *The Pius War: Responses to the Critics of Pius XII*. New York: Lexington Books, 2004.
Botwinick, R. S. *A (Brief) History of the Holocaust*. Saddle River, N.J.: Prentice-Hall, 2001.
Braham, Randolph. *The Politics of Genocide*. 2 vols. New York: Columbia University Press, 1981.
———, ed. *The Vatican and the Holocaust: The Catholic Church and the Jews during the Nazi Era*. New York: Columbia University Press, 2000.
Branche, John S. *Pius XII: The Laity and the Church's Mission*. Rome: Pontifical University Press, 1951.
Brands, H. W. *The Devil We Knew: Americans and the Cold War*. New York: Oxford University Press, 1993.
Braun, Robert. "The Holocaust and Problems of Historical Representation." *History and Theory* 33, no. 2 (May 1994): 172–97.
Brechenmacher, Thomas. *Der Vatikan und die Juden*. Munich: Verlag, 2005.
———. "Pope Pius XI, Eugenio Pacelli, and the Persecution of the Jews in Nazi Germany, 1933–1939: New Sources from the Vatican Archives." *Bulletin of the German Historical Institute* (London) 27, no. 2 (November 2005): 17–45.
Brennan, Anthony. *Pope Benedict XV and the War*. London: King, 1917.
Bressan, Edoardo. "L'Osservatore Romano e le relazioni interazionali della Santa Sede (1917–1922)." In *Benedetto XV e la Pace—1918*, edited by G. Rumi, 233–53. Brescia: Morcelliana, 1990.
Brophy, Liam. "Pope Pius and the Social Problem." *Social Justice Review* 51 (December 1958): 261–64.
Brown, M. L. T. *Eugenio: True Hero of the Holocaust*. Steubenville, Pa.: St. Andrew's, n.d.
Brownfield, Cindy. "Researcher: Catholic Church Spurred Anti-Semitism." *The News-Journal*, February 24, 2001, 5C.
Brown Wells, S. *Pioneers of European Integration and Peace, 1945–1963*. New York: Palgrave/Macmillan, 2007.
Bullock, Alan. *Hitler: A Study in Tyranny*. Chicago: Bantam, 1962.

Buonaiuti, Ernesto. *Pio XII*. Florence: Parenti, 1958.
Burgellini, Piero. *Pius XII: The Angelic Shepherd*. New York: Good Shepherd Publications, 1950.
Burke, Richard. *The Social Teaching of Pius XII*. Rome: Gregoriana, 1955.
Burleigh, Michael. *Ethics and Extermination: Reflections on Nazi Genocide*. Cambridge: Cambridge University Press, 1997.
———. *The Third Reich: A New History*. New York: Hill & Wang, 2000.
Burton, Katerine. *The Great Mantle: The Life of Giuseppe Melchiore Sarto, Pope Pius X*. New York: Longmans, Green, 1950.
Callahan, William J. *The Catholic Church in Spain, 1875–1998*. Washington, D.C.: The Catholic University of America Press, 2001.
Camilleri, Nazareno. "*Defensor puritatis*": PP. Pio XII e il problema della purezza nei giovani. Turin: Società Editrice Internazionale, 1959.
Camp, Richard L. "Corporate Reorganization or Co-management? The Reform Program of Pius XII in the Hands of the Commentators." *American Ecclesiastical Review* 164 (May 1971): 319–32.
Campagnari, Raffaello. *Chiesa e cultura: Secondo il pensiero di Pio XII e della Costituzione pastorale "Gaudium et spes."* Verona: Testi, 1969.
Canepa, Andrew M. "Pius X and the Jews: A Reappraisal." *Church History* 61, no. 3 (1992): 362–72.
———. "Zionism, Israel and the Vatican." In *Encyclopedia of the Vatican and Papacy*, edited by F. J. Coppa, 458–60. Westport, Conn.: Greenwood Press, 1997.
Carpi, Daniel. "The Catholic Church and Italian Jewry under the Fascists." In *Yad Vashem Studies*. New York: KTAV, 1975.
Carrillo, Elisa A. "The Italian Catholic Church and Communism, 1943–1963," *Catholic Historical Review* 77, no. 4 (October 1991): 644–57.
———. "Italy, the Holy See and the United States, 1939–1945." In *Papal Diplomacy in the Modern Age*, edited by Peter C. Kent and John F. Pollard, 137–51. Westport, Conn.: Praeger, 1994.
Carroll, James. "The Silence." *New Yorker*, April 7, 1997, pp. 52–68.
———. "The Saint and the Holocaust." *New Yorker*, June 7, 1999, pp. 52–57.
———. *Constantine's Sword: The Church and the Jews*. Boston: Houghton-Mifflin, 2001.
Casella, Mario. *L'Azione cattolica alla caduta del fascismo. Attività e progetti peril dopoguerra (1942–1945)*. Rome: Studium, 1984.
Castiglione, Luigi. *Pio XII e il Nazismo*. Turin: Borla, 1965.
Casula, Carlo Felice. *Domenico Tardini (1888–1961). L'azione della Santa Sede nella crisi fra le due guerre*. Rome: Studium, 1988.
Catella, Marino. *Gioventù cattolica ambrosiana nell'età di papa Pacelli*. Milan: NED, 1983.
Chadwick, Owen. "The Papacy and World War II." *Journal of Ecclesiastical History* 18, no. 1 (April 1967): 71–79.
———. *Britain and the Vatican during the Second World War*. Cambridge: Cambridge University Press, 1986.
———. *A History of Christianity*. New York: St. Martin's Press, 1995.

———. *A History of the Popes, 1830–1914.* Oxford: Clarendon Press, 1998.

———. "Pius XII: The Legend and the Truth." *The Tablet* (London), March 28, 1998.

Charguéraud, Marc-André. *Les Papes, Hitler et la Shoah, 1932–1945.* Fribourg: Labor et Fides, 2002.

Cheetham, Nicholas. *The Keeper of the Keys.* London: Macdonald, 1982.

Chelini, Jean. *L'Eglise sous Pie XII.* Paris: Fayard, 1983.

Chenaux, Philippe. *Chiesa e papato 2.* Laterza, 1990.

———. *Une Europe vaticane? Entre le plan Marshall et les Traités de Rome.* Brussels: Ciaco, 1990.

———. *Pie XII. Diplomate et Pasteur.* Paris: Cerf, 2003.

Cianfarra, Camille M. *The War and the Vatican.* London: Burns, Oates and Washbourne, 1945.

Clarke, Duncan L., and Eric Flohr. "Christian Churches and the Palestinian Question." *Journal of Palestine Studies* 21, no. 4 (Summer 1992): 67–79.

Clonmore, Lord. *Pope Pius XI and World Peace.* New York: Dutton, 1938.

Coen, Fausto. *16 ottobre 1943: La grande razzia degli ebrei di Roma.* Florence: Giuntina, 1993.

Confalonieri, Carlo. *Pio XI visto da vicino.* Turin: S.A.I.E., 1957.

Connally, Michael. "Pope Pius XII on Democracy." *Irish Monthly*, October 1945, pp. 407–17.

Conway, John S. "The Silence of Pope Pius XII." *Review of Politics* 27, no. 1 (January 1965): 105–31.

———. "The Meeting between Pope Pius XII and Ribbentrop." *Historical Papers of the Canadian Historical Association* (1968): 215–27.

———. *The Nazi Persecution of the Churches, 1933–1945.* London: Weidenfeld & Nicolson, 1968.

———. "The Vatican, Britain and Relations with Germany, 1938–1949." *Historical Journal* 16 (1973): 147–67.

———. "Myron C. Tayor's Mission to the Vatican." *Church History* 44, no. 1 (March 1975): 85–99.

———. "The Holocaust and the Historian" *Annals of the American Academy of Political and Social Sciences* 40 (July 1980): 153–64.

———. "The Vatican and the Holocaust: A Reappraisal." *Miscellanea Historiae Ecclesiasticae* 9 (1984): 475–89.

———. "The Vatican, Germany and the Holocaust." In *Papal Diplomacy in the Modern Age*, edited by Peter C. Kent and John F. Pollard, 105–20. Westport, Conn.: Praeger, 1994.

Conway, Martin. *Catholic Politics in Europe, 1918–1945.* London: Routledge, 1997.

Coppa, Frank J. *Pius IX: Crusader in a Secular Age.* Boston: Twayne, 1979.

———. "The Vatican and the Dictators: Between Diplomacy and Morality." In *Catholics, the State and the European Radical Right*, edited by Richard Wolff and Jorg K. Hoensch, 199–22. New York: Columbia University Press, 1987.

———. *Cardinal Giacomo Antonelli and Papal Politics in European Affairs.* Albany: State University of New York Press, 1990.

———. "The Hidden Encyclical of Pius XI against Racism and Anti-Semitism Uncovered—Once Again!" *Catholic Historical Review* 84, no. 1 (January 1998): 63–72.

———. *The Modern Papacy since 1789.* London and New York: Longman, 1998.

———. "Pope Pius XI's 'Encyclical' *Humani Generis Unitas* against Racism and Anti-Semitism and the 'Silence' of Pope Pius XII." *Journal of Church and State* 40, no. 4 (Autumn 1998): 775–95.

———, ed. *Controversial Concordats: The Vatican's Relations with Napoleon, Mussolini, and Hitler.* Washington, D.C.: The Catholic University of America Press, 1999.

———. "Pius XII between History and Controversy." *Journal of Modern Italian Studies* 7 (Summer 2002): 261–66.

———. "Pope Pius XII and the Cold War: The Postwar-War Confrontation between Catholicism and Communism." In *Religion and the Cold War,* edited by Dianne Kirby, 50–66. London: Palgrave, 2003.

———. "The Contessa di Castiglione: The Forgotten Figure of the Risorgimento." *Italian Quarterly* (Winter–Spring 2004): 47–53.

———. *The Papacy, the Jews, and the Holocaust.* Washington, D.C.: The Catholic University of America Press, 2006.

———. "Between Morality and Diplomacy: The Vatican's 'Silence' during the Holocaust." *Journal of Church and State* 50 (Summer 2008): 541–68.

———. *Politics and the Papacy in the Modern World.* London: Praeger, 2008.

———. "Pius XII's Cautious Diplomacy." *The Tablet* (Brooklyn), February 27, 2010, p. 25.

———. *The Policies and Politics of Pope Pius XII: Between Diplomacy and Morality.* New York: Peter Lang, 2011.

Cornwell, John. *Hitler's Pope: The Secret History of Pius XII.* New York: Viking Press, 1999.

———. *Breaking Faith: The Pope, the People and the Fate of Catholicism.* New York: Viking Press, 2001.

———. "For God's Sake." *The Economist,* December 9, 2004.

Coste, René. *Le problème du droit de guerre dans la pensée de Pie XII.* Paris: Aubier, 1962.

Coverdale, John F. *Italian Intervention in the Spanish Civil War.* Princeton, N.J.: Princeton University Press, 1975.

Crankshaw, Edward. *Gestapo.* New York: Pyramid Books, 1959.

Cummings, Owen F. *A History of the Popes in the Twentieth Century.* Lewiston, N.Y.: Edwin Mellen Press, 2008.

Curtis, Michael, ed. *Antisemitism in the Contemporary World.* London: Westview Press, 1986.

Curvers, Alexis. *Pie XII, le pape outragé.* Paris: Laffont, 1964.

Cushing, Richard. *Pope Pius XII.* New York: Paulist Press, 1959.

Dalin, David G. "Pius XII and the Jews." *Weekly Standard,* February 26, 2001, pp. 31–39.

———. *The Myth of Hitler's Pope: How Pope Pius XII Rescued Jews from the Nazis.* New York: Regnery Press, 2005.

D'Angelo, Augusto. *Vescovi, Mezzogiorno e Vaticano II. L'episcopato meridionale da Pio XII a Paolo VI*. Rome: Studium, 1998.
Davies, Alan T. *Anti-Semitism and the Christian Mind: The Crisis of Conscience after Auschwitz*. New York: Herder & Herder, 1969.
———. "Religion and Racism: The Case of French Anti-Semitism." *Journal of Church and State* 20, no. 2 (Spring 1978): 273–86.
Degli Esposti, Francesco. *La teologia del Sacro Cuore di Gesù: Da Leone XIII a Pio XII*. Rome: Herder, 1967.
Della Rocca, Fernando. *Papi di questo secolo. Da Pio XII a Giovanni Paolo II*. Padua: CEDAM, 1987.
Delzell, Charles. "Pius XII, Italy, and the Outbreak of War." *Journal of Contemporary History* 2, no. 4 (October 1967): 137–61.
———. *Mussolini's Enemies: The Italian Anti-Fascist Resistance*. Princeton, N.J.: Princeton University Press, 1961. Rev. ed., New York: Howard Fertig, 1974.
———, ed. *The Papacy and Totalitarianism between the Two World Wars*. Turin: Einaudi, 1974.
De Rosa, Gabriele. *Chiesa e comunismo in Italia*. Rome: Coines, 1970.
Desmurs, Ferdinand. *Pie XII le pape du silence toujours à l'affiche*. Paris: Berg International, 2002.
Dietrich, Donald J. *Catholic Citizens in the Third Reich: Psycho-Social Principles and Moral Reasoning*. New Brunswick, N.J.: Transaction Books, 1988.
———. "Catholic Resistance in the Third Reich." *Holocaust and Genocide Studies* 3, no. 2 (1988): 171–86.
Dinneen, Joseph F. *Pius XII: Pope of Peace*. New York: Robert M. McBride, 1939.
Di Nolfo, Ennio, ed. *Vaticano e Stati Uniti—1939–1952: Dalle carte di Myron C. Taylor*. Milan: F. Angeli, 1978.
———. *Paure e speranze degli Italiani (1943–1953)*. Milan: Mondadori, 1986.
D'Orazi, Lucio. *Pio XII (Eugenio Pacelli). Attualità di un papa inattuale*. Bologna: Conti, 1984.
Doyle, Charles Hugo. *The Life of Pope Pius XII*. New York: Diier, 1945.
Duce, Alessandro. *La Santa Sede e la questione ebraica (1933–1945)*. Rome: Studium, 2007.
Duffy, Eamon. *Saints and Sinners: A History of the Popes*. New Haven, Conn.: Yale University Press, 1997.
Dunn, Dennis J. "Stalinism and the Catholic Church during the Era of World War II." *Catholic Historical Review* 59, no. 3 (October 1973): 404–28.
Ellsberg, Patricia Marx. "An Interview with Rolf Hochhuth." In *The Papacy and Totalitarianism between the Two World Wars*, edited by Charles Delzell, 108–24. New York: John Wiley, 1974.
Esposito, Rosario F. *Processo al Vicario. Pio XII e gli ebrei secondo la testimonianza della storia*. Turin: SAIE, 1964.
Falah, Ghazi. "The 1948 Israeli-Palestinian War and Its Aftermath." *Annals of the Association of American Geographers* 86, no. 2 (June 1996).
Falasca, Stefania. *Un vescovo contro Hitler. Von Galen, Pio XII e la resistenza al Nazismo*. Cinisello Balsamo: San Paolo Edizioni, 2006.

Falconi, Carlo. *Il Pentagono vaticano*. Bari: Laterza, 1958.
———. *Luigi Gedda e l'Azione cattolica*. Florence: Parenti, 1958.
———. *Pio XII*. Milan: CEI, 1966.
———. *The Popes in the Twentieth Century: From Pius X to John XXIII*. Translated by Muriel Grindrod. Boston: Little, Brown, 1967.
———. *The Silence of Pius XII*. Translated by Bernard Wall. Boston: Little, Brown, 1970.
Fappani, Antonio, and Franco Molinari. *Chiesa e repubblica di Salò*. Turin: Marietti, 1981.
Fattorini, Emma. "Santa Sede e Germania alla vigilia della seconda Guerra mondiale." *Dimensioni e problemi della ricerca storica* 1 (1990): 99–117.
———. *Germania e Santa Sede. La Nunziature di Pacelli tra la Grande Guerra e la Repubblica di Weimar*. Annali dell' Istituto storico italo-germanico. Bologna: Il Mulino, 1992.
———. *Pio XI, Hitler e Mussolini. La solitudine di un papa*. Turin: Einaudi, 2007.
———. *Hitler, Mussolini and the Vatican: Pope Pius XI and the Speech That Was Never Made*. Cambridge: Polity Press, 2011.
Favara, Fedele. *De iure naturali in doctrina Pii Papae XII*. Rome: Desclée, 1966.
Feis, Herbert. *From Trust to Terror: The Onset of the Cold War, 1945–1950*. New York: Norton, 1970.
Feldkamp, Michael. *Pius XII und Deutschland*. Goffingen: Vandenhoeck & Ruprecht, 2000.
Felice, Renzo de. *Storia degli ebrei sotto il fascismo*. Turin: Einaudi, 1961.
Ferrari, Liliana. *Una storia dell' Azione cattolica. Gli ordinamenti statutari da Pio XI a Pio XII*. Genoa: Marietti, 1989.
Ferrari, Silvio. "The Vatican, Israel and the Jerusalem Question (1943–1984)." *Middle East Journal* 39, no. 2 (Spring 1985).
———. "The Holy See and the Postwar Palestine Issue: The Internationalization of Jerusalem and the Protection of the Holy Places." *International Affairs* 60, no. 2 (1987).
———. *Vaticano e Israele dal secondo conflitto mondiale alla Guerra del Golfo*. Florence: Sansoni, 1991.
Ferrera, Nazareno. *Pio XII e la pace*. Palermo: Tip. Fiamma Serafica, 1966.
Filteau, Jerry. "History of Pius XII and Holocaust Seen as Unclear." *The Tablet* (Brooklyn), May 14, 2005, p. 13.
Finkelstein, Norman. *The Holocaust Industry*. New York: Verso Press, 2000.
Fiorentino, Carlo M. *All' Ombra di Pietro. La Chiesa Cattolica e lo spionaggio fascista in Vaticano, 1929–1939*. Florence: Editrice Le Lettere, 1999.
Flannery, Edward H. *The Anguish of the Jews*. New York: Macmillan, 1965.
Fleischner, Eva. "The Spirituality of Pius XII." In *Pope Pius XII and the Holocaust*, edited by Carol Rittner and John K. Roth. Leicester, U.K.: Leicester University Press, 2002.
Flynn, George. "Franklin Roosevelt and the Vatican: The Myron Taylor Appointment." *Catholic Historical Review* 58, no. 2 (July 1972): 171–94.

Foa, Anna. *Ebrei in Europa*. Rome: Laterza, 1997.
Fogarty, Gerald, S.J. "The United States and the Vatican." In *Papal Diplomacy in the Modern Age*, edited by Peter Kent and John Pollard, 221–43. Westport, Conn.: Praeger, 1994.
Fontenelle, René, and Mary Elizabeth Fowler. *His Holiness Pope Pius XI*. London: Catholic Book Club, 1939.
Forbes, F. A. *Life of Pius X*. London: Burns, Oates & Westminister, 1918.
Forcella, Enzo. *La resistenza in convento*. Turin: Einaudi, 1999.
Fouilloux, Étienne. *Une Église en quête de liberté. La pensée catholique française entre modernisme et Vatican II 1914–1962*. Paris: Desclee de Brouwer, 1998.
Friedländer, Saul. *Pius XII and the Third Reich: A Documentation*. New York: Alfred A. Knopf, 1966.
———. *Nazi Germany and the Jews*. Vol. 1, *The Years of Persecution, 1933–1939*. New York: Harper-Collins, 1997.
Gajewski, Karol. "Nazi Persecution of the Church." *Inside the Vatican*, November 1999, pp. 50–54.
Gallagher, Charles R., S.J. "Personal, Private Views." *America*, September 1, 2003, pp. 8–10.
———. *Vatican Secret Diplomacy: Joseph P. Hurley and Pope Pius*. New Haven, Conn.: Yale University Press, 2008.
Gallin, Mary Alice. *German Resistance to Hitler*. Washington, D.C.: The Catholic University of America Press, 1961.
Gallo, Patrick J., ed. *Pius XII, the Holocaust and the Revisionists*. Jefferson, N.C.: McFarland, 2006.
Garzia, Italo. "Pope Pius XII, Italy and the Second World War." In *Papal Diplomacy in the Modern Age*, edited by Peter Kent and John Pollard, 121–36. Westport, Conn.: Praeger, 1994.
Gasbarri, Carlo. *Quando il Vaticano confinava con il Terzo Reich*. Padua: Messaggero, 1984.
Gaspari, Antonio. "Justice for Pius XII." *Inside the Vatican*, June 1997, pp. 20–26
———. *Nascosti in convento*. Milan: Ancora, 1999.
———. *Gli Ebrei salvato da Pio XII*. Rome: Logos, 2001.
Gilbert, Martin. *The Holocaust: A History of the Jews of Europe during the Second World War*. New York: Holt, 1987.
———. *The Second World War: A Complete History*. New York: Holt, 1992.
———. *The Righteous: The Unsung Heroes of the Holocaust*. New York: H. Holt, 2001.
Giordani, Igino. *Pio XII. Un grande papa*. Turin: Società Editrice Internazionale, 1961.
Giovannetti, Alberto. *El Vaticano y La Guerra (1939–1949)*. Madrid: Esposa-Colpe, 1961.
———. *Roma città aperta*. Milan: Ancora, 1962.
Glatz, Carol. "Pope: Pius XII Worked Bravely to Help Jews." *The Tablet* (Brooklyn), Sepember 27, 2008, p. 7
Goguel, François, and Mario Einaudi. *Christian Democracy in Italy and France*. South Bend, Ind.: University of Notre Dame Press, 1952.

Goldhagen, Daniel Jonah. *Hitler's Willing Executioners.* New York: Alfred A. Knopf, 1996.

———. "What Would Jesus Have Done?" *New Republic,* January, 2002, pp. 21–45.

———. *A Moral Reckoning: The Role of the Catholic Church in the Holocaust and Its Unfulfilled Duty of Repair.* New York: Vintage Books, 2003.

Godman, Peter. *Hitler and the Vatican: Inside the Secret Archives That Reveal the New Story of the Nazis and the Church.* New York: Free Press, 2004.

Gonella, Guido. *A World to Reconstuct: Pius XII on Peace and Reconstruction.* Milwaukee, Wis.: Bruce Publishing, 1944.

———. *The Papacy and World Peace: A Study of the Christmas Messages of Pope Pius XII.* London: Hollis & Carter, 1945.

Gotto, Klaus, and Konrad Repgen. *Die Katholiken und das Dritte Reich.* Mainz: Grünewald, 1990.

Graham, Robert A. *Vatican Diplomacy: A Study of Church and State.* Princeton, N.J.: Princeton University Press, 1959

———. *The Pope and Poland in World War Two.* London: Veritas Foundation Publication Centre, 1968.

———. "The 'Right to Kill' in the Third Reich: Prelude to Genocide." *Catholic Historical Review* 63, no. 1 (January 1976): 56–76.

———. *Pius XII and the Holocaust: A Reader.* Milwaukee, Wis.: Catholic League, 1988.

———. *The Vatican and Communism in World War II: What Really Happened?* San Francisco: Ignatius Press, 1996.

Graham, Robert A., and David Alvarez. *Nothing Sacred: Nazi Espionage against the Vatican, 1939–1945.* London: Frank Cass, 1997.

Gratsch, Edward J. *The Holy See and the United Nations, 1945–1995.* New York: Vantage Press, 1997.

Guerry, Émile. *L'Église et la communauté des peuples. La doctrine de l'Église sur les rélations internationales: L'enseignement de Pie XII.* Paris: Bonne Presse, 1958.

Gurian, Waldemar. "Hitler's Undeclared War on the Catholic Church." *Foreign Affairs* 6 (January 1938): 260–71.

Gurian, Waldemar, and M. A. Fitzsimons, eds. *The Catholic Church in World Affairs.* South Bend, Ind.: University of Notre Dame Press, 1954.

Gutman, Israel. *Encyclopedia of the Holocaust.* Vol. 3. New York: Macmillan, 1995.

Halecki, Oscar. *Eugenio Pacelli: Pope of Peace.* New York: Ferrar, Strauss and Young, 1951.

———. "The Holy See and the Religious Situation in Central Europe, 1939–1945." *Catholic Historical Review* 53, no. 3 (October 1967): 393–410.

Hales, E. E. Y. *The Catholic Church in the Modern World.* Garden City, N.Y.: Hanover House, 1958.

Handren, Walter J. *Pius XI.* Westminster, Md.: Newman Press, 1955.

Hanson, Eric. *The Catholic Church in World Politics.* Princeton, N.J.: Princeton University Press, 1987.

Harries, Richard. *After the Evil: Christianity and Judaism in the Shadow of the Holocaust.* Oxford: Oxford University Press, 2003.
Harrigan, William M. "Nazi Germany and the Holy See, 1933–1936." *Catholic Historical Review* 47 (1961): 164–98.
———. "Pius XII's Efforts to Effect a Détente in German-Vatican Relations, 1939–1940." *Catholic Historical Review* 49 (July 1963): 173–91.
Hassett, J. D. "Pius XII and the Political Order." *Catholic Mind* 60 (December 1962): 4–15.
Hatch, Alden, and Seamus Walshe. *Crown of Glory: The Life of Pope Pius XII.* New York: Hawthorne Books, 1957.
Hearley, John. *Pope or Mussolini.* New York: Macaulay, 1929.
Hebblethwaite, Peter. *The Year of Three Popes.* New York: Collins, 1979.
———. *Paul VI: The First Modern Pope.* New York: Paulist Press, 1993.
Hecht, Robert A. *An Unordinary Man: A Life of Father John La Farge, S.J.* Lanham, Md.: Scarecrow Press, 1996.
Helmreich, Ernst C. *The German Churches under Hitler.* Detroit, Mich.: Wayne State University Press, 1979.
Herber, Charles J. "Eugenio Pacelli's Mission to Germany and the Papal Peace Proposals of 1917." *Catholic Historical Review* 55, no. 1 (January 1979): 20–48.
Hilberg, Raul. *Perpetrators, Victims, Bystanders: The Jewish Catastrophe.* New York: Harper, 1945.
———. *The Destruction of the European Jews.* Chicago: Quadrangle Books, 1961.
Hochhuth, Rolf. *The Deputy.* New York: Grove Press, 1964.
Holmes, J. Derek. *The Papacy in the Modern World, 1914–1978.* New York: Crossroad, 1981.
Hughes, John Jay. "The Pope's Pact with Hitler: Betrayal or Self-Defense?" *Journal of Church and State* 17 (Winter 1975): 63–80.
Hughes, Philip. *Pope Pius the Eleventh.* New York: Sheed & Ward, 1938.
Hürten, Heinz. *Pius XII und die Juden.* Cologne: Backem, 2000.
Innocenti, Ennio. *Presenza di Pio XII.* Rome: Apes, 1967.
Irani, George Emile. *The Papacy and the Middle East: The Role of the Holy See in the Arab-Israeli Conflict, 1962–1984.* South Bend, Ind.: University of Notre Dame Press, 1986.
———. "The Holy See and the Israeli-Palestinian Conflict." In *The Vatican, Islam and the Middle East,* edited by K. C. Ellis. Syracuse, N.Y.: Syracuse University Press, 1987.
———. "The Holy See and the Conflict in Lebanon." In *Papal Diplomacy in the Modern Age,* edited by Peter Kent and John Pollard, 181–88. Westport, Conn.: Praeger, 1994.
Issac, Jules. *The Teaching of Contempt: Christian Roots of Anti-Semitism.* New York: Holt, Rinehart and Winston, 1964.
"Judging Pope Pius XII." *Inside the Vatican,* June 1997, pp. 12–19.
Kasper, Walter, and Hans Kung. *Christians and Jews.* Translated by John Maxwell. New York: Seabury Press, 1975.

Katz, Robert. *Death in Rome.* Cambidge, Mass.: Harvard University Press, 1967.

———. *The Battle for Rome: The Germans, the Allies, the Partisans and the Pope.* New York: Simon & Schuster, 2003.

Keefe, Patricia M. "Popes Pius XI and Pius XII, the Catholic Church, and the Nazi Persecution of the Jews." *British Journal of Holocaust Education* 2, no. 1 (Summer 1993): 26–47.

Kent, George O. "Pope Pius XII and Germany: Some Aspects of German-Vatican Relations, 1933–1943." *American Historical Review* 70 (October 1964): 59–78.

Kent, Peter C. *The Pope and the Duce.* New York: St. Martin's Press, 1981.

———. "The Vatican and the Spanish Civil War." *European History Quarterly* 16 (October 1986): 441–64.

———. "A Tale of Two Popes: Pius XII and the Rome-Berlin Axis." *Journal of Contemporary History* 23, no. 4 (October 1988): 589–608.

———. *The Lonely Cold War of Pope Pius XII: The Roman Catholic Church and the Division of Europe, 1943–1950.* Ithaca: McGill-Queen's University Press, 2002.

Kent, Peter C., and John F. Pollard, eds. *Papal Diplomacy in the Modern Age.* Westport, Conn.: Praeger, 1994.

Kerdreux, Miguel de. *Pie XII artisan de paix et la dexième guerre mondiale.* Paris: Nouvelles Editions Latines, 1972.

Kershaw, Ian. *Hitler, 1889–1936.* New York: Norton, 1999.

Kertzer, David I. *The Kidnapping of Edgardo Montara.* New York: Random House, 1998.

———. *The Pope against the Jews.* New York: Knopf, 2001.

Kirby, Dianne. *Religion in the Cold War.* New York: Palgrave, 2003.

Klein, Charles. *Pie XII face au Nazis.* Paris: S.O.S., 1975.

Klenicki, Rabbi Leon, and Cardinal Avery Dulles. *The Holocaust, Never to Be Forgotten: Reflections on the Holy See's Document, "We Remember."* Mahwah, N.J.: Paulist Press, 2001.

Klieman, Aaron S. "In the Public Domain: The Controversy over Partition for Palestine." *Jewish Social Studies* 42, no. 2 (Spring 1980): 147–64.

Kreutz, Anrej. *Vatican Policy on the Palestinian-Israeli Conflict.* New York: Greenwood Press, 1990.

———. "The Vatican and the Palestinians: A Historical Overview." In *Papal Diplomacy in the Modern Age,* edited by Peter Kent and John Pollard, 167–79. Westport, Conn.: Praeger, 1994.

Kühlwein, Klaus. *Warum der Papst schwieg. Pius XII und der Holocaust.* Düsseldorf: Patmos-Verlag, 2008.

Kurzman, Dan. *Hitler's Secret Plot to Seize the Vatican and Kidnap Pope Pius XII.* New York: Da Capo, 2008.

Lacroix-Riz, Annie. *Le Vatican, l'Europe et le Reich de la Première guerre Mondiale à la guerre froide.* Paris: Colin, 1996.

La Farge, John. *Interracial Justice: A Study of the Catholic Doctrine of Race Relations.* New York: America Press, 1937.

BIBLIOGRAPHY

Lamb, Richard. *War in Italy, 1943–1945: A Brutal Story.* New York: St. Martin's Press, 1993.

Lannon, Frances. *Privilege, Persecution, and Prophecy: The Catholic Church in Spain.* Oxford: Clarendon Press, 1987.

Lapide, Pinchas E. *Roma e gli ebrei. L'azione del Vaticano a favore delle vittime del Nazismo.* Milan: Mondadori, 1967.

———. *Three Popes and the Jews.* London and Southampton: Souvenir Press, 1967.

Lapomarda, Vincent. "The Jesuits and the Holocaust." *Journal of Church and State* 23, no. 2 (Spring 1981): 241–58.

———. *The Jesuits and the Third Reich.* Lewison, N.Y.: Edwin Mellen Press, 1989.

Lavi, Theodore. *La vie de l'Église sous Pie XII.* Paris: Fayard, 1959.

———. "The Vatican's Endeavors on Behalf of Rumanian Jewry during World War II." *Yad Vashem Studies* 5 (1963): 405–18.

Lawler, Justus George. *Popes and Politics.* New York: Continuum, 2002.

Lazarus, Joyce Block. *In the Shadow of Vichy: The Finaly Affair.* New York: Peter Lang, 2008.

Lehmann, Leo Hubert. *Vatican Policy in the Second World War.* New York: Agora Publishing, 1946.

Lenn, Lottie Helen, and Mary Rearson. *Pope Pius XII: Rock of Peace.* New York: Dutton, 1950.

Levai, Jeno. *Hungarian Jewry and the Papacy.* London: Sands, 1967.

Lewis, Paul H. *Latin Fascist Elites: The Mussolini, Franco, and Salazar Regimes.* London: Praeger, 2002.

Lewy, Guenter. "Pius XII, the Jews and the German Catholic Church." *Commentary,* February, 1964, pp. 23–33.

———. *The Catholic Church and Nazi Germany.* New York: McGraw-Hill, 1965.

Lichten, Joseph L. *A Question of Judgment: Pius XII and the Jews.* Washington, D.C.: National Catholic Welfare Conference, 1963.

———, ed. *Pius XII and the Holocaust: A Reader.* Milwaukee, Wis.: Catholic League for Religious and Civil Rights, 1988.

Lipman, Steve. "Wartime Pope's Reappraisal." *Jewish Week,* September 12, 2008, pp. 1, 68.

Littell, Franklin H. "*Kirchenkampf* and Holocaust: The German Church Struggle and Nazi Anti-Semitism in Retrospect." *Journal of Church and State* 13, no. 1 (Winter 1971): 209–26.

Low, Alfred D. *The Anschluss Movement, 1931–1938, and the Great Powers.* Boulder, Colo.: East European Monographs, 1985.

Lukacs, John. "The Diplomacy of the Holy See during World War II." *Catholic Historical Review* 60 (July 1974): 271–78.

Luza, Radomir. "Nazi Control of the Austrian Catholic Church, 1939–1941." *Catholic Historical Review* 63, no. 4 (October 1977): 537–72.

Magister, Sandro. *La politica vaticana e l'Italia (1943–1979).* Rome: Editori Riuniti, 1979.

Malgeri, Francesco. *La Chiesa italiana e la guerra (1940–1945)*. Rome: Studium, 1980.
Manhattan, Avro. *The Vatican in World Politics*. New York: GAER Associates, 1949.
Manzo, M. *Don Pirro Scavizzi. Prete Romano*. Cassale Monferrato: Piemme, 1997.
Marazziti, Mario. *I papi di carta: Nascita e svolta dell'informazione religiosa da Pio XII a Giovanni XXIII*. Genoa: Marietti, 1990.
Marchione, Sister Margherita. *Yours Is a Precious Witness: Memories of Jews and Catholics in Wartime Italy*. New York: Paulist Press, 1997.
———."Jews, Catholics and Pope Pius XII." *The Catholic Answer*, September–October 1998, pp. 36–43.
———. *Pio XII e gli ebrei*. Rome: Pan Logos, 1999.
———. *Pope Pius XII: Architect for Peace*. New York: Paulist Press, 2000.
———. *Consensus and Controversy: Defending Pope Pius XII*. New York: Paulist Press, 2002.
———. *Il silenzio di Pio XII. Papa Pacelli di fronte al Nazismo e allapersecuzione degli ebrei: Accuse, controversie e verità storica*. Milan: Sperling & Kupfer, 2002.
———. *Shepherd of Souls: A Pictorial Life of Pope Pius XII*. New York: Paulist Press, 2002.
———. *Man of Peace: Pope Pius XII*. New York: Paulist Press, 2003.
———.*Crusade of Charity: Pius XII and POWs (1939–1945)*. New York: Paulist Press, 2006.
———. *Did Pope Pius XII Help the Jews?* New York: Paulist Press, 2007.
———. *A Hand of Peace: Pope Pius XII and the Holocaust*. San Francisco: Ignatius Press, 2009.
Margiottto Broglio, Francesco. *Italia e Santa Sede dalla grande Guerra alla Concilizaione*. Bari: Laterza, 1966.
Marquina Barrio, Antonio. *La Diplomacia Vaticana y la España de Franco, 1936–1945*. Madrid: CSIC, 1983.
Marrus, Michael R. "The History of the Holocaust: A Survey of Recent Literature." *Journal of Modern History* 59, no. 1 (March 1987): 114–60.
———. *The Holocaust in History*. Hanover, N.H.: University Press of New England, 1987.
Marrus, Michael R., and Robert Paxton. *Vichy France and the Jews*. New York: Basic Books, 1981.
Martin, Malachi. *Three Popes and the Cardinal: The Church of Pius, John, and Paul in Its Encounter with Human History*. New York: Farrar, Straus, and Giroux, 1972.
———. *The Jesuits*. New York: Linden Press, 1987.
Martina, Giacomo. *La Chiesa in Italia negli ultimi trent'anni*. Rome: Studium, 1977.
———. "L'ecclesiologia prevalente nel pontificato di Pio XI." In *Cattolici e fascisti in Umbria (1922–1945)*, edited by Alberto Monticone, 221–44. Bologna: Il Mulino, 1978.

BIBLIOGRAPHY

Martini, Angelo. "Il Cardinale Faulhaber e L'Enciclica 'Mit Brennender Sorge.'" *Archivum Historiae Pontificiae* 2 (1964): 303–20.

———. "L'Ultima battaglia di Pio XI." In *Studi sulla questione romano e la conciliazione*, edited by A. Martini, 175–230. Rome: Cinque Lune, 1963.

Masse, Benjamin L. "Pope Pius XII Demands Economic Reforms." *America*, December 30, 1950, pp. 378–81.

———. "Pope Pius XII on Capitalism." *America*, December 2, 1950, pp. 277–79.

———. "Pius XII and the Social Order." *America*, November 1, 1958, pp. 130–32.

Mazzolari, Primo. *La Chiesa, il fascismo e la Guerra*. Florence: Vallecchi, 1966.

McDermott, Thomas. *Keeper of the Keys: A Life of Pope Pius XII*. Milwaukee, Wis.: Bruce Publishing, 1946.

McInerny, Ralph. *The Defamation of Pope Pius XII*. South Bend, Ind.: St. Augustine's Press, 2001.

Messadie, Gerald. "La Santa Sede e le deportazioni." *Spostamenti di popolazione e deportazioni in Europa, 1939–1945*. Bologna: Cappelli, 1987.

———. "Santa Sede e Chiesa italiana di fronte alle leggi antiebrache del 1938." In *La egislazione antiebraica in Italia e in Europa: Atti del Convegno nel cinquantenario delle leggi razziali (Roma, 17–18 ottobre 1988)*. Rome: Camera dei Deputati, 1989.

———. *Storia dell'antisemitismo*. Casale Monferrato: Piemme, 2002.

Miccoli, Giovanni. "L'enciclica mancata di Pio sul razzismo e l'antisemitismo." *Passato e Presente* 15 (1997): 35–54.

———. *I dilemmi e I silenzi di Pio XI*. Milan: Rizzoli, 2000

Michaelis, Meir. *Mussolini and the Jews: German-Italian Relations and the Jewish Question in Italy, 1922–1945*. Oxford: Clarendon Press, 1978.

Micklem, Nathaniel. *National Socialism and the Roman Catholic Church*. London: Oxford University Press, 1939.

Milgram, Avraham. *Os judeus do Vaticano. A tentativo de salvação de catolico nãoarianos—da Alemanha ao Brasil através do Vaticano (1939–1942)*. Rio de Janeiro: Imago, 1994.

Milkowski, Tadeusz. "The Spanish Church and the Vatican during the Spanish Civil War." *Polish Foreign Affairs Digest* 3 (2004): 207–42.

Minerbi, Sergio. *The Vatican and Zionism*. New York: Oxford University Press, 1990.

———. "The Vatican and Israel." In *Papal Diplomacy in the Modern Age*, edited by Peter Kent and John Pollard, 189–201. Westport, Conn.: Praeger, 1994.

———. "Pius XII: A Reappraisal." In *Pope Pius XII and the Holocaust*, edited by Carol Rittner and John K. Roth, 85–104. Leicester, U.K.: Leicester University Press, 2002.

Mondin, Battista. *The Popes of the Modern Ages: From Pius IX to John Paul II*. Rome: Urbaniana University Press, 2004.

Montclos, Xavier de. *Les chrétiens face au nazisme et au stalinisme: L'épreuve totalitaire 1939–1945*. Paris: Plon, 1983.

Moritz, Stefan. *Grüß Gott und Heil Hitler. Katholische und Nationalsozialismus in Österreich.* Vienna: Picus, 2002.
Morley, John F. *Vatican Diplomacy and the Jews during the Holocaust, 1939–1943.* New York: KTAV, 1980.
Moro, Renato. *La Chiesa e lo sterminio degli ebrei.* Bologna: Il Mulino, 2002.
Morozzo della Rocca, Roberto. "Unione Sovietica e questione comunista nell'opinione pubblica cattolica in Italia." In *Pio XII,* edited by Andrea Riccardi, 379–407. Laterza: Roma-Bari, 1984).
Morreale, Girolamo Maria. *La consacrazione al Cuore Immacolato di Maria nella dottrina di Pio XII.* Rome: Desclée, 1966.
Morsey, Rudolf. "Eugenio Pacelli als Nuntius in Deutschland." In *Pius XII,* edited by Herbert Schambeck. Berlin: Duncker & Humbolt, 1986.
Mugnaini, Marco, ed. *Stato, Chiesa e Relazioni Internazionali.* Milan: Franco Angeli, 2003.
Mulligan, Hugh A. "Pius XII's Deeds Spoke Volumes" *The Tablet* (Brooklyn) April 8, 2006, p. 22.
Murphy, Paul I., and Rene Arlington. *La Popessa: The Controversial Biography of Sister Pasqualina the Most Powerful Woman in Vatican History.* New York: Warner, 1983.
Murray, James. "Pope or Pilate?" *The Western Australian,* February 15, 2003, p. 22.
Murray, John Courtney. *Morality and Modern War.* New York: Council on Religion and International Affairs, 1959.
Napolitano, Matteo, and A. Tornielli. *Pio XII tra Guerra e pace.* Rome: Città Nuova, 2002.
———. *Il Papa che salvo gli ebrei.* Casale Monferrato: Piemme, 2004.
Nasalli Rocca di Corneliano, Mario. *Accanto ai Papi.* Vatican City: Libreria Editrice Vaticana, 1976.
Nassi, Enrico. *Pio XII. La politica in ginocchio.* Milan: Camunia, 1992.
Naughton, James. *Pius XII on World Problems.* New York: American Press, 1943.
Nemec, Ludik. "Stepan Cardinal Trochta: A Steadfast Defender of the Church in Czechoslovakia." *Catholic Historical Review* 64, no. 4 (October 1978).
Nichols, Peter. *The Politics of the Vatican.* New York: Praeger, 1968.
Nidam-Orvieto, Iael. "New Research: Pope Pius XII and the Holocaust." *Yad Vashem Quarterly Magazine* 56, Tevet 5770 (January 2010). Reprinted in *Association of Contemporary Church Historians Quarterly* 16, no. 1 (March 2010): 13–14.
Nobécourt, Jaques. *"Le Vicaire" et l'histoire.* Paris: Seuil, 1964.
Noel, Gerard. *Pius XII: The Hound of Hitler.* New York: Continuum, 2008.
Nordquist, Kjell-Ake. "Contradicting Peace Proposals in the Palestine Conflict." *Journal of Peace Research* 22, no. 2 (June 1985).
Novelli, Angelo, and Thomas Pasquale. *The Life of Pius XI.* Yonkers, N.Y.: Mt. Carmel Press, 1925.
O'Brien, Felicity. *Pius XII.* London and Bristol: Burleigh Press, 2000.

O'Carroll, Michael. *Pius XII, Greatness Dishonoured: A Documented Study.* Dublin: Laetare, 1980.

Olf, Lillian Browne. *Their Name Is Pius: Portraits of Five Great Modern Popes.* Milwaukee, Wis.: Bruce Publishing, 1941.

"The Origins of *L'Ossoveratore Romano.*" Vatican Online at http://www.vatican.va/news_services/or/history/hi_eng.html.

O'Shea, Paul. *A Cross Too Heavy: Eugenio Pacelli and the Jews of Europe, 1917–1923.* Kenthurst, New South Wales, Australia: Rosenberg Publishing, 2008.

Padellaro, Nazareno. *Portrait of Pius XII.* Translated by Michael Derrick. New York: Dutton, 1957.

Pacepa, Ion Mihai. "Moscow's Assault on the Vatican." *National Review Online*, pp. 1–7, http://article—2/22/2007.

Padoan, Gianni. "Pio XII: Con lui—disse Hitler—farò i conti doppo!" *Historia*, November 1989, pp. 19–27n144.

Paganuzzi, Quirino. *Pro papa Pio.* Vatican City: Tipografia Poliglotta Vatican, 1970.

Palazzini, Pietro. *Il Clero e l'occupazione tedesca di Roma: Il ruolo del Seminario Romano Maggiore.* Rome: Apes, 1995.

Papeleux, Léon. *Les silences de Pie XII.* Brussels: Vokaer, 1980.

Parisella, Antonio. *Clero e parroci.* In *Pio XII*, ed. Andrea Riccardi (Rome and Bari: Laterza, 1984), 437–59.

Passelecq, Georges, and Bernard Suchecky. *L'encyclique cachee de Pie XI. Une occasion manquee de l'Eglise face a l'antisemitisme.* Preface "Pie XI, les Juifs et l'antisemitisme" de Emile Poulat. Paris: Editions La Decouverte, 1995.

Passelecq, Georges, and Bernard Suchecky, *The Hidden Encyclical of Pius XI.* Translated by Steven Rendall. New York: Harcourt Brace, 1998.

Paulikowski, John R. "The Papacy of Pius XII: The Known and Unknown." In *Pope Pius XII and the Holocaust*, edited by Carol Rittner and John K. Roth, 56–59. Leicester, U.K.: Leicester University Press, 2002.

Payne, Stanley. *The Franco Regime, 1936–1975.* Madison: University of Wisconsin Press, 1987.

———. "Fascist Italy and Spain, 1922–1945." *Mediterranean Historical Review* 13, no. 1 (June–December 1998): 99–115.

Pellicani, Antonio. *Il Papa di tutti. La Chiesa Cattolica, il fascismo, e il razzismo, 1929–1945.* Milan: Sugar Editore, 1964.

Persico, A.A. *Mezzo secolo di dibattito su Eugenio Pacelli.* Milan: Guerini, 2008.

Peters, Walter H. *The Life of Benedict XV.* Milwaukee, Wis.: Bruce Publishing, 1959.

Pfister, Pierre. *Pius XII: The Life and Work of a Great Pope.* New York: Thomas Crowell, 1954.

Pham, John Peter. *Heirs of the Fisherman: Behind the Scenes of Papal Death and Succession.* Oxford: Oxford University Press, 2006.

Phayer, Michael. *The Catholic Church and the Holocaust.* Bloomington: Indiana University Press, 2000.

———. *Pius XII, the Holocaust, and the Cold War.* Bloomington: Indiana University Press, 2008.
Picciotto Fargion, Liliana. *11 Libro della Memoria: Gli Ebrei deportati dall' Italia (1943–1945).* Milan: Mursia, 1991.
Pichon, Charles. *The Vatican and Its Role on World Affairs.* Translated by Jean Misrahi. Westport, Conn.: Greenwood Press, 1950.
Pie XII et la Cité. La pensée et l'action politiques de Pie XII. Paris: Téqui, 1988.
Pio XII nel centenario della nascita. Il Suo pensiero sulla formazione del clero, la sua figura come vescovo di Roma. Rome: Città Nuova, 1979.
Pollard, John F. *The Vatican and Italian Fascism, 1929–1932: A Study in Conflict.* Cambridge: Cambridge University Press, 1985.
———. *The Unknown Pope: Benedict XV (1914–1922) and the Pursuit of Peace.* London and New York: Geoffrey Chapman, 1999.
———. *Money and the Rise of the Modern Papacy: Financing the Vatican, 1850–1950.* Cambridge: Cambridge University Press, 2005.
Poulat, Émile. *Une Eglise Ébranlée. Changement, conflit et continuite de Pie XII a Jean Paul II.* Paris: Casterman, 1980.
———. *Les Prêtres-ouvriers. Naissance et fin.* Paris: Cerf, 1999.
Preston, Paul. *Franco: A Biography.* London: Harper Collins, 1993.
Prévotat, Jacques. *Les catholiques el l'Action française: Histoire d'une condamnation, 1889–1939.* Paris: Librairie Arthème Fayard, 2001.
Pugliese, Stanislao G., ed. *The Most Ancient of Minorities: The Jews of Italy.* Westport, Conn.: Greenwood Press, 2002.
Purdy, William Arthur. *The Church on the Move. The Characters and Politics of Pius XII and Johannes XXIII.* London: Hollis & Carter, 1966.
Refoule, François. *The Church and the Rights of Man.* New York: Seabury Press, 1979.
Raguer Suñer, Hilario M. *Gunpowder and Incense: The Catholic Church and the Spanish Civil War.* London: Routledge, 2007.
Randall, Alec. *The Pope, the Jews and the Nazis.* London: Catholic Truth Society, 1963.
Redaelli, Cesare. *Spadolini Giovanni. Il papato socialista.* Milan: Longanesi, 1964.
Rhodes, Anthony. *The Vatican in the Age of Dictators (1922–1945).* New York: Holt, Rinehart, and Winston, 1973.
Rhonheimer, Martin, "The Holocaust: What Was Not Said." *First Things* 137 (November 2003): 18–28.
Riccardi, Andrea, ed. *Pio XII.* Bari: Laterza, 1985.
———. *Il Potere del Papa da Pio XII a Paolo VI.* Rome: Laterza, 1988.
———. *Il Vaticano e Mosca, 1940–1990.* Bari: Laterza, 1992.
———. *Pio XII e Alcide De Gasperi. Una storia segreta.* Bari: Laterza, 2003.
———. *L'Inverno piu` lungo, 1943–1944.* Bari: Laterza, 2008.
Riccobono, Salvatore. *Il diritto naturale nel magistero di papa Pacelli.* Palermo: Denaro editore, 1960.
Rittner, Carol, and John K. Roth, eds. *Pope Pius XII and the Holocaust.* Leicester, U.K.: Leicester University Press, 2002.

Rocach, Livia. *The Catholic Church and the Question of Palestine*. London: Saqi Books, 1987.
Roche, Georges, and Philippe Saint-Germain. *Pie XII Davant l'histoire*. Paris: Laffont, 1972.
Rota, Olivier. "Les 'silences' du pape Pie XII: Genèse et critique d'un process biaisé." *Revue d'Histoire Ecclésiastique* (Louvain) 9, nos. 3–4 (July–December 2004): 758–66.
Royal, Robert, ed. *Jacques Maritain and the Jews*. South Bend, Ind.: University of Notre Dame Press, 1994.
Ryan, Edwin. "Papal Concordats in Modern Times." *Catholic Historical Review* 16 (October 1930): 302–10.
Ryan, Joseph L. "The Holy See and Jordan." In *The Vatican, Islam and the Middle East*, edited by K. C. Ellis. Syracuse, N.Y.: Syracuse University Press, 1987.
Rychlak, Ronald J. *Hitler, the War, and the Pope*. Huntington, Ind.: Our Sunday Visitor, 2000.
Sachar, Howard M. *Israel and Europe: An Appraisal in History*. New York: Alfred A. Knopf, 1999.
Saint Varent, Anne. *Vida de Pio XII*. Barcelona: Brugnera, 1967.
Sale, Giovanni. "The First Anti-Jewish Measures and the Declaration of the Fascist Grand Council." *La Civiltà Cattolica*, September 20, 2008.
Sanchez, Jose M. *The Spanish Civil War as a Religious Tragedy*. South Bend, Ind.: University of Notre Dame Press, 1987.
———. "The Enigma of Pope Pius XII." *America*, September 14, 1996.
———. "The Popes and Nazi Germany: The View from Madrid." *Journal of Church and State* 38 (Spring 1996): 365–76.
———. *Pius XII and the Holocaust: Understanding the Controversy*. Washington, D.C.: The Catholic University of America Press, 2002.
Sarfatti, Michele. *Gli ebrei nell'Italia fascista: Vicende, identita, persecuzione*. Turin: Einaudi, 2000.
Schierl, Josef. *In Christus. Deutsprachige Stimmen zur Verbindung de Gläubigen mit Christus im Vorfeld der Enziklika Pius XII. "Mystic Corporis."* Regensburg: Pustet, 1994.
Schmid, Johanna. *Papst Pius XII begegnen*. Ausburg: Sankt Urlich, 2001.
Schneider, Burkhart. *Pius XII. Friede, das Werk der Gerechtigkeit*. Göttingen: Musterschmidt Verlag, 1968.
Scholder, Klaus. *The Churches and the Third Reich*. Philadelphia: Fortress Press, 1988.
Schwarte, Johannes. *Gustav Gundlach S.J. (1892–1963). Massgeblicher Repräsentant der Katholischen Soziallehre während der Pontifikate Pius' XI und Pius' XII*. Munich: Schöningh, 1975.
Schwaiger, Georg. *Papsttum und Päpste im 20. Jahrhundert. Von Leo XIII. zu Johannes Paul II*. Munich: Beck, 1999.
Segre, Bruno. *La Shoah. Gli Ebrei, il genocidio, la memoria*. Milan: NET, 2003.
Serrou, Robert. *Pie XII. Le pape-roi*. Paris: Perin, 1992.

Simpson, William. *A Vatican Lifeline*. New York: Sarpedon, 1996.
Smit, Jan Olav. *Angelic Shepherd: The Life of Pope Pius XII*. New York: Dodd, Mead, 1950.
Spadolini, Giovanni. *Il papato socialista*. Milan: Longanesi, 1964.
Speziali, Giacomo. *L'ascesi sociale alla luce del pensiero di Pio XII*. Alterocca: Poligrafico Terni, 1964.
Spicer, Kevin P. *Hitler's Priests: Catholic Clergy and National Socialism*. De Kalb: Northern Illinois University Press, 2008.
Spinosa, Antonio. *Pio XII. L'ultimo Papa*. Milan: Mondadori, 1992.
———. *Pio XII. Un Papa nelle tenebre*. Milan: Mondadori, 1992.
Stehle, Hansjakob. *Die Ostpolitik des Vatikans 1917–1975*. Munich: Piper, 1975.
———. *Eastern Politics of the Vatican*. Athens: Ohio University Press, 1981.
Stehlin, Stewart A. *Weimar and the Vatican, 1919–1933: German-Vatican Relations in the Interwar Years*. Princeton, N.J.: Princeton University Press, 1983.
Steigmann-Gall, Richard. *The Holy Reich: Nazi Conceptions of Christianity, 1919–1945*. Cambridge: Cambridge University Press, 2003.
Stevens, Richard P. "The Vatican, the Catholic Church and Jerusalem." *Journal of Palestine Studies* 19, no. 3 (Spring 1981): 100–110.
Sullivan, Brian R. "Fascist Italy's Military Involvement in the Spanish Civil War." *Journal of Military History* 59 (October 1995): 697–727.
Tapia de Renedo, Benedicto. *Pio XII. ¿Inocente o culpable? Confrontacion de documentos secretos*. Madrid: Iberico, 1972.
Teeling, William. *Pope Pius XI and World Affairs*. New York: Frederick A. Stokes, 1937.
Thavis, John. "N.J. Nun Presses for Beatification of Pius XII." *The Tablet* (Brooklyn), December 6, 2003, p. 24.
Thomas, Lucien. *L'Action française devant l'Église (de Pie X à Pie XII)*. Paris: Nouvelles editions latines, 1965.
Tinnenmann, Ethel Mary, S.N.J.M. "The Silence of Pius XII." *Journal of Church and State* 21, no. 2 (Spring 1979): 265–85.
Tittman, Harold Jr. *Il Vaticano di Pio XII. Uno sguardo all'interno*. Milan: Corbaccio, 2005.
Tornielli, Andrea. *Pio XII. Il papa degli ebrei*. Casale Monferrato: Piemme, 2001.
Townsend, W., and L. Townsend. *The Biography of His Holiness Pope Pius XI*. London: Mariott, 1930.
Tramontin, Silvio. *Un secolo di storia della Chiesa. Da Leone XIII al Concilio Vaticano*. 2 vols. Rome: Studium, 1980.
Trevelyan, Raleigh. *Rome '44: The Battle for the Eternal City*. London: Secker & Warburg, 1981.
Valente, Massimiliano. "La nunziatura di Eugenio Pacelli a Monaco di Baviera e la 'diplomazia dell'assistenza' vaticana (1917–1918)." *Quellen und Forschungen aus italienischen Archiven und Bibliotheken* 83 (2003): 264–87.
Valiani, Leo, Gianfranco Bianchi, and Ernesto Ragionieri. *Azionisti. Cattolici, e comunisti nella Resistenza*. Milan: Franco Angeli, 1971

BIBLIOGRAPHY 299

Van Hoek, Kees. *Pope Pius XII, Priest and Statesman: A Biography*. New York: Philosophical Library, 1945.

Veneruso, Danilo. *Pio XII e la seconda guerra mondiale*. Rome: Herder, 1969.

Vian, Giovanni Maria. "Il silenzio di Pio XII: Alle origini della leggenda nera." *Archivum Historiae Pontificiae* 42 (2004): 223–29.

Villa, Luigi. *Pio XII, papa calunniato e scomodo. Nel XX anniversario della sua morte (1958–9 ottobre 1978)*. Brescia: Civiltà, 1979.

Vogelstein, Hermann. *The Jews of Rome*. Translated by Moses Hadas. Philadelphia: Jewish Publication Society of America, 1940.

Volk, Ludwig. *Das Reichskonkordat vom 20. Juli 1933*. Mainz: Matthias-Grünewald-Verlag, 1972.

Von Albrecht, Dieter. *Katholische Kirche im Dritten Reich. Eine Aufsatzsammlung zum Verhältnis von Papsttum, Episkopat und deutschen Katholiken zum Nationalsozialismus 1933–1945*. Mainz: Grünewald, 1976.

Von Aretin, Karl Otmar. *The Papacy and the Modern World*. Translated by Roland Hill. New York: McGraw-Hill, 1970.

Waagenaar, Sam. *The Pope's Jews*. La Salle, Ill.: Open Court Publishers, 1974.

Walker, Reginald. *Pius of Peace: A Study of the Pacific Work of His Holiness Pope Pius XII in the World War, 1939–1945*. Dublin: Gill, 1945.

Ward, Leo R., C.S.C. "Pius XII and Man's Rights." *Ave Maria*, October 25, 1958, pp. 5–7.

Webb, Leicester C. *Church and State in Italy, 1947–1957*. Carlton, Australia: Melbourne University Press, 1958.

Webster, Richard A. *The Cross and the Fasces*. Stanford, Calif.: Stanford University Press, 1960.

Weisbord, Robert G., and Wallace P. Sillanpoa. *The Chief Rabbi, the Pope, and the Holocaust: An Era in Vatican-Jewish Relations*. New Brunswick, N.J.: Transaction, 1992.

Wenger, Antoine. *Rome et Moscou, 1900–1950*. Paris: Desclée de Brouwer, 1987.

Whealey, Robert H. *Hitler and Spain: The Nazi Role in the Spanish Civil War*. Lexington: University of Kentucky Press, 1989.

Wheeler Bennet, John W. *Il patto di Monaco. Prologo della tragedia*. Translated by Giuseppina Panzieri. Milan: Feltrinelli, 1968.

Williams, George L. *Papal Genealogy: The Families and Descendants of the Popes*. Jefferson, N.C.: McFarland, 2004

Williams, Paul L. *The Vatican Exposed: Money, Murder and the Mafia*. Amherst, N.Y.: Prometheus Books, 2003.

Williamson, Benedict. *The Story of Pope Pius XI*. New York: Kennedy & Sons, 1931.

Wills, Gary. *Papal Sin: Structures of Deceit*. New York: Doubleday, 2000.

Wilson, Evan M. "The Internationalization of Jerusalem," *Middle East Journal* 223, no. 1 (Winter 1969).

Wistrich, Robert S. *Hitler and the Holocaust*. New York: Modern Library, 2001.

Wolf, Hubert. *Pope and Devil: The Vatican's Archives and the Third Reich*. Translated by Kenneth Kronenberg. Cambridge, Mass.: Harvard University Press, 2010.

Wolff, Richard J. "The Catholic Church and the Dictatorships in Slovakia and Croatia, 1939–1945." *Records of the American Catholic Historical Society of Philadelphia*, 1978.

Wolff, Richard J., and Jörg K. Hoensch, eds. *Catholics, the State, and the European Radical Right, 1919–1945*. Boulder, Colo.: Social Science Monographs, 1987.

Wright, Quincy. "The Palestine Problem." *Political Science Quarterly* 41, no. 3 (September 1926).

Wyman, David S. *The Abandonment of the Jews: America and the Holocaust, 1941–1945*. New York: Pantheon Books, 1984.

Zahn, Gordon C. *German Catholics and Hitler's War*. London and New York: Sheed & Ward, 1963.

———. "Catholic Opposition to Hitler: The Perils of Ambiguity." *Journal of Church and State* 13, no. 3 (Autumn 1971): 413–25.

Zizola, Giancarlo. *Il microfono di Dio. Pio XII, Padre Lombardi e i cattolici Italiani*. Milan: Mondadori, 1990.

Zolli, Israel. *Before the Dawn*. New York: Sheed & Ward, 1954.

Zuccotti, Susan. *The Italians and the Holocaust: Persecution, Rescue, and Survival*. New York: Basic Books, 1987.

———. *The Holocaust, the French and the Jews*. New York: Basic Books, 1993.

———. *Under His Very Windows: The Vatican and the Holocaust in Italy*. New Haven, Conn.: Yale University Press, 2000.

INDEX

Abbot, Father Walter, 122
Abdullah, king of Jordan, 191
Acta Apostolicae Sedis, xxiii, 214, 224, 268
Actes et documents ... relatifs à la ... guerre mondiale, xviii
Action Française, 91, 134, 226
Ad Caeli Reginam, 12, 224
Adenauer, Konrad, 234
Affari Ecclesiastici Straordinari, xx
Albania, 137,
Alfieri, Dino, 141, 169
Allenby, General Edmund Henry, 176
Alsace-Lorraine, 65–66, 71
America, xiv
American Israelite, xiii
American Jewish Joint Distribution Committee, xiii
Angelini, Cardinal Fiorenzo, 26
Angriff, Der, 128
Annuario Pontificio (Annual Papal Directory), xxiv, 268
Anti-Judaism, xv, 48, 76, 91, 107, 169
Anti-Semitism, xii, xv, 48–49, 76, 91, 100, 169
Antonelli, Cardinal Giacomo, 7
Arab League, 193
Arabs, 181–82, 188–89, 191
Archivio Centrale dello Stato di Roma, xxv
Archivio della Congregazione della Fede, xx
Archivio della Nunziatura Apostolica in Berlin, xx
Archivio della Nunziatura Apostolica in Monaco, xx
Archivio ... del Ministero degli Affari Esteri Italiano, xxv
Arendt, Hannah, xvi

Armenian genocide, 25
Assumption of Virgin Mary, dogma of the, 11–12, 224
Attolico, Bernardo, 204n7
Auschwitz, 223
Auspicia Quaedam, 190
Austria-Hungary, 51–52
Aversa, Giuseppe, 62
Axis, 118, 130, 138, 141, 143, 145, 149, 158, 242

Balfour, Lord Arthur James, 177
Balfour Declaration, 177–79
Baltic states, 203
Bassi, Ignazio, 31
Bavaria, 62–64, 72, 80, 83, 89
Bavarian concordat, 86
Bea, Cardinal Augustin, 99, 231
Belgium, 54–56, 148, 164
Ben-Hur, Oded, 261
Benedict XV, Pope, xx, 52–54, 200; peace note of 1917, 68–70
Benedict XVI, Pope, xxi, 262
Benelux countries, 235
Benigni, Umberto, 44–45, 48, 225
Beran, archbishop of Prague, 211
Bergen, Diego von, 85, 114
Bernstein, Rabbi Philip, 195
Bertram, Cardinal Adolf, 129
Bethlehem, 187
Bethmann-Hollweg, Theobald von, 65–66, 68, 77
Bolshevik Revolution, 200
Bolshevism. *See* Communism
Bottum, Joseph, 281
Brazil, 164
Brokdorff-Rantzau, Count Ulrich von, 93
Bulgaria, 170

INDEX

Caillaux, Joseph, 61
Canon law, 225
Cappellari, Bartolomeo Alberto. *See* Gregory XVI
Carlen, Claudia. *See* Papal Encyclicals; Papal Pronouncements
Carroll, James, xv
Casablanca Conference, 205
Castel Gandolfo, 245
Castel Sant' Angelo, 30
Caterini, Maria Antonia 4
Caterini, Prospero, 4–5
Catholic Action, 115, 148–50, 215–16
Catholic University of America, The, 45
Cavour, Camillo Benso di, 56
Center Party, 83–84, 100
Central Powers, 61
Centurians, 72
Chamberlain, Neville, 125
Charles-Roux, François, xxv, 133, 138
Chiesa Nuova (Oratorian Fathers), 8, 27. *See also* Santa Maria di Vallicella
China, 209, 231
Chinese Catholic Patriotic Association, 209
Christian Democrats (Italy), 212–15
Christus Dominus, 229
Churchill, Winston, xvi, 149, 165, 213n25
Ciano, Count Galeazzo, xxv, 128
Cicognani, Amleto, 182
Civiltà Cattolica, La, xxiv, 79, 157, 180
Clark, General Mark, 194
Cold war, xi, 198–99, 201–11
Concordat with Fascist Italy, 147–48. *See also* Lateran Accords
Confederation of the Rhine, 52–53
Conway, John, 263
Cornwell, John, xi, 2, 52, 76
Counter-Risorgimento, 9, 14–15
Crimean War, 17
Czechoslovakia, 141, 209

Dalin, David D., xviii
Danzig, 132, 139, 183
De Gasperi, Alcide, 212, 215
Deiparae Virginis Mariae, 224
Della Chiesa, Giacomo Giambattista, 132–33. *See also* Benedict XV
Deputy, The, 124, 153, 219
Desbuquois, Gustave, 169. *See also Humani Generis Unitas*

Dietrich, Hermann, 82
Divini Redemptoris, 147
Divino Afflante Spiritu, 205, 227
Documents on British Foreign Policy, xxv
Duce, the, 88, 117, 122, 125, 128, 132, 145, 149. *See also* Mussolini
Duce, Alessandro, 253

Eastern Europe, 202–6
Ebert, Friedrich, 75, 87
Ecumenism, 222, 225, 233, 238
Eden, Anthony, 161
Egypt, 195–96
Eichmann, Adolf, xiv, 153
Einstein, Albert, xiii
Eisner, Kurt, 79–81
Erzberger, Mathias, 58, 67, 83
Estonia, 202
Ethiopia, 148
European Coal and Steel Community, 235
European Economic Community, 235
European Free Trade Association, 235
European integration, xii
European Recovery Plan, 209, 234. *See also* Marshall Plan
European Union, 235
Eurovision, 239
Evangelii Praecones, 233

Fascism, 144, 159–60
Fascist Italy, 97, 101, 103, 105, 107–8, 119–20, 123, 132, 137, 226, 263. *See also* Mussolini
Fatima, 63, 200
Faulhaber, Cardinal Michael von, 77, 80, 129
Ferrata, Cardinal Domenico, 53
Finaly affair, 222
Final Solution. *See* Holocaust
Finland, 148
First Vatican Council, 79, 102–3, 222
Fogli di udienza (Records of Audiences), xxi, xxiii, 24
Four Power Agreement, 132
Fourteen points, 70–73. *See* Wilson, Woodrow
Franco, Francisco, 130, 135, 159
Franco-Prussian War, 14
Franz Ferdinand, Archduke, 51
Franz Joseph, emperor of Austria, 58–59
French Revolution, 6, 149, 256

INDEX 303

Friedlander, Saul, 2, 146–47
Friends of Israel, 107, 195, 230
Führer, the, 108–9, 129, 143, 148. See also Hitler
Fulgens Corona, 224
Früwirth, Cardinal Andrea, 63

Gaeta, 7
Garibaldi, Giuseppe, 7, 56
Gasparri, Cardinal Pietro, 18, 41–42, 44, 47–48, 50–53, 58–59, 63, 71, 78–80, 84, 87, 93, 183, 247, 254
Gaza, 195
Gedda, Luigi, 213
Gerlach, Monsignor Rudolf, 64
Genoa Conference, 88
Gilbert, Martin, xviii
Gillet, Martin, 139
Gizzi, Cardinal Pasquale, 83
Goebbels, Josef, 128
Goldhagen, Daniel, xvi,
Graziosi, Filippo, 11
Graziosi, Virginia, 11, 15, 28
Greece, 148
Gregorian University, 34,
Gregory XVI, Pope, 6, 199
Gumpel, Reverend Peter, 217, 220
Gundlach, Gustav, 118. See also *Humani Generis Unitas*

Haigerty, Leo, 237
Haiti, 242
Halifax, Lord, 125
Hartmann, Cardinal Felix von 64
Herzl, Theodor, 176
Herzog, Isaac, 153, 261
Herzog, Jacob, 192
Hilberg, Paul, von Hindenberg, 66, 69
Himmler, Heinrich, 128, 143
Hindenburg, Paul von, 66, 69
Hitler, Adolf, xv, 90, 114–16 128–29, 146, 155–56, 162, 250; *putsch* of 1923, 89
Hlond, Cardinal August, 195
Hochhuth, Rolf, xiv–xv, 2, 159, 219, 246, 257
Holland, 144, 148, 182, 194
Holocaust, xiv–xv, 2, 13, 30, 124, 136, 152–55, 159, 165, 171, 174
Holy Land, 175–78, 188, 190, 192–93
Holy sites, 176
Hudal, Alois, 168, 202

Humani Generis Unitas, xxiv, 18, 119, 120n48 144

Impartiality, 54–57, 59, 78, 90, 102, 131, 135, 140, 152–57, 221, 249
Immaculate Conception of Mary (1854), 223–24
India, 231
In Multiplicibus curis, 192
Inquisition, 45
Israel, 174, 187, 189 190–91, 192–95, 197
Italian Diplomatic Documents, xxv

Japan, 145, 240
Jerusalem, 175–76, 186–87, 190, 194, 197; internationalization of, 183
Jesuits, xviii, xx, xxiv, 23, 28, 34, 54, 62, 98, 118
Jewish Advocate, xiii
John XXIII, Pope, xvii, 158, 222, 243, 245–47
John Paul I, Pope, 257, 268
John Paul II, Pope, xix
Jordan, 191–92, 194–96

Kaas, Monsignor Ludwig, 99
Karlsbad Protocal, 209
Katz, Robert, 290
Keeler, Cardinal William, 173n43
Kennedy, Joseph, 127
Kertzer, David I., 223n1
Kesselring, General Albert, 150
Kingship of Christ, 88
Korean War, 207, 212
Kremlin, 96
Krestinski, Nikolai, 93
Kristallnacht, xxi
Krupp, Gary, xviii. See also Pave the Way Foundation
Küng, Hans, 247

La Farge, Father John, 117–20. See also *Humani Generis Unitas*
Lagarde, Paul de, 110
Lais, Father Giuseppe (Chiesa Nuova), 28, 38, 40, 231
Lansing, Robert, 70
Lapide, Pinchas, xii–xiii, xvii
Lateran Accords, 18, 21, 95, 101–2, 121, 136, 140, 145

Lateran University, 261
Latin American countries, 168
Latvia, 92, 202
Law of Papal Guarantees, 19, 244
League of Nations, 71, 183–84
League of Saint Pius V, 44
Ledochowski, Father Vladimir, 118–19, 122
Lehnert, Sister Pascalina, xxv, 67, 72, 166
Lehrer, Abraham, 261
Lenin, 94, 204
Leo XIII, Pope, 17, 47–48, 51–52, 199, 232
Levai, Jenoe, xviii
Levien, Max, 81–82
Lieber, Father Robert, 23
Lithuania, 202
Litvinov, Maximilan, 94
Lloyd George, David, 182
Lombardi, Father Federico, 262
London, Treaty of, 61
Low Countries, 141, 191–92
Luciani, Cardinal Albino. *See* John Paul I
Ludendoff, Erich, 66, 69, 90
Ludwig III of Bavaria, 64
Lueger, Karl, 125

Maglione, Cardinal Luigi, 130, 138, 152, 168, 182, 205
Marchi institute, 30
Marchione, Sister Margherita, xvii, xxvi
Mariology, 223
Maritain, Jacques, 172, 185
Marshall, George C., 209
Marshall Plan, 209, 234
Martini, Father Angelo, xxvn37, 120–21, 126
Mastai-Ferretti, Giovanni Maria. *See* Pius IX
Maurras, Charles, 91, 134
Mazzini, Giuseppe, 6–7. *See also* Young Italy
McDonald, James, 155, 192
Mediator Dei, 228
Meir, Golda, xii
Memel, 183
Mendes, Guido, 30
Merry del Val, Rafaelle, 63, 176
Michaelis, Georg, 68–69, 70
Middle East, 231
Mihai Pacepa, Ion, 219
Mindszenty, archbishop of Budapest, 211
Mit brennender Sorge, xxi, 116–17

Miranda Prorsus, 239
Modernism, xxxix, 43–44, 48
Monnet, Jean, 234
Montini, Monsignor Giovanni Battista, xviii, xxii, 160, 169, 231, 243. *See also* Paul VI
Mooney, Bishop Edward, 172
Mortara affair, 222–23
Moscow, 200
Mühlberg, Otto von, 64
Munderlain, Cardinal George, 165, 172
Munich Agreement, 131, 133, 139
Munificentissimus Deus, 224
Muslim Turks, 175
Mussolini, Benito, xv, 91, 95, 103, 117, 121, 128, 149, 155, 250
Mystici Corporis Christi, 227

Nasser, General Abdel, 196
Nazism, 150–56, 159–60, 164
Nazi Germany, 105, 120, 127, 138, 142, 146, 148, 165, 173, 185, 225–26, 252; Nazi-Soviet Pact, 137
Neuilly, treaty of, 71
Non expedit, 17
Non licit, 17
North Atlantic Treaty Organization, 212

Oratorian Fathers, 27
Organization for European Economic Cooperation, 234
Orientales Omnes Ecclesias, 208
Orsenigo, Cardinal Cesare, 109nn14–15, 131, 138nn30–31
Osborne, Sir Francis D'Arcy, 141, 161
O'Shea, Paul, 2
Osservatore Romano, L', xxiii, 13, 60, 79, 141, 157, 180, 213
Ottoman Empire, 71, 181

Pacca, Cardinal Bartolomeo, 55–57
Pacelli, Elisabetta, 16, 21, 41
Pacelli, Ernesto, 20
Pacelli, Eugenio, 2; at Almo Collegio Capranica, 34; altar boy, 39; birth of, 16; cardinal, secretary of state, 98; childhood, 9, 26; Christmas message 1942, 160, 167; Christmas message 1944, 205; death, 245; *Defensor Civitatis*, 150; education, 2, 25; at Ennio Qurino-Visconti

INDEX

Institute, 31; eucharistic congress, 113; expresses desire to become priest, 33; first Holy Communion, 27; first Mass, 39; Germanophile, 201; nuncio to Germany, 75–79; nursery school, 29; plot to kidnap, 168; religious background, 10; revision of canon law, 42, 46; Secretariat of State, 49–50; secretary of state, 104–13. *See also* Pius XII
Pacelli, Filippo, 4, 6, 15, 28; transfers Eugenio to Ateneo Pontificio di S. Apollinare, 37
Pacelli, Francesco, 10, 95. *See also* Lateran Accords
Pacelli, Gaetano, 4
Pacelli, Giuseppe, 5, 21
Pacelli, Giuseppina, 16
Pacelli, Marcantonio, 4–7, 14, 17, 28, 238
Pacelli, Maria Domenica: marries Francesco Caterini, 4
Pacelli family, 3–22; family home in Onano, 3–5, 15, 37; name change from Pacella, 4
Pact, secret: with Mussolini's Italy, 126
Pact of Steel, 137
Pacha, Agostino, 165
Palestine, 174–78
Papal Encyclicals, xxiv
Papal infallibility, 102–3, 129
Papal Pronouncements, xxiv
Papen, Franz von, 109, 153
Palazzo Pediconi, 8
Pascalina Lehnert, Sister, 67, 72, 99, 166
Pascendi dominici gregis, 130
Paul VI, Pope, xvii, 32, 217, 222
Pave the Way Foundation, xviii, xxiii, 261
Pecci, Gioacchino Vincenzo Rafaelle. *See* Leo XIII
Peel Report, 181
Peron, Juan, 260
Phayer, Michael, 183n19
Pius IX, Pope, 6–9, 13–14, 17, 21, 269
Pius X, Pope, 48–51, 175–76
Pius XI, Pope, xvii, 88–89, 94, 105–6, 118–23, 248
Pius XII, Pope, xiii, xvii, 8, 12, 41, 136, 177, 183, 184–218, 234. *See also* Pacelli, Eugenio
Pius War, 2, 153, 246
Planck, Max, 237

Plombières, 98
Poland, 71, 92, 105, 164, 203
Pontifical Mission for Palestine, 195
Pope Speaks, xxiii
Preysing, Bishop Konrad, 163
Primo de Rivera, Miquel, 146
Pro Perfidis Judaeis, 230
Prussia, concordat with, 93–94

Quanta cura, 13
Quas Primas (1925), 88

Rampolla del Tindaro, Cardinal Mariano, 47
Rapallo, Treaty of, 88
Ratline, 202
Ratti, Cardinal Achille. *See* Pius XI
Ratzinger, Cardinal Joseph. *See* Benedict XVI
Redemptoris Nostri Cruciatus, 193
Reich Concordat, 44, 110, 112–13, 138, 154
Rerum novarum, 122–23, 232
Rhineland, 16
Ribbentrop, Joachim von, 143
Risorgimento, 6, 9, 46, 56, 109, 175–76
Ritter, Otto von, 60, 64, 86
Romania, 165, 170
Roman Question, 59–60
Romanus Pontifex, 29
Rome, xxiii, 6, 8, 13–15, 19, 27, 30, 34–35, 72, 119, 125, 150, 168, 214–15, 244, 271–72, 299
Roncalli, Angelo. *See* John XXIII
Roosevelt, Franklin Delano, xxv, 132, 135, 139, 165, 171 199–201, 216, 238
Russell, Odo, 90
Russian Orthodox Church, 21

Saint-Germain, treaty of, 71
Sanchez, José, xviii, 159
Santa Maria di Vallicella, 8, 27–28, 38–40
Sarto, Cardinal Giuseppe Melchiore. *See* Pius X
Scapinelli, Raffaele, 58
Schioppa, Monsignor Lorenzo, 66, 77, 82–83
Schulte, Cardinal Josef, 129
Schuman, Robert, 234
Second Vatican Council, xvii, 222, 245
Second World War. *See* World War II

Secretariat of State, xxiii, 40, 42, 45, 47–49, 53, 71, 79, 102–3, 108, 110–11, 115, 117–19, 125, 154, 201, 213, 251
Secret Vatican Archive, xix, 251
Serbia, concordat with, 51–52, 75
Sharett, Moshe, 184, 196
Shazar, Zalman, president of Israel, 240
Sheen, Fulton, 217
Siccardi Laws, 91
Sicut Iudeis, 11–12
"Silence," 221, 246. *See also* Pacelli, Eugenio
Simon, John, 111
Siri, Archbishop Giuseppe, 235, 246, 257
Slovakia, 170
Sonnino, Sidney, 61
Soviet Union, 147–48, 189–90, 203–5, 207, 243
Spain under Franco, 226
Spartacist revolution in Bavaria, 79
Spinoza, Baruch, 35
Stahel, General Rainer, 168
Stalin, 97, 202, 234
Stalingrad, 205
Stepinac, Archbishop Alois, 210–11
Suez Canal, 196
Summi pontificatus, 156, 200, 250
Switzerland, 175
Syllabus of Errors, 13

Tardini, Monsignor Domenico, xxi, xxv, 12, 130, 144, 193
Taylor, Myron, xxv, 142
Tiso, Monsignor, 165
Tisserant, Cardinal Eugene, 167
Tito, Marshal 210
Tittmann, Harold, xxv
Totalitarianism, 101–2, 255
Trent and Trieste, 58, 222
Truman, Harry S, 211
Truman Doctrine, 208

Ubi primum, 133
UNESCO, 222, 243
United Kingdom, 164
United Nations, xii, 187, 193
United Nations Relief Work Agency, 195

United States, xii, 51, 61, 142, 164, 189, 198, 202, 211, 240
United States Holocaust Memorial Museum, xxi

Valeri, Cardinal Valerio, 134, 137
Vannutelli, Cardinal Vincenzo, 47
Vatican City, 147–48, 156, 207
Vatican Information Service, 148–49
Vatican Radio, 160, 174, 190, 203, 226
Vehementer nos, 43
Verolini, Gennaro, 170
Vicar of Christ, 107, 121, 134, 149, 154, 162, 171, 250
Versailles, Treaty of, 71, 75
Vichy France, 164
Victor Emmanuel II, king of Piedmont/Italy, 55–56
Victor Emmanuel III, king of Italy, 141, 149

Wagner, Richard, 106, 146
Wannsee conference, 159
War Guilt Clause, 78
Washington, 144, 194
Weimar Republic, 75, 95, 98
West Bank, 191
Wilhelm II, 66–67
Wilson, Woodrow, 70, 73
Wittelsbach dynasty, 79
Wojtyla, Archbishop Karol, 231. *See also* John Paul II
World Jewish Congress, xiii
World War I, 51–52, 175, 249
World War II, xiv–xv, xix, 140–50, 186, 199–200, 204–7, 221, 233, 245, 252
World Zionist Organization, 176–77

Yad Vashem, 283–84
Yellow badge, 18, 25, 29, 34, 46, 59
Young Italy, 88

Zelanti, 48, 55–61, 83
Zionism, 175–77, 180, 182, 190, 196
Zolli, Israel, xiii
Zuccotti, Susan, 300